CHELSEA FC

THE OFFICIAL BIOGRAPHY

THE DEFINITIVE STORY OF THE FIRST 100 YEARS

Rick Glanvill

headline

First published in 2005
by HEADLINE BOOK PUBLISHING

First published in paperback in 2006
by HEADLINE BOOK PUBLISHING

5

ISBN 9780 7553 1466 9

Statistics provided by Paul Dutton *paul@dutton2004.fsnet.co.uk*
Edited and designed by Butler and Tanner, Frome, Somerset
Printed and bound in Great Britain by CPI Mackays, Chatham ME5 8TD

Headline's policy is to use papers that are natural, renewable and recyclable
products and made from wood grown in sustainable forests. The logging
and manufacturing processes are expected to conform to the environmental
regulations of the country of origin.

HEADLINE PUBLISHING GROUP
A division of Hodder Headline
338 Euston Road
London NW1 3BH

www.headline.co.uk
www.hodderheadline.com

Football, history and music writer, and a Matthew Harding
Upper season ticket-holder, Rick Glanvill has contributed to
Chelsea's official publications since 1993, even surviving a tunnel run-in
with Ray Harford over his particularly insulting programme 'pen-pics'
of Blackburn Rovers players. A broadcaster and regular on 'Chelsea TV',
Rick has written well over a dozen books, including the highly acclaimed
Rhapsody In Blue and several others on Chelsea FC, as well as the
Urban Myths series, featured in the *Guardian*.

His first football match was Chelsea v Arsenal in 1965 as a
toddler (2-1 win, George Graham brace), where he also mastered
how to eat a hot-dog over the stench of horse manure. Rick's
fascination with historical detail and genealogy has extended
as far as the search for a direct family link to
the Abramoviches. No luck yet.

'I find it unfathomable. The mystique of Chelsea.'
Albert Sewell, Chelsea programme editor 1948–79

'I have been an avid Chelsea supporter for more than 40 years.
During that long period, we have not been spoilt with success.
If one adds to that my membership of the Labour party,
I suppose that one can see that life appears to have dealt me
something of a bum hand. But, in politics as in football,
it is best to travel optimistically.'
Tony Banks, MP, 1996

In fond memory of Tony Banks, Scott Cheshire
and Peter Osgood

DEDICATION ·

To Alfie and all north London Blues

ACKNOWLEDGEMENTS

I am grateful to all those players, staff and fans who agreed to share their
Chelsea memories with me and provide a broader range of opinion than
my own limited viewpoints.

David Wilson, Lorraine Jerram – great to be on the same wavelength with a publisher.
Picture researcher, editor and fellow Blue Julian Flanders, you were brilliant.

Special thanks to true Blue writers Paul Mason, who undertook some vital interviews,
and Tim Harrison, for expertly researching the parts other luvvies just don't reach.
To Kenneth Quisgaard, Chelsea Legends Odense branch, for translating Middelboe.
To David Hellier and Paul Joannou for vital steering. Also to Neil Barnett for all-round
assistance, insight and telephone numbers.

Chelsea archivist Derek Webster and statistician Paul Dutton were great sources
of information and help. Scott Cheshire and Ron Hockings' superb books were a
constant source of inspiration and regulation. Thank you especially to the extremely
fast and accurate Alison Sieff (yes, you do have to type up the 'mature' lady talking
about her father), Peter Collins, Matt Rowan and Yael Glanvill for their timely
transcriptions. Much appreciation to Luc Torres at the *Guardian*; Luis Lorenzo; Carlos
Jones at MercoPress, Montevideo; Marcelo L. Aruda at RSSSF.com.br; and the British
Council, Berlin. Thanks to Bernice and Marguerite and all at Age Concern, Fulham.

To Ollie, well done for Googling out nuggets from the Internet
(even if it was just to keep you occupied).

I am grateful for the guidance of Patrick Newley, of the *Call Boy* magazine, Richard
Anthony Baker and Michael Kilgariff regarding Chelsea's Music Hall connections.

I always found the staff at the London Metropolitan Archives, the British Library,
the National Archives, the Westminster Library and elsewhere to be
extremely helpful. Thanks to them.

CONTENTS

FOREWORD

When I became involved in Chelsea, I had little idea how much joy and excitement it would bring me and I can think of no more fitting tribute to our centenary season than to enter it as the Premiership champions. That is like a dream come true.

Of course, it is 50 years since our last title, and I know that everybody at the club will be working hard to ensure that we will not have to wait that long again. This book tells the story of the great history and tradition of Chelsea and this is something I have the utmost respect for. It represents the heart and soul of the club and the values it was built on. I hope to carry this forward in the true Blue tradition of Chelsea, but also to build even stronger foundations to last us for the next hundred years.

Inside these pages are the people who made Chelsea, the players, the managers, the directors, the administrators, the staff and, most importantly, the fans. Each has made a huge contribution to a great club.

Most of all, this story is a homage to our fans, both young and old. I regard it as a great honour that I have been asked to write this foreword for you. Without our fantastic supporters there would not be a Chelsea Football Club and we will never forget that. In the future we hope to bring you more joy than you have experienced in the last hundred years.

In order to do this many challenges lie ahead. We aim to retain the Premiership title and, of course, challenge again in Europe. Maybe this year we can go one step better and get to the Champions League final. In the long-term our strategy is to build the most successful football club in the world and everything we have done so far is geared to this. We have this vision for Chelsea and we want you, our fans, to share that with us.

Roman Abramovich

INTRODUCTION

My starting point for this book was that I had never trusted any previous history of the club I love. That is no way a denigration of the contributions of Scott Cheshire and Ron Hockings – Chelsea's versions of the Venerable Bede – but is based on my knowledge of what poor source material all of us have had to work with.

Our club has rarely, if ever, celebrated its history and its failure to retain even the most basic club books, records, photographs and manuscripts has been shameful. The reported illicit flogging off in the late 1990s of what few items the club retained over the decades is nothing short of a tragedy that will, in the future, impoverish all of us who love to read or write about SW6's most interesting resident.

Ironically, the newest board of directors, criticised by some for being interlopers, have shown a keener sense of the club's early past than any in living memory. Let's hope that is backed up with a commitment to establish a permanent museum and archive, as seems certain.

Not many of Chelsea's fans or writers have shown much enthusiasm for Walham Green's longest-running soap opera back beyond the 1950s. The prolific Cheshire and Hockings apart, for a big, glamorous club we must have had fewer books written about us over time than any of our rivals. Perhaps the Music Hall connection really did intimidate us out of taking the old club seriously.

As a result of all this, the official *Chelsea Chronicles*, programmes and handbooks, plus one or two pre-war books and autobiographies are pretty much all there is to go on. The early *Chronicles* especially – erudite but understandably full of 'spin' from arch manipulator Frederick Parker – form what is a hand-me-down history of the pre-war years, stocked with dubious anecdotes and apocryphal tales that tells only half the story.

We lack the objective viewpoint that well-researched books from the 1930s and 40s might have provided. (Had we actually won something back then, they would, of course, have followed.) As a result, the club's history has had to be rehashed in the spirit of goodwill, as there are so few original sources at the club.

This book is a personal attempt to dig beneath the pleasantries and accepted sequence of events and bring to life the origins, the achievements, the people, the dealings, the events and the colour of Chelsea Football Club over its entire hundred-year history.

I have researched thousands of documents (some declassified for the first time), records, books, newspapers, photos, letters, films and websites, and interviewed dozens of players, board members and fans, here and abroad, so as to put together as full a record of what Chelsea is about as possible, and with as many different voices and opinions as possible.

In that sense I have tried to produce a social history of a football club.

The story is often laid down in themed sections rather than in chronological order. (I have already written a season-by-season history in the matchday magazine, so it probably would have been a more sensible idea.) This is because I wanted to examine the club almost as a person, with many consistent traits and habits that have recurred over time; one about which friends and enemies alike have very clear feelings; one that has been dealt severe blows – including the near loss of its ancestral pile – but has survived and now flourishes better, perhaps, than any other.

The 'same old Chelsea' remains just that, but it may not be exactly as you have been led to believe.

There have been surprises along the way. I had no idea, for instance, that the Chelsea team toured Germany at the most cataclysmic moment in that country's history; that the stigma of bigotry is a denial of the club's hidden past; that Chelsea legends starred in Britain's first great football feature films; nor that a billionaire was at the Chelsea helm long before our favourite Russian Oligarch.

There is an awesome (in the English, rather than the American high school sense) statistics section collated by Paul 'Dutto' Dutton, which many will find more entertaining than the rest (and certainly more useful). There are, hopefully, new colourful angles or rewrites of the stories we have come to know. There are new tales – and one or two small bombshells – revealed here for the first time.

Some of the truth may be painful, but then isn't that always the way with people we love?

That said it is almost certain that there will be many inaccuracies, oversights and personal opinions that will annoy people. I apologise for the first two but not the last; working on this, with so much new material, has felt a little like going on holiday, with a room full of clothes, hardly any of which can fit in the already-full suitcase.

It's been a great first hundred years. My aim now is to last at least till we've won the title three times.

Rick Glanvill, London, September 2005

THE BEST OF TIMES

The **champions**, 2005 and 1955

1
IT'S COLD AT THE TOP OF THE MOUNTAIN

They always tell you the hardest thing in football is to follow up a title win with another one, back-to-back. They don't warn you it might take 50 years. And in truth, despite certain periods – 1963–71, 1984–86, 1998–2000 – when the team showed something approaching the necessary consistency in the league, it never really looked likely. All the elements – squad, management and luck – need to be in place. There was never the complete combination of depth, mettle and managerial brilliance before 2004–05.

It really began in 2003 with the Abramovich revolution and the subsequent influx of players. 'I remember exactly where I was and what I was doing when I heard,' says Frank Lampard. 'I was in America on holiday, in LA, in a shoe shop buying sandals. And my dad rang me and told me. I'd been tipped off about a similar thing a month before and it never came true. It's funny I remember it exactly, but it was a big thing, a billionaire taking over.'

The arrival of the Russian's chequebook in July 2003, brought the possibility of far greater competition for a first-team place 'I can't remember ringing anyone like JT straight away to talk about it,' says Lampard. 'I just remember being in a cab with my missus, and discussing it, a mixture of amazement, happiness and a bit of worry. I was in my own world for a while thinking about it.'

He needn't have worried. Having been instrumental in the near-success of 2003–04 under Claudio Ranieri, both he and his great mate JT were immediate beneficiaries of the arrival in the summer of 2004, from Porto, of José Mourinho. One of the first things Mourinho organised was a team meeting and a session with each player. His soon-to-be legendary preparation immediately showed itself to the individual players. 'It's like an interview more or less,' he reveals, 'an interview where they can also put me questions. But I try to prepare, I tried to identify the points where I want to touch, what I want to hear. I want to show them immediately what I am and that I'm open, that I can be a sweetheart but at the same time I can be very nasty in my questions. So I could say for example to one player, "Hey, last two seasons, 11 matches – why? Why? You play nothing, you don't work, you don't sleep, you are always injured. The manager is shit? He don't like you? The manager is racist and did not like blacks? Why you don't play?"

'And the player he has to be open. So in this moment you know you can always get feelings from the players. There are some players that are never responsible for their failure – "manager doesn't like my face", "manager's training methodology is bad."

'Other players, they go straight to the point and they say, "I am guilty. I was not committed, I have to change myself, I have to start a new life." Other players they can say, "I don't like this tactical system. You think I'm a winger. I'm not a winger, I like to play inside." It is important to start an open relation with them.'

With some, like midfield fulcrum Claude Makelele, Mourinho knew what to expect. 'I think I not demonstration to José,' Makelele says in his faltering English. 'He has seen me for a long time. He has seen my function, he has seen my job, I never change my job.

'When a manager asks me to come to his team, I say what is my function? I never change my system when I play.

'I speak with José, I say, "You see me play. My system is this, I play this." He said the system that was in his head, and I say, "Okay, no problem."'

JT and Lampard soon proved themselves too. 'I think I could identify because of their style of play,' says José Mourinho. 'When you are outside and you see players on the pitch you can more or less smell it. I think what I did well with Lampard and Terry was to give them more power than they normally have in a dressing room. I give them the crown, you know? "You have responsibility."'

It's difficult to overstate the esteem in which Terry and Lampard are held. It's partly the respect they have in the wider football world, of course, but it's overridingly a result of the way they lead the squad, on and off the field. 'I think it was important for the group,' says the manager. 'And I think was important to have these players on your side ... to help you, not to disturb you. When I say breakfast 9 o'clock, if John Terry or Frank Lampard they are 9.10 then everybody thinks they can be 9.10. But they don't. So they were very, very good allies I had to hand with me. Very important for what happened to us. They play injured, operation last week. Why last week? Because the championship finish. So, everybody knows they play injured. I think we have very good players in the team, but these two personalities were very important to help me in my leadership.'

'When he first came,' says John Terry, 'the manager said to me and Lamps it was going to be me and him, we were going to be captain and we were both excited and both hoping.'

Mourinho left it open a few days, then made his decision.

'He made me captain and Lamps was vice-captain,' says Terry. 'He gave us responsibility round the training ground, on matchdays, you know, loads of little things for players, not only for me and Lamps, but for the whole squad. The manager gives everyone responsibility. He's got great trust in us and that's been brilliant for myself, Lamps and the other lads.'

No prouder man has worn the Chelsea armband than Terry, but he is quick to acknowledge two other legendary team-mates. 'Growing up at Chelsea, I was very lucky to have two great captains behind me to learn from,' he says. 'Wisey was really vocal and noisy around the place, playing jokes and with the things he done for the lads on and off the pitch. The way he was on the pitch, he got the fans going, he got the players going and that was Wisey and I learnt a lot from him. I would say I'm quite similar to Wisey. And Marcel [Desailly] was totally different. I'm not saying Wisey wasn't a ledg, because Wisey was probably the biggest that Chelsea's ever seen, along with Franco, but Marcel had that presence where he didn't need to shout. When Marcel spoke, everybody listened. So I had two different things, but growing up, those two were great role models for me to live and learn from.'

Terry brought that education to bear on and off the field. Before games there was the huddle, players taking it in turns to say something before kick-off, hopefully to inspire. He's always talking too. 'I don't want to make out I do everything for the lads,' says Terry. 'That's not the case, but certain things on the pitch, I'm just really loud and, you know, I like to organise, I like to be bossy. I think on the pitch the organisation is really a big key. I think there's a lot more talking on the pitch nowadays and I think that helps everybody in the whole team.'

Off the field there is a good atmosphere and plenty of bonding sessions. 'We had our Christmas party,' says Terry, 'we had a PlayStation tournament, we went paintballing, we went go-karting. There was just loads of things like that that we organised and hopefully we're going to do a few more this year. Things like that I just like taking responsibility for and dealing with them.'

Although he defends the record of predecessor Claudio Ranieri, who steered Chelsea to second in the league and gave Terry his first taste of captaincy, he eulogises about Mourinho's all-encompassing approach. 'It's so many different things,' he says. 'You know, tactically his coaching is spot-on. Physically his training's perfect. All of the work that he and his staff do around the place, going into games, at team meetings; we were more prepared about other teams. We knew a lot more about them.'

Mourinho always emphasises the importance of the carefully assembled coaching team, and is clear about the function of each. 'Rui Faria, I think now he is the only one who can share with me the methodology,' he says. 'He helps me on decisions, what we do in training. If I want to achieve this, we go this way. So instead of saying he is a fitness coach, I prefer to say he is like a methodologist. Because he understands everything about my methodology.

'Steve Clarke is the man who knows every player in English football. So if I'm before the game and I have the sheet of the opponents and there comes the subs – who is this player? He knows this player is from the academy, he has 179 centimetres, he is fast, he is slow, he is fat. He knows everything about that.

'He is someone I enjoy to speak with, because he always has an opinion. It's easy for me to ask him, "What would you do? Drogba's injured, do you play with Gudjohnsen or Kezman?" He always has his opinion. Sometimes it's not mine, but he always has an opinion and the reasons for his opinion. "I would play Gudjohnsen because he holds the ball better, he's more intelligent and he pass better. And for this game, I think it is important."

'Silvinho Lauro was a great player and more than that is a very good goalkeeper coach. So he cannot train other players, he cannot be involved in other things. I know the keepers with him only can be better. I think for Petr Cech it was fantastic to have him in this moment of his career. And Carlo [Cudicini], I think it is only possible with one goalkeeper coach like Silvinho: he doesn't lose his morale, his ambition, his potential. And you see every time he played during the season, he was always ready. So instead of become a bad man, because he lost his position, he was always top, which means the keeper coach is fantastic.

'Andreas Villas is a big help for me. He sees opponents, he discuss with me what he saw. He put in the computer all the information; I can show the players every slide and every piece of information. He is a very organised boy. Brito is a special guy too because I used to say this, "How is possible that somebody who can't speak English can communicate so well with the players?"'

It's true. Baltemar Brito, like some big, old, reassuring bear, influences players in a room simply by sitting among them, nodding, gesticulating, saying one or two words, a smile playing on his lips but never quite breaking. 'He has the players in his hands,' says Mourinho. 'The players, they love him. He can get from the players everything he wants. He doesn't speak English. He is from the psychological point of view very good, you know?

'The players trust him. They can say to him, the manager is a son of a bitch. They know he won't tell me. They trust him. He is a man of my confidence; he's a man of their confidence. Everybody loves him. He gets a great feeling from everybody.'

A Mourinho/Faria training session is different in character to anything seen before at Chelsea, but not necessarily in content. You can see why one of Mourinho's favourite teams was 'that beautiful Holland team in 1974, 78' and their 'fantastic way of playing football'. His is total football on the training ground too.

For Clarke, a Chelsea man since 1987, now one of the coaches charged with deploying the system, there is no one simple reason why the Portuguese triumphed where his predecessor, Claudio Ranieri, just failed. 'You can't say – "that's better, that's the reason",' he says. 'There's so many different factors, so many combinations of little things that all come together to make the package successful.

'I think the intensity the Portuguese staff generate in training, before matches ...' he muses, singling out what he considers the biggest change in coaching. 'They really work on players to demonstrate that the next game is going to be the most important game, or the next training session's the most important training session. Everything's geared towards that – people performing at their best at all times.'

It would be unfair to say that Ranieri, who, of course, achieved the Premiership runners-up slot and a place in the semi-finals of the Champions League, did not prepare the players tactically for opponents, but it was nothing like Mourinho. Ranieri had videos of set pieces prepared for team discussions and pinned the team on a board a few hours before kick-off. In the Mourinho methodology there is intensive tactical work tailored to the next match and in response to the last; what needs to improve and what to expect from an individual opponent. More often than not, the players know they are playing a day or more in advance and are given individual DVDs to watch. 'If I'm marking someone,' reveals John Terry, 'I know where he's going to run. I know he might have beaten me in the air, but I know where he's going to run to. I've got half a yard on him as a result.'

The players clearly benefit from this rigorously structured approach. The bond of trust so evident throughout Chelsea's title-winning season grew from an understanding and appreciation of the Mourinho way on and off the field. Villas's scouting insight and audiovisual materials are key and Faria considers personal training plans for each on a daily basis. It takes into account how much someone played or did not, and how much he will or won't play. Rolling schedules are drawn up deciding when and for how long each squad member will play in matches, and when they will rest. It is a source of annoyance to Mourinho that such careful considerations have not yet reached the training camps at national level.

The players work in groups according to their positions, with one or two specialist coaches taking charge according to Mourinho's plan. Three-a-side games are a popular way to fitness. Anyone who has watched these training sessions will be struck by the sergeant-majorly precision, each part of the session marked by a peep of the whistle. The contrast with any recent sessions in Chelsea's history is remarkable.

Claudio Ranieri's man, Roberto Sassi, was the last in a line of Italian fitness technicians who drilled and drilled the players. That was the reason why Sassi was always the first man to be thrown in a muddy puddle at Harlington as soon as one was formed.

'Just to run you don't need to think,' comments Mourinho. 'Sometimes you just close your eyes and you just do what they tell you to do. "Ten times 200 metres." On the seventh repetition, you are full of lactic acid, you close your eyes, but you do it. "They pay me for this, so I have to do it."'

Now, there is more ballwork than at any time since Glenn Hoddle's arrival. 'And because it is competitive,' says Mourinho, 'they compete every day and when you compete every day you become more prepared for that.'

'This way of working is not dissimilar to the way a lot of coaches worked in the past,' says Steve Clarke. 'Obviously you ran hard in pre-season but most of the rest of the time you played with the ball. Football players only remember what they did with the ball, they don't remember the running. They like ballwork; I think you get more out of them. If you have a group of 12 players and they say they're tired, if you throw a ball into them, they'll start playing whether they're tired or not. It's all in the mind.

'The philosophy's more about playing football. The football element of training is the most important element, not the physical element. If you do the football early and correctly, the physical element follows. It's automatic. There's no fitness testing, there's no strict diet – obviously, players at that level know what they can and can't eat and drink. They know how to prepare for a match. So you take all these things on trust. When they're together as a group, they have to eat what's put there, but it's not like dried chicken or dried fish or rice – there's a little bit more flexibility.'

The skipper approves. 'I'm not saying the previous managers didn't,' he says, 'but José treats us like men. If we're in a hotel, we can have a can of Coke the night before a game, we can do things the way we want to do and prepare ourselves right for the game. No, we're not going to sit up till three or four in the morning having 14 cans of Coke. It's a more relaxed regime but nowadays the players are so professional and we've learnt off the likes of Franco and Marcel. There's so many things that the manager's done.'

On the face of it this reverses a trend started in the Hoddle era. In 1994, faced with players who left Harlington straight after training and headed for the nearest fast food outlet, the new manager laid down strict guidelines about food and alcohol consumption, and even ran the rule over who sat at which table in the canteen at Harlington.

Now, although there is less nannying, there is more of a sense of self-reliance with which our Victorian founders might have empathised. Mourinho also accepts that his young men need to let off steam in the way other young men do. As long as they are on time for training, and as long as they are always able to give 100 per cent to him, it is something he willingly accepts. This is a more relaxed camp than any for more than a decade. 'In a place like London,' accepts Mourinho, 'I cannot have a bodyguard to each one of them. In London, if they want, they will always have a dark corner where they can do everything they want and nobody sees. So I cannot control their lives.

'The responsibility has to be: next day 100 per cent. And with the way we train during the season, I don't need somebody to tell me, "This player didn't sleep too much," because I know. "This player last night did a silly thing." I don't need that. I know already by myself.

'And with that there is a relation to the ambition of the players, they know by a silly night they can perform badly. Because they perform badly, next game I will change, and because the quality of the team is very, very high, maybe because of one silly night he lose his place in the team.'

How he handles the situation depends on the individual. 'I never defend the old headlines of football how everybody must be treated the same,' says the manager adamantly. 'I think the opposite. Everybody must be treated different. Absolutely. There are certain rules for everybody: 9 o'clock is 9 o'clock for everybody, 11 o'clock is 11 o'clock for everybody, but my relation must be different with everybody.

'Let me try and find two examples: John Terry and Lenny Pidgeley. If I say to John Terry, "You were a f**king shit, a disaster; next game if you do the same, out of the team," next game he is the best player. If I say to Lenny Pidgeley, "You have shit on your gloves, you cannot save a ball," next ball he have to save he drops.'

How could such cleverness, thoroughness and intensity fail?

John Terry noted an immediate psychological change. 'In previous seasons

I've gone to Arsenal and always felt we could have gone out there and won, but deep down in the back of my mind I felt that they were the better side. Last year, going into those games, we were better than Arsenal. And I felt that. There was no way we were going to lose those games and that's what the manager has instilled in us.'

The aspiration on the pitch at which this crescendo of preparation is aimed is emotional control. 'It's one of the keys,' says Mourinho. 'Without emotional control you cannot play, influence; you cannot react. You have to know what you have to do and not react. You have to be cool.'

In a season of many controversies – the UEFA tunnel incident, the Faria earpiece sham, the shooshing of the Scousers and the spats with Arsenal – coolness is not something always associated with 'cool'. That is how Mourinho likes it.

'Roman Abramovich coming in stepped the club up media-wise,' says Eidur Gudjohnsen. 'The players seem to be watched very closely whether they're playing for Chelsea or just doing their own thing. And I think with a manager now who's very interesting with his interviews, we're a hot thing for the press it seems. But he's taken the pressure off the players to a degree I think, without people realising. It always seems to be about him and just leaves the team to do its own thing and play football.

'In some cases he'll explain his motives to us. He has come out with some bold statements and he'll tell the team what lies behind it. But that's something that stays in the dressing room. The communication between us and the manager is very good. He expects a lot from us – and that's the pressure we want to be under.'

'He's very clever,' says Steve Clarke. 'He doesn't say much without thinking about what he's going to say. There's always a reason behind whatever he does, whatever he says. And 99 times out of a 100, that reason is for the good of the football club.'

In Chelsea's entire history, no manager arrived with the credentials of José Mário Santos Mourinho Félix. His predecessor Claudio Ranieri's legacy was to deliver the Champions League qualification in 2003 that helped convince Roman Abramovich to buy the club that summer, and then, under immense pressure following the Russian's arrival, to reach the semi-final in that competition and finish second in the Premier League. It was the first time Chelsea had ever managed that lofty position.

Despite no real playing career to speak of, Mourinho had won the league in Portugal twice, and the UEFA Cup and the Champions League in successive seasons. There was no higher gamble for him than taking on a club taunted by the fans of Manchester United and Arsenal for having won the league in black and white. Following his Champions League victory in May with Porto, Mourinho's options were open. The big appeal for him of Chelsea included a move to London and Premiership football. He had visited London as a tourist and as a professional with Barcelona and felt it was a good choice for his family. With the football it was the 'emotion, full stadiums, competitiveness, atmosphere'.

But then there was the challenge of taking on the poisoned chalice of Chelsea at the most exciting moment in its history. 'In Roman they have the ambition, the economical power,' he says. 'In Peter Kenyon you have the top power organisation in football, and I know he came from Man U, so I was immediately interested.'

Like everyone in football, Mourinho felt the impact of the new Roman empire. 'Everybody was speaking a lot about Chelsea,' he notes, 'the team of the moment. Everybody wants to join Chelsea, but at the same time Chelsea has the pressure that nobody wants. Nobody wants to go where you *have* to win. If you go to Milan or if you go to Manchester it is the routine of winning; or you go to a place where you have time and no pressure to win: you go to Liverpool – "40 points behind Chelsea, no problem". I connect immediately, the power of Chelsea and the pressure of winning. That's good, that's good for me.

'The final decision was when I met them personally. I listened for important things for me. They were saying, of course, when you want to create one of the best clubs in the world, you need to win. You go into Asia searching for commercial things and support, and you cannot go if you are a loser. If you want to take supporters from other English clubs: no victories, no chance.

'Peter Kenyon told something important for me: "We don't want to win one championship, we want to win the first, but we want to build Chelsea into one of the best clubs in the world."

'They showed me a PowerPoint presentation with numbers ... supporters in the world, supporters in England, Man United, Real Madrid, Barcelona, where Chelsea was, what Chelsea needs to do in sports terms to push all the other things, and I have got that responsibility in my hands. After that I showed them my PowerPoint presentation about my ideas about the team, and they were open for that. I could show them my way to win, my profile of players, of teams, of concepts, and they understood it well and we shared opinions and it was a nice two days.'

In a football world where a journalist can suggest that, 'Abramovich is the worst thing to happen in the English game in many, many years ... Unlike the sort of football-created wealth United, Arsenal and Liverpool built their success on, Chelsea's boundless bounty is not football money and that's why people resent it,' he realised his might be a thankless task. 'It's a risk I know I was going to have in a club like Chelsea,' he says, 'because you come, you change things, you work a lot, you do – in my opinion – a very good job, and in the end of the day some people can still think that with Abramovich behind him it is easy.'

Though it is not necessarily easy, in the summer of 2004 the Russian owner's money bought in the key figures of Paulo Ferreira, Ricardo Carvalho, Arjen Robben and Petr Cech.

A truly successful football season explodes like a neutron bomb in your social life, devastating friends, family and acquaintances indiscriminately and leaving only buildings – specifically pubs and stadiums – standing. That is how it was, from the moment Eidur Gudjohnsen's goal brought three points against potential challengers Manchester United in the first game of the 2004–05 season. It looked serious.

With the hard-working Damien Duff recovering from a shoulder injury and magical Arjen Robben injured in pre-season, Chelsea won seven games in various competitions by a goal to nil without the two wingers starting a match. Ever-prepared, Mourinho adapted to use a diamond in midfield. 'I was working during the pre-season for both,' he says. 'One and another. Because I know during a season you need that and you need to change during the game. You have injured players and you have no wingers and you have to play maybe the diamond, or you have wingers and you forget the diamond, and I always work two different ways of play to be ready for that.

'But almost in the end of pre-season in the US I was clear that Robben and Duff, they were special. And Lampard, I also spoke with him about it. He likes very much to arrive late into scoring positions and when you play with a closed diamond the concentration of players is bigger in the centre of the field and it is more difficult for him.

'I always try to bring the best qualities out of the players. I was thinking 4-3-3 is the best for us. After that, Robben injured, Duff injured, no wingers to start the season. We start 4-4-2.'

Once both were fit, Mourinho played them. 'I remember Arjen came on at half-time against Blackburn,' says Frank Lampard, 'and played so well with Duffa, who was on fire, and everyone realised they could play together. After that, people couldn't deal with their pace and skill, they were scoring and making goals.

'Those November games were important. That was the time we started banging in four goals against teams and it helped our confidence. We were playing so well then. Also we were putting to bed that whole boring 1-0 thing people were trying to put on us, even though it wasn't really true. We were showing we could dominate teams and kill them off.'

Either side of the critical Christmas period came games where TV coverage meant that Chelsea played ahead of Arsenal. In early November Chelsea went top by winning at Everton while Arsenal only drew with Palace; in January Chelsea won at White Hart Lane and fans in the pubs of the locality were delighted by Bolton's late winner over the Gunners. 'It's funny,' says Lampard, 'the year before it seemed to be the other way round and just when we had the chance to put pressure on them we always fell just short. We were playing so well, we built up a run and had become like they used to be – annoyingly consistent. Really, after that run of wins over Christmas I never had any doubt we would win the league.'

Mourinho places flexibility and intelligence alongside discipline as elements he looks for in a player. No one exemplified that more than Eidur Gudjohnsen, who finally scored his first hat-trick for Chelsea in the drubbing of Blackburn. 'I think I'd had 12 times up to then I'd been on a brace,' he smiles. 'Mainly because Ranieri always took me off when I had scored two goals! Yeah, I think out of the 12 times I was on two goals I must have been taken off about ten times. I dunno. I'm glad it came eventually.'

The Iceland international striker excelled in the second half of the season as an out-and-out midfielder. How he came to adopt that role is a fascinating insight into Mourinho's 'learning by discovery' technique. 'He was fantastic, in every position he played for us,' says Mourinho. 'He start as a striker. He played against Barcelona and Liverpool in the Carling Cup in that role behind the strikers, but after that he was transformed into a pure midfield player because we went back to our midfield triangle, and he was playing in the position where Tiago and Smertin and these guys were playing. But he is more an attacking player. When you don't have Robben you lose qualities in your team. But even without Robben, because of Eidur playing in that position, he gave us a little bit more flair. Holding the ball, passing the ball. Intelligent movement. I think he became a very good player for us. He's a team player. Tactically he wants to work for the team, a lot of ambition.

'After the game in Barcelona, I thought, of course, the result was not correct because of the eleven against ten situation. But at the same time I understood that we didn't play well. And my opinion was that one of the reasons was a little tactical mistake. So for the second game I want to make a change. Instead of playing with Makelele and the open triangle, for the first time we played Makelele and Lampard and Gudjohnsen in behind. And it's February or something like that, so we had eight months' of routine of playing with an open triangle and I want to change for this triangle. And I push the players to tell me what they think.

'They couldn't tell objectively. They felt something. And they were saying to me it was difficult to press Xavi. Why? "Because my distance to Xavi was too big. I want to press him, but when I arrive there the ball is not there. So I had to go there and I had to come back." So maybe it's better instead of playing with the open triangle, we play with Eidur in that position and Eidur is already on Xavi. So when we lose the ball, he's already there. "Yes that's for sure, if he's there he doesn't need to run 20 metres to go there, he's there. We have to change our shape, we have to think different." So we spoke one day, we spoke two days, on the third day I was saying to them my decision is this one.

'It's about experience and thinking. If you just say immediately, "We are going to change our system after eight months," you say "Why?" With my assistants when I need a real opinion I never give my opinion first. Because when I want to test them and to see which one is able to say a different thing than me I give my opinion before.'

When he first gave Steve Clarke his job, Mourinho revealed there were two sides to him: Mourinho the professional and Mourinho the man, 'When I work, I work, and we all know we're working. But when I'm not working, we can have laugh and a joke.'

'He's a different man when he's working,' says Clarke, 'but always a good man. He's hard but he's fair and that's the way it should be: he demands the best at all times.'

An example of when the two Mourinhos collided came in December. 'We were losing 2-1 at half-time and José wasn't happy,' relates Clarke. 'He gave them a rollicking along the lines of, "The best team is losing 2-1. We've been the best team, we've been better than Arsenal, we're doing this, we're doing that, but we're losing 2-1. How can this be possible? You come to places like this, you have to impose yourselves on the game." He was working himself up into a little bit of a frenzy. He picked up a plastic cup and assumed it was empty but it had some Lucozade in it. So the players are all that way and the staff are standing behind him – and he dropped it and volleyed it back towards the staff. The Lucozade came flying out right into my face. Carlo Cudicini was next to me and it's gone all over Carlo's clothes. And the boss is ranting and raving and then he's picked up a tub of Vaseline and he's heaved that as well, and it's bounced off the wall in the dressing room and there's a big blob of Vaseline stuck on the wall but slowly falling down towards the fitness coach's clothes. And I'm thinking, "What can I do? I can't tell the manager to f**k off."

'He just drowned me in Lucozade; it was running down my face. No one really noticed because the players were focused on the manager, but all the staff were looking at this Vaseline dripping down the wall. He was in the middle of his talk, so no one wanted to interrupt him because it was crucial. So I'm trying to grab a towel to wipe the Lucozade off my face and Carlo's trying to wipe the stuff off his gear and the fitness coach is trying to make sure the Vaseline doesn't fall on his clothes. And at the time it wasn't funny because you're so focused on the game. We're all as intense as the manager and we're thinking, "get them ready for the second half". But when you look back on it now, it was funny.

'After the game, he said, "I'm sorry, I'm sorry." It was one of those crazy moments – like Ferguson kicking the boot and hitting Beckham on the head. He didn't even know he did it. Then we came out for the second half and we scored within two minutes, so it worked.'

At the end of January, Chelsea were ten points ahead of Arsenal and 11 clear of Manchester United, with the two rivals still to meet at Highbury in what had become, remarkably, almost a play-off for second place. Mourinho was asked for his preferred result and, naturally, he opted for a draw. 'Since we achieved the five-point lead,' he said, 'I always say the same to the players: our objective every weekend is to keep the lead and head for bingo.'

February brought the first silverware of the Abramovich era at Mourinho's earliest attempt, the Carling Cup. The Band of Brothers had all now become winners.

At Blackburn the same month, Petr Cech capped an incredible season by breaking the all-time record for minutes without conceding a top-flight goal. 'For me the aim was always just to do my best,' he says. 'You know with Carlo Cudicini, who is a great keeper, it is going to be difficult, so in pre-season my aim was just to do my best and persuade the manager that I should be number one.

'I've done the record already when I was playing for Sparta Prague. It was 924 minutes or maybe more, so when we conceded a goal, I thought it was going to be very tough to do it again. It was ten games in a row and it was unbelievable, and when we did it here, it was 11. I was very proud and for me there was a moment and it was against Blackburn. When they had the penalty, I thought, "S**t, it's going to be finished!" And when I saved it, I thought then that we could go really far.

'Always the main thing is to win the title, to be successful with the club. The record was one of the bonuses. There were some difficult points or important points in the season. The first one was against Man Utd in the first game. It's always important to start well when you have a new squad, a new team and a new manager. This was the first point in the season. The second one was when we lost against Manchester City; everybody was saying that's it, now we're going to lose and drop points. The reaction was fantastic: we won all the games after this. And the third point was during the Christmas period: everyone expected us to drop points but we were marvellous during this period. It was not us but Arsenal and Man Utd that dropped points. That was the biggest difference between us.'

As a follower of the English game, Cech had watched Chelsea with interest from afar. 'I knew the club had big potential to be one of the best,' he says, 'but still they couldn't win the title or they couldn't win a place in the Champions League every year. But when I signed the contract they were still in the Champions League and playing fantastic. I thought they were going to go through the semi-finals when I saw their squad and the squad of Monaco. I was watching the game against Arsenal and when they went through the quarter-final in the last minute, I saw this was a big moment.'

Great as that Arsenal match at Highbury was, a bigger one in the career of almost all of the team would come in April at the Reebok Stadium. As a former Wanderer, it was Eidur Gudjohnsen's job to turn Henry V and deliver the pre-match rallying cry. 'Today,' he urged, 'we can make history and become champions of England.'

In the first half the 50 years of underachievement appeared to weigh heavy on the shoulders of the champions elect. Kevin Davies even squandered a free header at close range that had nerves jangling. At half-time, with the score 0-0, Mourinho delivered one of his most important rallying speeches. Steve Clarke sets the scene: 'We knew the team was tired. We were limping along, we were missing key players and we needed to win the game. We wanted to win it there and kill it. It was just motivation. José said, "I need more from you."

'How you choose to get that effort out of players is down to different managers. José's way was, "Give Stevie [Clarke] a jersey, give [Baltemar] Brito a jersey and for five minutes we will show you the passion needed to win a game like this." He did also say, "and after five minutes bring oxygen, call an ambulance and take me to hospital" – but that wasn't reported.

'He was having a go at them – that he'd do better for five minutes and then he'd be dead. It was key and they came out in the second half and played very well.'

'We were not good enough in the first half and he made that very clear to us and we responded,' smiles Gudjohnsen.

In the second half the history-maker was Frank Lampard. Coincidentally, he and John Terry had discussed what such a feeling would be like, just like any school kids in the playground might. 'Yeah, it was the night before the Bolton game,' recalls Terry, 'and we were saying "Imagine scoring the goals that win Chelsea the Premiership!" And the next day Lampsy did it. It's bizarre thinking about it now. You know, we'd often speak about things like that the night before games – and Lamps has got that forever. I wish it was me actually! But it's a great thing and just to be part of a great side, I'm privileged.'

Both the outstanding Chelsea midfielder's goals came from end-to-end moves. The first came when Cech's long kick was headed on by Gudjohnsen, the ball bouncing over Jarosik. The prowling Drogba, outmuscling Hierro, nodded the bouncing ball on into the box. Now Lampard, with a determination and clarity of thinking that was irresistible, stretched ahead of Candela to head the ball into space. Ignoring the French defender's desperate shirt-tug, Lampard was already adjusting his stride to wrong-foot Ben-Haim, the last line before keeper Jaaskelainen. What now opened up for him was not just the goal, but decades of disappointment. Lampard stared at the keeper, made as if to slot the ball to the far post, then tucked it inside the near one. The relief among the players and the fans, at whose end the goals were scored, was immense.

Lampard's second goal bore the trademark of champions. An excellent one-handed save at full-stretch by Cech gave Bolton a corner, which the Chelsea keeper palmed off Terry's head into the path of Gudjohnsen, whose first thought was a counter attack. His pass towards Makelele asked a lot of the pivotal midfielder, but he won the ball with his right foot, instantly swung 180 degrees and sent a glorious left-footed 30-yarder between Lampard and Carvalho, both breaking decisively into Wanderers' half unmarked.

'It was a strange moment,' says the midfielder. 'The only thing I can put it like is when there was the penalty shootout in the Euros and there's that long walk up to take it. Everything goes quiet. Luckily I'd scored one already so I had a safety barrier, but as I was running towards goal I felt confident.'

Lampard picked it up and drove forward on a solo run of seven amazing seconds, taking on and beating Jaaskelainen, driving the ball into the empty net. 'I joked afterwards about not passing to Riccy [Carvalho] but the truth is, looking back, I didn't really have any idea that he was actually there with me. I was so concentrated on taking the ball on, getting it past the keeper and into the net.'

At the final whistle, naturally, there were the incredible scenes of joy, relief and tears that accompany long-awaited achievements. The bonding of players, manager and fans at the away end lasted an age. The players had disappeared for a few minutes and returned in the now iconic T-shirts printed in anticipation. John Terry demanded that Roman Abramovich receive the acclaim the supporters wanted to show, strolling over with his arm around him, ruffling the Russian owner's hair. Long after the game, Joe

Cole and Didier Drogba cavorted on the top of the team coach. John Terry videoed the celebrating fans.

Like Peter Sillett, scorer of the famous penalty that brought the title in 1955, Lampard will forever be remembered for those goals. 'I had a lot of people say it to me,' he grins, still not accepting it fully. 'Friends were saying it to me that night: "You've made history." It was only when they said it that it sank in, "F**king hell, we have." I watch Chelsea TV and when those goal clips come on I get that feeling again, a bit of a tingle. It makes me proud to think that over a hundred years the club had won the league once and that we had won it again after 50 years; the importance gets to you.'

'Of course, it was magnificent,' says Petr Cech. 'You see all the people involved in Chelsea. They were with us in the dressing room and they were celebrating – all the squad, all the staff, everybody together with Mr Abramovich and the boss. I knew the club had only won the league once, but I thought it was in the 1970s. So when I saw in the papers that it was 1955, I knew this was a huge season because everyone has been waiting 50 years. I think this was a massive achievement for the club.'

For most supporters this was sheer, unreserved joy, a chance to head off to local bars, buy the best champagne, light an expensive cigar. To revel and reflect, play the mind games on the way home – 'Who do you wish had won the league for us but didn't? Zola? Kerry? Wisey? Ruud? ... Matthew?'

The majority of Chelsea fans were not at the Reebok, but watching from the pub – especially a rammed Shed Bar – or at home. 'I'm sure every Chelsea fan will remember the moment when Frank Lampard scored his second against Bolton and we knew we were going to win the championship,' says season ticket holder and TalkSport presenter Andy Jacobs. 'I'm welling up now I'm talking about it; I'm not ashamed to admit it. I was on my own, funnily enough. But I did, I burst into tears. I don't know what it was, I don't know whether it was all those moments, all those days, all that money you've spent, all that angst, everything just came out and I'm sure every Chelsea fan felt the same and I don't suppose anything we ever win again will feel like that. It was an incredible, incredible moment.'

In the Chelsea dressing room, as in 1955, it was a slightly different story – there was Liverpool to deal with in the Champions League on Tuesday. 'Maybe the people who've had the experience before would understand it a little better,' says Steve Clarke. 'But for the boys who haven't won anything, we just celebrated like crazy. And like I say, three or four hours after the game, everybody's tucked up in bed. It was a little bit like, "Is that it?" But when you have another game coming up, you have to get ready for that.'

'It was strange,' says Gudjohnsen. 'It took a while to sink in. Just amazing. Shaking the champagne and shouting and screaming and then after the game you have a moment when you sit on the coach and think, "Oh Jesus, we've won the league." That was something I've dreamed of since the day I started football – just to be a champion. And to give it back to the club I adore and love – that's not only great for me but everyone here.'

As Clarke suggests, the sense of professional anticlimax was no surprise to Mourinho. Everyone had been expecting dominant Chelsea to win the title at some stage. 'I tell you one thing,' he says, 'this is my third championship and never was there big emotion. I was champion in Portugal with seven matches to go, then with six matches to go and now, here, with three matches to go. So you know you are going to be champion. It's just a matter of when.

'You know you have 11 points, you have ten, you have nine, you have 12 … the only doubt here was just at home or away from home? Maybe Fulham, maybe Charlton, when? But everybody knows we are champions, so I think it's an emotion that you build. You almost can predict how you are going to react, you know?

'I went in a tracksuit to Bolton because I know there will be champagne. When you go home the feeling is the same. You know you are champion, you are proud, you have memories from the first day and what happened and so on, but in that moment is more a moment that you can control, you can control a little bit.'

The pain was more palpable, of course, after the stunning defeat at Anfield in the Champions League semi-final a few days later. 'Only football can put you on such a high and take you to such a low in three days,' says Clarke. 'That's why the game is what it is and has the following it has. At Bolton, the excitement … it's hard to put into words. Just the adrenalin of the day was incredible. One week on we'd calmed down a little – we'd had a big kick in the nuts; going out at Liverpool was really hard to take for the whole group.'

Winning the league with games to spare set up perhaps the greatest ceremony ever at Stamford Bridge for the arrival of Charlton. There was a playful atmosphere. If the Fulham Borough Brass Band had been invited, though, they failed to turn up, just as they had done in 1955.

Mourinho had conceded beforehand that if his side was winning and a penalty was won, the lynchpin – goal-shy Makelele – should take it. The late spot-kick was earned at 0-0, with points still to be gained, but the players insisted Maka take it anyway. The worst penalty by a Chelsea player since Pat Nevin's miss against Manchester City a generation earlier was saved, but when the France international responded well and just about hoiked in the rebound, he was mobbed like no other scorer that season.

'The game against Charlton was very strange. It didn't have the same intensity but the satisfaction was good,' says Clarke. The week before was exciting – winning the game, jumping around on the pitch, spraying champagne everywhere, not drinking any. No one drank champagne, there was no party. Three or four hours after the game, we were still coming down from the high of winning the league – but no party. Waking up the next day and immediately focusing on the next game ... Charlton was ... There's no adrenalin – just celebration; what you saw on the pitch [at Bolton] was just pure joy. Charlton was just satisfaction.'

At the end of the game, a proper presentation full of Chelsea pageantry had been organised and was played out without a hitch – another distinct rarity for the club. First, partly through the insistence of Tony Banks, the surviving 1955 players were allowed to do what had been denied them in the past: to parade the old Football League trophy. In a further reconnection with the club's heritage, there was a guard of honour of Chelsea Pensioners, including one special scarlet-jacketed individual, Joe Cusselle. A lifelong fan since 1920 who survived the Japanese PoW camps to attend the Moscow Dynamo match in 1945, he still attends matches as a Pensioner, works for Chelsea's education scheme and is living Chelsea history.

Through the guard of honour and the others came the backroom staff, the 2005 playing squad, then finally José Mourinho to hold the Premier League trophy aloft.

For Steve Clarke, veteran of the dismal days of the late 1980s, the short stroll to the platform was almost too emotional. 'Walking out in front of the crowd ... ' he begins, still moved at the memory, 'I've got to say I was determined to enjoy the day, but when I walked out and got the reception that I did, I had a little choke. That was a good moment. And then when you're walking to the podium and you see the Premiership trophy, the feeling was there. At last! For me to be involved after so long at the club – that was a great moment.'

After the ceremony, there were further celebrations on the pitch, the players letting go and playing the fool. Robert Huth commandeered a groundsman's buggy – and transported tens of millions of pounds worth of superstar perilously around the pitch at speed.

'I think maybe I could appreciate it a little more than some other players,' suggests Eidur Gudjohnsen. 'I'd been here five years and it means a hell of a lot to me. So I can imagine after 50 years ... This is a time when we're on the up, we've started to win things again and that's what we're all after. I'm just glad to be part of the team that won the trophy back. I've always been well supported by the Chelsea fans.'

Another favourite, Joe Cole, played football in the goalmouth with Didier Drogba's and Eidur Gudjohnsen's children. 'It was amazing going out for the presentation,' he says. 'It meant so much to me because I used to stand on the terraces when I was a kid. We worked so hard for it, though, did what we had to do, listened to the manager. I came here to win things and this season proves I made the right decision.'

It was a special moment too for the two title-winning skippers. John Terry met Roy Bentley two years earlier and has had 'a great relationship with him' ever since. 'He still comes to every game,' says Terry, 'which I think is fantastic. Every home game, he comes in the players' bar after and has a drink with the lads and he's on first-name terms with the players and the lads love him. It's great to see him about the place and he always says to me, "Good luck, I think you're going to do it – but remember, I was the first!" And after the presentation at the Charlton game he said to me, "I'm never going to let you forget that I was the first one to lift that."

There have been many critics of Chelsea, a team of which it is finally possible to be jealous. Midway through the season, when the flak was flying, Kenneth Quisgaard, a Danish friend of the author and Chelsea obsessive, produced the perfect response. 'We have a saying over here,' he said. 'It's cold at the top of the mountain, but the view is great.'

Not that the chill will affect our centenary manager. 'I'm preparing myself for next season,' revealed José Mourinho, speaking a few weeks after lifting the Premiership trophy. 'I think I will start the first meeting with the players by saying, "Why were we champions? Give me 20 reasons why."

'And we have to go through that, we have to speak about it so we were champions because of this and this and this. If you have it in your hands, if you know the reasons why we were champions, we have a very good starting point for the new season.'

And the new centenary.

2

THE COMEDY IS OVER

'The crowds massed around the stand for all the world as if this were the Oval and Chelsea had won the Ashes. There were speeches and sunny rejoicing and the Chelsea of the last 50 years were extinct. They had won something at last.'

The Times

If the trend in modern stadium design for spelling out words in seat colours had been fashionable in 1939 when the North Stand was built, it might have borrowed a phrase from the stoical Cockney working classes who were soon to face the Blitz, 'STILL.' it would have said,'MUSTN'T GRUMBLE, EH?'

'Even in the 1920s Chelsea were unpredictable,' says John Marsh, a fan who was taken to Stamford Bridge from Willesden by his father in 1921, and who can number Bob Turnbull, Ben Howard Baker and George Mills among his favourite players. 'Frequently they would beat the top sides but lose to the lower ones. Often they would find themselves a goal or two down in the first half-hour and somebody would say, "Turn around and look at Joe's face." This was Chelsea chairman Joe Mears, sitting on the front row of the stand. It would be a deep red, matching the colour of the carnation he used to have in his buttonhole.'

At least top-flight status has been reasonably secure since 1930. Chelsea was a wealthy club offering players – especially talented older ones – a great lifestyle. Everyone associated with the club was in the comfort zone. A pre-war fan, Peter Ralph's attitude was typical. 'I was always optimistic that they would win something,' he smiles, not altogether convincingly. 'And I always thought Chelsea were more entertaining than other teams. I was ever hopeful. However, there were always two or three players in the side not up to standard who needed replacing. One in particular I remember was the outside-left Benny Jones who, apart from a terrific shot, had nothing else to his game. I believe he ended up selling matches outside the ground later.'

It goes without saying that one of the main hobbies of residents near the King's Road is shopping. And, throughout the years, when money has been burning a hole in the club's pocket or people associated with the club have been in need of a boost, the board has been tempted to splash out on a nice new player or even a complete set of them. And they didn't need to be local.

The squad assembled by first manager John Tait Robertson, once a player with Glasgow Rangers where he was known as Jackie, boasted only one Londoner, Frank Wolff – 'a Chelseaite by birth', according to the 1905–06 handbook, bought from Hull City – and he only played once, in the FA Cup.

Most of Chelsea's stars between the wars were from outside the capital, like the Scots glamour boys Alec Cheyne, Hughie Gallacher, Alex Jackson, Bob McNeil, George Smith, Tommy Walker and Andy Wilson, the northern Irishman Joe Bambrick, the Geordie Jackie Crawford, or Barnsley winger Dickie Spence.

It was the arrival of new secretary-manager Billy Birrell in July 1939 that was to change Chelsea's strategy forever – eventually. It wasn't enough that he brought in a new trainer, South African Arthur Stollery, to replace Jack Whitley after 20 years.

'Billy Birrell was the manager when I started at Chelsea,' remembers Albert Sewell, who edited the programme for many years from the late-1940s. 'He was secretary-manager. It was a double job. And he had very little to do with the players during the week. He was an office man really. Not a tracksuit manager. He would watch the training for an hour or so and then go back to the office and do the office business. But he was very nice, a Scotsman, a very nice man.

'He joined in 1939 just before the war and he had all the wartime business to deal with, which must have been hard. He started the youth business; that was one of his credits.'

Birrell's far-sighted innovation was in taking the cream of young talent and providing specialist training and a disciplined environment on and off the pitch. In a departure from the habits of 40 years, the plan was to counter the escalating transfer fees facing clubs by producing players for 'free'.

Arsenal's Herbert Chapman had thought along similar lines in the early 1930s, but Birrell's approach, conceived on his arrival at Stamford Bridge in 1939 but delayed in its implementation by the onset of the Second World War, was a far more complete and exacting education for the youngsters. 'I wouldn't say it was the only one,' says Sewell, 'but it was very, very rare. He decided transfer fees were getting out of hand, and he set out to try and counter it and made plans to start this youth thing.'

John Graydon, writing in *The FA's Book For Boys* from 1949, agreed. 'The "Chelsea Scheme" is different from the numerous other junior football schemes,' he wrote, 'for it sets out to make youngsters not only good footballers, but first-rate citizens. Infinite trouble is taken in giving everyone a thorough chance and Chelsea's reward is a constant flow of young players from their Junior Club into their various senior teams.'

Soon the club bought part of the Welsh Harp training ground (in Hendon, next to the lake, on the North Circular Road) for its juniors to play games.

Once it had bedded in, and with proper investment, the system delivered a production line of talent that went unbroken from Bobby Smith, Mickey Harrison, Ron Tindall and Jimmy Greaves, through Barry Bridges, Bobby Tambling, Terry Venables, Peter Bonetti, Ron Harris, John Hollins and Peter Osgood, up to the era of Ray Wilkins.

Before the 1947 season Chelsea publicised the fact it was looking for applicants and thousands of letters poured in from all over the country. Eventually, 32 boys between 15 and 17½ were requested to attend three times a week and play against teams of their own age. The first Chelsea juniors team played under the name 'Tudor Rose'.

The curriculum covered 'physical development, mental alertness, speed and agility, coaching in the fundamental skills, team-work, tactics, technical knowledge, hygiene,' reported Graydon. The London County Council (the Greater London Authority of the day) advised the club on the boys' 'cultural and educational development'. Discipline was strict. 'Training begins at quarter-to-seven in the evening,' Graydon observed. 'If a boy arrives after the whistle has blown, he is sent home. If this happens again without a very good reason for not appearing at the appointed hour, he is politely told not to come again.'

Training was exacting too, a mixture of running and individual technical work with a ball. In the tactical room the youngsters were introduced to new ideas from the continent. 'What Chelsea, in fact, are really doing is to see that young players do not miss greatness because no one has taken the trouble to put them wise to their faults,' thought Graydon.

Birrell's lieutenants were the former players Dickie Foss and Albert Tennant, sometimes abetted by Dickie Spence, who spent most of his time with the reserves. 'Dickie Foss organised it very well,' remembers Albert Sewell. 'He was Billy Birrell's first right-hand man of the youth scheme. Dick Spence was a lovely Yorkshireman from Barnsley. His career had ended by injury – he broke a leg just after the war – and in his time he never became higher than about 13th trainer, always very much on the fringe. I always thought they kept him for his humour. He was terrific.

'He kept the whole place abuzz. He liked to dabble on the horses and the dogs and everything, and every year he backed Chelsea to win the cup. His bookmaker gave him way above the odds as a gesture. And in the year they won the FA Cup at last in 1970 he had said, "I've had enough of this," and he stopped – he hadn't backed them! He carried on telling that story against himself for a long time.'

So much for the future youth success. As a famous Scotsman once said on TV, you don't win anything with kids. After the Second World War Chelsea had only two pre-war first-teamers on its books and had to acquire a team fast. The big money signings were Tommy Lawton, Tommy Walker and Len Goulden, and later keeper Reg Matthews. 'In a way these purchases were isolated actions which didn't do us particularly great service on the pitch,' said the late Tony Banks, who saw his first match in 1949, 'and certainly in terms of our reputation did us positive harm. Because we would do that, it was like trying to distract attention from what the problems were. It's almost like Machiavellian stuff. What we do is, "Let's buy some big name and that'll distract everyone's attention." It didn't actually do anything for the team.'

While Lawton's cameo extends Chelsea's fantastic history of being home to Britain's greatest forwards, arguably the critical signings in that post-war period under Birrell were lesser-known players like John Harris, Ken Armstrong, Stan Willemse, Eric Parsons and Roy Bentley.

Still it was the same old Chelsea when in 1950–51 Birrell's boys needed to win the last four games to avoid being relegated. Even then results – especially Sheffield Wednesday's – had to go in their favour and it would all come down to the better goal difference – the figure arrived at by dividing goals for by goals against.

'They put Bill Robertson in goal for the last four games,' remembers Albert Sewell. 'He was a big, hulkish bloke, but he was like a jelly before those games. And Norman Smith, the trainer, before his first game, poured whiskey down him a quarter of an hour before the kick-off. Incredible.'

Peter Ralph was in the crowd at the end of April that season when Wolves came to the Bridge and Chelsea crucially won 2-1. 'The winner was scored by Ken Armstrong at the North Stand end,' says Ralph, who adored the fact that the right-half always gave his utmost. 'He clearly controlled the ball with his hand before scoring, but luckily the referee didn't see it. Handling the ball had been a bit of a feature that season. Earlier in the year, when Everton visited the Bridge, Jack Saunders punched a goalbound shot from Everton's Ted Buckle over the bar. Everton missed the subsequent penalty and Chelsea won 2-1.' Although Chelsea survived by a 0.44 better goal average, the club was once again a laughing stock.

Harris and Bentley almost quit Chelsea before the following season, 1951–52. Instead of the threatened Players' Union industrial action over wages, at Chelsea there was a two-man strike with two future members of the title-winning team refusing to agree terms with the club – the team was so bad the players were not earning enough. 'My team must have been the biggest joke in football, but I wasn't paid a comedian's salary,' said Bentley. He was paid £12 a week after tax. 'Johnny and I spent the pre-season training period playing golf,' said Bentley, 'although we talked football all the time.' A French team offered to take Bentley on the grounds of 'ill-health'. Another time Bentley revealed he had been offered £150 a month, plus all travel and other expenses, to coach a South American team, and received an offer to play in Bogotá.

'We walked along the Thames embankment, near to tears over Chelsea,' said Bentley. That's one experience at least many fans have in common with one of Chelsea's greatest players. But Harris and Bentley do seem to have shared the players' age-old love-hate relationship with the club. In one of the early season games in which he had refused to play, Harris, a non-swearing Scottish lay preacher and 'hard-as-nails' defender, even disguised himself in cloth cap and specs and paid to watch a game.

The 'Chelsea Two' held out for eight weeks without wages until early September. Finally the directors listened to their grievances and nearly all were dealt with. Harris had injured himself, but Bentley, restored to the team straight away, scored the winning goal in two successive games and scored in eight of his first ten games back.

At the end of the 1951–52 season, a tired and fed-up Birrell stepped down and Ted Drake arrived from Reading. Drake, who was to become Chelsea's sixth manager and the first to work closely with the players, had been something of a joker as a player. Once, in a team talk, the Arsenal manager had been using small tumblers of water to mark out team positions. Drake picked up one and drank the contents. Then he put back the glass and pronounced, 'The centre-forward's drunk.'

People wondered how the no-nonsense centre-forward, retired from playing after a spinal injury, would adapt to management. At Chelsea, it was noted by one who knew him that his 'natural humour and ebullience were strangely muted'. He put on a pin stripe suit and got down to business. But he couldn't stop himself lapsing every now and then. 'When Roy [Bentley] once missed a header in training,' says Frank Blunstone, 'the manager came on in his suit and got me to cross the ball. Ted nodded it in, saying, "That's how you do it." He was covered in mud. That's how he was. He certainly wasn't a tactician.'

Along with Peter Sillett, a £12,000 buy from Southampton, Drake regarded his best value signing for Chelsea as 18-year-old Frank Blunstone, £6,000 from Crewe. 'To sign Frank Blunstone in 1953,' marvels Albert Sewell, 'Ted had heard there was a board meeting going on at Crewe and he drove up there and he took the board meeting by storm with his offer. I think it was about £6,000 and to them it was money they couldn't refuse. He was the England-to-be left-winger.'

Blunstone stayed for years and became a lynchpin of the youth scheme under Tommy Docherty. He was a great servant. In digs, he actually had to share a double bed with Bobby Smith, later a member of Tottenham Hotspur's 'double'-winning side. The squad did not own a car between them.

They walked to a milk bar to spend their 3s 6d (17½p) luncheon vouchers or played billiards and darts in the old games room at Stamford Bridge. 'When I came down at 19 I went in digs,' remembers Blunstone. 'I went in digs with four of us. There was myself, Bobby Smith, Len Kell and Andy Bowman, and we lived in 11 Britannia Road, up the other end from the Britannia pub. Her [the landlady's] name was Mrs Scott and she was very good to put up four lads our age.

'But a lot of the youngsters didn't stay in digs because Jimmy Greaves and all that lot were London lads, Venables, Shellito, so they travelled. They got the tube in and out. They had season tickets given to them, all their fares were paid. It was mostly the senior players who were in digs. I'd never had a pint of beer in my life and in those days we didn't have enough money anyway. We were training by 10, though we had to be off by 11 when the whistle blew for the greyhound trials that were held at the ground.'

Drinking was not a big part of the Chelsea culture at the time and it was just as well because Drake was a disciplinarian and knew all the tricks footballers played on away trips. He'd get his trainers to check the windows to ensure no one was moonlighting. Once, Blunstone was rooming in Manchester with John Sillett and they kept hearing a toilet flush. On examination they found the toilet was flushing itself and the two youngsters cracked up laughing. 'Ted came in and asked what was going on,' recalled Blunstone. 'I tried to explain and he cuffed me – told me to get to bed, like I was a naughty boy.

'But he made sure he was part of his players' lives. When he went north to watch a player, he often got off at Crewe and walked round to our house. There was Mum and Dad, and all the kids, and there was the Chelsea manager. They sent round to the chip shop for his tea. Somehow I can't imagine Mr Mourinho doing that!'

Drake and Mourinho exuded a similar sense of calm confidence in the quality of their teams. 'We were very experienced,' says Stan Willemse. 'The whole team, without bragging, was all internationals. And Ted Drake was very quiet, very sober, and we liked him and we played for him.'

Willemse's steel was an important injection of spirit, but it wasn't just about players and hunger. In much the same way as José Mourinho has done at the club more than half a century later, Drake wanted a root and branch overhaul of Chelsea FC.

Part of his task, as he saw it, was to change the nature of the support at Stamford Bridge. Chelsea fans who went to Brentford versus Chelsea at the end of the war would have read the Brentford chairman berating his club's fans in the matchday programme for putting off opposing goalkeepers when taking a goal-kick. At Stamford Bridge, the opposite was the case. Strange as it may seem at the end of the century, the Chelsea stadium had always been regarded as a pleasant place where fair-minded supporters would generally applaud the opposition as much as the hosts.

Drake wanted to change all that and turn the ground into a more partisan and hostile environment, like other grounds, with hopefully a commensurate improvement in home results. He also wanted to ditch the association with the old Chelsea Pensioners, who since the earliest days had been allowed passes to matches at the Bridge. The classic Chelsea badge, an adaptation of which the club has now, featured the lion rampant (with forepaws raised as if attacking), reguardant (looking back in an act of vigilance), holding a crosier (a bishop or shepherd's staff). The big cat comes from the coat of arms of Lord Cadogan (adopted from the Sloane family of Sloane Square), whose name was associated with the club for 75 years. The crosier, or shepherd's staff, was taken from the arms of the Bishop of Westminster. Both were major landowners in the Chelsea area. Typically, it was not quite 'proper'. Chelsea FC is actually in Fulham, but it was inspired by the 1903 civic heraldry of the Metropolitan Borough of Chelsea.

Other players vital to Chelsea's eventual title success arrived at newly badged Chelsea. 'Seamus O'Connell was interesting,' says Albert Sewell. 'Because he came down from Carlisle, where Bishop Auckland were the top amateur team. The first time he came down to play for Chelsea he arrived on the train on the Friday to play on the Saturday and he had a brown paper parcel and inside that were his boots. Extraordinary.'

More experienced Chelsea fans had reached an accommodation with their team. As long as they put on some enjoyable football every week, no one would raise their expectations unreasonably. And if you learn more by failure than success, theirs was the best education in football.

But an unbeaten run of 14 games in 1953–54 – a Chelsea record – suddenly heralded a new defensive steel and teamwork. This, rather than the old flamboyance and flair, would be hallmarks of the title-winning side. As well as Bentley, Harris, Sillett, Blunstone, Willemse and O'Connell, Drake was also getting the best out of Stan Wicks, Johnny McNichol, Les Stubbs, Derek Saunders, Ron Tindall and Eric Parsons.

In that remarkable 1954–55 season a million people would surge through the turnstiles.

'They didn't shape like champions. In November they were halfway down the league,' remembers Albert Sewell. He would produce the definitive account of that title-winning season, *Chelsea Champions!* There were several factors, says Sewell, that made all the difference: defence and teamwork and spirit. The run began in November, during which they lost just three games and outstripped the opposition. There was a change of style throughout the club to what one reporter called a 'virile, aggressive, open and direct style'. It was no coincidence that Chelsea's reserves and juniors also won their titles that year.

In November 1954, with Chelsea meandering in mid-table, Army boy Blunstone became available for a run of games. 'I'm not being bigheaded,' he says, 'but someone pointed out that our results picked up then. It was because of the balance of the side. Jim Lewis, an amateur, had been playing on the left, but Jim was right-footed.

'West Bromwich Albion were FA Cup holders, a strong side, and we went 2-0 down. But Les Stubbs kept getting in front of their goalkeeper to stop him kicking, which you could do then. Eventually, the keeper kicked the ball and booted Les up the backside. The ref saw it. We scored from the spot and went on to win 4-2.'

'It was round about Christmas or just after that we started playing a bit better,' says Stan Willemse. 'There were about half a dozen teams in the running, but we ended up finishing quite easy. We had a good spirit, we were good friends.'

A remarkable goal in a vital game against Leicester City added to the collection of good omens. Leicester defenders Stan Milburn and Jack Froggatt are universally acknowledged to have scored the only joint own goal in professional English football. The match was on 18 December 1954 at the Bridge. It finished 3-1 and the incident is still fresh in Stan Milburn's mind – for all the wrong reasons. 'I don't know about the others involved but I was always embarrassed about it,' he says. 'You look back on your career and people always remind you about that goal, no matter what else you did. It's in the *Guinness Book of Records* – that didn't help!'

He appears to remember the actual own goal as if it happened last week. 'It was one of those things. Jack Froggatt was centre-half and I was right full-back and the ball was over on the right-wing and Eric Parsons crossed the ball and it came in around the penalty spot. We were both watching the ball and both kicked it at the same time and it flew in. We didn't say much. We just looked at each other; you couldn't say anything because it was a goal. Johnny Anderson in goal was speechless too.

'Chelsea then were always a hard team, always had flying wingers. The matches were always keen. Chelsea had the money and the big crowds.'

People were beginning to recognise the change under Drake – Chelsea were becoming an unusually mean and purposeful team at Stamford Bridge. 'In every sense this was a new Chelsea,' marvelled *The Times* after one display. 'Not a weak link anywhere and a line of forwards who found each other with penetrating passes.'

But there was still a sense of disbelief in the dressing room. 'We didn't think we could win it,' admits Blunstone, 'until we suddenly found ourselves top with a few games left.'

On Easter Saturday, Chelsea met their main rivals, Wolves, at Stamford Bridge. Chelsea hadn't won an Easter game for seven seasons. 'They'd beaten us 8-1 at Molineux the year before,' says Blunstone. 'We finished with nine men because of injuries, yet their manager, Stan Cullis, was urging them to go for ten. Ted Drake wasn't happy with that. So it was sweet when we beat them 4-3 away in December 1954 and now we were meeting in almost a title decider.' After that Molineux game, Drake's tunnel confrontation with Cullis would have been admired by Chelsea fans today, much as José Mourinho's contretemps with the likes of Arsène Wenger or Rafael Benitez would be 50 years on. Supporters love managers who show they care.

In the home match in front of a staggering 75,043 it was 0-0 with a quarter of an hour remaining. 'Parsons, Bentley and O'Connell all had good chances but were denied by Bert Williams,' recalled Mick Mears, a long-standing supporter and box-office staffer. 'And then Billy Wright stopped a certain goal from Seamus O'Connell with his fist and 75,000 people yelled, "Penalty!"

'We were stunned when the referee gave a corner, but then he consulted his linesman and pointed to the spot. Our hearts were in our mouths as we watched Peter Sillett step forward to take it, but ice-cool Peter smashed the ball into the net. The last 15 minutes seemed to last 15 hours.'

The penultimate match was at home to already relegated Sheffield Wednesday. A win in that and Portsmouth failing to win at Cardiff City would make the new Blues champions at last. With so much at stake it was a miserable match played out by a nervous Chelsea side. But a Parsons header, a fumble by a full-back-turned-keeper and a debatable penalty brought the two points in a 2-0 win.

In the programme for the Fulham match in 2005 was a historical photo depicting the pitch invasion after the final whistle. The photo stirred up many memories. 'We used to stand halfway between the West Terrace and the South Terrace,' says lifelong Blue Alan Tomkins, 'and on the Pathé News, after winning the game, you see this eight-year-old kid jump over the fence and run across the pitch. That was me. And actually I'm also in the photo in the Fulham programme. When I first opened it up and saw the photograph, I thought, "Am I in this?" And I'm looking everywhere in this photo to see if I'm in it and I came to the front and bang, here I am.

'I haven't got a clue who the people are next to me in the photo. The only thing I remember of that game is everyone starting to run across the pitch at the end, and I thought, "This is great!" I climbed the little wall and started running. My old man said, "Come back here," but I ran and I got lost in the crowd and I can remember first of all they came out with one of those big old-fashioned microphones, saying, "We want everyone to be quiet, because we haven't got the result [from Cardiff] yet." So everybody just stood there and it was like you could hear a pin drop. I can remember the tension was unbearable.'

Albert Sewell remembers waiting for the result of Portsmouth's game at Cardiff like everyone else. 'We got the result.' He smiles wistfully even now. 'It came through to the club. They were able to announce it and everybody went mad. I was up in the press box. I went down to the dressing room and it was all bubbling away and going on. I don't think there was champagne, I don't remember that, but it was just a general melee of happiness and "We've done it!"'

'We were in the bath when the Pompey result came through,' says Blunstone. 'We stuck bathrobes on and went back up into the stand because the crowd were calling for us. Roy Bentley, as captain, said a few words.

So did Joe Mears, the chairman, whose father founded the club. There was no trophy there, no champagne, no lap of honour. After the fans dispersed, I had a cup of tea and a cheese sandwich with my uncle and auntie, then went home.'

There was not the same restraint among the fans. 'I thought to myself, "I've found the right club to support,"' thought the young Alan Tomkins, whose aunt Ethel had attended the first Chelsea game in that same stadium 50 years earlier. 'I mean in 1951, 52, 53, we didn't do a lot. But it was my local club and that was it. When you're a kid you nail your colours to the mast and that was it. That was me, lifelong Chelsea.'

After the match Albert Sewell indulged himself for once and obtained the autographs of everyone on the team line-up page of his own copy of the programme he edited. It is his most prized possession. 'Ted Drake too,' he smiles, 'they've all signed ... And what I also find interesting, you can look at those signings and you can read the names. Autographs now... [he sneers and mimes a squiggle]. I think it's poor.'

Sewell felt strongly for Roy Bentley in that moment of triumph and redemption. 'Not just because he was captain,' he says, 'but because he'd come down from Newcastle and he'd had a difficult start because he'd been bought to replace Tommy Lawton, and how do you replace Tommy Lawton? Things didn't go for him. And then he finished up being top scorer for seven seasons and I thought, well, you know, if anyone deserves it, he does. He was a bit above your average footballer, intelligence-wise, I would say.'

The players weren't allowed to hold the championship trophy on the day. Instead they simply received their medals from Joe Mears in an ad hoc ceremony. 'I don't remember the trophy ever being shown at the Bridge,' says Albert Sewell. 'They had to be more careful in those days. If there hadn't been the right result at Cardiff, Chelsea wouldn't have won the title that day. The league were much more careful back then; they wouldn't have a trophy waiting to be handed over, in case it didn't happen.'

Others recall it being carted around the pitch before the first home game of the following season in a wheelbarrow.

Even the pressmen all but dropped their traditional sneering attitude towards the Fulham Road's overpaid underachievers. 'It was a red-letter day at Stamford Bridge on Saturday,' reported one. 'In years to come men will tell their grandchildren that that was the afternoon they saw Chelsea gain their very first major prize in football by becoming champions of the Football League. To those generations already passed, who in their time have been a faithful part, rain or shine, of the great cosmopolitan gathering on the Chelsea terraces, this would sound like some beautiful fairy tale. But it now happens to be true and it has come to pass, most happily, in Chelsea's year of Golden Jubilee.'

The media always look for a stick to beat Chelsea with, though, and they soon found it. 'They were slammed a little bit,' recalls Sewell, 'as being not great champions because they only had 52 points, but they still won it by four points. It went against them that they were the poorest of champions since the war, or whatever. It doesn't alter the fact that they did it.'

It is also a fact that Derby County won the same title with just one more point, 53, in 1975. No one mentions that Arsenal accrued the same winning total in 1938 either. The ultimate conspiracy theory of media bias against Chelsea came towards the end of that glorious campaign. On 25 March maintenance electricians and engineers in London opted for strike action that virtually wiped out national newspapers for a month.

Since Chelsea had gone top of the table for the first time that season two days earlier, on 23 March, the unions were quite clearly dominated not so much by Communists, as was alleged at the time, but by the Red hordes of Old Trafford and Highbury in their ranks.

Maddeningly, the new Blues' nervy march to the championship went virtually unreported in the press. Even this little gem from *The Times*, appraising the 2-1 win over Sunderland, was written but has remained unpublished until now: 'Chelsea as much resembled champions as the Battersea power station looks like a painting by Cézanne.'

It would have been another graceful and gratuitous Chelsea insult to add to the long list. Although perhaps there is a hidden compliment there after all. Looking at the structure now, there are compelling arguments for the French painter's Modernism actually having influenced Sir Giles Gilbert Scott's industrial 'upturned snooker table' beside the Thames. Miraculously, as if the grinding play of Wicks, Armstrong and Saunders had worn down even the unions, on 21 April the presses rolled again, so Fleet Street was able to give proper coverage to our title-winning triumph, two days later, against Sheffield Wednesday.

Chelsea fans nursing hangovers were able to salve the pain with headlines such as: 'DRAKE'S WARRIORS SAIL HOME', 'GENTS, THE TOAST IS CHELSEA' and 'CHELSEA, CHAMPIONS! JUBILEE CURE FOR THE BLUES'.

Coincidentally, when the team finally repeated the feat in 2005, BBC technicians' threatened strike action over restructuring could have wiped out *Match of the Day* on the night Chelsea lifted the Premiership trophy. Happily, it came to nothing.

Unfortunately, so did the title win in 1955. Chelsea started their defence poorly and never competed under Drake again. 'It did rather run down,' says John Battersby, club secretary at the time. 'Having got there you'd have thought this is the start of something that's going to last, but it didn't, did it? Whether it was because Ted had signed a lot of players from lower divisions I don't know. There were quite a few he went around the divisions for: Derek Saunders from Walthamstow; Blunstone from Crewe; Stubbs from Southend ... there were no mega-signings. Now whether they couldn't react to being champions, perhaps ...?'

The team began to break up as Ted Drake tried to bring more of the first proper fruits of Birrell's youth scheme through. Despite the arrival of stars like Greaves, Drake was increasingly viewed as a man out of time. When Greaves left in 1961, Drake was soon to follow.

With six years of a ten-year contract still to run, in 1961 came the headline: 'LACK OF SUCCESS LEADS TO DRAKE LEAVING CHELSEA'. Joe Mears announced that, 'Ted Drake's contract has been cancelled by mutual consent. We are making no appointment to replace him in the near future. Tommy Docherty will have charge of all matters to do with the playing staff, but he remains the coach.

'Ted was with us when we discussed the present state of the club and its lack of success since we won the championship. It was agreed by everybody, including Drake, that it is best for us to part. Drake will be generously compensated for the balance of his contract. He left today on a long holiday. Docherty will be in sole charge of the teams. He has a free hand in selecting them, although the teams will be discussed in committee [ominously]. It will be two or three months, I expect, before anything is done to replace Drake as manager.'

The board had been disappointed that their wonderful youth sides over the years had not blossomed into a league team. 'You could say that it is the general lack of success that has caused this parting,' Mears continued. 'Ted is a personal friend of mine. He did not ask for this job. I went after him. His departure has nothing to do with Jimmy Greaves. Greaves insisted on a transfer. There is no friction between Drake, myself or the board.'

Drake, only 49 at the time, said, 'I love the game and I love the Chelsea club. I have been 32 years in soccer and I have been very loyal to it and to Chelsea. We part on the best of terms and if there is anything I can do for Chelsea I shall be only too pleased to do it.'

Albert Sewell remembers Drake fondly. 'Oh, a lovely man. Very nice man, Ted, a lovely Hampshire dialect. He'd had a bit of managerial experience at Reading. And he moved to a house at Wimbledon and he lived in that house until he died, I think. But he lost all his medals, pre-war with Arsenal, Chelsea's championship medal and his five England caps, when his house at Wimbledon was burgled.'

John Battersby also remembers that Drake had another passion by then. 'Ted was mustard keen on golf,' he says. 'He was the first bloke who dragged me out at Chelsea golfing. He cooked up some story about going and looking at some property in Reading, where he'd come from, and he wanted me to go with him and bring my golf clubs, and we played a round. I don't think that pleased the chairman.

There is another, possibly apocryphal, story that reveals the level of detachment Drake felt after the title win. He was driving his car along the King's Road with Peter Sillett as passenger when the lights turned red. Drake stared ahead of himself into the distance. Sillett watched as the sequence went through amber-red and green to amber and then red again, without Drake driving off again. A passing policeman is said to have tapped on the window and asked, 'Are you all right, sir?'

'Oh Peter,' said Drake suddenly. 'I thought you were driving!'

Whatever the aftermath, Drake's legacy is immortal. It was sad that before he died in the 1990s he was only once introduced on the pitch to the later generations of fans, as the greats of 1955 were all but forgotten.

In more recent years that has been put right, with Tony Banks in particular a great supporter of Chelsea's first champions. Back in 1955, Geoffrey Green, the veteran correspondent from *The Times*, got it absolutely right, 'So, 50 years of indeterminate struggle, of hopes and disappointments, of fickle behaviour have at last found a point of solid achievement. The taxi driver, the artist, the chimney sweep, and the actor who rubbed shoulders at Stamford Bridge – "we go usually to cheer the other side" – can at last ride roughshod over the gibes aimed for so long at "dear old Chelsea".

'Perhaps all this strange transformation can be traced to the moment three years ago when, under new management, that affectionate old emblem of the Pensioner disappeared from the Chelsea crest. With him went the dilly-dallying of old, a Chelsea reputation for friendly and gentle, sometimes doddering, artistry, but a Chelsea who was exasperated by their failure to achieve results. Now much of that old wayward charm has gone out of them and they are quite altered in character, a team – if not quite without character – at least without outstanding personality.

'Looking back at some of the great Chelsea names of the past one recalls Windridge, Hilsdon, V.J. Woodward, N. Middelboe, the Dane, Warren, Andy Wilson, the cavalier Jackson, and Gallacher, one of the great and artistic centre-forwards of any era. Yet none of these brought real success. The streamlined Chelsea of today have outstripped the past and now they have to take themselves seriously. So do we. The comedy is over.'

EARLY DAYS

The **formation** and **location** of the club

3
ORIGINS

Chelsea Football Club is 'a riddle wrapped in a mystery inside an enigma.' Winston Churchill coined the phrase to describe his difficulty in understanding the Russia of Stalin and the post-war era. But it applies equally to the Chelsea of Gus Mears and Roman Abramovich, the two moneyed patriarchs at either end of the club's first hundred years.

To begin with, Chelsea FC is not in the borough of Chelsea, which starts at the railway line that runs behind Stamford Bridge's East Stand. It is situated in the parish of St John, Walham Green, Fulham, now in the London borough of Hammersmith and Fulham. Even in its very name lies a contradiction.

The questions on supporters' lips are eternal ones, ones you cannot regenerate with new bricks and mortar or new flesh and blood. They are in the soil, the dust, the air ... the soul of the place. Why, when undoubtedly some of the best footballers of each generation have played for the club, has it failed so dismally to bring home silverware? Why has such a big club so regularly lacked consistency? What makes it such a big club anyway? Despite the decades of failure, how has it managed to project an aura of glamour, of wealth and success, and attract a galaxy of stars and celebrities? Why did 28 million TV viewers tune in to watch the Leeds v Chelsea FA Cup final replay at Old Trafford in 1970?

There are many other curiosities to explore about the club of Foulke and Cech, Harrow and Terry, Middelboe and Lampard, Hilsdon and Greaves, Calderhead and Mourinho.

To understand the club's personality and its history, it might be useful to think of it as some great party to which you have been invited. Before accepting the invite, you would want to know three things: where it's taking place, who's organising it and who else is going along. In Chelsea's case, that means examining in turn the neighbourhood of the club, the people who have run it through the years and those who have followed it from its earliest days. Once we have looked at those aspects, you can make up your own mind about the Chelsea mystery.

The magical location and the communities that lived there is as good a place as any to start. In 1904, the local newspaper, the *Fulham Chronicle*, was in reflective mood about the spiritual decay of the area. 'Casual observation of the crowd which assembles on Saturday evenings at Walham Green has often prompted a curious query in our minds as to what those fervid souls who figured in the William and early Victorian periods would think of it all, could they rise from beyond the grave.

'When the spirit of political reform strode through the land with giant strength, our fathers and grandfathers were assured that the intellectual advance of the race must be maintained with the political. The worker was to be wise as he was to be free ...

'... And here we are with the bankruptcy of the theatre and the bounding prosperity of the music hall, the failure of the working men's institute and the glory of the *Daily Mail*. Verily our anticipations are often better than our realisations.'

The use the grounds of the London Athletic Club were put to since the mid-Victorian era had varied greatly. There were athletics events ranging from the record-breaking – the first black footballer in Britain, Arthur Wharton, famously broke the world 100 yards record there in 1886 with a 10-second sprint – to the corporate – company sports days were a regular feature on the calendar. Everyone from civil servants to laundresses held sports days on the grounds, where clowns and people on stilts mingled with participants.

It was a place of novelty and of giving new ideas a go. In November 1901 a balloon of the Aero Club of Great Britain lifted off and reached a height of

10,000 feet before landing comfortably at Maidstone. A year later on the same fields, John Tickner fell 100 feet to his death from the trailing rope of another balloon. It had just carried Rev. John Bacon and others engaged in a race with some cyclists on the ground, but suddenly took off again once people had got out. As poor old Tickner was lifted into the air bystanders yelled at him to let it go. He did, but only after reaching a height that gave him little chance of survival.

After such a tragic conclusion to a frivolous exercise, what must the upholders of common sense in SW6 have made of the imminent arrival of a new football team at Stamford Bridge, in 1905? By then Stamford Bridge was well established as a London playground, and perhaps a sense of 'not taking sport too seriously' has remained in the dusty corners, untouched by new brooms, ever since.

On 11 March 1905, *The Times* announced, 'It has been decided to form a professional football club, called the Chelsea Football Club, for Stamford-bridge. Application will be made for admission to the first division of the Southern League.' Three months earlier it had been called Kensington FC. They also considered London and Stamford Bridge FC.

In May there was a Football League meeting at the Tavistock Hotel in Covent Garden plaza. Representing the new club were Frederick Parker and Claude Kirby, both former officials at the London Athletic Club. Parker was honorary financial secretary, while Kirby had been elected as chairman. The night before the meeting, Parker ensured delegates were plied with drinks during intense after-hours lobbying. Then, with Kirby making his excuses, Parker delivered an inspirational speech to win the day before the voting. Chelsea were in.

The details could be finalised. Season tickets would be £1 1s for gentlemen, 10s 6d for ladies and 'schoolboys' for the grandstand, 10s 6d and 5s 6d for the ground only.

It would later be characterised as 'a team of talents that doesn't always blend together well'. The reporter was actually writing in the 1930s but, with one or two exceptions, it has applied to most of the ten decades since 1905.

Perhaps the spirit of adventure and fun infected the people who attended Chelsea FC a hundred years ago. Supporters would come from all over the capital – that had happened ever since the London Athletic Club's sports ground had opened on part of the old market garden site on Fulham Road in 1877. And it was in the club's interest to promote Chelsea as the best-connected team in the capital.

'All roads lead to Stamford Bridge' proclaimed Chelsea's first handbook, pointing out the rail links to Walham Green (now Fulham Broadway) and Chelsea and Fulham station (opposite the main entrance), that omnibuses 'pass the Grounds every few minutes of the day from all parts of London', and that 'River Thames Steamboats call at Chelsea Pier'.

Fulham Road had formed part of London's main route west for centuries. The London General Omnibus Company ran three buses along it: numbers 5, 14 and 15; the 11 and 19 then served the King's Road. By 1937 the number of daytime services to the area had risen to nine, and in 1993 there were 11.

Chelsea and Fulham railway station had been renamed in 1903, but it closed in 1940 and was mostly demolished in 1955. Housing was later built on its site, butting up to what is now Wandon Road, by the side of the surviving commercial parade with the old Rising Sun. Photographs taken in 1913 15 minutes before the start of a match indicate that great crowds of passengers would use this popular route, which brought supporters from Willesden Junction and beyond in the north to Putney Bridge.

The steamboats were actually run by a Chelsea director, J.T. Mears. During the transport strikes of 1919 that brought London to a standstill as the buses failed to cope, Mears, 'the Thames steamboat owner ... sent four of his pleasure steamers to London, where they landed at Westminster Pier.' Overcoming some difficulties using London County Council piers, 'the first three boats were crowded and the first four conveyed over 800 to town', along a route from Richmond, stopping at Hammersmith and Putney. The cost was 2s 6d return, 1d a mile.

Such a wealth of transport links placed Stamford Bridge firmly on the capital's map, and the club has always drawn from the great London well for its support. However, in the early years, the people living nearby would be the ones who established the club on the terraces. The area, and especially Chelsea, is amongst the best known places in the world. The very name is talismanic. There are hotels, songs, consumer goods; what other English football club's name is sufficiently beautiful to serve as a girl's name? The nearest rivals – Preston, Everton or Chester are better suited to cattle, West Indian batsmen or northern comedians. No one is called Arsenal.

There are more than a hundred compositions of popular music with 'Chelsea' in the title. Only Liverpool comes remotely close to competing with that musical muse. There are only just over a dozen titles including the word 'Arsenal' and little more with a 'Manchester'. And as for Tottenham?

And what attracts all the associations to Chelsea? Class, fashion, romance and style, obviously. The world knows Chelsea for the nearby King's Road designer outlets, Sloane Square, and the music and street culture of the 1960s and 70s; the Bohemian excesses of the Arts Club balls, dating from 1908; the flower show at the Royal Hospital, first staged there in 1913; the music halls; and those timeless emblems of selfless service, the scarlet-jacketed Pensioners.

All have garlanded the reputation of the football club, good or bad, and the associations are not merely geographical. The area has always long mixed the privileged and the penniless, the influential and the indolent.

To Tony Banks – or Lord Stratford, a different kind of Chelsea peer – occupying one of London's top addresses hasn't always been a blessing for the Blues, especially in the image it projects to the wider football world. 'I suppose in a way they've always sneered at us,' said the former Brixton boy who travelled to matches on the 45 bus. 'They've always thought we were effete, you know, not real footballers and not real football supporters. We were mincing weirdos and real Flash Harrys or showbizzy, glitzy – all the sort of things that don't sound like you're really good, solid football people. We've always suffered from that.

'It comes from our location, that's the first thing. When you think about it, that part of Fulham which we occupied, the old borough of Fulham, that was very working-class. Fulham and Battersea were very much the working-class part, but we were also rubbing shoulders with Kensington and Chelsea after all. There is no football club I can think of who were, as it were, located so close to one of the most affluent parts of the city and indeed one of the most affluent parts of the world. There are titled people and all sorts of things literally just down the road.

'And because of our location we attracted quite a lot of showbizzy type people. We've always had more than our fair share of famous names supporting our club and that brings you other problems.

'You could be a middle-class kid or family from down the road, but you'd also get quite a lot of students because there were quite a lot of bedsits in the Chelsea area. And then into the 1960s of course, clearly we were literally where it was all happening, the King's Road set, all this sort of stuff. And, of course, the very name Chelsea, when we weren't actually really in Chelsea, has all those associations with the literary set, Bohemia, the arts people, showbiz.

'And indeed that was reflected in the way that some of those suites in the rebuilt West Stand were named after various literary figures. I don't think that was the most satisfactory thing, and indeed many people thought the Zola suite was actually Emile Zola rather than Gianfranco, you know.'

But what of the more down-to-earth inhabitants of the area back in 1905? We are lucky that plenty of clues exist in public records, for instance, in the Liverpudlian philanthropist Charles Booth's 'Survey of Life and Labour in London' (1886–1903). In the spring of 1899, just five years before the club was founded, Booth surveyed Chelsea and Fulham. He coloured streets on a map according to seven grades of 'poverty classification' – from 'Black: Lowest class. Vicious, semi-criminal' to 'Yellow: Upper-middle and upper classes. Wealthy'. His notebooks also described what he saw as he walked around, leaving evocative pictures of neighbourhoods.

Even at its birth the club's feet were in working-class Fulham, but its head was in prosperous Chelsea. The immediate vicinity of the Stamford Bridge grounds, according to Booth, was largely middle-class, with small, surprising colonies of wealthy and criminal classes in the various courts and squares lying here and there.

Looking further afield the well-to-do areas blanketed north from a line drawn roughly between West London (now Brompton) Cemetery in the west and Elm Park Gardens, near King's College on Fulham Road, in the east. Its northern boundary was Kensington Gardens. Lords and ladies, diplomats and dilettantes, industrious directors and London's most fashionable socialites always lived here.

The idling pleasure-seekers who had set up the Chelsea Arts Club on Old Church Street (a mixed area on Booth's map) in 1891 included the famous painter Whistler and his sculptor, writer, dancer and architect friends. They liked a 'bit of rough' for authenticity in their unconventional lifestyles and their association with the area, especially through the club's annual balls that came to scandalise decent society, left an indelible mark on public perception of the area.

Chelsea retained something of a village feel and west London has never quite had the edginess of similar areas across town, such as Clerkenwell. There, an arty fringe to swathes of slums attracted intellectuals such as Karl Marx and created a seed-bed for British Communism.

Perhaps a proximity to water helped keep things cool in the west. Up in Hammersmith, Booth found a group of Russian nihilist writers with shelf loads of revolutionary books utterly untroubled by their neighbours because 'they are very quiet and don't cause any trouble.' The same could not be said of the pamphleteers and radicals of Clerkenwell.

The year after Chelsea FC was founded, Liberals made significant local gains in the area and across the south and west, while the north of England moved towards Labour. (The Chelsea board – including the Mears family that would dominate it for the first 75 years – was staunchly Conservative for many years.)

In the more working-class Fulham, as well as Chelsea, ranks of ancestral wealth and hand-me-down poverty stood side by side. One side of Queen's Club (founded in 1886) was comfortably middle-class; the other, straddling Field Road, exhibited 'chronic want'. It has since partially been absorbed by the elite tennis club.

Between Fulham Road and King's Road, in the parishes of St John and St Luke, Chelsea as well as Fulham, there were streets here and there forming an island chain of deprivation. Booth considered Slaidburn Street 'one of the worst streets in Chelsea, and I should say one of the worst in London'. He followed a police officer on his beat and described drunken, lawless hordes frequently in trouble with the law and 'drink-sodden women' of ill-repute hanging out of patched-up windows. Even in the 1940s, there were three families to every three-storey house in the road and prostitution was prevalent. But 106 years on from Booth's survey, a Slaidburn Street house sold for in excess of £800,000. However, as if some grim memory of the past remains, Slaidburn still lags behind other streets in Fulham and Chelsea.

Back in 1899, access to the nearby workhouse of St George Hanover Square or the infirmary might be considered a bitter sanctuary to the worst off, but other forms of relief were available. Until 1908, when it moved across town and river to Lambeth, James Burroughs and Sons' distillery loomed on Cale Street, producing Beefeater gin and methylated spirit.

There was more poverty in the St Augustine parish, an area trapped in the corner created by the conjunction of Lillie Road and Munster Road. Nor would a respectable person wander in the area between Sandilands Road and Furness Road, deeper into Fulham, where the worst crime in the area was evident. The same could be said of the streets draining into the Thames from the King's Road between Lots Road and Millman Street. 'Altogether this is rather a depressing district,' commented Booth of this patch, 'which has, I should think, afforded a refuge to a good many who have been displaced in slums further West.'

Perhaps, though, some of their wealthy neighbours' stardust had rubbed off on them. 'What the reason may be I know not,' Booth wrote, 'but I have certainly seen more life in the poorer parts of Chelsea than in any other district: children especially.' He was struck by the robust health of the youngsters playing in the streets – 'almost without exception they have been well-nourished'. There was, though, an inordinate number of 'low people who drink to excess and indulge in hawking'. Cheerfulness in adversity, a useful spirit for a football supporter.

The southern line drawn under this lair, overlooking the shimmering Thames was, of course, Cheyne Walk, the ultimate symbol of success to the Victorian gentleman, and sometime home of James McNeill Whistler, J.M.W. Turner, Marc Brunel and David Lloyd George.

Chelsea's directors were sprinkled around the area. Chairman Claude Kirby's neighbours on Wardo Avenue ranged from shoemakers, postmen, coachmen and a Harrods office boy, to hotel managers, interior designers, book-keepers and those of independent means. Gus Mears, founder and first owner of the club, lived at 444 Fulham Road. Ever the go-ahead type, his brother Joseph Theophilus, universally known as J.T., commuted from the Old Ship Hotel, Richmond, in his early Model R Ford car. He would later own Ford dealerships and make a pile. Whip-maker and saddler to the privileged, George Schomberg, a grandee among the new money, lived on the Brompton Road. Edwin Janes and his uncle Alfred ran local drinking houses.

Alfred is also probably the only Chelsea director who was thought to have haunted a building. He lived in one of the last remaining big old Victorian properties, 'Chesterfield', on Streatham High Road. He was the subject of intense pressure to sell, but held out for years, refusing to sell. Then finally, in his dotage in 1929, Janes reluctantly accepted an offer he couldn't refuse and moved to Clapham. The developers built the cinema on Streatham's main drag that still stands to this day, first called the Astoria. Janes died in September 1930. In 1933 the cinema's fireman, Lewis Amis, was doing his rounds late on Christmas night when he saw a figure advance towards him. He shone a torch on the shape and saw an old man in a long white gown with a hood over his head and a wizened, wrinkled face with a short beard. The figure then turned away and moved through two heavy and firmly fastened doors, floated over the orchestra pit and stood in front of the curtains wailing, in a weird husky voice, 'I won't sell, I won't sell!'

Back in 1905, though, there was plenty to offer those with the leisure time besides the Janes family's pubs. Music Hall will forever be associated with Chelsea. The Granville Theatre of Varieties was built in 1898. Its shell still stands opposite the old entrance to Fulham Broadway tube station (renamed from Walham Green in the early 1950s after representation from local traders).

Twenty-three years later Chelsea star John 'Jack' Cock, renowned for singing lustily all the way from the dressing room to the pitch before games, would make his public debut there. After the war it served as independent TV studios and the Beatles rehearsed and recorded three songs for *Shindig* there in 1964. In 2005 it was draped with a massive banner celebrating Chelsea's second title triumph.

If the bill there didn't appeal, in 1905 there was always the Chelsea Palace on the King's Road, with its two performances nightly, 6.40 and 9.10 – 'the principle stars are under contract', or Alfred Butt's Victoria Palace, tickets ranging from 6d and 2s 6d, opposite Victoria Station.

Chelsea are more closely connected with that variety tradition these days than the club has ever thought, or hoped. The ritual celebration song since the early 1980s, 'Celery', is in part derived from the old knees-up number 'Ask Old Brown'. It's a song probably familiar to any working-class Londoners over the age of 60, including Mr Knapp, a Chelsea season ticket holder who died in 2004 aged 83. He remembered his mother and the rest of the family singing it when he was much younger. It went:

'Ask old Brown for tea
And all the family
If he don't come

We'll tickle his bum

With a lump of celery.'

Another who had the same experience at family get-togethers was Chas Hodges. He always loved the song, which was always thumped out on the joanna. That's why he recorded it in 1981 on an album called *Christmas Jamboree Bag*. If we believe the story, it was the famous Chelsea fan Mickey Greenaway who picked up the cassette version during a Chelsea tour of Sweden in August the same year. On the journey over and throughout, he played the tape to death and 'Celery' came out of that as a new Blues anthem.

In case you haven't guessed, Chas Hodges is one half of Chas and Dave. So Chelsea fans probably owe one of their most self-defining songs to a couple of Spurs fans and a music hall ditty.

The Chelsea/Music Hall connection is actually quite natural. Besides the Granville, renowned entertainment impresario Oswald Stoll (of Stoll-Moss fame) actually planned to build another theatre on the Fulham Road. Being a teetotal non-smoker made him pretty much unique among his kind, but here was a Music Hall director with no perceptible sense of humour, who 'only ever swore twice' and who was notoriously mean.

Stoll ran many theatres in London, including the Hackney and Shepherd's Bush Empires, and he built the Coliseum and the Hippodrome. And at none of the venues he managed did he allow the blue jokes or raw humour that was meat and drink at others.

The plans in Walham Green, though, revealed the philanthropic side of his character. Having repeatedly applied for planning permission for his new theatre to no avail, he and others built the War Seal Mansions in 1916, intended as a self-contained community for disabled ex-service personnel and their families. Since 1937 they have borne his name and remain a landmark on the route to Stamford Bridge. The theatre was never built – the Granville must have wielded more influence on licensing authorities than Fulham FC could on the Football League when trying to redevelop Craven Cottage.

Mears sold his delightful home at 444 Fulham Road, along with the premises next door, 446, and the land behind, to Stoll in 1910 – a cash-in of unwanted land from the original acquisitions from a Mrs Poisson on 5 October 1903. Stoll passed on the land to the War Seal Foundation and work here did not start until 1917 when the first 72 flats were built – these cost £17,000. They have just built a new block of 20 flats that cost £2.2 million.

The focal points of Walham Green were a big draw. In an age when some lacked proper cooking facilities eating out was cheap and readily available. There was the Redcliffe Cage Restaurant at 276 Fulham Road run by Mr Giandoni, serving Apollinaris table water, or the Red Lion at number 490. In the parade opposite the Stamford Bridge ground were John Lawrence's coffee rooms, Mrs Laidler's confectionery (her husband was also a plumber) and the premises of Albert Collier, a beer dealer. Alongside were George Simmons's tobacconist and the dairy counter of the Graham Brothers.

The buildings would be recognisable even now to those who went to the first games. On the corner, the Rising Sun pub would play a lengthy role in Chelsea history, mostly in quenching the thirsts of generations of Chelsea supporters, but in the early days as a venue for board meetings. It was at what was described in the *Fulham Chronicle* as 'another meeting' there on 14 March that they named the club Chelsea and considered applications for the post of manager. The paper found it a curious choice of name since 'it will be no more connected with the neighbouring borough [Chelsea] than with Timbuctoo'. Perhaps the name indicates simple lack of imagination; when the club launched their matchday programme, it was called the *Chelsea Chronicle*. How did that go down in the *Fulham Chronicle's* newsroom?

No one went without drink in the area. As well as the Janes family pubs near the ground, the Rising Sun and the Black Bull, the family ran the Duke's Head in Parsons Green and the King's Head next to Walham Green station. But there was also the White Swan at 571 Fulham Road (now Brogan's), the White Hart across the road and the Britannia, 40 years later the meeting point for the first Chelsea Supporters Club. In case that wasn't enough, bottles of Worthington were also available inside the ground.

Remarkably, much of the old Victorian infrastructure of the area remains. The biggest change is to Walham Green station itself. It changed its name in 1952 (much like Ted Drake and Chelsea sadly ditching the association with the Pensioners), under petition from local traders, to Fulham Broadway. The modern shopping complex that straddles it replaced a shabby parade of small commercial properties which for a long time included a sports shop and the

Stamford Bridge Café, where the likes of Charlie Cooke would grab a fry-up. There also used to be a George Best Café a few hundred yards to the right outside the station, but that was subsumed in an earlier redevelopment.

It is instructive to stand and watch the traffic pass by there. The luxury sports cars and the buses. Even though few people know it's proper name, Walham Green is what it always was – a vibrant mixture of the very rich and the very poor living almost uniquely cheek by jowl, with each end of the scale displaying an unusual spirit and lust for life in utterly different ways, coexisting relatively politely.

The same children Charles Booth noted for their vigour in adversity would marvel at the latest local diversion, rush to the stadium with their parents, rub shoulders with the Arts Club fops and families of professional people from north, south and east, along with the capital's elite from Kensington and Mayfair, all flocking to see London's newest football team.

Chelsea FC, though, would rarely be perceived as a working-class club. From the outset it was seen as the rich man's plaything and the team of London's elite. If its feet stand in earthy Fulham, its head has always been in airy Chelsea.

4
THE FINEST GROUND IN THE KINGDOM

'The Chelsea ground, one knows, has magnetic properties.'
The Times

As we enter the second hundred years of Chelsea Football Club, we look around at a magnificent stadium – and wonder why it isn't bigger. One of the marvels of Chelsea FC had originally been the scale and grandeur of its ancestral home. I still recall the enchantment at the moment, as a toddler, that I first walked up the steep steps at the side of the Shed End to be confronted by the magical landscape of massed humanity ranged around the gloriously undulating open bowl of Stamford Bridge. And I dare say it had the same effect on everyone.

In later years, particularly the late 1970s and 80s, the thrill was tempered by uncertainty as to what size crowd we would be part of – Chelsea had again become a 'walk-up' attraction on the day by then. But the magnitude of the ground was always remarkable and it helped make Chelsea what it is today. Nevertheless, by the mid-1960s, when I first went to games, the stadium was in need of regeneration. It had long been a mixture of unspoilt Edwardian grandeur and latter-day compromise. Some of its facilities evoked the grim conditions behind the Iron Curtain described in newspapers.

A group of us actually called the cowshed-like toilets behind the old West Stand 'Poland'. But like a spouse in a seasoned relationship, we had reached an accommodation with its faults and even developed an affection for some of them.

But gradually charming and quirky became shabby and unworkable. New stadium licensing legislation arrived, and the club's finances ebbed and flowed. Three distinct, ambitious redevelopment plans were raised since 1960. One never got off the ground, the second could only be implemented in part, and the final one is largely what we see today.

There was rarely the coincidence of capability off the field and success on it. It took nearly 20 years to recover financially from the setback of the East Stand development, during which time the entire ground was almost lost to developers. But at the end of Chelsea's century, the club boast a stable, clean, world-class £100 million stadium that comfortably accommodates 42,400 spectators with fantastic facilities. We have hotels, restaurants, bars, executive office space, an underground car park and an in-house TV station. We even have environmentally friendly roofing material on the North Stand.

For long periods in our history we boasted the largest club venue in England, setting records yet to be beaten. Now, our capacity lags behind Newcastle, Sunderland, the Manchester sides and Arsenal. It soothes neither the romantics nor the realists among us to know the club's current owner is as rich as Croesus. A smaller stadium means lower status as much as it prompts higher entrance fees. And the seeds of what we have at the close of the century – including the restrictions on ground capacity and threat to its future – were sown by the people who built the first grandstand.

The history of Chelsea's ancestral home is every bit as intriguing and twisted as that of any thousand-year-old castle. And although the football saga began in 1904, the Stamford Bridge ground's roots on the site go back to April 1877, when wealthy financiers the Waddell brothers, James and William, freeholders of the grounds, built the first basic stadium as a home for the London Athletic Club. 'Miss White, the daughter of the Lord Mayor, performed the opening ceremony, and there was a very notable gathering,' according to the *Fulham Chronicle*.

In a few years, though, the Waddells, former athletes who became LAC officials, suddenly absconded leaving the LAC with substantial debts, and in 1883 John Stunt, a boot maker on the Strand who had owned a market garden, houses and stable buildings covering around two and three quarter acres adjacent to the stadium since the 1830s, stepped in as freeholder to secure its immediate future. (It wouldn't be Chelsea without a Stunt being involved somewhere along the line, now would it?)

It was soon after this that the Mears brothers arrived on the scene. Their Hampshire-born father, Joseph, a well-known London building contractor, died in the 1890s, leaving them financially well set for the future. Both had entered the same profession as their father and were well used to buying up land or property for commercial redevelopment. When they approached Stunt, though, he was unwilling to sell what was already a prime piece of real estate. The Mears brothers would have been well aware that wherever the underground went, a property boom followed. The District Line extension to Putney Bridge, taking in Walham Green, was built in March 1880.

Stunt died in 1902 and his relations, Robert and Charlotte, were involved in the negotiations as early as December 1902 that would lead to the freehold of the stadium lands transferring to Gus Mears – on 29 September 1904. The complication was that John Stunt had bequeathed that athletics should continue on the purpose-built grounds for two years after his death.

In the meantime, in October 1903, Mears snapped up the adjacent parcel of land formerly owned by Stunt, and leased by Augusta Poisson (née Dillon) of Southampton. Mears and his family were living in one of the houses on that estate, 444 Fulham Road, in 1905. In between his home, called 'Bellwood', and number 446 (formerly 23 and 24 Stamford Villas) was a pleasant garden with some outbuildings. To the left of 446 was a private road leading to the rest of Stunt's market garden triangle, which bordered the District Line track on the north-west and the Stamford Bridge ground to the north-east. This is the space, approaching three acres, that the Oswald Stoll Mansions now occupy. The private access lane down where Stunt's horse and trap passed is roughly where the entrance road under the Stoll Mansions arch goes today.

The fact that Mears had bought this extra land next door to the popular arena at all – presumably not just to live there – added to local concerns. And then there was the involvement of his brother J.T., an even more active speculator. Although he didn't appear on any documentation, J.T.'s closeness to the negotiations is borne out by the witness signature of Tom Lewin Kinton, his manager at Crabtree Wharf, and a future Chelsea director, on the leases. What would two property developers do with 14 acres of highly valuable brownfield land? To some Londoners, if the pleasure grounds were lost to concrete it would be like losing a lung.

At February 1904's annual meeting of the London Athletic Club, the committee announced it was looking for a new ground within a few miles of the present site at Stamford Bridge, which would be handed over to 'the builder' Mears on 24 June that year. The deeds were drawn up in the name of Henry Augustus Mears, founder and sole proprietor until his death in 1912.

Once the LAC's lease ran out, there were fears for the future of leisure in Walham Green, as voiced by the *Fulham Chronicle* of 30 September 1904. 'Although the *Sporting Life* has suggested that the Stamford Bridge Grounds may yet be saved for metropolitan and other athletes,' it said, 'it is generally thought that the estate will be quickly realised for building purposes.'

Athletics, it felt, would seek a new home and 'upholders of the sport in the most legitimate sense of the term are naturally grieved at the prospect of transfer to the "rapacious builder". It is pointed out that the ever-advancing tide of bricks and mortar has already devoured grounds at Catford, Wood Green, Kensal Green and Ilford. Paddington would have gone the same way but for the vigilance and public spirit amongst the municipal authorities.' But it seems the Mearses were not yet 100 per cent certain what to do with the site and kept their options.

In 1961, 79-year-old John Smith, known for the 50 years he'd kept turnstiles at Stamford Bridge as Jack, sent a typewritten account of his 'True Story of Chelsea Football Club' to the club. It was his brisk, informal and often half-remembered take on some (but not all) of the important events he had witnessed, and the various people at the club he had known. Jack lived at Ancill Street, off Lillie Road, and worked as a carpenter at Crabtree Wharf, run by J.T. Mears and his brother-in-law Henry Boyer. His account suggests that football, and indeed a stadium, were an afterthought to the Mears brothers. According to Smith the first thing they did was sell off a vast amount of sand on the Stamford Bridge site to the building trade. It extended from a foot underground as far as the water table. Smith was roped in to help do it.

Other than clearing it for house building, there were two options being considered for the land. The Great Western Railway were said to have tabled a lucrative offer to use the space as a coal and goods yard.

The second possibility was explained, retrospectively, by Chelsea's first secretary-manager, John Tait Robertson. 'Mr H.A. Mears, who is the son of the late Joseph Mears, the well-known contractor, conceived the idea of turning the Stamford Bridge Athletic Ground into a football arena,' wrote Robertson. 'He and his brother, Mr J.T. Mears, have played football all their lives, and being as fond of sport as they are wealthy, determined to buy the piece of ground that seemed to them so eminently suited for their purpose. It was more centrally located than any other existing ground, and it was large enough, when treated by a skilled architect, to hold the biggest crowd the most ambitious club-manager ever dreamt of.'

In 1904 the Mearses publicly pledged to spend up to an incredible £100,000 to ensure that the Stamford Bridge stadium was the best around. No doubt this was to support their intention of creating a national stadium to host lucrative cup finals and other events – an idea that may have subsided with the opening of Wembley Stadium in 1923, but which was actually resurrected in SW6 56 years later.

In 1904 it had validity as the doyen of football stadiums, Simon Inglis suggests in his book *Engineering Archie: Archibald Leitch – Football Ground Designer*. There was, Inglis notes, dissatisfaction with the existing national stadium, Crystal Palace, which could hold 115,000, but was 'inconveniently located and appallingly designed'.

Stamford Bridge was always superbly served by transport. The Mearses' main revenue generation lay in paid-for leisure and bricks and mortar, so building a sports stadium for the masses was in harmony with their business strategy. As it turned out, the driving force behind this visionary scheme would become Frederick W. Parker. The original idea was not to create a new football club but to offer the ground to nearby Fulham FAC. J.T. Mears's company had actually laid out their stadium at Craven Cottage in 1896 but Fulham were now looking for another solution.

In July 1904 the *Fulham Chronicle* revealed that 'arrangements have been made to remain at Craven Cottage during the greater part of next season. At the expiration of that period the tenancy of the club terminates, when it is hoped they will take possession of their new ground, which is quite near to the scene of their operations.' The new ground presumably being Stamford Bridge, which offered 11 acres compared to Craven Cottage's six and close proximity to Walham Green (now Fulham Broadway) station.

In January 1905, the famous Glasgow stadium architect Leitch was called in to examine and redesign the four Mears-built wooden stands at Craven

Cottage, one of which had been pronounced unsafe by the police and ordered for demolition.

Gus Mears was looking for Fulham to take root at his site, offices and all, for a sum of £1,500 per annum, but as landlord he would retain all monies accrued from other rentals, such as cup games and internationals. Fulham's Chairman Henry Norris gave him short shrift but John Dean was confident Mears could be hammered lower. Wealthy as the Mears brothers were, though, they were actually seeking outside investment to get the Bridge project off the ground and it was proving hard to raise. Take the annual £1,500 out of that and you have a 'deal-breaker'.

In the meantime there was relief on Christmas Eve 1904 when the LAC 'arranged terms with Mr Mears, the freeholder of Stamford-bridge grounds. The members will enjoy all the privileges, to which they were accustomed when the club was in full possession of the ground, as to training, lawn tennis, and the use of a club dressing room.'

Parker urged Mears to hold firm against Fulham, saying, 'They have the club, you have the finest ground in the kingdom; if they won't come to terms tell them we will start a new club that is bound to become one of the best in the country.' It was the first step on the road to Chelsea Football Club, but almost a false one. Fulham eventually rejected the Stamford Bridge option and Mears was convinced by that to sell to the GWR after all.

Parker was a good friend of sport as well as the Mears brothers. He drew up figures projecting that Stamford Bridge could reap £3,000 a go from major events alone. Parker had a head for figures and a way with words. Aged 41 in 1905, Lambeth-born Parker was passionate about sport (in 1912 he agreed to become Chief Athletic Adviser, travel the length of the country and advise on team selection ahead of the Stockholm Olympics). He lived with his wife Rosabelle and daughters less than a mile from Stamford Bridge, at 11 Foskett Road, near Hurlingham Park, and he was an official of the London Athletic Club, setting the handicaps and scheduling the races. But as the son of a banker, he'd left school as soon as he could to become clerk to a coal agent and his head was in the commercial world. His brother was a stockbroker and it was to the Parker brothers that the Mears siblings now looked to offload their investment.

The famous dog-bite story that is said to have changed the course of football was later related by Parker in this way, 'I met him by appointment one Sunday morning when we had the whole of the old grounds and adjoining vast market gardens, also purchased by him, to ourselves. He told me no one else would "come in with him", so he would accept the GW Railway offer for the whole site ...

'Feeling sad that the old ground would be no more, I walked slowly by his side when his dog, coming up from behind unobserved, bit me so severely through my cycling stockings as to draw blood freely. On telling the owner, "Your damned dog has bitten me, look!" and showing him the blood, instead of expressing concern he casually observed, "Scotch terrier; always bites before he speaks."

'The utter absurdity of the remark struck me as so genuinely funny that although hopping about on one foot and feeling blood trickling down, I had to laugh heartily and tell him he was the "coolest fish" I'd ever met.

'A minute later he surprised me by slapping me on the shoulder and saying, "You took that bite damned well. Most men would have kicked up hell about it. Look here, I'll stand on you; never mind the others. Go to the chemists and get that bite seen to and meet me here at nine tomorrow morning and we'll get busy.'

The stadium plan that delivered Chelsea FC would be put into action on the whim of an entrepreneur after the bite of a mutt.

The two men must have met Leitch while he was in London for the Fulham hearing, and now paid a visit to him in Glasgow, touring his creations at Ibrox, Celtic Park and Hampden, newly opened in 1903 for 80,000 spectators. Gus's sister-in-law may even have put in a good word. J.T.'s former barmaid, now his wife Henrietta or 'Ettie' (née Watt), was born in that city too.

Leitch, the son of a blacksmith, was the dominant grandstand architect in an era bookended by the disasters at Ibrox 1902 and Hillsborough 1989 – both stadiums of his design. 'From conception to inauguration,' wrote Simon Inglis, 'the new Stamford Bridge would be ready for use within just eight months.' J.T. Mears's own men built the banks for terracing with soil from work on the Kingsway tram tunnel and the Piccadilly Line. The wily contractor was actually paid handsomely to take the clay and soil off their hands at a shilling or more per load.

When Leitch's plans were submitted to the London County Council on 23 February 1905 they consisted of one grandstand and three banks of terraces, to a template he used elsewhere. The East Stand would consist of 4 to 6,000 seats, covered by a steel-framed roof with pedimented gable, and fronted by a terraced enclosure; 50,000 would be accommodated on the terraces. The stand was the same dimensions as Craven Cottage – 120 yard long, roof suspended from 70 foot high iron columns, accommodating 5,000 – built the same year, though theirs was finished with brick and Chelsea's was corrugated. Opposite, on the West Stand, Leitch proposed a roof cover with a gabled arch, suitable for a press area – something that was becoming increasingly important for bigger games. This was never built at Stamford Bridge, but a replica was fitted to Leitch's new stand at Anfield a year later.

The long-term idea had been to cover the whole ground so that '50,000 enthusiasts will be enabled to watch Chelsea pulverise their opponents, well sheltered from bad weather.'

There were extra dressing rooms for athletics use too, though that was not good enough for the London Athletic Club's Dr E.B. Turner who, in January 1906, disclosed the inconveniences caused by the rapid expansion of the ground – despite the landlord, Mears, doing all in his power to help them. He then chastised what he called 'degeneracy in sport': too many lookers-on and not enough 'doers'. Twenty thousand people, he scoffed, would go to see 22 people play football at the Bridge. He would rather have had 22,000 playing and 22 looking on.

To fund the launch of the new club and ground, the Mearses launched a 5,000 share issue, which was snapped up enthusiastically – unlike the similar event at Southern League Fulham around the same time. The board soon worked itself out: the Mears brothers, J.T. and Gus; Henry Boyer, husband of their sister Beatrice; J.T.'s manager at Crabtree Wharf, Tom Lewin Kinton; John Maltby, clerk of the club's solicitor, Slater & Co; the pub-owning Janes family, Edwin (of the Rising Sun, opposite the ground) and Alfred; and upper class whip-maker and saddler, George Schomberg. William Lewis was lured from Brentford to be the first club secretary. A shipping clerk, great amateur sportsman with Finchley Harriers and lifelong LAC member, William Claude Kirby became chairman; Frederick Parker maintained his connection with the LAC but was made honorary financial secretary at Chelsea.

As work progressed on the stadium, the Glasgow connection, already strong – what with the architect Leitch and co., J.T.'s wife Ettie, new manager John Tait Robertson and many of his recruited players – grew stronger.

It was like little Caledonia on the site. All the steelwork came down the Great North Road from Glasgow. Grass for the pitch was grown in Winchester but laid by Scottish labourers.

Stamford Bridge opened for business for the friendly against Liverpool on Monday 4 September 1905, two days after the renovated Craven Cottage. At that game, reported Ernest Edwards of the *Liverpool Echo*, 'When I told the Chelsea half that his Kop did him well he said, "They're only just starting on it really. It won't be finished until the end of the season."'

'Good, goodness, gracious!' spluttered Edwards in reply. 'It'll hold a mighty crowd when it is finished.'

He was right. When Manchester United visited on Good Friday 1906, it was in front of the largest league attendance at a football match up to that point in London: 67,000.

Following promotion in 1907, Chelsea became the nation's best supported club, consistently averaging over 30,000 at home and proving a box office draw on their travels.

In December 1910, having paid Mrs Poisson £2,000 seven years earlier, Gus Mears sold over additional land to the west of the Bridge to Oswald Stoll for £8,500. It was a nice profit, and recouped some of the investment from the development of the ground (and just maybe helped fund the purchase of the players Jack Harrow, Tom Hewitt, Geoffrey Johnson, William Read and Robert Buchanan the following spring).

Simon Inglis rightly points out that there were inherent weaknesses in Stamford Bridge's design. As time passed there were too few seats added. Worse, the stadium lay on a north-south axis and on sunny afternoons those in the main East Stand, until 1939 the only place to sit down in comfort, were staring straight into the sun.

But with soil banking and terracing at the north and south ends increased to match the enormous swelling on the west side, a capacity of 80,000, then 85,000 was achieved, and it became the largest stadium in London. And when Crystal Palace (still recovering from its use by the forces during the 1914–18 war) became unavailable for football, the FA Cup final of 1920 was offered for Stamford Bridge to host.

It may have been overdue, and there had been many international, inter-league, cup semi-final and Charity Shield matches there (the last of these being Everton 2 Chelsea 1 in 1970), but it was very welcome.

Apart from the raised terracing, between January 1920 and April 1921 there were alterations to the Royal Box and the press seats, with improvements to lavatory facilities costing nearly £8,200.

The 1920 final finished Aston Villa 1 Huddersfield Town 0 after extra time. But attendance was restricted to 50,000, in part by apparently overpriced tickets. There was also inflation and the threat of unemployment as Britain headed into recession. Chelsea staged the finals until 1922 but the opening of Wembley in 1923 killed off Parker and Mears's dream. Parker appears to have left Chelsea in 1915 anyway. Sadly, too, Gus Mears had died on 4 February 1912. A notice was placed in *The Times* with the date and time of his funeral at Brompton Cemetery: 'Friends are asked to accept this as the only invitation.'

Hundreds turned out to see him off in the rain, and as the cortege passed by Stamford Bridge, it paused for a moment for him to enjoy his creation one last time. His catchphrase had been 'Don't worry' and his absence was a major blow beyond simple morale. His brother J.T. became the dominant influence on the board and a series of events had ramifications that would nearly kill the club half a century later.

The first great Chelsea scandal would erupt in 1921 over the handling of Gus Mears's estate, which included the freehold on the land on which Stamford Bridge stands. It was serious enough to prompt an FA inquiry, which concluded that the way Mears was running the club was damaging to its interests.

The issue came to light in a letter to the FA in July 1921 from founder director Henry Boyer, husband of Beatrice Adelaide Mears, Gus and Joseph's sister. He alleged that his brother-in-law was attempting to overcharge and rip off the club and that he had effectively been excluded from the board of directors because he was the only one who knew all the damaging facts.

The FA took the concerns seriously and made a polite exploration. They were disturbed enough by what they found to order a commission of inquiry under Mr J. Howcroft which uncovered a very detrimental state of affairs. In Gus Mears's will he passed on the Stamford Bridge freehold in trust to his sister Beatrice, one of its trustees, along with all rents payable on it from the club. For eight years Beatrice made no move, then in July 1920 she sold to the club properties adjacent to the ground: numbers 418, 420 and 440 Fulham Road. The club paid £1,250, and eight months later, in April 1921, were in negotiations with the Trustees for the purchase of the ground itself.

They were told at first that it would cost £50,000. Since Chelsea at the time had around £8,000 in the coffers, they would have to borrow from the bank. Then out of the blue came an announcement the same month from board member J.T. Mears that he had bought the freehold and was the new landlord – all cheques should now be payable to him.

He offered a choice as to how the club might proceed with its lease on the site: either carry on with a year-round lease for the rest of the agreement at the cost of £3,000 per annum, with the corollary that he should be given sole catering rights on the site; or to extend the lease to 99 years with an additional rent premium of £2,000.

The board opted for a 99-year lease with no signing over of the catering. Mears wrote back asking for the £2,000 premium and £100 per year for providing the refreshments. The board backed down on the lease extension but not the catering, and the next thing they heard from him was an offer to sell them the ground for £42,000; £7,000 upfront, and the balance payable over 14 years at £2,500 a year with ten per cent interest. He also demanded that the recently re-elected Henry Boyer, the Trustee's husband and his brother-in-law, be kicked off the board for 'non-attendance'.

Here is where Boyer intervened, revealing that he had not even been invited to board meetings, and alleging that Mears wanted him out of the way because he knew how much the Trust had sold the ground to him for: £35,750.

The board mustn't have known who to trust – before selling to her brother Beatrice Mears had been trying to charge the club £8,000 more than that! Even so, J.T. was slapping on an instant mark-up of £6,250, or 17.5 per cent. In his defence, he pointed to the construction in the past of bars around the terraces that he had built at his own expense, and reminded people that he had failed to get a licence for them during the war years and that he had frequently lost bar takings when thieves took advantage of the big crowds.

The investigation shifted to the way Mears had been dictating things at the club since his brother's death. The stadium improvement work in 1920–21 now came under particular scrutiny. There had been no tendering process, no estimates or plans had been subjected for assessment, and there had been few progress reports. Moreover, the work had been given to Mears' own company with a 20 per cent profit margin, was supervised by Tom Kinton (a Mears employee as well as club director), took an age to complete and was deficient.

'The Bridge's embankments had been raised and terraced so hurriedly that the material had not been allowed to settle,' wrote Simon Inglis, 'causing the rakers on which the barriers were bolted to shift. This meant that a programme of continual running repairs was necessary.'

The FA's report was damning, and made three main demands: that the gene pool of the board should be broadened by the addition of members unconnected in any way with the Mears family; that all future stadium work be closely monitored by the FA or its approved agents; and that the catering contract should be open for tender.

Needless to say, the vital opportunity for the Chelsea board to buy its own stadium had passed. Ten years later another opportunity overlooked would have an impact that is felt no more than in the present. Today, the ground's capacity is capped almost entirely by health and safety issues because there are no egresses other than those onto the Fulham Road, and the concentration of too many people all using one thoroughfare at the same time is deemed dangerous.

Even in April 1905 pedestrian walkways to provide alternative exits from the stadium had been in people's minds. The railways talked about extending the platforms between West Brompton and Chelsea stations, with a footbridge over the lines to the ground. The District Line promised something similar from Walham Green. The only new access carved out back then was the path through Mears's own beloved garden at 'Bellwood', probably roughly where the Britannia Gate is now. Manuscripts from 1934 in the London Metropolitan Archives, including a perfectly drawn plan and map of the area, show how keen the police were at the time to find another direction to convey people from the ground. Bruce Buck, the current chairman, now has a copy.

The police's case was simply put in a police report dated 28 March 1934: 'At the conclusion of each match the spectators commence leaving and until the actual finish of the game little difficulty is experienced. There are three large exits on Fulham Road and a small one in Stamford Bridge. From these gates the whole crowd enter Fulham Road and for a period of a quarter of an hour in less important games to a much longer time in those of more important [sic], vehicular traffic is completely stopped and diverted from Fulham Road to enable spectators to depart in comparative safety ... It is bad enough on Saturdays when traffic is light but if there happens to be a Cup Tie replay in mid-week the congestion is serious.

'The Undergound Co. was approached by the Commissioner [of Police] and asked to make an internal communication between Walham Green Tube Stn and the ground, and also the London Midland and Scottish Railway Co. asking similar facilities at the station of the West London extension. These efforts were not successful at the time on the ground of expense, but as control of the underground system has now been vested in a public body, the London Passenger Transport Board, the time would seem opportune to make further endeavours to obtain more sympathetic consideration of a scheme, which would, it is estimated, absorb 40 per cent of the spectators who now enter and leave the ground from the Fulham Road.'

'All we are concerned with,' wrote Chief Inspector Day, 'is the fact that people are brought there by railway, dispatched into the streets only to enter the ground and vice versa, whereas with structural alterations it would be possible for large numbers of people to proceed direct without using the streets.' But he immediately spotted the key issue: 'One can read between the lines that it will be a question of who should pay. This is no matter concerning the police ...'

The Ministry of Transport saw no reason to dig into its pockets to pay for the walkways. The London Passenger Transport Board treasurer initially warned, 'I must point out that the trouble to which you refer is not caused by the Board but by those who are responsible for attracting large crowds in the vicinity of Walham Green Station without providing adequate facilities for handling and dispersing such crowds.'

But then in November 1934 the Board relented, commissioning and presenting fully specified architectural plans for a walkway and footbridge at Walham Green, even taking into account the placing of new turnstiles and the position of the dog kennels at the north end of the stadium – Stamford Bridge had become a greyhound racing venue two years earlier.

They estimated costs of the scheme as £8,000 and were prepared to stump up three grand of it. 'It is to be hoped that this improvement will not be delayed unduly,' wrote Chief Inspector Day, having seen the plans.

It now came down to whether Chelsea would stomach the £5,000, or at least part of it, and in January 1935 the police met with Chelsea chairman Claude Kirby. A Mr F. Gentle of the Stamford Bridge Greyhound Racing Club was also present, which tells you something of the influence the dog racers had quickly acquired.

Kirby was a mustard keen golfer and from the memo in the LMA files, it sounds like he might have had to give up a day on the links for the meeting. He was withering about the LPB proposal, claiming it 'would not be of much use ... as it would only serve one portion of the ground and it would mean the club having to double the staff at the additional turnstiles.'

He then stated that where they used to have 60 to 70,000 gates it now rarely reached 35,000. 'As regards the dispersal the 20-foot footpath would only accommodate 3,000 people,' he said, and he thought that it would be a happy hunting ground for pickpockets. Outside the kennels he feared that the cross-streams of pedestrians would be such as to cause great congestion and that would-be train passengers would prefer to leave the ground and enter trains by way of the railway station proper.

For this reason he thought the scheme doomed to failure. Mr Kirby also said he felt sure his club would not be prepared to contribute to this scheme but he undertook in due course to examine any improvements to evenly distribute the crowds on the highway. Mr Kirby added that the crowds clear in 20 minutes and that this happens only about 15 times a year, a total of five hours a year. He then instanced Twickenham, the West End Theatres and other football and dog racing grounds.

What improvements Claude Kirby had in mind we may never know: Chelsea's resolute first chairman succumbed after lying ill for several weeks on 24 October 1935, aged 67. Three months later, the night of a 0-0 FA Cup draw at home to Fulham, 19 February 1936, his successor C.J. Pratt, 70, also died. This sudden flurry of bereavements at the club had begun with assistant secretary Bert Palmer's death and been swiftly followed by that of the domineering Joseph Theophilus Mears, who fell unconscious with a blood clot in the heart on 27 September 1935 at his grand home, Royston House, opposite Kew Gardens. Gus's wheeler-dealer older brother had done very well indeed out of his contracting business, his wharf and pleasure cruisers, the cinemas, the Ford car franchise and Chelsea FC.

According to his grandson, Brian Mears, in his will he left a trust fund (including, of course, the keys to Stamford Bridge) worth just under £30 million. As a guide, in 1926 Lord Rothermere was rated the richest man in Britain with a personal fortune of £5 million short of that. Staggeringly, in today's money the 'Mears Trust' would be worth roughly £1.5 billion. A J.T. and a billionaire at Chelsea. Now that has a familiar ring, doesn't it?

5
FOUNDERS, KEEPERS

'Speculative stadiums built for profit seldom prosper. Stadiums built with heart endure.'
Simon Inglis

As landlord, having lost major athletics events because of the state of the track, and experimented with cinder track racing (early speedway) and other novelties, J.T. Mears had forced greyhounds on the club whether they liked it or not. It is interesting that this change in tack from the wealthy, vulnerable Mr Mears should come at a time when the all-pervasive, murderous Clerkenwell razor gang of 'Darby' Sabini was most active in their protection racket of entertainment impresarios. Two of the most notorious Sabinis, Joe and Harry, were shareholders in the White City, Harringay and Stamford Bridge Greyhound Racing Bookmakers Association that controlled the betting pitches on the terraces.

Whatever the reason, the greyhounds arrived, compromising the players' training sessions and dictating stadium policy. Back in 1904, the unruffled reaction of Frederick Parker to a dog bite had helped make up Gus Mears's mind to go with Parker's idea of creating a football club. Now it was as if Mears's dog was biting all over again, but this time it was drawing blood from the club, not Frederick Parker. Most of the planning applications that went in during the 1930s were related to the greyhounds, including more and more Tote booths buildings, kennels and the like. In 1930, a roof was at last built over the south end, but in its size and bizarre orientation it only served the purposes of the racing fraternity.

When J.T. Mears died in 1935, the ground once more became the property of a trust, benefiting his three children and their heirs, and vulnerable to the whims of the trustees. The battle of Stamford Bridge was far from over.

Things didn't improve when, under the chairmanship of Lieutenant-Colonel Crisp, the application for a long-overdue new stand on the north side came through in 1939. It was always ramshackle and poorly conceived and stood unfinished for five years of war. When it was completed it looked embarrassed for itself, standing out all alone and different, nestling up against the East Stand for comfort. And it was appallingly designed. 'Spectators in the nearside corner,' reports Simon Inglis, 'had their view of the far goal blocked by the glazed screen [installed to provide shelter from the weather], while a section of the roof [a rectangle of several square yards on the south-east edge] had to be cut away for the benefit of those sitting at the rear.' It held only 2,483 and was demolished after less than three decades' use in 1976.

The son of Chelsea's original architect, Archibald Kent Leitch, masterminded these developments. Inglis characterises them as 'cheap, utilitarian additions to the plan, especially behind the main stand'.

Joe Mears, son of J.T., took over in 1940, and was the first chairman to see the championship won on his watch. He was a powerful, impressive, dominant personality, a man of great influence. 'Dad was an incredible man,' says his son Brian. 'He was completely autonomous. Of course, he needed a board of directors to advise him, but he was the chairman and he would make decisions sometimes without others, because they weren't available. You had to. He always said to me, "If you have a decision to make, make it. You can't sit around waiting for people to come along and say, 'I didn't know about it.'"

But he merely tinkered with the big questions being asked at Chelsea about the stadium. The £150,000 West Stand, built in 1964–65, had another completely different feel, with its 6,300 reserved seats and 3,360 concrete 'benches' at the front. Stamford Bridge now had the look of a shantytown.

It might have been very different. As early as 1961, plans were resurrected to transform Stamford Bridge into a national stadium and sports centre. 'I'd been talking with Charles Brown,' says club secretary John Battersby, 'who had a wonderful scheme to redevelop the entire stadium. I'd been in long discussion with him about a scheme to redevelop the stadium as a national sports centre – it was very like what Ken Bates developed in fact. It was a wonderful scheme with some fantastic ideas.'

The plans were published in March 1961. 'There is in this country an architect who has a vision,' enthused *The Times*. 'Mr C.B. Brown [is] a lifelong supporter of Chelsea Football Club, wearing all the ups and downs of Stamford Bridge over the years surprisingly lightly. He sees the whole area surrounding Stamford Bridge as a perfect site ready to be developed as a super new sports centre, containing at its heart a new National Football Stadium, three-tiered and covered in by a cantilevered roof, to hold 150,000.

'The site in mind is a triangle formed by West Brompton Station, Fulham Broadway Station, and the Fulham Road ... The Mears Trust, holders of the freehold of the Chelsea ground, are willing to negotiate; the Greyhound Racing Association, who also have a finger in the Stamford Bridge pie, have been put in the picture.'

It was noted that a new stadium would benefit Chelsea too. 'Lacking the intimacy of Craven Cottage or the claustrophobic compactness of White Hart Lane, Stamford Bridge needs epic deeds if any genuine rapport is to be established between players and spectators.'

It was something Tommy Docherty was pushing for. 'Stamford Bridge is our biggest enemy,' admitted Docherty in April 1965. 'It lacks warmth and intimacy. The players themselves feel remote out there in the middle, detached and watched from a distance as if they were puppets; as if the audience was placed too far back from the footlights.'

'He [Brown] told me he had options on all the property surrounding the ground,' says Battersby. 'In order to make it work financially, he wanted the FA to commit to holding the cup final there for the next ten, 20 years. And the FA wouldn't do it. So without the guarantee he couldn't finance it.'.

Joe Mears and the board now began to wrestle with other schemes. A while before he died in an Oslo park on Friday 1 July 1966 aged 61, Joe Mears had had a heart attack, and was warned not to take alcohol (a warning he ignored). There were signs that his famous judgment was not infallible, too, when in March 1966 the World Cup was stolen from a stamp exhibition. It was later found in Norwood by a dog called Pickles, whose owner, Thames lighterman David Corbett, claimed the £6,000 reward money. But privately, Mears put in a personal claim for the reward, based on his assistance to the police and the fact that part of the trophy had been sent to him. He later withdrew it, but as one FA councillor put it, 'As chairman of the FA he was responsible for the safety of the trophy at the time it was stolen.'

Mears had inherited the family wharfing business and garage and motor distribution concerns and was able to devote much of his time to football. But during the war he had been with the Royal Marines, and one of his responsibilities for a time was the security at Winston Churchill's bunker in Whitehall. Mears had initially defended his actions, 'A man telephoned me about nine days ago. As a result I told the police. My home became a headquarters and several times the man telephoned me giving various instructions during the following days. He has now been arrested and that is the basis of my claim.'

His wife spoke later, 'The assessors say he does not have a claim and that is the end of the matter. He is very upset about all the publicity. I do not think the assessors should have told Mr Corbett my husband's name.'

Tommy Docherty later suggested that Mears was intending to pass on the money to a youth charity. It was shame this wasn't spelled out at the time. In the event Corbett got his money and Pickles won a year's supply of dog food and a film contract at double the normal rate for dogs.

After Mears's death a few months later, Bill Pratt Jr assumed control, followed by Joe's son Brian Mears, the third in his line to captain the Chelsea ship. Many people considered the latest in the Mears line weak, as he says himself, 'When I became chairman, the first thing everybody said was, "You're not as good as your father as chairman" and I think that's what they would have said to father. It's strange isn't it, that although I wasn't as good as he was, I won more trophies than he did. So if that counts for anything then I was at that time the most successful chairman ever.' Chelsea won the FA Cup and the European Cup-Winners' Cup in his time and became one of the biggest clubs in England. It gave him the confidence to think expansively.

'They excluded me from the new stadium completely,' says Battersby. 'It was one of the reasons I resigned [in 1971]. George Skeets had worked wonders in stopping the authorities closing down the stadium. The old stand desperately needed replacing. And they went to see contractors all on their own – they didn't take me. I was the secretary and I'd been in football since 1934.'

An awkward piece of business that had remained unresolved for over 40 years now came to a head. The younger generation of beneficiaries of the lucrative J.T. Mears Trust – worth £30 million in 1935 – wanted it carved up. Part of it was the freehold on the land upon which Stamford Bridge was built. Beneficiaries of the J.T. Mears Trust included Chelsea board members Brian, David and Leslie Juan Mears.

In the meantime, the stadium was patched up. Chelsea was one of the first clubs to provide permanent TV facilities with the 30-foot gantry (later extended to 70 feet) in the West Stand. The light provided by Chelsea's new tall floodlights was also appreciated by the BBC crews. The first floodlit game had been against Sparta Prague eight years earlier.

By the late 1960s discussions for an ambitious redevelopment were underway with various firms. In October 1969, 'after prolonged negotiations' mostly by Len Withey, Chelsea signed a new lease on the Stamford Bridge ground. It was not the purchase that was expected.

Then, a year later, on 14 October 1970, there was a statement from chairman Brian Mears, 'I am pleased to inform you that contractual arrangements have been made for the purchase, from the J.T. Mears Trustees, of the freehold of Stamford Bridge Grounds for the sum of £475,000, with completion due no later than May 1974 (although it is hoped to complete the purchase before then).

'Plans are now being drawn up for the necessary re-development of the accommodation at the Grounds, so as to afford the most up-to-date facilities for the club's supporters, and steps are also being taken to raise the not inconsiderable amount of finance necessary to complete the purchase and pay for the improvements.' The purchase and redevelopment was estimated at £1 million and was the board's 'number one priority'. Already it sounded an optimistic estimate.

While Chelsea worked on the new stadium, the old one fell apart. 'The old North Stand,' laughs Albert Sewell. 'The rail track was along the back there and when the trains went along that whole stand shook.' Fans reported 'murmurs' which prompted a GLC inquiry in December 1971. The result was the North Stand was closed for safety reasons.

It became clear around this time that Chelsea were opting for an extremely ambitious 'super stadium' to be built by a company, Darbourne and Darke (D&D) of Richmond, inexperienced in this type of development. The extensive and extraordinarily ambitious proposal document of January 1972 makes a fascinating read now.

Among the 'considerations' were, 'The optimum growth of the stadium [thought to need to be 80,000 to stage internationals], the value of the overall property, present and future planning policy and restraints, the effect on the locality, status of the club and future trends.

'Social factors (such as increased leisure time) and factors outside the Chelsea Football Club's control (e.g. development of a special league) would also have to be considered in the definition of stadium capacity.

'The survey indicates a growing number of women spectators. Improved facilities, safety, seating conditions, etc will assist in continuing this tendency.

'It appears that Chelsea is drawing support from a very wide region, the bulk of which is in the South-West and the Home Counties. This is still a growth area where incomes are above average.'

Facilities to be contained within new buildings included: 'Improvements to players' accommodation and ancillary functions, Vice-Presidents' club and restaurant, Directors' accommodation, administrative section, ground staff, certain car parking, TV, radio and Press facilities, Private viewing 'boxes', bars and lavatories, public restaurant, indoor practice area.'

If the stadium size needed to be increased, the pitch could be 'sunk below ground level and re-orientated east-west' from the existing north-west/south-east. As to stadium sightlines, 'It is apparent that existing conditions are significantly better than the majority of stadia (excluding Barcelona and the Azteca),' but the facilities added over the years were 'generally acknowledged to be inadequate both in size, scope and relationship one to the other' resulting in a 'somewhat poor image of the club, both on arrival and within the site'.

The new stadium would be the same height as Camp Nou, and way above Wembley, White Hart Lane and Highbury. There would be plenty of eye-catching innovations too. 'An in-built concourse system within the stadium all the way round' would solve the lack of surrounding land, but escalators were considered 'uneconomic as peak times occurred so infrequently'.

There would be heating for spectator areas, including eco-friendly 'radiant heaters in the roof'; air would be conducted around the feet of spectators at the cost of £3 to £6 extra per seat, and two electronic scoreboards with '18-foot high characters' and 'a clock' were on the list.

A massive 330 square-metre restaurant in the South Stand would overlook Fulham Road with views of London. There would be six supporters' bars and an exclusive 'executive box level' tier circling the ground. An underground sports centre, an indoor practice area and the best lux floodlights for those glory, glory European nights.

But what did the fans want? According to a survey of 1971, they wanted, in order of preference:

1. All terraces covered
2. Low-price bench seating
3. Restaurant facilities
4. Club car parking facilities
5. More licensed premises
6. Other activities

None of the first five were achieved until the Chelsea Village complex was built. One can only presume the mysterious 'other activities' were dealt with by the Village too.

Helpfully, 85 per cent of respondents also included at least one suggestion of their own, namely:

1. Improved entrances and exits
2. Stands closer to the pitch
3. Covered stands and terraces
4. Improved toilets
5. Electronic scoreboard
6. Pre- and post-match entertainment
7. Supporters' and social facilities
8. More season ticket facilities
9. Boys' enclosures and entrances
10. More low-price bench seating
11. Direct link to the underground

And, straight in at number 11 after 66 years on the charts, everyone asked for 'alternative access points'.

D&D recognised four possibilities for these:

'To the West: Direct pedestrian link to Fulham Broadway Underground Station along the embankment.

'To the North: Pedestrian connection over the existing bridge, across the underground railway, to the area north of the site.

'To the East: Direct link to British Rail. This may entail construction of platforms, etc.

'To the South/East: Possible pedestrian links along the alignment of the West Cross Route, which could avoid existing public roads.'

The Fulham Broadway link was estimated at a cost of £80,000; a ten-fold increase since Claude Kirby and the man from the Greyhound Racing Club saw fit to ridicule the scheme when it was first mooted in 1934. Now, the LTA was not prepared to ship in a penny.

The last, but perhaps not final, attempt to resurrect the access issue was in the Chelsea Village scheme. 'We talked planning permission to build a walkway to West Brompton which really opens it up,' says Ken Bates, 'and somebody said they'd found a bloody rare, unique orchid or something. But since you couldn't get to the bloody place, how could they possibly know?

'I put in 11 planning applications and that was the only one the inspector turned down. I suppose he had to do something.

'Fulham Broadway was too difficult and too expensive, and all you're doing anyway is feeding the people back in the same place. Whereas West Brompton, we could have opened it up to the north. There was a huge car park where they could have parked their cars, but they could have also picked up the Earl's Court station which could have reduced the congestion at Fulham Broadway.

'Then I thought of another scheme whereby they were going to incorporate some exit over to Brompton cemetery. They had a regeneration plan.

'They wanted to renovate the cemetery and make it up to date, and I offered to pay a lot of money to them for the renovation provided they did us a footbridge over the railway. But they wouldn't do it. So we tried all of these things. For every good idea you put to fruition, nine fall by the wayside.'

We live now with the consequences of successive failures to resolve a problem first 'solved' in 1905.

The costs of the 1972 stadium were estimated, of course. A phased 'B2' plan offered the 'greatest economy':

East Stand: £1,470,000 (£122.50 per seat)

SE Quadrant: £620,000 (£112.73)

South Stand: £660,000 (£94.29) More on bars, less on toilets and boxes.

Completion (i.e. the rest of the stadium) £3,500,000.

A total of £6,250,000 for the best stadium in the world. Then again D&D warned, 'Building costs are rising at between ten and 12 per cent per annum. Should this continue, then assuming the stadium will be completed by 1980 some 40 to 50 per cent should be added to the above cost.' Never assume.

With the 'tremors in the North Stand' investigated by structural engineers, the water drainage not functioning and soakaways silted up, and the East Stand's annual licence from the GLC expected to be denied 'unless considerable work is carried out', a decision was already made for the club.

In June 1972, work began on the 'first phase', the East Stand. It became the first phase in a total of one. Industrial disputes, poor project management, inexperience, loss of gate revenues, escalating costs, massive delays, squad unrest ... and then relegation in 1975, followed by promotion, and the drop again in 1979. These were Chelsea's darkest days. In 1977 debts were at £4 million and the liquidators were poised. Martin Spencer, an accountant brought in by Chelsea to balance the books who then became chief executive, set up schemes to 'Save the Bridge'. Lost somewhere amid the financial horror was the fact that Chelsea FC was not actually able to buy the freehold from the J.T. Mears Trust.

A lot of the joy of going to games leeched away in those funless days of austerity. In the 1950s, Chelsea often had a brass band that would play old and modern favourites for a singalong on the terraces for half an hour or so before the game, and then a march round the pitch at half-time. In the 70s this had been reduced to a 'Pre-match spin with Pete & Dave'. On one occasion, Pete Owen went off to Nashville and got hooked on the music there, imposing a whole 'programme' of country and western on his captive audience. The morbid strains of dying dogs and 'D.I.V.O.R.C.E' might have suited the wrist-slashing times at the ground, but no one was going to go and buy a Stetson at the club shop, even if the New York Cosmos could draw 40,000 to the stadium in 1978.

Before the East Stand debacle of the early 70s, board member Richard Attenborough had mused, almost longingly, 'When I look across the ground, I sometimes see it as it was before the West Stand was built – a vast, uncovered terrace, with me arriving before one o'clock for a big match to get a place by a crush barrier for the girl I was courting. On fine days, we'd bring sandwiches and have a picnic lunch; other times we got frozen or drenched. My two love affairs, with Sheila and Chelsea, have lasted ever since.

'We [the board] come on from our jobs, get down to business and talk on into the early hours when there's a lot on the agenda, as there is now with this vast re-development programme underway. I believe we are coming to the most exciting period in Chelsea's history.'

He was sadly mistaken. It is easy to be scornful in retrospect. The men who embarked on the plan were sincerely trying to do their best for the club, and the fans had always chastised the Mears family for a lack of ambition. Chairman Brian Mears, buoyed by the on-field success, must have felt confident that his would be the greatest legacy of his family's connection with the club. It was not to be and he still lives in his father's shadow.

But for the fans, worse was to come.

Chelsea, under guidance from Martin Spencer, had acted to offset debts by separating Stamford Bridge (S.B.) Properties Ltd, the company that now owned the freehold of Stamford Bridge, from the football club. So when Ken Bates famously bought Chelsea for £1 in 1982, he bought the club, but not its assets. 'There was only one story,' says Bates, 'and that was that we did the deal. I was going to buy S.B. Properties and S.B. Properties had the debt. I took the club and we transferred the ground to S.B. Properties and we began there as tenants.'

Here was a decision that would return to haunt the club. Lord Chelsea and David Mears, on behalf of S.B. Properties, gave Bates a seven-year lease on the ground while its future was decided. 'David Mears had the biggest proportion of the shares,' says Bates. 'He had 44 per cent. I mean everybody else was irrelevant almost. And I said, "Okay well I'll buy it but I don't trust Barclays Bank, I've got to make sure that they're happy."

'So I went in to see them and we did a deal that we paid them off £1.5 million over four years. And then the guy said – because he was in the intensive care recovery department of the bank – he said, "Look you've got to appreciate you're not our client, so if we're going to have a payment plan it's got to be put to the board. So get them to ask us, we'll say agree it, and then you can come in and borrow it." And I said, "Okay."

'It took a while, but eventually I'd done a deal. David Mears was going to get £5,000 a year for five years plus a Volvo estate car – it's amazing how giving people cars swings them, you know? – plus a seat in the box, all the usual things. But it all took so long. He always says he couldn't get me to come to the table, but Sheila Marsden [Bates's secretary at the time] will tell you it was the other way round.'

Bates was trying to buy the assets (S.B. Properties and the land) for £450,000 cash, and assume liability for the £1.6 million debt within it from the East Stand.

Meanwhile, in September 1983, David Mears and Lord Chelsea agreed to sell S.B. Properties, including the freehold of Chelsea, to Marler Estates for redevelopment. Marler, a property company with roots in west London going back decades, was chaired by David Bulstrode and included Patrick Noonan and John Duggan amongst its major shareholders. 'I only found out because we were playing Crystal Palace reserves and Ron Noades came to the game and said, "'Ere, do you know – what's this about you ground-sharing with us?" "What you f**king talking about?" And Lord Chelsea had been round there talking to him.' The idea was that Chelsea would move out to Selhurst while Stamford Bridge was 'redeveloped'.

'So the next Saturday,' says Bates, 'Mears came in and I said to him, "What's this about, you?" And he huffed and puffed and I said, "Listen, when this gets out you'll be a f**king leper, nobody will ever want you at Chelsea'.

In fact S.B. Properties rejected a cash offer and instead took one million Marler shares at a hefty premium above listed price, giving Mears, Lord Chelsea et al a stake in the profits accruing from the redevelopment of the ground. It looked a lucrative investment before the property collapse of the late 80s. In 1983 Barratts were building residential properties adjoining the stadium.

In his plans Bulstrode talked of a 'much smaller and more compact stadium. The old ground is too large and deteriorating. [It] is all wide open spaces and difficult to police.' With Chelsea removed, assuming interest from a large supermarket retailer, the value of the 14-acre site (including pitch) would rise to £50 million if developed.

Bates, like most fans, felt betrayed. 'My comment on the way Mr [Leslie] Mears has changed his mind would be that his great grandfather built the club but the current generation presided over its decline,' said Bates at the time. But the critical issue now became whether Chelsea could stay after any redevelopment took place.

In January 1985 Marler shares jumped to a high of 145p after Hammersmith and Fulham Council gave permission for the planned redevelopment of Stamford Bridge. In May Marler offered £3 million to buy Selhurst Park so Chelsea could share it while they developed a £32 million housing and office complex. It was the high water mark of Marler's attempt to concrete over the famous turf.

There was a clause in the lease from S.B. Properties that the club move, by mutual agreement, so that the stadium land could be redeveloped, providing a new 'home' stadium had been found. Many felt that if they left, they would never get back to their ancestral home. Marler were trying everything to get Chelsea out, says Bates, and then 'honest broker' David Dein [from Arsenal] got in touch with Chelsea, talking about attendances and capacities. 'I said to him, "Why don't you f**k off? Nobody asked you to be an honest broker,"' says Bates.

It now became a battle of wits, with Bates fighting a rearguard action, buying 20 per cent of S.B. Properties shares, anything to stall any development and groundshare, and Marler Estates trying to realise the value of its asset without overreaching itself financially. At the end of the lease Chelsea were served notice to quit in 1989. The club was stuck in an inert position, unable to move forward and losing cash in the battle to stay put.

Presumably exhausted, Marler sold out to another developer, John Duggan, of Cabra Estates, who also owned Fulham's Craven Cottage. There was no change in their desire to redevelop the Bridge, but the tide had turned. The market downturn of the early 1990s made a quick return on the investment less likely. As things dragged on Chelsea were able to exploit a mistake by the football authorities to their advantage in December 1992.

'Things were getting messy,' says Bates. S.B. Properties were claiming Chelsea owed them £6 million. 'So I was trying to set up as many awkward obstacles in their way to bring him to the table, because I knew that Duggan was running out of time.

'It coincided with the Premier League formation. We all had to resign from the Football League and join the private Premier League and that was the time I switched it over. So Duggan won all his [liquidation claim] case against the Chelsea Football and Athletic Club, and we just had an empty shell there - the players' contracts had all been registered with Chelsea Football Club Ltd instead of Chelsea Football and Athletic Club ... It was just bad typing at the League. For want of a nail... '

Chelsea Football and Athletic Club went into administrative receivership, and at Chelsea 'The Liquidator' became, once more, just a clap-along tune on the stadium PA.

It was a 'combination of factors' that eventually won the day, reckons Bates, but 'basically our war of attrition against them. For example, Duggan had boosted his shares up to a ridiculous level anyway and I'd bought 29.9 per cent off of Ashraf Marwin, who's a very good friend to me, or a very good friend to Chelsea actually.

'And what I did then, I started selling the [Cabra] shares on the market or pretending to. Do you remember going to a Hereford pre-season game [8 August 1990] when they hadn't cut the bloody grass and Gordon Durie kicked the ground and he got this bloody great bruise in his groin?

'Then what happened is that the Midland Bank got taken over by HSBC and they just pulled the plug on Cabra. So we lost about £3 million [in Cabra shares], but I just regarded that as key money to get in.'

In 1992 the battle was won and Bates set about ensuring the pitch would not be a battlefield again. He devised a scheme, the Chelsea Pitch Owners [CPO], designed to make it too messy for any future predators to remove the football club from its ancestral home. 'It definitely served its purpose,' counters Bates. 'Because there were two or three approaches to invest in the club before [Abramovich], which never got in the papers, and as soon as they looked at CPO, it was a poisoned pill, they ran away.

'Well, they wanted to move Chelsea out and knock the place down because it's so valuable.

'The CPO sold shares all over the bloody place and no matter how many shares you bought you could only have a few votes. The idea was no matter the number of shares you controlled; just a few determined people could f**k it.

'Oh, and the other thing which I think was really the cleverest of all, we transferred the name Chelsea Football Club Limited to CPO. And the company that has the license to Chelsea Football Club, which is Chelsea Football Club Ltd, the condition is they have to play all their first-team games at Stamford Bridge.

'So when they talk about Abramovich moving the club to east London or the new Wembley or whatever, you say, "Great, off you go, rename it Neasden United, give us our pitch back, we'll sign tomorrow and we'll name it Chelsea Football Club Limited, just as Wimbledon have." That's what I mean, the ultimate poison pill.

'Now obviously Chelsea Village had kind of lent the money to CPO, but there's no repayment date. It's almost perpetual. So no one can come and demand the money. It's absolutely foolproof,' claims Bates – as long as CPO keeps its house in order, of course. There was already one problem with a former CPO official selling priceless club memorabilia on the market. The fact is, as Inglis says, that Stamford Bridge remains 'the most valuable piece of real estate in football, which means that its future can never be entirely assured'.

Even after the development of one of the best-appointed stadiums in the country, with a complex of leisure facilities, Bates feels defeating Cabra was his finest hour. 'Nobody really appreciates how important that was,' he says. 'That was the basis upon which everything could take place. We couldn't develop the ground, it was owned by somebody else. And the Royal Bank of Scotland was fabulous, they gave it a 20-year lease with an option to buy any time at a fixed price, and that was December 1992. In 1993 we started to build what was later to be called the Matthew Harding stand.'

The Chelsea Village complex divides people. It divided Chelsea – Colin Hutchinson [the club's then managing director] was on the original board, but resigned because he felt he couldn't fight the football club's corner. He wanted to guard against football club money being used for other activities. 'I think there came a point,' he says, 'when in certain quarters there was an obsession with the Village, and me, after Matthew died, trying to be the sole protector of the football club. Because, don't forget, Ken was chairman of Chelsea Village *and* the football club.

'I felt I was honour-bound to the club and the supporters to try and protect Chelsea Football Club and that's why I came off the Chelsea Village board. In later years it was perhaps something I regretted, inasmuch as the Chelsea Village board became all powerful and the football club was just talking about issues, making decisions that could be rubber-stamped or overturned or had to be approved by the Village board.

'I have reservations about the whole concept of the development. I did a paper in 1995 where I questioned the economics of building the hotel because I estimated that the lost capacity of the Shed End would cost the football club £800,000 a year in lost gate revenue, which at the time was calculated at about £12 a seat. And in that paper I raised a lot of issues that have never been answered to this day.

'I think at that time we would have got permission for the extra seats, the 6,000 or whatever. I made the point over the lost capacity that I could not believe the hotel would make £800,000 profit – and that was without all the peripherals of people buying merchandising and so on. Every time I hear tongue-in-cheek comments about knocking the hotel down, I have a little smile and remember my memo.'

The majority of fans would probably have been in the camp of fewer hotel rooms, more seats. One of the first things Roman Abramovich's people looked into when they took over in 2003 was the stadium capacity. 'If we had to do it over,' says Bates's successor as chairman, Bruce Buck, 'we would have just built a top-notch stadium. We would not have built the hotels and certainly not the flats. We would have built a bigger stadium, or a stadium that could have more easily been capable of being expanded.

'We have the hotels and other things, and we're going to make them profitable. But if we had it to do over, we wouldn't go the Chelsea Village route.

'There's a basic fallacy in that structure. It's a good idea in the sense that you've got 15 to 20 acres and you're only using it 30 days a year – it doesn't seem right. There ought to be a way to use it. In the US some stadiums are used for two sports or maybe they have 50 rock concerts a year. We have problems doing that because of planning, but in other situations there are ways to make more use of a big stadium. But we are where we are and we're going to make it work. But we found out that by and large football fans want football.'

Back in 1904, the *Fulham Chronicle* had reservations about Gus Mears, the new freeholder of John Stunt's old market garden, who now resides, along with the first chairman and man of sport, Claude Kirby, in the adjacent Brompton Cemetery. His 'commercial instincts', it maintained, would give him 'a keen eye for the shekels'. And yet he built a club that did, eventually, stagger humanity.

It would be nice to think that we have heard the last of the 'rapacious builders' on the saintly old grounds. But somehow you doubt it.

6

THE MAGNETISM OF STAMFORD BRIDGE

'In 1904 they did not exist,' said John Tait Robertson, Chelsea's first manager. 'Now everyone interested in the game has heard of their splendid ground, their fine 11, and the great chance the club has of getting into the league proper at the first time of asking.

'Chelsea have come in on a huge tidal wave of popularity. The game is booming as it has never boomed before. London is now as enthusiastic as Birmingham, Manchester, Liverpool and Glasgow.

'I may be biased, but I believe, and a large number of men who have had a vast experience of the game think with me, that Chelsea is destined to be the leading club of the metropolis.'

One of the great characteristics of Chelsea has always been extravagance: gestures, purchases, innovation for its own sake. That 'let's make a splash' mentality. Is it any wonder, when the location, with its posh houses and artistic pursuits, lets you dream the dream? The Fulham Road can make you feel, for an instant, that anything is possible.

Chelsea is not just a club with money now. It has nearly always been a rich club. The penury of the years between 1974 and 1994 is the anomaly. It's Okay to spend a lot, Chelsea thinks, but it's better to spend a little and dream a lot. Successive boards have bought big – in 1910 to stave off relegation, in

1930 to exploit promotion, in 1946 to rebuild a team, in 1966 to push on to greatness, in 1998 to conquer Europe, in 2003 to make a start. It has hardly ever worked out as it was planned. When Chelsea won the league in 1955, or the FA Cup in 1970, it was a few tweaks on a good basis that did the business. When it *did* work, in 2004, it was a manager that was the best buy.

Chelsea's first manager was a player-manager. The club seems to have had more of this species of gaffer than any other. Colin Hutchinson explains the flurry of them in the 1990s as pragmatism. An entirely new coach would have wanted wholesale changes. José Mourinho was the first managerial appointment to have previously won a league title as a boss.

All through its history the club has spent money only when it would make a 'splash', cause a sensation. In 1907, the sensation was strong, 'the huge amorphous crowd, 30,000 or 40,000 strong, is an amazing phenomenon. Quite half of it is composed of pale, weedy lads, who ought to be playing football themselves ... ' said *The Times*. 'The poor fellows are chiefly drawn from the vast brick-and-mortar ambuscades of Fulham, Wandsworth, and further westward and southward – parts of London much more dreary and monotonous than the East End of 20 years ago.'

Another trait of the Chelsea personality is innovation. The club's first board, especially the Mears family, brought a commercial flair to the club that often strayed into opportunism and which got woven into the badge. First in the south to publish a programme, first to use ball-boys, first to wear numbered shirts, first to publish a magazine-style programme, first to fly to a domestic away game, first to exploit live closed circuit TV rights, first to do this, first to do that ... It was almost as if innovation was part of the mission statement of the club. 'I think it was,' says Albert Sewell, a former programme editor. 'They couldn't win prizes, but they could do firsts, eh?'

To Tony Banks this was in the nature of where the club is and the people who follow it. 'We do come out with these very creative and imaginative initiatives,' he said, 'but we've never done enough groundwork and that's the point. We never really laid a firm basis for going forward and even when we got a good team together it got broken up mainly because of the pressures of being where we were. It's like there's no follow-up ... "I've bought you a bloomin' player, now d'you expect to train and manage him properly?"'

Innovation without groundwork is novelty. Roll in the glamour and Bohemian image of Chelsea and you have frivolity. Punk and Sloane,

History maker Frank Lampard scores the second of his goals that won the title at Bolton in 2005 – as discussed with John Terry the night before.

Mourinho's magician Joe Cole emerged as world class under the manager's uncompromising guidance. Here, with Ronaldinho-esque skill, he twists past three United players to score in the 3-0 title decider at the Bridge.

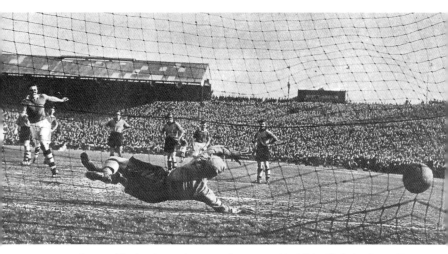

Spot on 'Our hearts were in our mouths as we watched Peter Sillett step forward to take it, but ice-cool Peter smashed the ball into the net.' It was the goal that knocked the stuffing out of Wolves's 1955 title challenge.

Skipper Roy Bentley leads the applause for much-maligned winger Eric 'Rabbit' Parsons in the short ceremony after the Sheffield Wednesday match that sealed Chelsea's first ever championship. Manager Ted Drake hogs the mikes.

Albert Sewell's prized back page of the Sheffield Wednesday programme. 'I went down the dressing room and got everyone to sign it. What I find is interesting, you can look at those signings and you read the names. Autographs now ... it's just a squiggle.'

Head and shoulders Roy Bentley heads athletically towards goal at Fulham in January 1952. Chelsea's 2-1 win was their first in five league games. A Fulham back signals a touchdown in an unsuccessful distraction.

Cup glory at last Bobby Tambling (above left) helps win the 1965 League Cup and Peter Osgood (above right) converts Charlie Cooke's cross to set up the FA Cup replay triumph in 1970 at Old Trafford. Chelsea's board finally has to order the Brasso in.

The Real thing Keith Weller (left) makes sure as Peter Osgood wheels away to celebrate his second goal against Madrid's 'Ye-Ye' boys in three days. 'A great goal to score in the final, that was the main thing. I had a knack of doing that.' The 1971 Cup-Winners' Cup is Chelsea's.

Above 'I thought to myself maybe I will shoot' – Roberto Di Matteo thinks his way into the history books with the fastest ever cup final goal at Wembley. Happy days are here again in 1997.

Left Gianfranco Zola borrows a hat from a Swedish leprechaun – and it fits! The goalscorer and all-time great celebrates the 1998 European Cup-Winners' Cup win in Stockholm over Stuttgart with fellow Italy international Roberto Di Matteo.

Left Modern architect? Player-manager Glenn Hoddle dragged the club out of the dark ages into the modern era, and here indicates how tall he likes his strikers to be: John Spencer and Mark Stein are in the squad.

Below From Hod to god: the majestic Ruud Gullit in action as a player. His presence drew other greats and, as a manager, he brought 'sexy football' to Stamford Bridge.

Left Elementary, Watson: Juve's European Cup legend Gianluca Vialli was revered at Chelsea, and scored five times past the poor old Barnsley keeper in two attempts in the 1997–98 season.

Below 'Oh Dennis Wise ...' the goal that launched a thousand drunken chants, and that showed the new Chelsea had arrived with a mesmerising 1-1 draw with Milan at the San Siro. The skipper led Chelsea into the European Cup for the first time in 1999.

Mourning the King

The fans' heartfelt response at the Hawthorns (below) to the death of all-time great Peter Osgood – 'the King of Stamford Bridge', pictured left, before his broken leg in 1966 – bonded the current success to a glorious past.

champagne and chav, plummy and estuary English – all rub shoulders within a borough firmly connected to the 1960s, the King's Road set, art, models and photographers. Recent years have been no different with the development of Chelsea Harbour, quirky hotels, the Chelsea Cruise, posh restaurants, exclusive nightclubs, expensive antique shops, turned-up collars, designer clothes and the Chelsea Tractor. Chelsea has always been London's Bohemia.

Imagine the contrast. On 7 August 1918, Florence Horsburgh, manageress of Chelsea Town Hall kitchen, found a novel way to ensure the poor of the locality received the appropriate nutrition in harsh times, and at a reasonable 2d to 6d a time. 'Hiring a coster's donkey and cart she packed up her stock in trade of sausage rolls, fish cakes, and apple dumplings, and drove into the districts where the kitchen was little known,' marvelled the *Daily News*. 'Everywhere she was surrounded by crowds, and sold out within the hour.'

However, a year earlier the bright young things of Chelsea had prompted the headline 'And In War-Time Too!' when one of the fortnightly New Arts fancy dress balls (tickets 4s, including buffet) was raided by Military Police. Sixty officers were caught dancing a two-step, 'with a rag-time band grinding out a kind of bunny-hug'. 'Others were going through almost monkey-like antics' ... 'bizarrely-dressed females', a male dancer wore 'a sleeping suit with gaudy floral designs down the front', with 'pantaloons or silk knickers' and whiskey bottles smuggled in in mufflers.

Austerity brought boredom and here was the place to let it rip. Where better than Stamford Bridge for football?

But the location had its own attraction even before the club was formed, and the very fact that Gus Mears called it Chelsea shows which side of the class divide he wanted fans to think of. It seems clear that the location dictated the fanbase. If you went to Chelsea you were making a statement. It was a holiday from your usual haunt. You were lording it for the day, unless, like the club's first president, Arthur Cadogan, you were a lord already.

We are privileged in that we know what at least one person who went to the games thought, because she only recently passed away. Ethel Tomkins, born in 1897, travelled to one of the first games at Stamford Bridge with her family – policeman father Walter, mother Eliza and older brothers Fred, William, Arthur, Victor and Bertie. It says something of the allure of the new club that they came all the way over from Hampstead in north London, next to Gospel Oak station, on matchdays. It must have been easy to get the connection at Willesden Junction to the ground. Ethel remembers men handing out flyers with the team names on outside the Chelsea railway station – she still believes she has one stashed away somewhere. It was a new thing that the family wanted to try out – a novelty. As an eight-year-old she remembers the crowds and the noise. The family enjoyed it enough to go many times again, including to the 1915 FA Cup final, which few other Chelsea fans managed because of travel restrictions.

One of the uniting factors of the club was the fact that Gus Mears decided to build such an immense stadium. It was always possible to get in – a long trek was never wasted by a lockout. It was closer to the stations than most London clubs and there was plenty to do before or after the match. It was a proper day's entertainment.

For those attending the first game at Stamford Bridge, a friendly against Liverpool, there should have been even more enjoyment, but the Fulham Borough Brass Band who had been invited to play, failed to show. (Perhaps they thought they were playing out of their manor.) According to the local paper, the ceremonial first kick was made by six-year-old Joseph Augustus Mears – the son of 'father of the club' Gus.

But Chelsea has always seemed to be too off-the-cuff and last minute a club to go into matchday entertainment in a big way. The fans are often cool and non-participatory anyway. In 1963 the media loved it when Stamford Bridge fans were treated to a display of high-stepping baton twirling by drum majorettes before the start of the Chelsea-Sheffield United match. It may even have been one of the first clubs to do so ... but no one really gave a damn.

It might be different at Christmas. West London would have a knees-up during the festive football programme. Think of the great football matches at that time of years gone by. Remember the crisp air, the dramatic open skyline, a nice sunset and a laugh in the Shed. 'My aunt used to live on Lillie Road,' says lifelong Fulham resident Roy Simpson. 'Christmas time, it wasn't one game, they used to play three. One time I got dressed up in great big top hat and tails, and my aunt said, "You're not going to the game like that are you?" I said, "Yeah!" and my brother Reg, my brother Frank, we had a couple of beers and went down there and you'd see lots of other people dressed up in different colours, sort of a carnival atmosphere. Boxing Day, that was what it was like. Football matches were like carnivals.'

To Tony Banks Boxing Day meant luxuries and gifts more than dressing up. 'All the men and the boys would go over to the match,' he said, 'because I think it used to kick-off usually at 11.30 a.m. so you could get off and you could come back for your Christmas dinner. If someone had a car, we'd all pack into it, and you'd see people walking around wearing their new yellow gloves that they just got. It was one of the traditional Christmas presents, new yellow gloves and Wills whiffs.

'Everyone was feeling very expansive. And sometimes, of course, you'd take whiskey with you, not for the kids, but they'd take a tot of whiskey and they would pass the whiskey round and smoke the Wills whiffs and everyone felt really affluent, and you know, it was a great feeling.'

The open, expansive layout of Stamford Bridge and the lack of roofs to reflect the hubbub meant that, unless it was a really big gate, it was difficult to create the throbbing atmosphere evident at some away games.

Roy Simpson remembers the post-war mood at Stamford Bridge well. 'You had a brass band out in the middle of the pitch,' he says. 'Everybody respectful, standing, singing – the old singsongs. It was different people in them days, different people. You had songs for the players like now, everybody sung their songs. But it was always good fun songs, a laugh.'

Even today the general nature of the Chelsea crowd is passionate but quiet, with vociferous noise-generation reserved for games where it has been felt a contribution was really necessary: a London derby, a top-of-the-table decider, or, especially, a big European night.

This selective switch-on is not, as today's webchat ranters would like to believe, a phenomenon just of the modern days of crustacean-based hospitality. When he took over as Chelsea manager in 1952, part of Ted Drake's root-and-branch reform of the club was an exhortation to supporters to ditch the legendary fair-mindedness and become more vocal and partisan. 'Let's have more people eating, sleeping, drinking Chelsea,' he urged in the programme.

Chelsea won the league three years later, but in the stands the earth still didn't move. 'We were more of a restrained crowd, that was always a reputation that we had,' said Tony Banks, a veteran of the early Drake days. 'One of the reasons being that, don't forget, you were a long way back from the pitch because of the greyhound track, which was unusual. I remember that it was only when I went to away games like Birmingham, where my father's family was, and you were really up close, you suddenly realised how ugly the players were!

'God almighty I've seen some horrible things done on football pitches, but at Chelsea, you were way back from the crowd and that was definitely a "limiter". It would create a culture in terms of what's the point of two or three of us singing when it just goes up in the heavens? There's no point. That's why we tended to be polite, and in many ways, you know, some fans actually took that as being an attractive feature. In other words there was a lot of clapping. I remember there was a lot of applauding. You would be very fair and you would applaud a lot of what the other side was doing as well, which is probably one of the reasons why so many away teams liked visiting Chelsea and why people used to say, "Why haven't we got the killer touch like Arsenal?" We never seemed to have the killer touch you know. And it's only relatively recently that we got ourselves away from that.'

'We always tended towards a combination of inconsistency and a lack of fervour. I'm talking about the last 20 years or so – though our inconsistency lasted until much more recently than that.'

But then Banks always represented the silent majority. 'I've never been one for singing, not now and not then,' he said. 'Mainly because I was too f**king nervous to be honest with you. I had to conserve all my energy to will the team on. I couldn't expend it on singing because for me singing was a waste of energy. I'd be bottling it all up just waiting for a goal.

'Because I was so nervous, there were times when it really got bad and I'd pull my duffle coat up and just sort of peer out of it like when you feel frightened and you go under the bedclothes.'

Perhaps Chelsea's ancient ability to self-harm at vital stages has bred a variety of fan personified by the quivering Banks.

In 1957 Dorothy Bright of the Chelsea Supporters' Club did her best to raise a racket. 'It has always amazed me how lacking in vocal support our supporters are,' she wrote in the club's journal. 'I thought the only way to make more noise was to get some rattles, and now I have got them.' It had taken her six months' trawling round London shops just to get hold of 27 of the things, and now people could buy them, three bob a pop, at the Supporters' Club room at the Britannia public house.

Hopefully she shifted them all.

For those too young to know them, rattles were handheld wooden ratchets that make a clacking sound when whirled round. They had been handed out in the First World War to alert people of gas attacks. It was nostalgic to hear two of the old contraptions 'duelling' in the Matthew Harding Upper at the end of the 2004–05 season.

'You'd have whistles, you'd have rattles,' remembered Banks. 'But mostly it would just be roars.'

Regularly in the Chelsea programmes over the past 40 years there have been letters criticising the inferiority of those roars at the Stamford Bridge ground. The comments made by Pat and Ruby Mullan ('supporters for 20 years') and published in the Atvidaberg programme of November 1971 were typical, expressing their disgust at the 'pathetic lack of support from the so-called "spirit of the Bridge" – the Shed' during a recent Arsenal match. Others said virtually the same thing in the 1960s, 80s and 90s, except the blame would be shifted from the Shed to the West Stand, the West Stand to the East. Chelsea fans just accept that's how it's always been and that it's unlikely to change except for special occasions.

Typically, José Mourinho was quick to notice this aspect of Chelsea's character. 'I think Chelsea's are not the crazy fanatic supporter who push the team to the victory,' he says. 'But the feeling is there, and you go on the street and they are polite people and very nice people. Always showing the happiness and the relation with the team and "We have to win tomorrow."'

After he arrived Mourinho, like Drake, didn't just ask for more noise and hostility at the Bridge; he demanded it. He wants total commitment from everyone. 'I think it is important to create a club,' he explains. 'When I say create a club I say it must not be just me and the players. It must be me and the players and the fans and everyone in the club. That is one thing I'm never happy about, when people do this thing to me: I walk in the club on Monday and someone says to me, "Congratulations." I always say, "Congratulations to you also." I like people to feel part of it, everybody with a little contribution, some more, some less. But everybody – even with a good feeling – they are participating in something.

'So I think it's very important this kind of relationship we create with the fans, you know. I think especially here in Stamford Bridge we have a certain style of supporter. It's the same in Portugal. We have for example in Lisbon,

I used to say Sporting supporters are supporters with a tie and a jacket, and Benfica supporters are the supporters with a loud voice and a T-shirt and a scarf.'

José feels that the club's support at away games is different – louder, more effective. He has singled out the Chelsea fans at Fulham, Newcastle, Bolton and elsewhere for praise.

Until the 1950s, away fans would rarely travel other than for special occasions. The motorways we all get stuck on now only began to appear in the 1960s and it could take five hours to travel by train to Birmingham. 'My memory is of travelling to away games on my own,' says lifelong Chelsea fan Peter Ralph, whose first game was against Bolton in 1939. 'I don't recall many fans going away, and definitely no large followings to specific games, although there was no segregation of fans in those days, so it would have been difficult to tell. The fans who did go were mainly men in their 20s and 30s, along with the odd girlfriend. The older fans couldn't afford to travel away as they were all married.'

In the early 1970s away rail travel was organised by the club on the 'Chelsea Train'. It wasn't popular. It was a 'dirty old train not fit for animals' according to one user, who claimed fans wanted Chelsea to use the more luxurious new 'League Liner'. On its maiden voyage in February 1974 for the trip to QPR, Burnley fans on the liner enjoyed TV, piped music and a disco. It sounds right up Chelsea's street.

A GLC travel survey for the new stadium development was conducted after the Chelsea v Leeds match of 27 March 1971 and provides an insight into where Chelsea's traditional fan base lies. Nearly 9,000 of a crowd of 58,000 responded. Here's where they had travelled from:

North 108
Wales 100
Leeds 548
Midlands 800-ish
South West 519
Hants 852
West Sussex 935
East Sussex 985
Surrey 1,782

West Berkshire 256
East Berkshire 1,252
South Bucks/South Oxon 1250
North Bucks/North Oxon 561
North Beds 158
South Beds 247
North Herts 345
South Herts 1,284
West Kent 1,312
East Kent 1,373
Essex 1,672
East Anglia 399
GLC area 39,389
   Harrow 1,539
   Feltham 1,291
   Surbiton 1,388
   Weybridge 1,040
   N2/6 805
   SW19/20 1,219
   SW12/16/17 1,598
   SW 3/6/7/10 1,285
   SW5 1,794
   SW1 902
   SW11 1,540

The breadth of support is enlightening. Of course, some Leeds fans may have responded, but excluding the north and midlands, the results chime with anecdotal evidence of our appeal along the M4 into Wales and the South West and deep into Kent.

Gabriele Marcotti, one of many Italians with a fondness for Chelsea, now UK correspondent for *Corriere dello Sport* and European football writer for *The Times*, first went to Stamford Bridge during the 1989–90 season – the start of the current unbroken stint in the top flight, and one that brought a fifth-place finish. 'At the time, I was in school here in London and Chelsea were simply the nearest club to my house,' Marcotti says. 'I was 16 and wanted to watch football so my friends and I simply wandered down there.

The following season, 1990–91, we had season tickets.

'Back then, Stamford Bridge was a right dump compared to grounds in Italy or Spain. There was a huge new East Stand, which was totally out of proportion with the rest of the ground. The West Stand looked okay, in sort of a quaint way, though it was rather decrepit too.

'The Shed was great if you were a twenty-something male who enjoyed singing and rowdiness. And the North Stand as far as I could tell was just a pile of rubble. As I recall, the fan base was mostly male, mostly white, but that might have been simply a function of going to the Shed.

'Obviously, the atmosphere was quite different [then]. In terracing like the old Shed, you can move around freely and what generally happens is that the loudest fans tend to congregate there. Now that Stamford Bridge is all-seater, the "loud" fans are sort of spread out and that changes the atmosphere somewhat.

'Funnily enough, when you see Chelsea away, the fans are much louder and I think that's because the more passionate fans tend to travel and they tend to be compressed into one area at away grounds. Having said that, when I go to games (as I occasionally do at most London grounds, not just Chelsea) as a "civilian" (i.e. not in the press box) I notice that the Matthew Harding Lower stand is still the loudest. I guess a lot of the guys who were in the Shed 15 years ago have ended up there.'

It is interesting that the Chelsea support has often been at its best at northern venues. Preston Blue Paul 'Iggi' Higham, born in 1975, is one of those who especially enjoys games on his 'home patch'. 'I think away games create a different atmosphere, fans travel in larger numbers, meet up at pre-arranged pubs for a pre-match beer,' he believes, 'and they are generally more of a day out than a home game where fans do the same things week in week out.

'I think the games "oop norf" have a better atmosphere as it's not the same people that go to all the games nearer London. By that I mean it's northern supporters that can't get to as many games in London so they are more determined to create a good atmosphere and enjoy their day.

'We're very well organised up here. There's always somebody organising travel to games. There is Chelsea North-West that has travel arrangements made for all games outside the area, as well as local groups that travel independently that all keep in contact with each other.'

Iggi has a football-mad dad to thank for his Blues allegiance. His first game was Preston-Chelsea when he was four: Division Two, Nobby Stiles v Geoff Hurst, 1-1. Lovely.

Hooked ever since, it's understandable that within the catchment area of so many successful local teams, he's often asked: why Chelsea? 'I usually tell them that geographically they are the nearest half decent team,' he laughs. 'That tends to shut people up. I've lived in the same area for 30 years so everyone around here knows I've been a Chelsea fan for years and therefore don't get much stick from anyone.'

Most of Chelsea's friends in the north though were originally captivated by the stylish image of the King's Road swingers of the 1960s. The glitter and glamour contrasted with gritty, industrial northern England with its dour icons like Don Revie. It was simplistic, but it worked for the Blues. Chelsea led the way in fashion and football.

In 1971 Mark Evans of Bolton appeared in the programme desperate for a 14 or 15-year-old girl pen pal 'to keep me informed about the smoothie or suede head fashions'. Another, 16-year-old Stamford Bridge season ticket holder Mike Bracegirdle from Manchester spent £500 in 1970–71 following the Blues. 'I've had lots of girlfriends,' he chirruped, 'but lost them all through Chelsea.'

London-based Chelsea fans have always been aware, and mostly appreciative, of the image the club, as well as the wealth associated with and projected since the late 1960s and early 70s. Playing up to it can lead to extremes of behaviour. During the Premiership match at Old Trafford in May 2004, in which Chelsea won a point to confirm second place and the last Champions League group stage place, there were the usual enjoyable jibes, 'You'll have to qualify,' 'Channel 5, Channel 5, Channel 5' and the like. But when the United fans retorted, and the response of 'Loads and loads o' money!' began, a hefty middle-aged man in the middle of the Chelsea seats stood up, turned to the home fans and reached into his pocket. Then, with a gaze of fixed indifference, he began stripping loads of £50 notes, one at a time, from the huge wad in his left hand, and slowly slapping them flat on his bald head with his right. Each note quickly blew away in the riffling breeze, but he betrayed no immediate concern as to where the money flew. It was a bizarre demonstration of Abramovich-era bravado and it made some Reds incandescent with rage.

'The north/south divide is great if you play it right,' says Preston lad Iggi. 'For years I travelled to the Bridge and never bought a pre-match round. I would always be told to put my money back in my pocket by Londoners in the round, as they didn't have the heart to take a northerner's cash! Sadly now they've changed their ways. But I still tend to find that northerners know a lot more about the south than vice versa.'

Chelsea's age-old Champagne Charlie image might have its spin-off benefits for the northern Blues, but how the club could entice more money from fans often seemed to elude them. In the 1960s it was almost impossible to come by a replica kit. If you wanted Chelsea's highly desirable numbers on shorts, you cut them out and stitched them on yourself. Or, if she really loved you, your mum would do it for you.

Happily, in the mid-60s, at the same time as coaching the youth team, Frank Blunstone –Ted Drake's best value signing – set up the first outlet for official Chelsea merchandise. The premises were on Lavender Hill in Clapham, close to the junction with Queenstown Road, Wandsworth Road and Cedars Road. 'It such a massive industry now and we were the first to start it,' says Blunstone with some pride. 'We actually employed two or three Chelsea players. Tommy Doc opened the sports shop for us and we had Peter Bonetti working for us, advertising goalkeepers' kit. We started a Peter Bonetti goalkeeper's pack – green shirt, green shorts, socks and green gloves – because Catty always wore gloves.

'We sold hundreds of them, particularly at Christmas. Bobby Tambling advertised the boots for us. From memory – you're talking 1964, 41 years ago – the shirts cost about thirty bob [£1.50], something like that. But we were the first ones and we were sending them abroad and everywhere.

'We had to get an old boy in, a pensioner, just to take them to the post office because there were that many orders coming in from Chelsea supporters abroad who wanted them. We were sending them to Australia, New Zealand, everywhere.'

Blunstone's Chelsea emporium was the only place to buy proper Chelsea kits with embroidered badges and all the trendy little details that Docherty introduced. The shorts were numbered, but sadly so were the days of Blunstone's exclusivity. 'Obviously like everything else, you can't stop other people cashing in,' he shrugs. 'Other shops started to sell the stuff and then Chelsea themselves started to do it.'

There have been a number of Chelsea merchandise shops around Stamford Bridge since then. There was one, for a long time, on the walk from Fulham Broadway tube. Once a small one had opened within the new East Stand, the club was at pains to point out that the previous outlet was 'unofficial'.

In the early-1980s there was a semi-permanent portacabin inside the main entrance. Since July 1997 there has been a massive megastore to supply the insatiable demand for licensed products. The statistics are larger than Frank Blunstone had to deal with, but the quirks remain. With 10,500 square feet of floor space over three floors it was, at the time of opening, the largest football club store in the world. It is visited by between 8,000 and 11,000 people on matchdays and has shifted 135,000 shirts with names printed on the back, with 'Zola', naturally, the most popular. As the century closed, it was Lampard who was shifting the most of the current squad, followed by Terry, Robben, Drogba and Duff. Coincidentally, the most popular girl's name on shirts is 'Chelsea'. And 91 people have bought Chelsea-branded frying pans (or one accident prone, Chelsea-supporting chef).

Bringing the club's commercial activities in-house in the 1970s was an obvious and sensible move. What was less predictable was the sudden blossoming of self-published fanzines by die-hard supporters, frequently critical of the club to which they owed allegiance and the way it was run. These were reflective either of the oafish, up-for-it hooli culture or the views of those on the politicised left.

How Chelsea's fans approached it and how the club treated it is instructive. A catalyst was the battle to keep Chelsea at Stamford Bridge and stop Marler Estates' plans for a groundshare with their west London rivals. Back in the late 1940s a few supporters had formed their own supporters' club, which was not recognised by the Chelsea directors. 'The board weren't interested in the fans,' says Peter Ralph, 'only their money – they saw the fans as a nuisance. The supporters' club used to meet in the pub opposite the West Stand entrance, the Britannia. They used to hire a coach to away games and I remember going to away matches on it when there were only about 30 of us fans.'

By the mid-80s, though, the old supporters' club had become official and, in the eyes of some younger fans, not outspoken enough about supporters' issues. Twelve fans, including Nick Brown, Peter Collins,

Paul Roberts and Mike Ticher, got together to set up an independent supporters' club, the Chelsea Independent Supporters' Association (CISA), in April 1987, and along with it the *Chelsea Independent* fanzine. They produced more than a hundred issues over 13 years and it was for a while a must-read for a certain type of socially aware supporter. Chelsea's terraces had been cowed by violence and their publications suggested that there were fans with a different, softer perspective on support. Their anti-racist stance gave confidence to those who wanted to tell the bigots to shove it. CISA also paid for balloons and fireworks at matches to bring a little joy to the terraces.

The club – and in particular Ken Bates – publicly took the view that fanzines such as the *Independent* were ripping fans off. He often appeared obsessively opposed to them, which suggests he was as concerned with their effect on the club's image and coffers as on fans' pockets. Bates used the advantage of his public platform in a vehement campaign. Once CISA chairman Ross Fraser had committed his organisation behind Matthew Harding rather than Ken Bates he joined the rota of targets, many of whom were editors of Chelsea fanzines, that Bates wrote about in his always entertaining programme notes. Fraser was more shaken, though, by a carefully planned violent attack on him and other CISA members in a post-match pub by a group angered by the *Independent*'s anti-racism campaigns.

Added to all this there was the rare event of a loyal supporter taking the club's chairman to court for libel. Another CISA member, Dave Johnstone, challenged Bates's description of his organisation as 'parasites'. The litigation lasted two years and Bates settled out of court.

With the old chairman out of the way, in 2005 Johnstone was employed by the new regime as an archivist of memorabilia for the Chelsea Centenary Exhibition. It could just be an example of the club adopting the old adage of keeping your friends close, but your enemies closer. But for the first time, under Trevor Birch Chelsea pledged to create fans' forums to air and exchange views between fans and the club, and current chief executive Peter Kenyon made it one of his first actions on taking up his post.

But perhaps the biggest change has come in how the remote Chelsea community keeps in touch with the club. Fans can be fervent, well-informed supporters without ever knowing or caring where Walham Green is.

Chelsea's history of always harnessing new media to increase its fan base and revenue opportunities continued in the Bates era with the sudden availability to clubs of broadcast rights and cheaper production and broadcast technology. But the tradition stretched way back to the very beginning.

In the club's very first season they produced two publications: a small format handbook of fixtures, player profiles, editorials and adverts that came out at the start of the season and persisted for many years; and the *Chelsea Chronicle*, the first four-, then eight-page pamphlet-style programme in the south. It was a mixture of high-minded humour, gossip, word play and lots of competitions, alongside team line-ups and player profiles, all printed in blue ink on white newsprint. It was a community-builder, an interactive medium.

It proved very popular. The club had requests for copies to be sent out to armed forces in Gibraltar in 1906, and on a break while out cycling with a friend, Frederick Parker – who wrote the publications himself – was gratified to come across a copy of the *Chronicle* lying inside a bus shelter. The word was spreading.

Other than expressing the Chelsea board's point of view and entertaining fans, it was, of course, intended to make money. The board soon noted that among the many hawkers who lined the streets on matchdays were men selling inferior, unofficial copies of the *Chronicle*; they even wore blue and white armbands to suggest authenticity.

Then, in the mid-1990s came the advent of accessible new media – although it wasn't all a success. The problem of piracy faced by the *Chronicle* didn't trouble Radio Chelsea when it launched on a restricted licence. The main reason it wasn't copied was because no one could hear it, except in the stadium concourse. In time-honoured fashion, here was a great new Chelsea innovation that was not planned and executed with the necessary rigour.

'I loved Radio Chelsea.' Andy Jacobs, a Chelsea media type who produced TV's *Fantasy Football* and is a presenter, with Paul Hawksbee, on TalkSport was an early recruit. 'I got involved because I heard about it and I wrote to Alex Connock who owns Ten Alps with Bob Geldof, one of the biggest production companies in this country – don't ask me how, but they do! I wrote to Alex. He was the head of programming for Planet 24 and they produced the station for Chelsea.

'But the whole thing about Radio Chelsea, it seemed to typify Chelsea at that time. It was a bit half-arsed; you couldn't even hear it in Fulham Road. It had a transmitter that didn't transmit.'

The early commentary team included Andy Saunders, the PR man for Oasis and Creation records, whose boss, Alan McGee, is also a Blue. Saunders was laconic and extremely biased, just as fans wanted. Jacobs continues, 'Paul Hawksbee [Chelsea's short-lived media and PR manager] often reminds me of the fact that its early broadcasts were relayed around the pitch on the PA and one day while the players were warming up on the pitch they had some guests in the studio saying, "So-and-so, I don't know why he's in the team!" slagging off a player, and Paul had to rush up and say, "Look, they can hear this, you know!"

'Then there was the time with stadium announcer Carl Chapman and his player introductions – it's legendary. I remember when he'd been doing it a long time and he basically had this idea that it would be good fun to build up the players, "He's played 25 times this season, scored ten goals, such and such." And it came to Chris Sutton and he said, "He's only scored one goal in 35 appearances – Chris Sutton!" And I thought, that's really going to boost him up! After a while we'd sort of make up our own, you know, to join in with him. We'd do like, "He's only got one trick, but it's very good – Eddie Newton!" or "He's only scored one goal, always hits the post, never likely to make it – Mateja Kezman!"

'Also, one of the guys before Carl was funny. He found out I was a Chelsea fan (it's a true story, this) and he said to me, "I do the stadium announcements at Chelsea, come and be in the box before the match." I said, "Oh, that would be nice."

'So we go into his box, and he starts smoking a joint! And he's like away with the fairies this guy, and he's shouting over the PA, "Stamford! Take your head off!" It was a slightly less professional club in those days, but that's all part of the fun.

'Carl was off one week in 2001 or 2002, and I got a phone call saying would I like to do the PA before the match? It was just when I'd joined TalkSport. And I said, "Yeah, I'd love to do it, why not?"

'Well, I'm a broadcaster and a producer, but technically I'm absolutely useless. So I go up there and he goes, "Well, here are the carts, so you play these disks ..." and I said, "What are you talking about? All I have to do is talk, don't I?" He said to me, "Oh no, you have to do the ads and stuff ... " And I said, "I can't do that! I'm Andy Jacobs from TalkSport, how dare you!"

'And in the end somebody came in to do it and I said, "Oh good". And he said, "No, you're out, you're fired." So before I even started I got sacked as the PA announcer. It's a great moment and I'm very, very proud. About 25 minutes and I never got to say anything, so there you go!'

The media channel that seems to have tapped into the jugular of obsessive fans is Chelsea TV, 'the home wrecker'. Spouses not used to seeing their other half on a matchday are alternatively amazed and appalled by the capacity of a person they thought they knew and understood to withstand the same news repeats, or hang, rapt, on the reserve team boss's post-match interview, or endure ten minutes of the thumping testcard music before programmes start at 4.30 p.m.

The now globally-available Chelsea TV started rather amateurishly as matchdays-only Channel Chelsea in 1994, with Capital DJ and Chelsea fan Graham Dene as its host. After the two big Glasgow clubs and Manchester United, it was the first club TV station. It is addictive viewing for Chelsea fans anxious for full-length reserve games or revealing chats with a club masseur, alongside exclusive player interviews that indicate where the power and value in players' 'image rights' are moving. The thrice-weekly phone-ins are often populated by the same gaggle of fans week-in, week-out, much like parts of the old ground before seating. 'Chelsea TV, long may it continue, I think it's tremendous ... it's great for the fans to have that,' says Jacobs. 'But there is a slightly in-bred feeling about the phone-ins. And I don't understand how "Tony Chelsea from Wigan", "Gel Emery" and "Susan McKnight from Belfast" – "Hello there, Neil! I'm looking forward to coming over" – how do they always get on? I can't get on.'

After the players had won the title, several of them, led by John Terry, invaded the studio during a live phone-in and covered presenter Neil Barnett completely with flour. 'That was a great Chelsea TV moment,' says Jacobs. 'He's a Chelsea fan through and through and he has the players' trust. That was what was shown in that moment. They wouldn't do that if they didn't like him, they wouldn't have come on there and done that.' Most fans watching felt the same. It showed that club TV can help fans bond with the players, understand them better. The phone-ins help the fans to understand themselves too. What unites them, what differentiates them.

It's also noticeable that there is a greater proportion of ethnic minority callers, more from Ireland, the north, children, women.

TV, the king of media at the time of Chelsea's centenary, helps the fans realise how inclusive Chelsea can be. Like that big old lovely stadium, there's room for everyone.

REPUTATIONS

'We're all playing **Championship** Manager on our PCs; **Roman's** doing it for real'

7

RUBBING SHOULDERS WITH GREATNESS

'Chelsea, the home of actors and artists, provided a nesting place, a gathering at the village pump, for the Bohemian element. Stamford Bridge, indeed, achieved a gay cosmopolitan clientele from the lowest to the highest in the land, who gathered under its roof for entertainment, as much to cheer the opposition as their own Blues – the owners of antique shops; the showbiz element and garrulous taxi drivers, one of whom once drove Laurence Olivier, his wife Vivien Leigh and myself away after a night match. Happy, carefree days.'
Geoffrey Green, 1982

There was a sense of come-one, come-all at the pre-1993 Stamford Bridge. Its terraces were like some old public park, a place to lose yourself among the leisuring classes. Its high banks afforded rare views of London; on a clear day you could see a championship. Supporting a club is like contracting a virus and it can infect anyone 'from the lowest to the highest in the land'. It was a privilege that you were a carrier and going to the Bridge back then helped ease the suffering. And, as we have seen, if one thing has been a factor that influenced all others and sat at the root of the club's strengths and its weaknesses it would be its location.

That is true right from the way the club was created through to today, to Abramovich, who was attracted by the very positioning of Stamford Bridge.

'If you look at the mix of housing round West Chelsea and Fulham, you've got a road with millionaires living in it next to a World's End or a Lord Attlee estate and that kind of stuff. So I think that they're probably slightly more affluent than other clubs, but against them I also suspect that people are working class round Fulham and Chelsea more than in, say, Islington,' said Tony Banks.

Chelsea has always infected more fashionable and showbiz types than other clubs, but has also always been a club of the masses. The crowd at Stamford Bridge is a congregation of opposites, the club of Cocky Dick as well as Hooray Henrietta. 'We are so close to the fleshpots and the fashionable areas of London, the restaurants and the theatres and the shops and all that, and I don't know of any other club in that position,' continued Banks. 'Certainly Tottenham and Arsenal and Charlton aren't. Not Fulham, because they're more residential where they are.

'You had glimpses of greatness on the pitch and at the same time had a continuing sense that "Wow that's the King's Road where fashion happens, that's a posh restaurant that we've heard about." At the very least we were the club with the closest proximity to all those events, particularly in the 1960s, the Rolling Stones and stuff like that.

'The club actually did nothing to try and counter that, probably the reverse – they thought that was a sign of strength. It's certainly meant that we were always a famous club, but I think in many ways that stopped us from being an effective club. In terms of where we got our support from and the players that we attracted, I think we probably attracted more than our fair share of "Good time Charlies". Let's face it; you're just down the road from everything you want. The hotels, the restaurants, the theatres, all those things.'

The interest in any form of celebrity today, whether manufactured or merited, reveals how associations with glamour and fame would have helped Chelsea. But if you embrace the slightly shallow world of showbiz, you must be prepared to be tarred with the same brush. It has been a source of wonder and pleasure over the years to see George Robey, King Alphonso of Spain, Ronnie Corbett, Raquel Welch and Damon Albarn in the stands at Chelsea. But it has created a perception to some outsiders that showy Chelsea is not in the gritty mainstream of football. Not a proper football club.

'If you want to take the piss out of the club, there's your ammunition,' laughed Banks, 'they're all standing there. It's not fair, but if you're a sort of famous personality you're not really supposed to be a football fan. You're a bit of a poseur, because we're seen as a poseur's club.' It's almost as if, rightly or wrongly, they're assumed not to be passionate and committed, but simply there to be seen.

Most people assume that the double-edged sword of celebrity was first unsheathed at Stamford Bridge by Music Hall's biggest star of the day, George Robey, who helped organise and played inside-left in a benefit match for the widow of Chelsea's Scottish international trainer Jimmy Miller, who had died suddenly, in 1907.

The benefit match was between Chelsea and an All-Star XI. According to football curio collector Bryan Horsnell, 'So well did Robey perform, that after the match he was signed on as an amateur. The club having won promotion to the First Division of the Football League, George would say in his act, "I just wanted to make sure that Chelsea stay in the First Division." This was the first known occasion on which the club was mentioned on the music hall stage.'

Peter Cotes, Robey's biographer, wrote that this 'started the long series of comedians' jokes about Chelsea Football Club, of which we have surely not heard the last'. So the cudgel with which Chelsea have always been beaten appears to have been picked up by others.

The Music Hall connection was sealed when in 1933 Norman Long, a popular comedian, actually performed a song called 'The Day that Chelsea Won the Cup', satirising their lack of silverware, and the first verse went:

'Now a little while ago I dreamed the most amazing dream.

It tickled me to death when I woke up.

Now you know just how impossible the things we dream of are.

But I dreamed that Chelsea went and won the Cup.'

The 'Music Hall jokes' jibe hung around for decades – even Ted Drake referred to it as a bind in the early 1950s. But the 'Chelsea sensation' – the money, the location, the novelty – had been felt even before Robey sealed the showbiz link. With excellent commercial heads such as Frederick Parker and Claude Kirby on board, the club bought media-friendly players such as Willie Foulke, who generated publicity wherever he went, and it also produced the wordy *Chelsea Chronicle*, which set out deliberately to create a buzz about the club and its 'brand', carrying cartoons of Chelsea Pensioners and gossip painting Chelsea in a good light. Parker, writer and editor of the programme for 30 years, was Chelsea's first 'spin-doctor'.

At one away ground (possibly Blackpool) Foulke was amazed to see locals standing outside the railway station with sandwich boards advertising the presence of Foulke in town, 'COME AND SEE THE TWENTY-FOUR STONE GOALKEEPER'. You get the sense that Chelsea might have organised it themselves.

The 6 foot 2 inch, 22-stone Foulke was larger than life in many ways. One of his party tricks was to carry a boy off the field of play at the end of the game – Chelsea had introduced small 'ball-boys' to accentuate Foulke's size. In team photos he was nearly always deliberately placed next to his smallest team-mates for contrast.

He dominates the *Manchester Guardian* match report of Chelsea's very first match at Stockport on 2 September 1905. 'Chelsea brought some very famous men to Edgeley Park,' it cooed. 'Foulke stood in the goal with his 20 stone of lusty manhood, McEwan was in front of him and McRoberts at centre-half. Forward there were Copeland and Kirwan of Tottenham's Cup-winning eleven ... Foulke played as well as ever. "As active as a cat," the crowd said, and his nimbleness was indeed astonishing.'

This amazing-agility-for-a-fat-lad quality and his outgoing, quipping personality meant that 'as a draw alone Foulke is worth his weight in gold,' as one paper eulogised. Commentators spoke of him 'arousing almost a fever of interest in the doings under the bar for the Chelsea club.'

'He stops low "daisy cutters" and high dropping shots with equal ease,'" bragged his manager, Jackie Robertson, 'and his punch despatches the ball to a distant point of the horizon. He has accomplished many good performances this year, but perhaps his best so far was his fine fantasia at the close of the match against West Bromwich Albion. The "Throstles" tried strenuously to equalise and sent in a perfect bombardment of shots, but Foulke was as imperturbably calm as he was adequate. The crowd gave him an ovation after the game.'

Ninety-eight years ahead of Real Madrid's acquisition of David Beckham, and with a noticeably different physique, 'Fatty' Foulke was bought for his marketability. He only lasted one season at Chelsea. The last ever football match he attended was the 1915 FA Cup final between his two old clubs,

Sheffield United and Chelsea. His nephew played for the Blades and he favoured them in the 3-0 win. Contrary to popular belief, Foulke did not see out his life as a poverty-stricken seaside attraction saving penalties in a sideshow tent. He did it once, briefly and for a laugh, at Blackpool, but kept a reasonably successful corner shop on Matilda Street, Sheffield until dying of cirrhosis, diagnosed two years earlier, in 1916.

His full-length photographic portrait, in profile to show his stomach in all its glory, is one of the Chelsea-related displays at the National Football Museum in Preston. In 2003, on a salsa club noticeboard, I saw the same image used alongside a call for new players for a Sunday league team – 'any standard'.

The press were attracted to the millionaires from nowhere who had started from scratch. One newspaper's stop press section carried a febrile piece of gossip reserved these days for former *Big Brother* contestants, 'The Chelsea team are now enjoying a luncheon of roast mutton and dry toast.'

As young opportunists entering a competitive industry, the Chelsea board looked to distance themselves from their competitors, especially the grimy hotbeds of the north. When the club achieved promotion in 1907, they commemorated the team with a carefully constructed photo in front of a posh hotel. All the players wear superbly tailored three-piece suits with fob watch chains, and they are nattily coiffed, dashing and hatless. It was a long way from the black clay pipe, check caps and woollen mufflers of their contemporaries. The image suggests: it's a good life down at Chelsea.

It was fun in the stands as well. In April 1914 football was officially trendy – *The Times* decreed it so – and at the centre of it was the Fulham Road. 'In the last two or three years, League matches at Stamford Bridge and elsewhere have been attended even by persons to whom the dangerous epithet fashionable might be applied,' it wrote. 'Professional football of the best kind is no longer regarded as a spectacle only for the proletariat.'

It is odd, in these post-Princess Diana days, to imagine that royalty might be thought of as the most glamorous people. But in the 1920s, they still enjoyed lifestyles and status that were unattainable to others. New fashions were first seen adorning princesses and queens. They went to all the most exclusive parties. In that context, incredible enthusiasm greeted the King's appearances at Stamford Bridge to shake hands with the players and war veterans around the pitch at games in 1920. At the 3-0 cup victory against Leicester in February, he arrived by car and was met outside the ground by the man who owned much of west London, Chelsea's club president, Earl Cadogan. Chairman Claude Kirby escorted King George inside the ground and the Irish Guards band played the national anthem. After the player presentations, the King watched the game and apparently exchanged technical observations with Kirby.

The visit gained national coverage, adding to Chelsea's lofty reputation. Manchester's *Athletic News* joked that the club had become something like footie's Fortnum & Mason, 'If these kingly favours be continued the Chelsea club will soon be entitled to alter the sign over their gateway, and in golden letters blaze forth, "Royal Chelsea, Purveyor of Football to their Majesties King George of England and King Alphonso of Spain".'

After King Alfonso XIII of Spain paid a visit to the Madrid Club de Fútbol in 1920, they were allowed to change their name to Royal, or Real, Madrid. The same monarch watched Chelsea beat Bradford Park Avenue 4-0 the previous year, but the only royal association the club is left with is the blue of its shirts; for the first few years they had been a light 'Eton' blue colour, as worn by horse racing fanatic Cadogan's jockeys.

After royalty, and even more than Music Hall stars, society turned for its glamour fix to the cinema. And, again, Chelsea was ahead of the rest. You can forget the regularly trotted-out *Arsenal Stadium Mystery*. The Pensioners' Cornish-born centre forward John 'Jack' Cock, who won the Military Medal for gallantry in the First World War, was signed to Chelsea in 1919 having starred in a benefit match at the Bridge.

Cock was an England international and another superstar who took football to a different level. Supremely skilled and graceful, he had a powerful shot in either boot, was great with his head, striking-looking with a big, open face, not unlike a young Robert Shaw, and was known to take to the pitch singing. When fans then saw him doing the same on stage at the Granville Theatre, they must have wondered if there was anything he couldn't do.

The fact that at one stage Cock's team-mates sometimes included a Hampton, a Dickie, and a Bell – and an Armstrong – at least gave the terrace wits something to have a dig about.

Cock became Chelsea's first matinee idol in 1920 when he starred as himself in the originally titled silent movie *The Winning Goal* (no twist at the end there then). It was directed by George Samuelson, who saw professional sports as a growth area for the silver screen and covered them one by one.

Unfortunately, no copy of the film can be traced. Happily, Cock's next feature *The Great Game* (1930) is in the British Film Institute's archives. It's a typical football movie: chairman has daughter, young player meets daughter, young player can't get in cup team, daughter pulls strings, young player wins the cup – huzzah!

More than that, though, it's an attempt to convey for the first time some of the age-old conflicts within the game. An old-style secretary-manager wants to give young, hungry footballers a chance; his chairman wants to buy established players, of which the key one is Jack Cock. When the manager sneers of his chairman that he 'would like to buy an entire new team at fancy prices' it resounds all the way down the years to the present.

Less so the grizzled old trainer, played by Wally Patch. 'In my day,' he says, 'all you did was to eat well, sleep well, work well, and play up like 'ell! And that's good enough for you lads to train on, I give you my word!'

'I still believe,' says the manager, 'that a team with a good heart and will to win can beat £50,000 worth of players.' (I'm not sure, but I think I saw a few of the Chelsea players in the cast look at each and nod at this point.)

Although Cock was by then a Millwall player, many of his former team-mates do feature in it, including the popular internationals Andy Wilson, George Mills and keeper Sam Millington (who is shown making one of his occasional costly lapses), as well as Albert Thain, George Smith and Willie Ferguson. In the film there are great shots of what looks like the old Stamford Bridge boardroom, the dressing rooms, the East Stand and wonderful scenes of the players training at Stamford Bridge, running along the track and knocking the ball around in the goalmouth. They are even seen playing golf. The football action is real, possibly filmed at Millwall's ground. It is shot in black and white, but it appears that our heroes – Manningford FC – are playing in Chelsea strips, with a strange badge on them – 30 years before the real team adopted the habit.

The greatest moment, though, comes when the newly bought Cock is asked to demonstrate his skills. He calls over the young hero, runs at him with the ball, dips his hips, does a dummy stepover of the kind we thought Zola had patented, and drags the ball round his team-mate with the outside of his boot. He must have been a great entertainer on the pitch.

The same can be said about the legendary amateur from Corinthians, Benjamin Howard Baker, known as 'HB', who holds the distinction of being the only goalkeeper to score from that position in a competitive match for Chelsea. It proved the single, decisive goal of a bad-tempered First Division game at home to struggling Bradford City and was from the penalty spot. He also set the world record for high jump at 6 feet 5½ inches. He was 6 feet 3 himself, and only became a keeper after a wartime explosion damaged his ankle. He was a striking figure, renowned for his playfulness. Fans remember with delight HB bouncing the ball round his box, basketball-style, and over opposing forwards' heads, while instructions to the players were bellowed from the directors' box through a loudhailer. Off the field his party piece used to be to kick out the lightbulbs from chandeliers eight feet off the ground. The trick puts later Blue Duncan McKenzie's standing leap over a Mini into the shade.

Nearly 60 years before Yugoslavian Petar Borota surprised his defence and the Chelsea fans by spurting out of his goal in his tracksuit bottoms, HB became one of the first goalies to enjoy roving his way upfield. On one occasion, towards the end of the 1922–23 season in which every point was vital, he scored a bizarre own goal, toeing the ball into the net as he ran back into his box following one of those forays. 'I couldn't help being a little bit spectacular,' he recalled as an old man.

It was said that the dandy socialite was 'as well known to wine waiters and hall porters as Douglas Fairbanks', the great film star and Lothario. People like HB made Chelsea the draw they remain to this day and he always said he had his greatest days at the club.

In 1930, four years after the colourful HB had moved on, newly promoted Chelsea was acquiring an all-star line-up, with Scotland's 1928 Wembley Wizards forward line being shipped south to the club. What better for a club with a long Scottish affiliation? With their ball play and sensitive short passing, they brought the artistic side of the game.

In December 1930 Caledonian Chelsea slaughtered Sunderland 5-0. 'There was never a doubt about their winning, once it was seen that Gallacher was in his best humour and Jackson as lively as a bucking bronco,' wrote The Times. Sunderland's beanpoles easily dealt with high balls, 'while pygmies, such as Gallacher, Cheyne and Crawford, could get nowhere near. Yet it was the clever footwork of these players that did the trick.' Jackson 'made a somersault over the goalkeeper, and performed other tricks which won the heart of the crowd.

'Chelsea showed themselves to be a powerful team as they were placed on Saturday, and it is much to be hoped that they will now at last be allowed to develop the team spirit and understanding.'

Symptomatic of the way the club's brilliance has shimmered like a mirage were the financial disputes with the board that meant it didn't work out for Cheyne and Jackson. Gallacher was a star who glittered long in posterity, as fondly remembered as Zola to those who saw him play. He brought fantasy and infamy to the Fulham Road, where football and entertainment were already mingled.

The club's first £10,000 signing was only with the Pensioners for just over four seasons starting in 1930, but at 5 foot 6 the centre-forward packed a lot into his time at the Bridge – except silverware. Chelsea's celebrity status brought media attention. In 1932, Gallacher presented the Chelsea players to Edward, Prince of Wales, on the occasion of the opening of the West Stand at Highbury (built, by the way, on top of rubbish donated by local people). He inadvertently caused a sensation by breaking protocol in putting his arm round His Royal Highness's waist in a most familiar fashion. 'I had to put up with a great deal of chaffing over the incident,' he recalled later.

Less amusing was an incident involving Fulham fans near Stamford Bridge. Gallacher had been out with some team-mates and stopped at a coffee stall for a snack. The Fulhamites began provoking him 'being very uncomplimentary about the Chelsea team and me in particular'. A scrap ensued, broken up by a policeman, who arrested Gallacher for being disorderly. He managed to arrange for a very unhappy Chelsea trainer to bail him out, but next day attended the magistrates' court. Gallacher protested his innocence and there was no conviction, but he was asked to put ten shillings in the civic poor box and club secretary Harry Palmer told him he was dropped for the next game.

That evening, a London paper screamed, 'CHELSEA'S DRASTIC ACTION'. The problem was that around Walham Green, Gallacher was well known for his drinking and enjoyment of the vibrant nightlife. 'Hughie Gallacher,' recalls Roy Simpson, 'before he played football, used to go in the White Hart and have his pint or his whisky and then go to play the game. That is true. Then he'd arrive in the ground – "Yeeeaahh!" – and get going.'

Opposing players out for stroll once saw him slumped drunk in a doorway the night before a game. As legend has it, he surprised them all by running rings round them the next day and scoring.

But there was a self-destruct mechanism triggered by alcohol. In January 1931 the FA Council suspended Gallacher for two months for 'using filthy language to the referee' in a Grimsby match the day after Boxing Day, in the aftermath of an incident involving Andy Wilson. It was one of several lengthy enforced absences that robbed the public of his performances and him of his money, which infuriated and frustrated him further.

His private affairs became even more public by that October when 'Hugh Kilpatrick Gallacher, of Dewhurst Road, Kensington, and lately of Bellshill, Lanarkshire' was adjudged bankrupt with liabilities totalling £787, made up entirely of solicitors' costs relating to his suit for divorce from his first wife. Gallacher's statement laid bare the star footballer's basic salary: from 29 August to 6 May he received the playing wage of £6 a week, but after that he was on summer rations of £4. He remarried ten days before the receiving order was made at Hammersmith Town Hall, with huge crowds and newsreel teams in attendance. When Gallacher received his signing on fee from Derby in 1935, it went straight to Carey Street Bankruptcy Court. In his suicide note, before throwing himself in front of an inter-city train in Gateshead in June 1957, Gallacher blamed drink for his downfall.

After their partially successful experiments with high-profile players in the 1930s, Chelsea had begun to exploit another fashionable aspect of its persona: the upper-class Englishness of its shareholders. This was especially effective once radio had become a national obsession, full of the plummy public school accents heard in the boardroom at Stamford Bridge.

When a young Joe Mears was elected to the Chelsea board in 1931 he became the youngest director in the game. (He would succeed Lieutenant-Colonel C.D. Crisp as chairman in 1940.) After his father's death in 1935, he and his two siblings had access to the bottomless pit of the 'J.T. Mears Trust' – it was almost 'old money', except that with various interests such as the Ford dealership and cinemas, he still needed to work. Mears had kept goal in two Arthur Dunn Cup-winning finals for Malvern School, and his son Joseph Brian was among those who would follow him there. Elsewhere on the board was Henry Boyer and Beatrice Mears's son Henry.

There were notable sports personalities in the executive boxes too. Chairman until 1935, Claude Kirby had been an outstanding runner, Vivian Woodward was a sensation as an amateur player, and long-serving director (1922–30) and Olympic water polo champion Jack Budd was on the board from 1931 to 1952. Among Chelsea's first ever vice-presidents had been a record holder in the seven-mile walk, Mr H. Venn, two justices of the peace (Colonel Leslie Powell, alderman and leader of Richmond Conservative Party, and Major W.F. Woods), two Tory members of Parliament (William Hayes Fisher, MP for Fulham, and C.A. Whitmore, for Chelsea) as well as Arthur, the Earl of Cadogan, Conservative MP for Stowmarket.

Until the Second World War threw social order up in the air, establishment figures could be almost as fashionable as royalty. Though the Great War had ended with America having leapfrogged Britain as the supreme world power during the 1930s, the global empire on which the sun never set was still enormous. At the hub of empire was London and London's elite had Chelsea FC as a neighbour. The club remained 'well connected'.

Lieutenant-Colonel C.D. Crisp (Chelsea chairman 1926–40) and C.B. Fry, a founding vice-president in 1905, were both regularly asked onto the radio to share their views on sport, life and everything.

Fry and Crisp may sound like a brand of home-cook chips today, but in the 1930s each epitomised the successful, sporty Edwardian gentleman. Fry was the bigger personality, representing England at cricket (he knocked a half century for Sussex the day Chelsea played their first match at Stockport), football and athletics, in which he set a world long jump record. The veteran cricket sage John Arlott, another regular at Stamford Bridge, wrote of him as 'a most incredible man ... the most variously gifted Englishman ... the pre-eminent all-rounder, not merely of his own age, but, so far as is measurable, of all English history.' He was possibly the greatest sportsman of all time.

At Oxford Fry met lifelong friends of the English intelligentsia, such as Hilaire Belloc and Max Beerbohm, wrote many books, represented India at the League of Nations and was once offered the throne of Albania. His nicknames included 'Charles III' and 'Almighty'. In the 1930s he went to Hollywood hoping for a film career and met Mary Astor, Basil Rathbone and Boris Karloff. He was also a friend of many Labour and Liberal politicians, but flirted with Fascism, before returning to Liberalism.

Crisp was alderman and then mayor of Lewes, Sussex, from November 1938. He'd been a director of Arsenal too and was an all-round athlete, a football referee and an FA councillor until two years before his death, aged 92 in 1956. He owned the Franche estate in Lewes and one of the little perks of being a Chelsea player was the regular days out there for fun and games. Richard Branson does the same thing for Virgin company employees today.

In 1936 the BBC's enormously popular radio magazine show *In Town Tonight* dedicated itself to London's trendiest football club, Chelsea. The half-hour show, with its evocative 'Knightsbridge Theme' music by Eric 'Dambusters' Coates, ran for 27 years from 1933 and in that time established an enchanting image of London life in listeners' heads.

In its introduction was the sound of a flower-seller repeating her familiar street cry: 'Violets, luvly sweet violets!' A newsboy called out 'In Town Tonight! In Town Tonight!' followed by a good old London Bobby shouting 'Stop!' then, 'Once again we silence the mighty roar of London's traffic to bring to the microphone some of the interesting people who are In Town Tonight!' On this occasion the nation listened in to Crisp, manager Leslie Knighton, and at least two players – Harry Burgess and his close friend and long-throw expert Sam Weaver, who told the audience, 'One day I threw such a particularly long ball that the distance was measured and found to be 48 yards!' The whole thing was tightly controlled, and Harry Burgess's son Martin still has his father's script – ad libs and all.

The intrinsic value of being the most central London club has mostly served Chelsea very well down the years. Since 1995 it has been one of the key attractions to overseas stars such as Gullit, Vialli, Zola, Leboeuf and Desailly ... even Abramovich and Mourinho. Conversely, it has meant to outsiders that the capital's faults – snobbishness, self-importance, undeserving wealth – became entwined with the image of Chelsea FC. In the inter-war years, being at Chelsea had the kudos of a visibly affluent lifestyle compared to other clubs, even if the trophies were elusive. Stamford Bridge was the prize move for older stars on the wain. Some of them took their status too seriously.

Audrie Swain was a young girl living near World's End in the mid-1930s. She was always playing with the boys of the area and they used to go up to the cemetery in Fulham Road, climb over the wall, cross the railway track and bunk in to the Chelsea ground. 'We never got caught,' she chuckles.

'When she grew up, though, Audrie gained a slightly different inside view of the club. 'I used to work as a bus conductress during the war and just after,' she says. 'We used to pick up the players on the number 96 bus. And you'd think they didn't need to wipe their bums, some of them.

They looked fit young men, of course, but I didn't know who they were. I'm looking at them asking for their fare, and they're looking at me as if to say, "What d'you want?"

'Passengers would say to me, "Don't you know who he is?" I'd say, "No – I'm just trying to get his fare." Perhaps they thought one man was going to pay for all of them.'

The club's regular habit of buying its way through life increased the perception that it had more money than style. The case of Tommy Lawton is instructive. In 1939, new Chelsea manager Billy Birrell had publicly pledged to contest the inflationary spiral of players' transfers and bonuses. But the war left London grey, ravaged and gasping for breath. So as if to make everyone feel better about themselves in the days of austerity following the Allied victories, Chelsea splashed out on glamour boys Len Goulden, Tommy Walker and the biggest star in the game, the recently demobbed England centre-forward Lawton.

According to the player in his autobiography, Everton earned nearly £14,000 from the deal, which had been precipitated by a lengthy illness suffered by Lawton's wife Rosaleen and medical advice to 'move south for the climate'. After just one full, record-breaking season, like Foulke, Joe Bambrick, Alex Jackson and other big name successes before him, he disappointingly moved on, two years and one week after joining. Perhaps there were contractual problems or Chelsea had failed to meet his expectations. In September 1947 Ken Armstrong, usually a half-back, deputised up front for Chelsea against Everton while Lawton was away with England, scored twice, and retained his place when Lawton was available again. The striker left two months later.

Like those others, though, his memory is inextricably linked to one momentous game. In his case, it was the visit of Moscow Dynamo just under a week after his transfer in November 1945. In fact, Moscow Radio imagined that Chelsea had signed the world-famous forward just so that he might face the Russian team. There is in that simple fact a suggestion of the hype surrounding this incredible occasion, the first match of the Soviet side's short British tour. Its impact on the footballing public's imagination should never be underestimated. It had mystique, brilliance, controversy and record-breaking magnitude. And it probably did more to seal Chelsea's reputation as 'big box office' than any other.

The buzz about the game around London and beyond was remarkable. For 13-year-old Brian Mears, son of then chairman Joe, it would be his first ever match. 'Curiosity,' he says. 'That's the word. They'd never seen Russians before and they were curious to see these people that had come from near extinction to push the Germans right back to Berlin – and those Russian tanks, they were fantastic, they blew the German tanks out of the water, didn't they?

'The Russians were a power to be reckoned with, and our allies, so they were heroes – before we knew what was going to happen afterwards, the Cold War, and all that sort of thing. They were heroes and they were bloody good footballers.

'Anyway, I should have been at school, but I wasn't. It was when my father said, "Would you like to come to the match?" I was very nonchalant. I said, "Who are we playing?" So when he told me and asked again, "Would you like to come to the match?" I said, "Yes, please!" It was a huge thing. It was fantastic.'

For those children outside of the board's immediate family the interest was as high, if not greater, but access to the game was more of a problem. Fulham resident Roy Simpson was a schoolboy at the time the Russians came. 'It was something different,' he recalls. 'It was a new team, from Russia. They'd given the Nazis hell in beating them back. Partly we were curious at what the Russians were like, but also we wanted to see what sort of football they played, see if it was at all different.

'So when they came over, people were well interested, wanted to see them. That's why you get the 100,000 and more at Chelsea. Everybody was talking about it – "Why not go? Let's go!" We were all bunking off school to go and see the Dynamos.'

Inside, children rolled down to the front on the hands of supporters and nestled round the pitch. Outside, when the gates were shut at 75,000 (the official capacity), people found any way to get in. Some gates buckled under the pressure. Some estimates of the crowd are as high as 125,000 with people visible like starlings massed on telephone lines atop every climbable construction – hoardings, nearby buildings and everything else. It was the biggest show in town for years.

Memories of the Moscow game swiftly passed into football folklore. For a start there were the bouquets of flowers the Soviets handed to their embarrassed hosts before kick-off. 'The huge crowd roared, first with laughter, then with applause,' recalled Tommy Lawton later. 'I felt like a film star at a première. We were all glad to hand over our floral decorations to luckless Norman Smith, the Chelsea trainer, who went off looking like a harvest festival.'

Then there was the impact of the Russians' play against a Chelsea side which included several Fulham players for the occasion. 'The Dynamo were one of the fastest teams I have ever seen in my life,' recalled Lawton. 'The Russians do not dribble. They flash the ball from man to man in bewildering fashion, often while standing still.'

Only the visitors' finishing let them down and Chelsea went 2-0 up through sheer physical persistence. Lawton tipped the ball out of keeper 'Tiger' Khomich's hands to set up Len Goulden for the first and a panicky clearance rebounded off Reg Williams' body for the Blues's second. The Russians had a goal disallowed (it had rebounded off a spectator!) and missed a penalty, and the score remained the same until midway into the second half. Then Kartsev whacked one in from outside the box, followed seven minutes later by Archangelski's equaliser. The diplomats in the Foreign Office and the Kremlin must have been delighted, until Lawton chased a long, high ball and headed past Khomich to make it 3-2.

The England centre-forward noted in his memoirs at this point that the stadium was audibly backing the Russians – typical of Stamford Bridge. So that when Bobrov, standing five yards offside, received the ball and converted to make it 3-3, few complained.

It was, football writers agreed, one of the most entertaining matches on English soil, a night of exuberant joy in a difficult period for people in post-war Britain. But not everyone was happy that night. Residents of properties adjoining the stadium knew only too well that football fans had done anything to get a glimpse of the game. Fences, gates, gutters and drainpipes were broken, and some chimneystacks, roofs and windows were in a state.

Mr John Munday of 432 Fulham Road claimed for and eventually won compensation under section two of the Riot (Damages) Act 1886. He won a total of £175 plus costs. The Metropolitan Police denied riot but accepted 'extensive trespass' had taken place 'regarding damage done on 13 November 1945 to Nos. 404, 406, 410, 412, 414, 420, 422, 424, 426, 428, 430, 432, 434, and 436 Fulham Road', all premises owned by Mr Munday.

'On this date,' said a police memo, 'the Russian football team, Moscow Dynamos, visited the Chelsea football team. A very large number of people were unable to gain access to the ground and in endeavouring to gain entry the crowds made their way over fences and walls into the gardens and onto the roofs of these premises causing damage.

'Police evidence indicated that the damage resulted from extensive trespass and the necessary elements of a riot were not present. A claim under the Act was accordingly refused.'

However, Mr Munday pursued his claim and Mr Justice Pritchard heard the case on 20 January 1949. The judge decided that all the necessary elements of a riot had been in place after all: 1. There must be at least three people (there were thousands locked out); 2. with a common purpose (seeing the game); 3. who execute or incept that common purpose (doing anything to get a view of it); 4. and have interest to help one another, by force if necessary, against any person who may oppose them in the execution of their common purpose (who's gonna stand in their way?); 5. and use force and violence not merely in demolishing, but displayed in such a manner as to alarm at least one person of reasonable firmness and courage.

The 'person of reasonable firmness' in this instance was Mr Munday's very own Alan Titchmarsh. 'It was clear from the uncontradicted evidence of Mr Munday's gardener,' said the judge, 'who had met with violence when he had tried to recover his ladder from those who had climbed onto a garage, that there was a riot there.'

So there you have it: Chelsea v Moscow Dynamo was a riot – official.

With such a buzz about Chelsea its position as post-war glamour club was in the bag.

'I remember Tommy Walker,' enthuses Roy Simpson. 'Marvellous player! What a player! Tall and lean he was, brave, used to get in with his head, and was a wonderful passer of the ball, lovely 30-yard balls and great to watch. But because he was lean he got knocked off the ball quite a lot.'

Walker, the 'Ace of Hearts' (he'd been bought from Hearts, where he returned as manager years later), was another of Chelsea's media darlings. Lawton described him as 'smooth as silk and as easy to get on with, who is at his best on a losing side – the hallmark of a great footballer'. Pathé seemed obsessed by him, filming him putting wealthy foreigner Maharajah Lokendra Singh through a private training session at Stamford Bridge in

1947 (even teaching him how to kick the ball) and using him as a rather stilted guest reporter for an international match exactly as *Match of the Day* do now, making him the prototype Alan Hansen.

The mood in Britain at the time was for renewal and change. Chelsea wasn't immune and the ageing Billy Birrell asked for help to deal with the increased demands of the game. 'Stanley Rous told me that Billy Birrell was looking for an assistant secretary,' says John Battersby. 'He'd hung on right through the war. I understood from some things that were said that he'd agreed a cut in wages during the war years.

'Billy was saying he wanted an assistant secretary and he'd got in mind a friend of his, Arthur Green, who ran the matchday staff, the turnstile men and the stewards and things like that. So Arthur was on the shortlist, as was I and a couple of other fellas. We were duly interviewed by the full board, one at a time and I was quite impressed because Joe Mears, the Chairman, he sat with his back to the window, typical psychology.

'As I sat facing the window, there was Len Withey, Bill Pratt and Leslie Mears. And the big 6 foot 8 vice-chairman, who was the champion water polo player, Jack Budd. He was sitting next to me, charming fellow, and he pulled out a packet of cigarettes halfway through my interview and offered me a smoke. I said, "Thanks very much Mr Budd."

'And Joe Mears had a letter from me in front of him which I'd typed out myself on FA notepaper, the record of my career, such as it was, mostly army stuff, and I didn't know it at the time he had been a major in the Royal Marines. I was Royal Artillery Ack-Ack and a PT instructor. Anyway, they said they'd let me know and the next day. Somehow I got the job. I was told Arthur Green was meant to have the job and I was only put in the selection process as a makeweight.'

The young Battersby would become full secretary on Ted Drake's appointment as out and out manager in May 1952 and was largely responsible for taking Chelsea into the brave new world of the 1950s. He looked immediately at how Chelsea could capitalise on its media outlets, including updating the programme and the season handbooks, which since their innovative launch in 1905 had not kept up with trends.

'I think John Battersby was a lot to do with it,' says Albert Sewell, who was soon brought in to help. 'Chelsea decided they'd have a magazine programme, do away with the pamphlet they had, that folded out. They went to a firm called Programme Publications off Piccadilly to do it. They did big golf events, they did circuses, Ascot Racing. They were top level.'

The publication would be football's first 16-page magazine-style programme and it sold for 6d. 'It was a proper programme,' emphasises Sewell, 'all football. They started on a Christmas Day, Tommy Walker's farewell match. There's a cartoon of him on the front. But the *London Evening News* gave them hell about doubling the price of the programme, "It's outrageous and it'll never last," they said.

'Anyway, they ran from Christmas to the end of the season and they were so successful that Arsenal said, "Oh, we must do some of that." And the chap who'd been doing the Chelsea programme, Gordon Ross, moved to do the Arsenal one. I'd worked with him before at the PA [Press Association] and he asked would I go and join Programme Publications and do the Chelsea programme? So that was it. I went there for the start of the season 1949–50 and that was the start of a very long relationship, until 1978.

'I was 24. I was mighty lucky to get involved with a big club. Of course, I did programme notes for Ted Drake, Tommy Doc and Dave Sexton. Ted, he was a lovely man and you worked easily with him. Tommy Doc was like a whirlwind, absolutely.'

And if Albert needed to find the players for an interview, he always knew where they'd be – in the billiard room, built in 1919, near the East Stand next to the railway.

Sewell's steady hand, backed by Battersby's sure-footedness, would bring out fantastic publications that were functional and commercial, but also helped build a sense of a Chelsea family with fans' letters, features on the players' families, insider gossip and Sewell's renowned excursions into memory-jerking club statistics, 'Between Ourselves'. (The 'specials' published around the time of the cup wins, 1970–75 are gems of astute marketing.)

But glamour – even of the variety as charming as Tommy Walker – doesn't survive well starved of the oxygen of publicity and the adrenalin of success. Without sustained periods of achievement, Chelsea's box office appeal diminished. By the turn of the early 1960s, Manchester United had stolen the show. When Susan George was asked to star in her first film, 1965's *Cup Fever*, about a kids' football team, the real-life soccer stars came from Old Trafford, not Chelsea.

That was all about to change, as a youthful culture of creativity in music, fashion and the arts exploded in London, with the King's Road at its epicentre. Coinciding with 'Swinging London' was the emergence of a sharp, fast, young team at Stamford Bridge under manager Tommy Docherty. In the ten years from August 1961 Chelsea spent £1.25 million (Spurs were next with £1.2 million). But this was not like the 30s, when there was no return on the investment. Chelsea's player sales earned £1.24 million over the same period.

Oddly, Chelsea have never broken the transfer record for an outfield player. Lawton's £20,000 transfer to Notts County in November 1947 was the highest of its day, while the £20,000 Chelsea paid to Coventry City in November 1956 for Reg Matthews was a record for a goalkeeper. But even when the club spent £100,000 on Keith Weller it was eight years after Man Utd splashed the same amount in bringing Denis Law back from Torino. The thing that sustained the Chelsea team over the decade from 1963 onwards was its home-growns, some of whom – Greaves, Venables, Bridges, Tambling, Bonetti, Osgood, Hudson – became crowd favourites every bit as popular as the bought-in Cooke or Baldwin.

Now came the age of the fur coat and diamonds at Chelsea, and the biggest names in world entertainment could be seen in the stands. Stamford Bridge was the place to be seen. At one stage, in a baker's in Thames Ditton, you could even buy a 'Chelsea loaf' with the names of the classic 1971 team imprinted on it. Chelsea let you get away with anything, it seemed. Ten-year-old Southampton schoolboy David Puckett was set the classroom task of writing five sentences beginning 'I hope ...'

He wrote:

'I hope Chelsea win the League.

'I hope Chelsea win the FA Cup.

'I hope Chelsea win the League Cup.

'I hope Chelsea win the Cup-Winners' Cup.

'I hope you approve of this homework, sir.'

'As a true blue Chelsea fan,' explained his teacher in a letter to the Chelsea programme, 'all I could write was "very good indeed".'

Then Alan Hudson's wife Maureen revealed, 'I can't grumble ... Alan's very generous. He bought me an [Austin] 1100 when I passed my driving test and now he's just replaced that with a Mini.' And Charlie Cooke wrote an article for top people's couture magazine *Vogue*. 'To tell the truth it didn't feel very glamorous,' says Cooke, 'though people outside might have thought it was. But it was a fun time. The country was doing well economically, things were looking up. The film business was at its peak, loads of things were happening in London. It was exciting, it was the time of the Beatles.'

For Brian Mears, who became chairman after Bill Pratt in 1969, they were special times too. 'We were nearer the West End than any other club,' he states. 'Allegedly, Michael Crawford, when he was working on the London stage in the 1970s, used to say to the cast, "You'd better hurry up because I want to see the last 15 minutes of the Chelsea game."

'Whatever people say about me, whatever, they were the most glamorous, fabulous times, when I was chairman. I enjoyed the friendships I made with all the club chairmen and directors. That's something that you can never erase. I knew everybody in football. Everybody. And they used to say "You're inviting us to lunch?" because my father started this, having lunch with the directors and their ladies at Stamford Bridge before the game. It was an innovation and the other clubs started doing it.'

To increase Chelsea's association with high society, Albert Sewell's programme series 'Stars in the Stand' catalogued all the glitzy show business associations. Ronnie Corbett's favourite player, we learned, was Charlie Cooke. He was born Edinburgh and was a Hearts fan who loved former Chelsea glamour boy Tommy Walker. He also knew Tommy Docherty. The West Stander from the *The Likely Lads* TV series, Rodney Bewes, once wrote a fan letter to Keith Weller. (We don't know if it was about those tights he famously wore on cold days.) Charlie 'Hello my Chelsea darlings' Drake switched from his Millwall origins and had a seat on the front row of the East Stand. 'I know the team's the thing,' he said, 'but it's the top names who switch the rest on, win games, pull the crowds ... someone like Osgood, a man of uncommon talent. Arrogance goes with genius.' Wise words from the man whose boomerang wouldn't come back.

We can leave to psychiatric profilers what it means that, of the comedy double act Mike and Bernie Winters, the charming, good-looking one supported Chelsea, while the goofy fool with the big dog who went 'Eeeeee' all the time preferred Arsenal.

Bill Oddie went to West Bromwich Albion games as a youth but watched Chelsea once he moved to London in 1965, enjoyed the Docherty team and stuck with them. 'The whole team was exciting to watch,' said the star of *The Goodies*, now a TV presenter, 'with Bobby Tambling and Barry Bridges in tremendous form up front. I decided this was the football for me. That was nearly such a great side. Then, sadly, it got broken up and we went through a couple of very dull years.

'I come to be entertained, to enjoy the superb skills of players like Peter Osgood, Charlie Cooke, Alan Hudson – especially him this season.'

For once there were more comedians in the stands than on the pitch, and it didn't stop there. Elsewhere at the Bridge you could find comedy writer and character actor Lance Percival, who would pop up every now and then with his Chelsea-related calypsos. Or *Cider with Rosie* writer Laurie Lee, who would get drunk with his literary mates in the Chelsea Arts Club and totter down to see his team at the Bridge. Or Steve McQueen or ... there were so many it would be impossible to name them all.

But undoubtedly the greatest glamour of the time was generated by the passion for Chelsea shown by two 1960s sexpots.

In March 1971 *The Times* arts critic Michael Billington, who died in June 2005, visited the best known of the two on set in Spain. 'Crouching on the floor of her caravan clad only in the figure-hugging vest and shorts of a Chelsea footballer,' he wrote, 'Raquel Welch pulled a gun from her holster, pointed it at me and fired. And if this sounds like the erotic fantasy of the masochistic soccer buff, I can only assert that it is gospel truth. For Miss Welch is playing the gun-toting heroine of a Burt Kennedy Western, *Hannie Caulder*, being made in Southern Spain and she was proudly demonstrating her speed on the draw.

'The Chelsea gear? This was to oblige a photographer and to demonstrate her new-found passion for soccer. "Tell them," she said, "Osgood is not forgotten on the plains of Almeria."'

Half Bolivian, part English, Jo Raquel Tejada once claimed 'the female mind can be an erogenous zone'. With her slightly wild eyes and leonine hair, we could see what she meant. 'I never wanted to be a nurse or social worker,' she told Billington. Affordable housing's loss was the male population's gain.

The photographer in Spain in 1971 was her old friend and a great Chelsea fan, Terry O' Neill. He shot four rolls of film that day. She looked amazing, kicking a ball, crouching, standing with a holster on her hip, taking throw-ins ... all in Osgood kit. 'I knew Raquel very well,' says O'Neill. 'She knew I'd been a Chelsea fan all my life and she went along with me to quite a few games. Back then I knew Ossie, Alan Hudson, Dave Sexton.

'So I took Raquel to meet Ossie, who was her idol. She had quite a thing for him. And I bought her the shirt with the number 9 on it and took it out to Spain for the shoot.

'Nowadays I don't go to the games. They're all on TV anyway and I think you see more of the game really. And I'm a Chelsea TV subscriber so I don't miss anything.'

In November 1972 Jimmy Hill (no, I don't know either) brought Raquel to Stamford Bridge where she was the centre of attention at a 1-1 draw with Leicester that Chelsea should have won 6-1. Brian Mears had not wanted her to come because the East Stand development was happening and it meant she would have to sit in the temporary directors' box of the rickety old North Stand, which wobbled whenever a train went by.

'Everyone could see her walking past the hoarding in front of the building work,' remembers Mears, 'and there was the most awful fuss as she tried to get to her seat. Then she demanded a brandy and I told her it wasn't possible but she kicked up such a fuss ... I got here the brandy, and she's sitting there, in the stand holding this bloody brandy. I'm thinking, "Oh my God".'

The film star had to leave before the end and Peter Osgood liked to relate that she waved and called out to him on her way out. Of course, he was supposed to be concentrating on the game at the time, but you can't blame him for noticing.

Raquel Welch was responsible for creating several Chelsea fans of my knowledge. In the late 1960s, my brother Gary had a den in the garden shed and inside was that iconic poster of the sex-goddess and her incredible shrinking animal skins from *1,000,000 Years BC*. To get in the den you had to join the 'Raquel Welch Fan Club', entry open only to fans of Raquel Welch *and* Chelsea. He successfully converted a Tottenham fan, John Skinner, and a West Ham fan, Nigel Vernon, both of whom now have children who are Chelsea fans and remain as ardent as ever about the Blues, if not Raquel.

The second sex kitten came through the local youth system, in keeping with the times. Judy Geeson sprang to fame in the film *To Sir with Love* and became a massive sex symbol with her pouting King's Road look. Her favourite players were Bonetti, McCreadie and Paddy Mulligan. But that didn't stop her making a famous gesture towards fellow fans. In 1971, when Peter Osgood was notoriously put on the transfer list, supporters staged an all-night vigil at the ground. Geeson turned up to serve the protestors hot coffee. She lived in a studio flat on the Fulham Road a stone's throw from the stadium and, as Sewell put it, she was Chelsea's very own Girl Next Door. 'I particularly enjoy the floodlit matches,' she mused. 'For a start the colours look special under the lights and the whole atmosphere is somehow different. Yes, I love watching Chelsea most of all at night.'

Her enthusiasm was not even dampened when a senior club director strangled her! Well, it was in the film *10 Rillington Place* and Richard Attenborough was such a nice bloke when he wasn't playing the murderer Christie.

Showbiz agent Harold Davison, who looked after Engelbert Humperdinck and Tom Jones, had a box at the Bridge in the 1960s and 70s. He'd just got back from the game one Saturday when there was a phone call from the States. Who was it? Why Frank Sinatra, of course, ringing from Palm Springs, anxious to know how Chelsea got on. 'I'd brought him to the Bridge once when he was in London,' explained Davison, 'but even so it was strange that he should ring from the States about Chelsea.'

The reason soon became clear. 'I've got someone sitting by the pool,' Sinatra crooned, 'who is desperate to know the Chelsea score – Richard Attenborough.'

How great is that? Arsenal can keep that bitter comedian Alan Davies, and Man Utd are welcome to Patrick Kielty – Sinatra was a Chelsea fan.

Ol' Blue Eyes had no rivals for his crown in the team that put 'Blue is the Colour' near the top of the UK charts. There is a truly fantastic full-length video of the recording session for the song. It starts with the players being asked how they feel. Marvin Hinton declares he's better at partying than singing. John Hollins says he'll be more nervous than on a matchday. A half-cut Charlie Cooke, wearing a tartan tam o'shanter, declares he's heard there is crate of beer inside so it should all be fine. Peter Houseman licks his lips and looks the female reporter up and down. And in the background, from a school playground, a high-pitched choir of children trill, 'What a load or rubbish!' It was never like that for Slade.

Then, after the well-known song footage, comes a priceless slice of cocky Chelsea. Four of the players, Houseman, Ossie, Alan Hudson and Eddie

McCreadie, arms round each other, are singing a terrace medley starting with a version of Anne Shelton's 'Lay Down Your Arms' to the blonde reporter.: 'Come to the station/Jump from the train/We've come to see the Chelsea/ Win away again/There on the terrace/We'll do some rock and roll/Come on big Ossie/Let's have another goal/After the ball was centred/After the whistle blew/Charlie got his medal/And down the wing he flew/He passed the ball to Huddy/And Huddy passed it back/And then old Charlie knocked the goalie flat/Where was the goalie/When the ball was in the net/He was hanging round the goalpost/With his balls around his neck/[Inaudible]/The goal was easy/Now we're Chelsea's pride and joy/When the ball was in the net/When the ball was in the net/It's a goal/It's a goal.'

'Well!' peeps the reporter, 'that one will chart if the other one doesn't!'

Later the enduring Chelsea anthem was adapted in 1978 as 'White is the Colour' by the Vancouver Whitecaps, who included Steve Kember in their ranks, and in 2002 a new version was recorded and released on a flexi-disc by the Proclaimers, who played it live at the Whitecaps' opening game that season.

The music connection eventually eclipsed others at Chelsea. Mods were seen at the Bridge first, and then skinheads, bequeathing Harry J. and the All-Stars' evergreen rocksteady tune 'The Liquidator' to subsequent generations. And when punk arrived, Stamford Bridge was, as usual, the home of early adopters. Joe Strummer fell in love with Chelsea after the 1971 European Cup-Winners' Cup. His widow took a banner commemorating him to an away game in the 2003–04 European Cup campaign. Drummer Paul Cook was seen at Chelsea even when he was still with the Sex Pistols, and is still a face at the Bridge. People reckoned they saw one of the band members of The Alarm being escorted out of ground at the Sunderland game in 1985.

Then there are the likes of Bryan Adams, the Canadian rocker, introduced by season ticket holder and former head of PR at Warners, Barbara Charone; and Damon Albarn, introduced by actor and Chelsea fanatic Phil Daniels, and absorbed by it on a philosophical level, but probably unable to recall who passed the ball to Zola at Highbury against Wimbledon in 1997.

MTV presenter Trevor Nelson went to his first Chelsea game when he was ten years old. 'It was a Second Division match against Bolton at Stamford Bridge,' he says. 'Ray Wilkins was our captain and he really stood out. He was quite flash for us at the time because he could pass the ball more than

20 yards and he was also a massive pin-up boy. I used to want to be like him – he had a full head of hair back then and the women were swooning over him.' His BBC Radio One producer banned him from monitoring matches on teletext during Saturday afternoon shows because Chelsea's fortunes were being reflected in his voice.

No one in music has become as associated with Chelsea, though, as Graham 'Suggs' McPherson, formerly of Madness (whose drummer, Woody, is another Blues fan). It is Suggs' 'Blue Day' that is played at matches and it receives a far better reception than the dirge played there in 1984 when Culture Club arrived to shoot a video for 'The Medal Song'.

'I seem to remember that the filming, which was going to take place at half-time, was announced before the kick-off and that was followed by the introduction to the crowd of Boy George,' says eyewitness Blues fan Julian Flanders. 'I remember him being greeted with a mixture of boos, catcalls and applause. I think he flicked the Vs at the Shed End but what do you expect?'

'The show at half-time was truly bizarre. As the teams walked off, on came an army of Carolines and Sarahs complete with Alice bands, frilly white shirts and clipboards. They assembled in front of the Shed. Two teams of six or seven players, one set in Chelsea shirts and the other, I think, in yellow shirts. The idea seemed to be that they wanted to film Mikey Craig, the black bass player, scoring the winning goal for "Chelsea".

'They had clearly rehearsed as the players all seemed to know what they were doing. Play started at the halfway line and Craig was to score in front of the Shed.

'However, his first shot missed. The crowd hooted with laughter and everything started over again. His second effort was worse than the first.

'The crowd were now laughing even more loudly and making exactly the wrong noises. The players were looking more and more embarrassed, Craig in particular, who even missed the ball completely at one point.

'It all took so long that the second half was held up. He must have scored in the end, but I think by then any cheer that he raised was in relief rather than anything else.'

Thankfully, the last 'showbiz' event at a matchday, when Laurence Dallaglio and Sir Clive Woodward paraded the Rugby World Cup round their beloved Stamford Bridge, went down perfectly. By then, the team and the stadium had become glamorous again. Ruud Gullit's 'sexy football' set a standard of technical play that has been maintained ever since, and the ground is the sort of place where a sex goddess can comfortably enjoy a brandy behind closed doors, with or without Jimmy Hill as an escort.

Among actor fans now there are lots of EastEnders and Joseph Fiennes, teased about Chelsea by Gwyneth Paltrow during the filming of *Shakespeare In Love*, but most of all there is our cherished Life President, Lord Attenborough. The man affectionately dubbed 'Lordie' started going to games during the war and got to know players such as Len Goulden, John Harris and Tommy Lawton. He was even invited to train with them for two weeks by manager Billy Birrell, when his part in a new gangster film based on a novel by Graham Greene required him to be super-fit. In fact, *Brighton Rock* drew on the real-life story of the Sabini family who ran the greyhound bookmakers' protection racket at Stamford Bridge and elsewhere.

For stage work he would insist on Saturday matinées not starting till 5.30 p.m., giving him the chance to get away from games in good time. But directing films was less flexible and he missed the Cup-Winners' Cup final replay while filming *Young Winston* in Wales.

It's sad, that with a heritage in film going back the 1920s, no one has considered Chelsea for modern treatment other than for hoolipics. Laughably, for 2005's *Goal!*, Newcastle beat off Man Utd and Chelsea for the privilege of appearing as a club that signs a young Hispanic wonderkid from LA, who will become the greatest player the world has ever seen over the planned trilogy of films. If they've properly researched the history of Latinos in the north-east, though, the second part might comprise of a month-late return from the Rio Carnaval followed by a cut-price move to Turkey. It is only a matter of time before the silver screen attaches itself again to Chelsea. But don't expect much quality to come of it.

As the century closed, it was a mark of how much a part of the old establishment Chelsea has become that so many politicians of opposing hues had nailed their team colours to the mast. As we can see by the Tory-influenced first board members at the club, Chelsea and politics have always mixed. At the FA Cup final in 1970, one fan even waved a banner hopefully proposing: 'CHARLIE COOKE FOR PRIME MINISTER'. And, as Peter Hain, MP, says, 'In the Ken Bates era there was a brash air of Toryism about the directors' box but that is no longer the case. Richard Attenborough and Joe Hemani are both strong Labour men, as are countless other Chelsea fans.'

As of 2005, of course, the club had three great and active supporters in Parliament's Upper House: Lords Attenborough, Coe and Stratford. Peter Luff (Worcestershire Mid) is the latest recruit in the House of Commons. Former Prime Minister John Major has been away from Stamford Bridge so long that he might consider filming a video like the famous election one, in which he drives down the Fulham Road, winds his window down, stares at Stamford Bridge and whispers, 'It's still there!' A Brixton boy and genuine fan, he would be welcome back now that the 'bad luck' streak of losses when he attended is a thing of the past.

His former colleague David Mellor, now an acerbic and compelling columnist, has a Chelsea connection that is legendary. I happened to be filming a TV music series in Berlin, Paris and Prague throughout September 1992. We were bombing around the sweltering banlieues of France's capital and – despite a mobile phone the size of a baguette – only receiving occasional news from England late at night at our hotel. On one such occasion a sudden flurry of notes required us each to ring home urgently. It appeared that interest rates were going through the roof and we were all much worse off than we had been the day before. England's economy was in crisis. It would become known as Black Wednesday, but we didn't have time to think. There was a plane to catch to Czechoslovakia.

The first thing we did at our accommodation in Prague was ask for any messages for us. 'Ah, yes,' said the receptionist. 'For Mr Glanvill.' And she handed me a fax. News that the pound was to be replaced by the Nigerian naira? A list of what I'd have to forgo in order to pay the mortgage?

No. Instead, the faxed front page of the *Sun* from a week or so earlier, with the headline 'Mellor Made Love in Chelsea Strip', accompanied by a mocked-up photo and, scrawled neatly on top by a calligrapher friend of mine, 'AND I THOUGHT CHELSEA COULDN'T SCORE AWAY FROM HOME??!!' We were 13th at the time, and had just lost 3-2 to Norwich at the Bridge with Dave Beasant's notorious goalkeeping howlers helping to squander a two-goal half-time advantage. Then came Ian Porterfield's dishonourable post-match outburst that the keeper would never play for Chelsea again. It wasn't great being a Blues fan.

The *Sun* cover picture was all speculation, of course. Mellor has since denied this detail of his illicit affair with Antonia de Sancha. And Max Clifford, for the record, is an Arsenal fan. Chelsea could have supported a Music Hall comedy revival all by itself at the time, without props or devious publicists.

But Hansard still yields some nuggets proving that nothing comes before Chelsea, even for our governing executive. Witness the dialogue in the Parliamentary record between two of the club's great champions in the House, a couple of weeks before Chelsea's vital Champions League clash at the Bridge with Bayern Munich:

Mr Tony Banks (West Ham) (Lab): '[I] draw my Right Hon. friend's attention to early-day motion 956 on the extraordinary attacks by UEFA, the European football governing body, on Chelsea coach José Mourinho. Whether or not we have a debate, will he make sure that the business on 6 April ['Opposition Day'] is as light as possible so that he can go to Stamford Bridge with me to watch Chelsea play Bayern Munich?'

Mr Hain (Leader of the House of Commons): 'I would love to have the opportunity to watch Chelsea secure another fine victory over a leading European club, but whether that is possible depends on my Right Hon. and Hon. friends ... As for the UEFA attack, I would call it a full frontal assault on José Mourinho. I find it extraordinary. The football authorities ought to conduct themselves with a little more dignity in these matters. When I look at the politics around international football, the politics around Government seem positively sombre and boring by comparison.'

 **8**

HOOLIFANS

'I would say that the scrappers knew more about the team and went to more games than anybody else. To us it was a religion. And if anybody said anything against Chelsea, to us that was blasphemy and you died!'
'Garrison', Chelsea hoolifan

It wasn't clever, but it was big. The story of Chelsea FC cannot be told without mention of the hooligans who tarnished the name of the club for two decades between 1969 and 1989. Their behaviour, for a while, was synonymous with it. They were a counterpunch to the image of posh, glamorous Chelsea. And their savage radiance appealed to many people who may not admit it today.

Garrison, a Chelsea fan now in his late 50s, has no such qualms. To him, the fighting was a significant aspect of the matchday experience. The rucks at Spurs, Stoke and Millwall almost rival David Webb's winner at Old Trafford in 1970 or Di Matteo's scorcher at Wembley in 1997 for the gilding of memories. He was one of the few – the lunatic fringe, to some – who influenced the various stages of escalating violence involving Chelsea fans. His career as a hooligan is the timeline of the club's fall from everyone's favourite underachievers – poor old Chelsea – to west London 'Neanderthals'.

Garrison – not his real name, for obvious reasons – first watched the Blues just before the championship win in 1955, and shortly after Ted Drake had demanded the fans provide a more hostile setting for visiting players. Stamford Bridge had been known as a venue where opponents were cheered as fervently as the home stars. Drake naturally had no intention of stirring up the trouble that came a decade later, but society was on the move and, as always, Chelsea were at the forefront of the changes in fashion.

'The very first fight I can remember was in 1963 or 64,' recalls Garrison. 'We all stood on the halfway line in the west terrace, before the West Stand was built. I can remember it was Burnley and they had loads of people in there – why, I haven't got a clue – but there were about three or four hundred Burnley supporters and they're all blokes, and we were all kids.

'It was unusual to see that many away fans. And we all started shouting "Chelsea!" and they were shouting "Burnley" and it verbally went off, pushing and shoving, and then the fighting started. And because we were kids and they were blokes we got a right hammering. That was the first fight I can remember at Chelsea.'

The seed was sown and revenge was planned. 'So everybody got together and we thought we're going to Burnley. And Burnley was the first away game we went to as a mob. Burnley's lot stand on the side terrace and there's a great big long terrace.

'We'd just paid to get in their end, because in those days they weren't used to away supporters. We walked slowly towards them and when we saw them we just charged, just gone through there like a hot knife through butter because they didn't expect us.'

But, like a shadow of the glory on the pitch, the Chelsea mob really made its mark for the first time as Docherty's Diamonds won the first major trophy at Leicester in the 1965 League Cup final. 'We took hundreds up to Leicester and it just went off,' recalls Garrison. 'It was a huge battle and we thought, this is great, so we started going to away games and that's how Chelsea's reputation started, because we'd turn up at away grounds and all the local supporters thought, what the hell's going on here? We never went with the express intention of causing trouble, but as soon as we turned up, that was it – it went off.'

A new fashion for teenagers going to away grounds in numbers was starting. Garrison and his Mod mates would travel to stadiums around the country on scooters or by train. An offshoot of this new culture were the new terrace songs to immortalise the mayhem caused there.

'"... and Leicester" comes from about 1965 or 66,' claims Garrison. 'There was a Combination game on a Friday night, a reserve match. There were about 70 of us; any excuse to have a go at Leicester really. We turned up there and it was absolutely pissing down with rain. We had a go at them and we got drenched. The police wouldn't let us into the train station until the train came. The next day it was a home match at Stamford Bridge and everybody sang, "We hate Nottingham Forest ... " and then my lot just shouted out "and Leicester" to say, like, "We bloody went up there!" But it stuck for a few games and then it died out and then in the 1980s it started up again.'

Garrison suggests that, like gangsters such as the Krays before them, he and his scrappers mostly only gave it to those who were also up for it, and that actually a benefit of this minor version of organised crime was that order of sorts was maintained. 'We'd go to the away games and deliberately go in their end,' he says, 'but at the end of the game that was it. The Luton train, we caught the guys that set fire to it. The whole point of having a train is so you can go to the game. If you smash the train up or you set it on fire, what's the point? You're not going to get to the games. We caught 'em and kicked the shit out of 'em and that's how the police got them – they [the arsonists] couldn't get off the train.'

As the fighting increased, another 'milestone' was achieved, a cracked mirror image of the club's progress on the field. Tottenham beat Chelsea in the 1967 FA Cup final – the first London derby at that stage of the competition – and Garrison and others meted their own revenge. 'At the end of the game we've come out of the terrace onto the concourse inside Wembley,' he relates. 'Everybody's sort of leaving and we've said, "Come with us!" And we've run down the other end along the tunnel and onto the terracing where Tottenham were and just massacred them. And that was the first time there'd ever been fighting at Wembley. And then we went out into the car park and smashed all their coaches, all the windows and that. I'll never forget that.

'We went up to White Hart Lane for the first game there the next season and we got up there about 11 o'clock. The Cockerel pub had just opened and we've got in there before any of the Tottenham. And in those days, taking a pub over, no one had done it, because it was still in its infancy. So we're all in this pub, getting the beer and the manager's looking at us. None of us had colours on; we're all in normal clothes. And then some of the Tottenham started walking in and that was it, wang, wang, wang, and the manager realised what was going on.

'So we wrecked the pub, put all the windows out, then ran round the side, because the police were chasing us, and climbed over a wall into the ground about 20 minutes before the gates opened. Into the Park Lane, which was their end. So we were all there before the Tottenham got into the ground and as they were coming in it just all went off. It was mental. The start was delayed 20 minutes because of the fighting. That was a classic battle.'

This was a growing aspect of football support in the late 1960s. Some were drawn to the unpredictable excitement. Others shunned it. The violence was nearly always appeared avoidable, but it was always a nagging distraction none the less.

In April 1969, there was a more sinister development when a kind of special forces mob was recruited from the hoodlums in the Shed. It made its home in the North Stand, next to where away supporters stood. For years afterwards the nasty chant, 'North Stand, North Stand, do your job' was a Shed mantra. These were the people you genuinely didn't want to meet in a dark alley – such as the one away fans had to walk along to get to the terraces at the time.

Garrison and his cohorts would socialise with the players – the likes of Baldwin, Hudson and Osgood – and the celebrity hangers-on who hung out with them at the Ifield pub, the other side of Brompton Cemetery from the stadium. 'We didn't really know any of the showbiz people,' he says. 'We didn't like them. They were false and egotistic. The players weren't like that. The players were genuine. That's what surprised me most, the players were genuine, down-to-earth people.'

There was a confrontation one evening between one of Garrison's mates and Jimmy Ellis, the actor from the TV police show Z-Cars. 'He was always slagging us off for fighting,' Garrison recalls. 'And one day my mate was winding him up and says, "You're so into this slagging us off for fighting. I agree with fighting, and you don't, so what you going to do – hit me?" And he says, "Yes, I will." And my mate says, "Well you're as bad as we are then!" We got him to the point where he was going to hit one of us. "Right, that's it, you're as bad as we are then."'

At a Monday night game, which Chelsea incidentally won 2-1, an Arsenal crew had 'taken' the Shed and the likes of Garrison were unhappy at the low level of resistance shown. 'And afterwards I said, "I've had it with the Shed bloody running. I'm going down the other end." And my mate said, "That's the away end." And I said, "So what?" We went down there and just took on all comers.'

Never mind that families or neutrals used to gather at the higher banked western corner of the North Stand, near the pylon. This would soon become a no-go area for them. Stamford Bridge was losing some of its magnetism for broader society.

Garrison's original team of four ruckers expanded after about a year into a hardcore of 30 or 40 intent on attacking opposition fans. 'When the North Stand split from the Shed,' he explains, 'we used to go on the away games. We'd like shadow them and when it went off – and this is true – we used to look after the normal supporters.

'If we saw any normal supporters getting hit we'd go in to rescue them, and that's how we got the reputation. We used to guard them. A couple of times we saw some Shed boys hitting normal civilians of other teams and we've gone up and kicked the shit out the Shed boys. I mean we did it as a sport,' says Garrison. 'This might sound stupid. To us it was a sport. But what's the sport in hitting someone who's not up for it?'

To those 'normal supporters' for whom football is a gentler obsession, this is anathema. But Garrison's story is important to an understanding of how Chelsea and its fans came to be viewed by others in the last quarter of the century.

It's a far cry from the denizens of Stamford Bridge that Ted Drake publicly implored to be more partisan and aggressive. Supporters had changed. Society had changed too.

By the late 1960s police massing outside Fulham Broadway station to stop trouble as crowds headed for the tube home was a dismal and regular sight. Authorities banned half-fares on trains on matchdays, knowing that youngsters formed the greater part of the mob. By then, however, a thousand miles of motorway was providing alternative awayday transport. And like an out of control driver, the hooligans seemed to accelerate into the skid. The trouble spread abroad – the 'English disease' was exported.

'The first time it ever really went off abroad was in Bruges in 1971. And that was a classic battle. That's up there with Stoke and Tottenham in 1967 as one of the all-time bests. Millwall in 1977. Those four are like classic.'

'Classic' was not a word on veteran football writer Geoffrey Green's lips. 'As deplorable as anything,' he recorded, 'was the behaviour of rival supporters in Bruges. Goaded into retaliation by the taunts of the home fans, there were running fights during and after the match between Belgian and Chelsea mobs that needed the intervention of police batons and dogs. Such are the violent passions of this game.'

'We had no idea of what was going to happen,' says Garrison. 'As we're getting closer to the ground, we're looking out the back window and there's like 30 of our coaches, coming from god knows where. It was like a wagon train.

'And they stopped just outside the city at a great big roundabout and a park and all these coaches parked up and everybody started drifting off and we got everybody together and said, "Don't drift off, you know what's going to happen, keep together." And we've marched them down the main street to the ground. The club had sold tickets at different prices. We thought get the 110-franc ones; we'll probably get a better view. So all the North Stand bought the 110-franc tickets for a better view. When we're showing the tickets outside the ground, the police are going, "That's in that entrance." And what we didn't know was it was in their end.

'The club sold us tickets for their end. And we didn't even know. Tiny little ground and even the terraces weren't all that wide. Their end was terracing, it was like the Shed but smaller. So we got split up, the Shed's gone down the other end.

'In their end I'd say there was about 70 altogether, but about 40 of the North Stand. So we've gone in and we've walked down this little lane at the side of their stand and then you come to the pitch and there's a wall and you have to walk along the wall and then there's the terracing to your left-hand side and we've looked up and it was just blokes. I mean blokes, 30 and 40, going, "We hate Chelsea, we hate English. English f**k off" – in English. And I've looked at a Scottish mate of mine and I says, "This is their end." So he said, "What are we going to do?" I said, "I'm staying here. We'll walk along and then go up".

'So we walked up this gangway and they were throwing stuff, coins and little bricks. And we've got up to the back. We hadn't expected any of this.

We're totally like, "Hello, what's going on?" I mean if we'd have expected it, we'd have steamed in straightaway but we just stood there and thought, "Oh my god, it's their end."

'So we've got to the back, where no one can take us from behind, and all of a sudden they've just steamed us. They've come up the terrace, the whole end have steamed us and there was knives, everything. We didn't have any knives. They did. So it was like a battle. My best mate, he had this great thick sheepskin coat on and one of the guys had a Stanley blade and he's just gone whack, down his back and just opened up the coat and if he hadn't had a coat on his back would have been ripped to shreds.

'So I got in and dealt with him and then we'd got quite a few knives off 'em. So I've just gone, "Draw sabres. Charge down to the bottom, across the pitch and down to the Chelsea end." There was no way we could handle it because we were kids. So we've just got the knives and slashed our way down, on to the pitch and ran down to the other end and for 20 minutes there was all these stretchers coming out with people on. It was down to them. We never went for the fight. We went to watch the game. But, you know ... '

After the game there was even more trouble. 'What was funny, we'd heard all about these ferocious police dogs, and there was a kid, a Chelsea fan, about 12 years old, he's gone up to one of the police dogs, started stroking it, kicked the copper in the nuts and got the lead and walked off with the dog. You never saw him again. Seriously! This 12-year-old kid's walked off with the bloody police dog.'

Between 1975 and 1984, however, a lack of on-field success boiled away the Chelsea following, leaving a concentration of young men for whom kicking up a rumpus was still a matchday thrill. Forty-eight people were charged after Millwall's visit to the Bridge in February 1977 and in May 1977 Denis Howell, then Minister for Sport, banned away fans from travelling after trouble at Luton and Charlton. Manchester United's fans were banned too, though Dennis Mortimer, Luton's chairman, announced some Chelsea supporters had acquired the reputation of being 'the most undesirable lot in the country – worse even than Manchester United fans'.

British Rail openly flouted the ban on away travel anyway, announcing, 'We know Chelsea fans have tickets for the Wolves game, for the last match of the season.'

'Mickey Greenaway was a clerk at British Rail,' explains Garrison. 'And after the Luton riot when we got banned and everybody else in the country got banned, someone put up the money for Greenaway to hire a train, specifically for us. So Greenaway hired a train! We all went round and sold the tickets and we sold the train out.

'Wolverhampton was the last game away. We've turned up and like every supporter in the country has been banned because of Chelsea, and then Chelsea turn up. There's 500 of us and they had to let us in. And we just kept on hiring the train and selling the tickets and that's how we broke the ban and we were the only club in the country that used to get trains.'

If ever proof were needed that, for better or worse, those heavily involved in fights at games were fans too, it came in the shape of Mick Greenaway. He was, perhaps, Chelsea's only true terrace legend, a cheerleader with a bad side. His influence is still captured in song now, according to Garrison.

'Greenaway was never a fighter,' he says. 'He was a figurehead. He was the one that led all the songs and the chanting. He was the one that started the "Zigger Zagger!" He was the one that first sang "Carefree" – that was on a Swedish trip in 1982 – and also "Celery", he started singing that as well, the same pre-season trip to Sweden.

'He was always in the middle of the trouble, but he was never fighting. He was always "Come on Chelsea!" He was always the figurehead. Everybody knew him.'

Greenaway's infatuation with the rucking got him into situations he was ill equipped to deal with. 'If he ever got involved in fighting he used to get killed,' says Garrison. 'I don't like to talk ill of him – he's dead, and he was a good bloke and I liked him – but he was a bit of a prat. I picked him up and threw him over a dinner table once.

'He had his nose broken twice by Man Utd. He got it broken in about 1967 or 68 and it took him about two years before he had the operation and it was in 1969, it was before the Cup Final, and we got word that Man Utd were taking the Rising Sun. We were up in the Wheatsheaf, so we've come down that road and we've got the mob to go in through the front door, and as soon as we've heard the mob going in at the front, we've gone in the side and took 'em from behind.

'And Greenaway's in there going, "Come on! Over here!" One of the Man Utd supporters picked up a three-legged bar stool and just smashed it in his face and it broke his nose again. And then a mate of mine came up with the song, "You've heard him sing, you've seen him pose, it's Greenaway with his staircase nose." It was so funny. He'd just spent a fortune getting it done, straightened out, and it was about a month after the plaster had come off and then it got broken again.'

At around that stage 'Chelsea fan' became a pejorative term, a byword for troublemaker. It was a watershed in how the media and other supporters viewed the club. *The Times* noted in 1981 that, 'The record of Chelsea's supporters is worse than most.' The fallout from disturbances at Derby had prompted an FA ban on travelling Chelsea fans that only evaporated in the heat of a threatened legal challenge.

Matters were coming to a head on and off the pitch. The board was finding the hooligans as difficult to handle as the club's finances. Then in early March 1982, having beaten Liverpool in the previous round of the FA Cup, Second Division, mid-table Chelsea faced favourites Tottenham from the top flight in the FA Cup quarter-finals in front of a massive 42,557 at the Bridge.

In other circumstances this would have been a romantic encounter to savour. That Spurs returned a thousand tickets told another story. Trouble had erupted on the terraces towards the end of that Reds' match. With the away ban on Chelsea fans only recently lifted, the Chelsea board, under then chairman Viscount Chelsea, took a dramatic step. The front page of the matchday programme for Spurs's visit was painted a dense, solemn black and a message pleaded with the 'small lunatic fringe who persist in causing trouble for the club' to stop or face private proceedings and a claim for damages from the club.

On the day, a supporter from each end shook hands on the pitch.

That image was only really challenged with the joyfully extended celebrations of men, women and children decked in blue at Wembley after the 1997 FA Cup final. Other fans could finally empathise.

When Ken Bates took over at Chelsea in April 1982, crowd trouble was still widespread. But his new and energetic response to the issue had a telling effect on the club's image and its approach to relations with the fans. The new chairman consistently fought against Chelsea being singled out and punished for crowd trouble, while at the same time trying to isolate offenders. He quickly realised that more public action, as well as gestures, would be required to tackle the escalating problem. In January 1983, after the FA Cup match at Derby, Bates was compelled to walk onto the pitch and call for calm as fighting went off.

In September that same year there was more at Brighton, even after a 2-1 win. An FA Commission watched footage of the pitch invasion filmed by a resident living in a flat overlooking the ground. Four policemen were injured and four supporters were arrested.

'It's all right for people to say, "ban Chelsea, shut the club",' warned Bates, 'but that attitude does not solve the problem.' Both Chelsea and Brighton were absolved of blame for the Brighton 'riot'.

Well known terrace icon Mick Greenaway, however, was alleged by the *News of the World* to have been one of the ringleaders in the south-coast fracas, and is said to have lost his job as a result. He was never the same again.

Ken Bates met Greenaway several times, fell out with him over his behaviour, but met him again. 'I got him in my old room one day, you know, in the old directors' room in the ivy-covered building,' Bates remembers. 'I said, "Mick, let me ask you a question." He said, "What's that?" I said, "Why are you doing it at the club you claim to love – that's the first question. You're not f**king unintelligent; you've got a reasonable job in British Rail.

'"What are you going to do in ten years' time?" I said, "Nothing will be worse than a clapped out, balding has-been ex-f**king tearaway, will it? Why don't you work with me, to take the club to where we both want it to be instead of causing so much aggravation?" He said, "I'll work with you." To be fair he slightly changed. He used to send me letters to print supporting the club and urging good behaviour. That's why in the West Stand you've got the Zigger Zagger bar – somebody wrote in and suggested it:

'Fair enough, he was the old Chelsea and he had as many good points as faults. He just needed directing and I think I managed to do it, and we became good friends in the end.'

When Bates believed some Chelsea supporters were wrongly accused of violence, the club used to pay for their defence. 'I said, "If they are found guilty then put them into bloody jail." But if they were innocent we would back them to the hilt.'

Among the pressing reasons why the chairman needed to weed out the troublemakers was the cost. Official figures show it cost £108,000 to police Chelsea in 1984 and £168,000 in 1989. And this, of course, was on top of the legal costs of trying to win control of the ground.

Bates remained a maverick in the hooliganism debate, applying drastic sanctions at Stamford Bridge, while simultaneously challenging the media and politicians for blaming Chelsea fans for a wider social malaise. He was once disgusted with the officer in charge of policing Stamford Bridge when she casually suggested that disturbances in the West End 'must have been Chelsea fans'.

'The fact of the matter is I took on hooliganism and Maggie Thatcher didn't want to know,' he says. 'My famous electric fence was in fact one strand of electric wire on top of a 6-foot 9-inch fence that, of course, hit the *Sun* headlines, and caused a big debate.'

Installed for the visit of Tottenham on 27 February 1985, Bates's 12-volt cow fencing was supposed to deliver a short, sharp shock (to use the then contemporary buzz phrase for punishing youth offenders) to those planning to invade the pitch. The GLC warned the club that it would apply for Stamford Bridge to be closed as a hazard to public safety and the club backed down.

In any case, as Rodney Drake of Tamworth-in-Arden advised, if it was the same system he used to keep pigeons off his pea plants, it is 'childishly easy to short out, and I should imagine it will take the Chelsea fans about five minutes to discover just how to do it.'

However, the fence caused a furore in the press and the whole episode reinforced the perception of Chelsea fans as animals to be caged.

Nevertheless, Bates maintained his crusade. 'After that I believe that they [the government] started to wake up and think they had to do something, because all they used to do was wring their hands and say how disgraceful it was that football blah, blah ... But it wasn't just football, it's a society problem. I believe that's why Ted Croker never got his knighthood. Traditionally when secretaries or chairmen retire from the FA they become a knight. Maggie Thatcher held this summit, organised by her daughter, Carol Thatcher, and they went in and said, "What are you doing about your hooligans in football?" Ted Croker said, "Prime Minister, what I want to know is when are *you* going to get *your* hooligans out of my football grounds?" She didn't like being talked to like that. But he was right.'

As the media played up the gang names, Chelsea's 'Headhunters', with their notorious calling cards, took on a glamorous burnish, eclipsing the old fashioned North Standers, who 'never carried weapons' according to Garrison. And some of the worst ever scenes of violence occurred when Middlesbrough won the relegation play-off at Stamford Bridge in May 1988. Yet the following January Bates told fans, 'We must be careful that our rational feelings are not carried away by reaction to media comment. At our match with Middlesbrough last season we had 53 arrests within the ground and this was described as a riot.'

There were several high-profile trials and many convictions over the years. Garrison, like others, was eventually put away for a lengthy stretch at Her Majesty's pleasure. But some investigative tactics sometimes proved controversial. In March 1986 seven alleged Chelsea Headhunters, including Stephen 'Hickey' Hickmott, who used to arrange away coaches for fans, were woken up by a police raid and prying TV cameras. The trial focused on Operation Own Goal's use of officers to infiltrate the mob, their questionable methodology and their lack of evidence, and it collapsed.

The BBC documentary *Macintyre Undercover* filmed Chelsea fans Jason Marriner and Andrew Frain arranging rucks at Leicester in 1998 and attending far-Right rallies. They were jailed for six and seven years respectively in December 2000 for conspiracy to commit violent disorder and affray. Marriner had claimed that Macintyre 'set up' stunts for the show. Others were amazed that the reporter chose to have the despised 1980s lion-wearing-socks badge tattooed on his arm rather than the classic 1950s one.

Following the attentions of the law, many of the hoolifans moved abroad. Indications of their presence are visible outside a bar in Thailand which advertises, for example, 'Footie tonight – Yids v Boro'.

Arrests and bans eventually took their toll on the crews, but it was the shocking scenes at the Liverpool-Juventus match and at Hillsborough that seemed to shake many hangers-on out of the tree. The blossoming of an almost old-fashioned style of support around Euro 96 fostered a softer atmosphere at English stadiums, and the new, all-seater Stamford Bridge lacked the freewheeling edginess of old. Imagine a smoking ban or ejections for racist language in 1969.

The bad name, though, persists. In the aftermath of Heysel, Liverpool's local newspapers carried eyewitness accounts claiming that the disaster was really the work of Chelsea fans. And so in April 2005 John Williams, the foremost authority on football culture and a lifelong Red, still felt comfortable contrasting the idea of being a 'scally' Liverpool fan with 'the kind of pointless destruction which neanderthals like Leeds or Chelsea or England fans went in for'. It must be a comfort to Bulgarian waiters everywhere that Scally violence is less pointless than that of ex-Headhunters.

Another long-term legacy has been a fundamental lack of trust in Chelsea fans along the corridors of football power; perhaps even those at Stamford Bridge. Our reputation is in the hands of others. The only thing we can control is our character.

Thankfully, trouble in the stadium since then has been rare and isolated. Millwall in 1995 and West Ham in 2004 were flashbacks to the bad old days. But it was the away match at Upton Park a few seasons earlier, where drunken, marauding gangs of mature men threw obscenities and 'come on thens' at each other from behind police escorts outside the ground that showed how trouble is 'managed' not extinguished. Nasty as these instances were, they felt nothing like the maelstroms of previous eras.

When Greenaway died destitute in 1999, fans clubbed together to pay for a gravestone. Garrison, still the most fanatical of Chelsea supporters but with no wish to return to a bygone age of terror, may even have the season ticket next to yours.

'It's a different club now,' says Garrison. 'Since Abramovich came in the parameters have changed. It's totally changed. I mean there was yesterday, then since Abramovich came in, there's today. Because we've got all that money we have to become a world dominating club, so everything is now geared to the business side. And the business side will ensure that the team is good. We've got to win the Premiership back-to-back, and we've got to win the Champions League. There's so much pressure now that there never was. It's totally different and a lot of supporters don't realise that. Chelsea's got to be marketed on a world stage.

'It's like us when we were fighting. That's all over and done; we're dinosaurs, because we were the ones that were fighting. Nowadays it's nice that there's not that. Because that was then, this is now, and it's nice to go to the ground and see women and children, and I think that's great.

'There's very little fighting and the only fighting now is wannabes anyway. "Oh, oh, we want to do what you used to do." That's bullshit.'

9

THE RUSSIANS ARE COMING

'He's a devoted fan like any you've ever seen at Stamford Bridge. He has the luxury of being able to do something about the results. We're all playing *Championship Manager* on our PCs; he's doing it for real.'
Bruce Buck on Roman Abramovich

'I first started going in 1987–88 and bought three season tickets in 1991. I wasn't the type of fan who memorised statistics, knew everything about every player. I came to be entertained and I was entertained. There were plenty of highs and lows in those days. But my kids really got into it.

'I was concerned sometimes to take young kids. I remember we played Bruges one evening – the number of police on horseback. It was a little concerning sometimes.

'It was never any problem getting tickets. It was quite relaxed.

'I was nostalgic about the Shed End. I'm not big on change, even though I'm not a long-term fan. It was always East Upper, Row 5.'

It was understandable that New Jersey-born Bruce Buck was more enthusiastic than most Chelsea season ticket holders when he heard that wealthy Russian Roman Abramovich had bought his club. Firstly, unlike his fellow fans, he knew quite a lot about the so-called 'billionaire from nowhere'.

Secondly, the news meant that he had done his job. With his corporate lawyer's hat on Buck was in on the deal to transfer ownership from the beginning and was quickly named as chairman of the 'new' Chelsea.

He paints the picture of the takeover in June 2003 from the Abramovich side. 'Mr Abramovich went to the Champions League quarter-final of Manchester United versus Real Madrid and he was enchanted ... ' Buck says, '... fell in love with football. He asked his advisers to find out what clubs in England might be available. Some people have asked, "Why not Spain or Italy?" But most of those are community or shareholder owned.

'An investment bank was hired to see what was available. Secrecy was very important at this stage because you're talking about buying public companies – if there was a leak the price goes up.

'They came back with five clubs – three were Man U, Chelsea, Spurs. I can't recall the others. Two meetings were set up – one with Chelsea and one with Spurs.'

Trevor Birch was chief executive of Chelsea at the time. An ex-Liverpool footballer, and an insolvency expert who had helped resurrect ailing community organisations, he felt great empathy towards the club he'd joined. He was a popular boss even though he was charged with handling Chelsea's debt, run up in order to build the stadium, the Village complex and the squad. 'We needed to reschedule and stretch some of the commitments that we had,' he says. 'The [£75 million] Eurobond was a lump payment each year. There were other commitments, football commitments with players who had been bought but who hadn't been paid for, that needed to be rescheduled.

'I think the financial side [at Chelsea] would have become an issue if certain actions weren't taken so all the plans were geared around stabilising the position, while certain contracts unwound. Chelsea had been caught by the acceleration of the transfer market which then left us with probably more players than we needed on probably more lucrative contracts than was prudent and therefore we had to try to untangle all those, contain things in order to rejuvenate the club.

'Which in the summer of 2002 was the reason why we made the one free transfer, Quique de Lucas, my one and only signing until I splashed out! I think that's the way football seems to work: you have a little spurt, then a rest, then a spurt again, and I think it was probably that rest period.'

It had also become clear that if an investor could be found, Chelsea would listen. 'That had been ongoing,' says Birch. 'I had feelers out there and one of the banks that we had been talking to on our possible securitisation of all the debts, consolidation of all the debts, Abramovich had been talking to them. So he came in by a couple of sources really and it just so happened that he popped up in June two years ago.

'There were two calls that came in to me, just to say, "Do you want to meet …?" I wasn't told his name, "… a very rich person, foreign", who was interested in investing.

So within a few days of that contact, I then met them. They were all there: Mr Abramovich, Richard Kreitzman, Eugene Tenenbaum, German Ktchadchenko [a friend and informal advisor to Abramovich]. We met at Stamford Bridge. I took them into one of the Millennium boxes and within about 15 minutes we'd done the deal in outline.

'They knew all about Chelsea. They had been looking at other clubs and they'd done their homework on all those other clubs as they had about Chelsea, so they were under no illusions as to what they were buying.

'He was keen, he was obviously keen to buy a football club.'

What had attracted them to Chelsea? 'The London location was a plus,' says Buck. 'In terms of creating an international brand, to me a London-based brand has a better ring to it than a Manchester or Newcastle brand. Just like a New York brand is better than a Cleveland brand. But what was most important was that we were already in the Champions League.'

Then Birch broke the news to the chairman. 'I said I'd met these Russians,' Birch says, 'who were keen to buy the club. In Ken-speak, he said he was amazed. Ken's the coolest character in the world, "Yeah, I'll talk to them," he said. So he wasn't particularly giving anything away at that stage.'

'I'm told he said he wanted more money,' says Buck, 'and Trevor said, "Don't be ridiculous, this is more than you could have imagined."'

That night, Trevor Birch, Eugene Tenenbaum, Richard Kreitzman, Ken Bates and Roman Abramovich met in a bar at the Dorchester hotel, chosen by Ken. They met for 20 minutes. Mr Abramovich and Eugene Tenenbaum had water – I believe Ken had a bottle of wine. Mr Abramovich is teetotal.'

'Well, he's very quiet and very self-effacing,' says Ken Bates of 'Mr A', as his friends call him. 'I found out later, of course, he spoke much more English than he let on. Usual thing, very clever, pretend you don't understand then it gives you more time to think. Anyway, Trevor Birch had been dealing with it and he kept me out of the scene. The thing is I'm very philosophical. I probably realised times had changed and I kept telling other people that.'

They agreed a price and Bates eventually pocketed a cheque for his Chelsea shares of at least £17 million.

Normally in an acquisition of this scale the thorough investigative process called 'due diligence' would kick in for a few months. Not here.

'For the next five days,' says Buck, 'lawyers worked day and night and the deal was announced on 30 June or 1 July [2003]. As part of the process they gave us a lot of financial information, so we understood there was an urgency. They never said that. Trevor was a very good negotiator. It was clear he'd been holding things together superbly for a year. He had obviously done a great job. The club owes him a great debt of gratitude.

'Once we had the meeting on the Thursday it was really only a matter of time and we were anxious to do it quickly. We were nervous there would be a leak. The first part of the transaction was to get over 50 per cent together, then make an offer for the rest. Over the next few days I was working with Mark Taylor [Ken's lawyer, who was on the board] and they got 50.1 per cent together. Then we made an offer backed by Citibank and slowly got to a point where we could squeeze out the minority. Once we got to 90 per cent of the remaining 49.9 per cent, we could squeeze them out. By the end of September it was done.'

The initial Abramovich investment to buy Chelsea was near enough £140 million – £60 million for the club, £80 million to cover its debts. The speed of the multi-million pound deal amazed Birch. 'But this is a man with exceptional wealth,' he reasons, 'and I have to say I've not done many deals with people of his wealth, so maybe this is the way they act normally.'

To Buck this was far from new. He took it all in his stride. 'We signed the agreement at 8 or 8.30 at night,' he says. 'Ken had left. Not much of a celebration. I walked home from Stamford Bridge. Two of my sons were home. I said, "I've just represented the Russian gentleman who's bought Chelsea Football Club."

'"Sure you did," they said.

'"No – watch it on the news."

'They watched and were dumbstruck. My youngest was away in July in Nepal. He came back and my wife said I'd represented Mr Abramovich who'd bought Chelsea and he said, "Sure you did."

'I said, "There's a game on Saturday. Put on a shirt and tie and I'll take you in the directors' box, you'll meet Ken Bates." He said, "I get it. Put on a shirt and tie, you take me to the East Upper, and all the yobs laugh at me." He comes to the directors' box and I walk in, then Ken says, "Bruce, sit over here ..." The world had turned upside-down.'

Soon the new regime was able to examine the state of Chelsea's finances closely. 'I personally was surprised,' says Buck, 'but those in the know weren't. They had a £75 million Eurobond outstanding and it was perfectly clear to the markets that they might have trouble making the July payment. Trevor Birch had been in discussions for some time about restructuring that bond. The financial community as opposed to the football community knew there were some real issues.

'Fans did not know that in January the club had mortgaged, if you will, the TV revenues. It borrowed against the TV revenues that were to be handed out in August. I didn't know as a fan that the club owed money to the Harding family and they wanted it back. As a fan I was naive. I knew the club had financial problems, but didn't know the specifics.'

As of 1 July 2003 Abramovich's billions set such issues to one side, and his passion for the club meant that one of the biggest experiments ever in world football kicked off with the sudden signing of as many top quality players as possible in a matter of days. The board swiftly felt the Chelsea pulse and responded accordingly. Within 24 hours of taking control they made it a mission to try to lure the beloved Gianfranco Zola back to the Bridge for £3 million. He had been disappointed to leave when his contract elapsed on 30 June – the day before the takeover had been concluded.

Had he known of the possibility, Zola might never have agreed to pledge his future to hometown club Cagliari. But since he had, and he is such an honourable man, he respectfully declined Chelsea's offer. 'I feel bad,' said the Italian at the time. 'I feel sad. It was a painful decision for me to leave. When Chelsea came back in, it was a very difficult couple of hours for me.'

That was one knockback but there were many rapid purchases; perhaps too many. 'You have to remember Mr Abramovich bought the club when we were already well into the transfer season,' says Buck. 'Even in the days of negotiating, there were already discussions about players. Ken was making suggestions – I don't know if anyone was listening to him.'

Now insolvency specialist Trevor Birch found himself spending a fortune in a matter of days. 'I think I realised it was going to be something pretty special because he was going to invest whatever it took to be the most successful club in the world. You could just tell. And money was not going to be an object and therefore you couldn't help but be excited about what was going to be achievable.

'Within six weeks I think I'd spent more than any other chief executive had spent in their entire life! I think it got to about £120 million, all things thrown in – you know, with agents' fees in there. So, with only the experience of having signed a loan player, it was a remarkable turnaround, but a very exciting six weeks, very exhilarating with the prospect of watching great players at work during the season.

'You thought of all the great things that you could do with the money, in terms of the training ground, which I'd identified on day one we'd better do something about and I'd got Cobham organised – I believe it's fantastic now. We secured that and the prospect of all those things. It was great to take the club forward. You had the freedom to do all the inhibitive things you might have wanted to do, to take the club onto the next level.'

'They [Abramovich and his advisors] realised they had to act quickly,' Buck says. 'I think it was a case-by-case basis. I don't think it was as haphazard as it looked in retrospect. I think there was a structure and a philosophy. In retrospect there were some mistakes, where some players did not turn out as well as you would have liked.

'Having said that, if you go to Man United and look at their transfers over the past 10 years, several of those did not work out. I don't think our rate of those that didn't live up to expectations is any greater than Newcastle, Liverpool or Man United over past ten years. I don't think we've spent any more than these other guys – more in a short time, yes, but we were playing catch-up. I don't look at this as "the management didn't know what they were doing." Some didn't work out and that's what always happens.

'Eugene Tenenbaum went on holiday in August and he was on the phone 50 times a day because he was the financial advisor.'

'Once we were in the Champions League qualifier against Zilina,' says Buck, 'we sort of looked at things and thought, "This could be really good!"'

Once the flurry was over, the buzz began. 'I went to the press conference for Veron and Joe Cole. I was pretty impressed – as a Chelsea fan. That was a *real* excitement for me. When the team came back from Malaysia, I was having a drink with Trevor Birch in Fishnets, when Geremi came over and chatted to us, and I thought, "This is pretty good."'

One of the biggest surprises for the new proprietors of Chelsea was that they thought the Russian owner would be major news for two weeks and then he would go back to being unseen Roman Abramovich again. 'I guess we were a little naive,' says Buck. 'We didn't realise how cataclysmic this was. It was an earthquake. We knew it would be a big story today, tomorrow the next day. We didn't realise the story would never end. It also wouldn't have been an issue if we hadn't spent all that money.'

Trevor Birch cannot remember a great deal of mail to the club either for or against the sudden deal. Maybe people were just letting it all sink in. 'I think most people understood the significance of what was happening in terms of hard cash coming into the club,' suggests Birch. 'There may have been a few people feeling slightly nervous about what it would all mean. Then it started to dawn on people as they saw the signings, with a mixture of disbelief and incredulity I suppose. It was a heady time.'

Abramovich swiftly earned the appreciation of Chelsea fans and envy of others. Although he appreciated the clever gesture of playing the clap-along Russian folk song 'Kalinka' before games, he asked for it be shortened, then stopped altogether. Now, he has to be virtually dragged out so that supporters can show their affection for him.

But he does appreciate it. 'He's touched,' says Buck on his behalf. 'He was very surprised. He wasn't expecting the kind of prominence and publicity all this has brought. He hasn't done this for the glamour or so the great and the good will want to mingle with him – although they do. He's done it because he's unbelievably enchanted by football and is honestly and truly in love with Chelsea.'

In the meantime, amid all the new arrivals, three familiar faces bid farewell. Chairman Bates left in a huff mid-season, becoming a tax exile in Monaco. 'There were problems as with any deal,' confides Buck. 'Ken's contract was one – there was a lawsuit [settled out of court] over it.

'The truth is we have a lot of respect for what Ken did for this club. He can take a lot of credit for Chelsea winning the championship, for example. We feel he would not have been able to take it the extra mile. But he did take it a long way and deserves a lot of credit for that.

'He was hurt, insulted, because once the club changed ownership, his involvement was severely limited, and he was not involved in any of the transfers that first summer. That bothered him. But the point is that he did sell the club and there was a new owner.'

Then Trevor Birch, the man who had massaged Chelsea's stiffening arteries enough to ensure the club was still a catch, was replaced, after a period of enforced 'gardening leave', by Manchester United's chief executive Peter Kenyon. Few people understand the modern commercial world of football at the highest level better than he does. Uncomfortable as it was for the likeable Birch, his core skills were different and less critical in the new 'Chelski'. 'Yeah, I was disappointed,' sighs Birch. 'I look back on my time at the club with pride, huge fondness and affection for the people there. The greatest moment in my life was walking round the pitch against Tottenham and people starting to applaud. That'll live with me till my dying day. It had been announced that I'd resigned the previous day and it was just overwhelming, absolutely overwhelming. I was very, very sorry to go.'

It was soon widely accepted that the days were also numbered for manager Claudio Ranieri. Ironically, by achieving the Champions League qualification that was so important to Abramovich in a club he might buy, he had almost authored his own passing. He maintained dignity under pressure but was not felt able to take Chelsea where the new board wanted it to be. 'We're trying to build a successful business,' says Buck, 'but it's clear you cannot have a successful football business if you're not successful on the pitch. You can have the smartest marketing people, but if you're 19th in the league you're not going to sell a goddam shirt. The things go hand in hand. You need the best marketing people, but in the first instance you need a top-notch team.'

And so the board bought the best young manager, with the right profile – José Mourinho.

'I think Roman changed the club,' says Mourinho. 'He changed the image of the club around the world. He changed the eyes of every person when they look to Chelsea. Chelsea becomes the team in fashion, you know. Like a fashionable team – in Portugal you say team of *la moda*. Like in Spain, it's Chelsea, Chelsea, Chelsea, Chelsea. But for the manager, pressure, pressure, pressure, pressure.'

The best prepared coaching staff in the Premiership showed what can really be done with a billionaire's plaything. Fundamentally the same side as in 2003–04 ran away with the Premiership in 2004–05.

Another plank of the strategy to become the best club side in the world was in place. As a fan rather than a director, Buck still found it nail-biting to watch. 'Since the Blackburn game probably a lot of people were saying Chelsea were going to win the league,' he says. 'I never believed that. I'm too superstitious. I'm more a Yogi Berra type – "It ain't over till it's over." I was nervous up to the 92nd minute at Bolton. There was incredible relief for me when it happened, but I was also unbelievably happy for Mr Abramovich. He devoted two years of his life to this. He really wanted this. I'm really pleased for him and for everyone who has waited for so long.

'I feel funny when people say "well done" to me. I didn't do anything. I think about the 25-year-olds who are out there every day in rain, sleet, snow, day in, day out. It's a real slog. They're paid well, but it's tough. I was happy for them and for Roman Abramovich.'

With immense financial clout, a global strategy for acquiring the best young players, a more integrated fan base and the best manager and squad in its history, it is just left for champions Chelsea to be recognised as a major force in the game around the world.

So why haven't Chelsea been welcomed with open arms into the G-14 group of Europe's 'top clubs', having been offered a sitting at the lunches back in 1955? 'Funnily enough,' says Gabriele Marcotti, *The Times* columnist, 'in October 2004 I went to Brussels and asked Thomas Kurth, the G-14's managing director, that very same question. He said, "It's normal for clubs to be suspicious of Chelsea. Some of our members believe it's an unorthodox club. They want certain questions to be answered. Is everything clean and legitimate? Is it a solid club or does it depend on the whims of its owner?"

'Kurth is actually a good guy, he's simply relaying the concerns of some other members. The idea of Abramovich being "clean" or not I think is ludicrous. The guy has been in this country for several years now, he's had people scrutinizing his every move, if there were anything untoward, at least on this end, I'm sure we would have found out by now. In fact, I personally think that some of the suspicion directed his way is purely a function of him being a Russian nouveau riche guy [and Jewish at that] ... It's the usual stereotypes, Russian mafia and all that rubbish.

'You either give yourself hard and fast rules or you don't. And if you're going to question Abramovich's money, the words pot, kettle and black come to mind. The truth is that the G-14 is a political organisation as much as anything else. If you look at the original members – Barcelona, Real Madrid, AC Milan, Inter Milan, Juventus, Bayern Munich, Ajax and Manchester United, you can see that these are all huge, important clubs. They have big fan bases, they have considerable amounts of money and they've been big for a long, long time.

'Lazio weren't admitted and yet there was a point when they were outspending everyone else in Europe [like Chelsea are now], winning European trophies and Serie A titles. It all fell apart, of course, but people remain mindful of that.'

'Over time we'll be in the G-14,' says Bruce Buck. 'They have to. We're an upstart, a new boy on the block and we're doing well. The established hierarchy doesn't like that because it knocks them down a step. We have to understand that. It's human nature. Arsenal and Man U are used to trading the cup every year. They don't like trading it off to someone who might hold it for a while. But this is not a Blackburn situation. We're building a dynasty here. We're not going to win every trophy every year. It's impossible. But we're going to win a lot of trophies, and that means others that have been winning them are going to win less. And it's natural that they don't like that.

'You're looking at the kindergarten years of the Abramovich era,' says Buck, Chelsea's tenth chairman in a hundred years. 'The best is yet to come. Mr Abramovich is here for the long haul. He's 38 or 39. I wouldn't look at two seasons, two fantastic seasons, and try to characterise the Abramovich era. When you write your next book at 200 years, you can characterise the Abramovich era.'

Remember, winning things doesn't guarantee popularity. For the first time in its history, Chelsea is popularly hated for being successful, not popular for being the famous home of glamorous, glorious losers.

We'd better get used to it.

GREAT TEAMS

The **managers** and players,
1905 to the present

10

THE FIRST XI

'My work has not been without its amusing side,' wrote John Tait Robertson around Christmas 1905. Apart from constructing Chelsea's first ever squad, he had to sift through improbable submissions from utter no-hopers. 'Among the many applications I received,' Robertson revealed, 'was one from a man who said he was a splendid centre-forward, but if that position was not vacant he could manipulate a turnstile. Another wrote, 'You will be astonished to see me skip down the line like a deer.' A third was willing to 'be linesman, goal-keep, or mind the coats'.

Robertson was 28 when he became Chelsea's foundation signing. His role of secretary-manager itself deserves explaining. There had always been trainers – what we might term coaches today. Trainers were nearly always former players, and by the turn of the century most club boards had come to the conclusion that such men were incapable of management in the football business. The popular replacement became the 'secretary-manager', someone with experience of the game and happy to do the board's day-to-day bidding on the football side. Boards loved to pick the teams themselves, but had companies to run, committees to sit on and fortunes to count elsewhere.

Secretary-managers were tied to their desks, applying themselves to transfers, publicity and commercial and administrative chores, while the cloth-capped trainer put the players through their paces. The last post for the secretary-manager at Stamford Bridge was sounded with the departure of Billy Birrell after the Second World War, when the role was split. But in Robertson's role of *player*-secretary-manager, we see a sign of the 'tracksuit manager' of which Ted Drake, Birrell's successor, was Chelsea's first.

J.T. would miss only five League games himself, suggesting an unusual closeness to the players that must have helped build team spirit in that first season. Robertson had come from Rangers but had also played for Everton and Southampton and had considerable contacts in the game. It also helped that he was a seasoned Scotland international, and planned to continue playing at left half-back, something between a left midfielder and a full-back in today's game.

Aware of his responsibilities towards the board as well as the football team, he appreciated that Chelsea was a project requiring something a little special to meet the expectations of its young, entrepreneurial directors. As a result, there was a sense of impulsive destiny, of a club in a hurry, of a runaway express train. 'In the whole long history of football,' he wrote, 'no club has rushed into fame with such sensational suddenness as Chelsea.'

Robertson had played his part in that 'suddenness' by helping the club secure a berth in the Football League. On 19 April 1905 he and director Frederick Parker had canvassed four Manchester and Liverpool clubs ahead of an election. The following day it was Lytham, Preston and Blackburn. Robertson had to play for Rangers that evening, so Parker saw Blackpool, Bolton, Derby, Small Heath and West Bromwich alone. Lytham's league president J.J. Bentley chided Chelsea, saying, 'Your new club [is] trying to run with the hare and hunt with the hounds. Which are you really going for, the Southern League or us?' Parker said all would be made clear in the press the following day – and promptly rang the London Press Agency to release a statement of no interest in the Southern League.

Bentley returned the compliment by running the line at the first Chelsea match ever at Stamford Bridge, a friendly against Liverpool on 4 September, where the first goal (a Liverpool strike having been disallowed) was scored by Bob McRoberts. Robertson himself scored Chelsea's first league goal, a winner at Blackpool.

He had arrived at Stamford Bridge in April 1905, as soon as league status was confirmed. 'We then set to work at once on the engrossing and intensely difficult task of marshalling a strong side. In football, as in war, the crux of the matter is the men. So far, the players we have engaged have more than fulfilled expectations.'

Then, as now, those who brought the players in had at least one eye on the box office. The first of a line of crowd-pleasers, stretching through every generation up to Arjen Robben and Shaun Wright-Phillips, was also named captain: Willie Foulke. 'He is already one of the most popular players in London,' wrote Robertson. 'When people first come to Chelsea, they fall to admiring the proportions of the ground, then the proportions of Foulke, and next his unquestionable skill as a goalkeeper. He weighs 22 stone 3 pounds, only one pound less than both backs put together, yet is as agile as a kitten.'

Beyond that Robertson built his team to a blueprint, and key to its success was the players' ability to carry out the basics, but also show that little flash of something a bit different. Needless to say this was most important in front of goal. It has been remarked of Chelsea teams throughout the decades that the quality of its strikers has outweighed that of other positions, and that philosophical bias was decided by our first team-builder.

'One hears club managers on every side bemoaning the lack of forwards who possess initiative,' Robertson observed. 'The player who can get rid of the ball tamely whenever he is tackled, and who always does the same thing every time, is easy enough to find. He will never help win a cup tie or a league match. It is the player who can do things his rivals do not anticipate, and who is above all not afraid to shoot when he draws near goal, that we all are hunting for, and these we think we have found.'

'The forwards are an accomplished set of players. They can play the three-inside game, or indulge in those long, swinging passes out to the wings that are more effective against some teams. R. McRoberts, of Small Heath, is in the centre. He was the first player signed by the club. He is a splendid shot, and when he does not score a goal a match one hears rumours that he is not well. But that is only because of his sad expression. Nothing is more cheering to 'Mac' than scoring a goal.

'[Martin] Moran is outside-right. He made a big reputation while with Hearts. He has never played so well in his life as he has in the light-blue jersey of the Chelsea club. His sensational centres are quite one of the striking features of the game.

'[David] Copeland, of Tottenham Hotspur, generally acts at inside-right. It was Copeland and the left-wing [Jack] Kirwan that played such an important part in gaining the Cup for Tottenham [in 1901]. James Robertson [no relation] is a clever player and a fine shot at goal, and can also play in the latter position. [Kirwan's partner] is [Jimmy] Windridge, of Small Heath. Both combine well together, yet do not fail to keep in close touch with the rest of the line. We have secured a number of other well-known players. Among them is [Tom] McDermott, of Everton. He is regarded as one of the cleverest inside-forward players in the country, and several League clubs were anxious to secure his services. He first made a reputation while wearing the colours of the Celtic club, but while playing before the critical crowd at Everton he won fresh laurels. He is essentially a polished player, with a mastery of those deft touches one expects of an Everton man.

'Another new man, who has a brilliant past, but should have a still more brilliant future, is [Frank] Pearson, of Manchester City. He plays effectively at centre-forward, and has the happy facility of being able to combine well with his wings, and yet never misses an opportunity of threading a way through opponents by himself.

'Our idea is to have a strong body of reserves, so as to ensure Chelsea always having a first-class side in the field. The regular backs are [Bob] Mackie, of the famous Heart of Midlothian team, and [Bob] McEwan, late of Glasgow Rangers. They are reliable kickers and tenacious tacklers, and play together with a nice understanding. Mackie has a happy facility for getting in his kick, no matter in what attitude he may be, when the ball comes his way.

'[George] Key, from the Heart of Midlothian Club, plays half, and last year got his cap for Scotland. Those who have seen him act as a sixth forward and then assisting the defence, and generally making himself exceedingly inconvenient to opponents, are not surprised. [James] Watson, another clever Scotsman, or [James] Craigie, Manchester City, generally plays centre-half. Both are good, and I am the third of the line.'

Unfortunately, J.T.'s reign was troubled. As early as November 1905 the board removed some of the manager's responsibilities by passing a motion 'that the Team be selected by the Directors'. The second season he played a handful of matches before any remaining managerial duties were taken away from him in November 1906, including 'to apportion the work of trainers, groundsmen and others'. The same month he had resigned and asked for a free transfer, and in January, Chelsea's first secretary-manager was gone to Glossop, to be replaced temporarily by former Brentford manager and Chelsea club secretary Bill Lewis. One of his first duties was to discipline club captain Davie Copeland for drunkenness.

Amazingly, despite the upheaval, Chelsea achieved the longed-for promotion to the First Division in 1906–07. A great deal of the credit must go to forwards George Hilsdon and Jimmy Windridge, as well as keeper 'Pom Pom' Whiting, who had filled the considerable boots of Willie Foulke and had conceded just 34 goals all season. Nineteen-year-old Londoner Hilsdon was one of the head-turning attractions, perhaps the club's first 'discovery', and an England international. Fast, mobile, muscular and with bullets in either boot, his presence was announced in the pre-season handbook: 'Another West Ham product. A centre-forward of great ability, keeps his wings together well and, in addition, is a prolific scorer. In the late Continental tour he placed 19 goals to his credit.' That was the 'Danube' tour of Denmark, Austria and Hungary. Although details on this are sketchy, it seems there were 23 goals scored in total.

Hilsdon destroyed poor Glossop – who'd left Stamford Bridge with a point on the opening day of the 1906–07 season. 'Gatling Gun', as he was soon dubbed, rattled in five during our auspicious 9-2 win and within weeks scored a hat-trick for the English League team's first international, against Ireland. The glamorous George scored 27 of 80 league goals in the campaign.

The self-evident ambition, on and off the pitch, of this star-studded club also earned plaudits even if the team's erratic away form didn't. But with Stamford Bridge becoming a citadel (one defeat, no draws), Chelsea were always favourites for one of the two promotion slots, and an excellent Christmas run of four away games without defeat set up a comfortable conclusion: nine points clear of rivals Leicester Fosse; three behind champions Nottingham Forest. Chelsea FC was promoted to the top flight and the big time.

Once promotion had been gained, Chelsea team-building strategy became clear: spend, spend, spend. The lucky man who could spend was new manager David Calderhead, from Lincoln City. Unfortunately, other than league titles and a cup during wartime, the investment didn't bring glory.

It brought popularity, however. In 1909 the handbook noted some records set by the club in its first three seasons: biggest gate at any Second Division match, v Man Utd, Good Friday 1906; biggest gate at any First Division match, v Woolwich Arsenal, 9 Nov 1907 – £1,626; record takings at any cup tie outside the final, Southampton v Wolverhampton Wanderers, 1908 – £2,788 9s 0d; record sale of programmes at league match, Chelsea v Villa, 26 Sept 1908 – £97 3s 9d; and record gross of programmes – £1,161 19s 10d, or 278,878 copies.

This self-marketing of Chelsea's success provoked hostility, not least from London rivals, who presumably felt they were losing custom to the new 'babes'. And when Gus Mears's club hit the skids through a devastating injury list during its third top tier season, 1909–10, there was scorn, not sympathy. And when Chelsea fought against potential relegation by forking out the then incredible sum of £3,300 on last-gasp deals, many in football must have said "Good!" when it failed.

The registration problems connected to these transfers led to the FA imposing a time limit on player transfers. The transfers had to be clear by the fourth Thursday of March at 3 p.m. and after that the FA could influence the deals by, for example, only allowing players to play league games.

At the start of a season back in the Second Division, Frederick Parker's anger was barely disguised in a bitter satire on journalists and other clubs' officials under the name the 'Philosophical Pensioner'. It takes the form of a conversation, with a father reassuring his sad son that, unlike 'The Spur', not all people like to kick a man when he is down. 'If you knew human nature, my son, you would understand that you cannot gather the flowers of sympathy in the garden of those who double-bolted the garden against you. Nor can you expect their own particular scribes to look beyond their noses for an excuse for your calamity. They write, "The Pensioner with all his money bags could not save himself from the doom of the Second Division." Never a word of the accidents and illnesses which incapacitated nearly a third of my whole team.'

Parker, as the Pensioner, then addressed the moneybags issue, in a way that is all too familiar in 2005. 'Some there were who unburdened themselves in reams over "the power of the purse", forgetful of the fact that my purse was made and filled by my friends and supporters. It was my duty to these friends and supporters to expend the money which they made for me in their interests. I had more followers than any club in London ... I did not spend my cash, I assure you, for the mere fun of enriching other clubs. "Enriching other clubs, Dad? I scarcely understand you. Some of the scribes wrote that the purchasing of players was unfair to the poorer organisations." Mark me, my son, the name of Chelsea has never been sweet to the ears of those who prophesied and hoped for my failure.'

Parker's prose might equally be applied to those who suggest Chelsea's investment in players today is 'killing football' or that the club is, as Wenger put it, 'financially doped'. Ask West Ham, Porto, Marseille or Lyon whether Chelsea's money is less viable than that of other clubs.

For the 1911–12 season promotion was the main target again and was narrowly missed. In the words of one football writer, 'Chelsea's was a glorious failure'. Eight injured players missed the critical last two matches: Betridge, Warren, Taylor, McConnell, Calderhead, Douglas, Hilsdon and Windridge. At the annual meeting, Chairman Kirby answered those who said the FA Cup campaign, where they'd reached a semi-final for the first time, losing 3-0 to Newcastle United, should have been sacrificed to ensure promotion. 'It is not the policy of the Chelsea directors to tell our players not to try to win any competition we enter,' said Kirby. While Parker, in the *Chelsea Chronicle*, wrote, 'There is a 7lb coke-hammer waiting for the next idiot who asks a Chelsea official, "Why didn't you go up last season?"'

Now Chelsea went for reliable players in defender Jack Harrow and forward Bob Thomson who joined from Croydon Common, and both became excellent club servants. Harrow – a prototype Ron Harris – played 333 times and won a brace of England caps. Bob Thomson was, famously, one-eyed. When secretary-manager Calderhead asked him, 'How do you manage, Bob, when the ball comes to you on your blind side?' He replied, 'I just shut the other eye – and bundle into the nearest back.'

Calderhead achieved Chelsea's second promotion on the back of Bob Whittingham's 26 goals in 32 league games. One opponent said of the powerfully built inside-forward, signed by Chelsea from Bradford City for £1,300 in 1909, that he 'would rather face his Satanic majesty than Whittingham'.

Although top-flight status was never certain, in 1913 the board felt confident enough, even after the death of founder Gus Mears, to try something of an experiment, hiring the 'Great Dane', the legendary Nils Middelboe. Middelboe was a willowy 6-foot-2-inch half-back with a stride that ate up the turf and an intelligence on the ball that was unusual for the time. His natural sportsmanship quickly made him popular. The Dane had played in two Olympic tournaments – 1908 (in London, when Denmark were beaten in the final by a Great Britain team) and 1912 (in Stockholm, when he was skipper of the side who again lost to Great Britain in the final) – and was the first player ever to score in an Olympic Games, against France on 9 October 1908.

He was not the first 'foreigner' ever to play for Chelsea, though. That distinction goes to Max Seeburg, who was born in Germany in 1884, but moved to London as a boy and played for Chelsea's reserves in 1906 – though the *Chelsea Chronicle* had him down as 'Seeberg'. Things didn't work out for him at Chelsea, though. During the First World War he was temporarily interned at Newbury (he was not, as he thought, naturalised), despite his father Franck fighting for the British.

Less convincingly, there were three Indian-born professionals at Chelsea before Middelboe, all of British background: Charles Donaghy, Hugh Dolby and George Hunter. Donaghy, born in Dalhousie, Fort William, in the Himalayas, in 1890, was the son of an Irish sergeant in the British Army and a Lancastrian mother, and he joined the club in 1905. 'Cocky' Hunter was born in Peshawar and signed in February 1913. Adventurous and undisciplined, he played for the first team but moved on to Manchester United for £1,300 before joining the secret service in the First World War. Dolby, born in Agra, never broke through and moved to Brentford.

If you thought Gianluca Vialli was ahead of his time as a manager when he fielded an all-overseas XI on Boxing Day 1999 against Southampton, think again. On 6 November 1905, Chelsea's team consisted of one Anglo, Frank Pearson, for a friendly against First Division Everton in front of 3,000. The remainder were Scots and Irish.

Middelboe's stay would be a long and influential one. He was met at the station on his arrival in London by Vivian Woodward, a friend from amateur internationals, and a car owner. He had actually signed forms with Newcastle, but the United director Mr Graham allowed him to switch to Chelsea. Middelboe made his bow in autumn 1913, having starred in a reserve match and received glowing praise in the *Chelsea Chronicle*. 'It was a great encouragement for me to be mentioned in such a nice way in the programme,' he wrote in his autobiography, 'especially as it was the day I would make my debut for an English First Division team in a proper league game. It took place on 15 November. Our opponents were Derby County, a good footballing team that people always wanted to see, and there were over 40,000 there that day.

'Of course, everything was very exciting, and in the morning I felt exactly the same as I had six months earlier when I sat my final examination to become a lawyer. Before the game everybody was incredibly kind and understanding. Woodward, who played the same day for the amateur English national team against Holland in Hull, sent me a telegram with his best wishes; I also got a couple of letters from fellow countrymen as well.

'Just before we were to enter the field, Chelsea's chairman, Mr Kirby, came to me and gave me the ball. He explained to me that it was the players' wish that I should be captain. It was really great news – because I didn't have to dwell anymore on whether the players wanted me to be part of the team.

'When you are captain of a team in England you always enter the field of play first with the ball in your hands. Here I already made my first mistake. It was the players' belief that the goal to the right as you entered the field was the "lucky" one – something that was pointed out to me, even though we only ran out for some preliminary exercises before the game. Of course, on this occasion I had just chosen at random the goal to the left. Even if it was simply superstition, from then on, and for the sake of my team-mates, I always chose the goal to the right. Then I lost the toss of the coin. Despite these "mistakes" Chelsea played a very good game and won 2-1, and all was well.

'I have always found it very difficult to judge my own performances, and this game was no exception to the rule. But the crowd were entertained by what my long legs could reach, either on the ground or in the air, and I got some applause. At the same time they were not so happy at my hesitation in making a tackle. Amazingly, I didn't really take too much notice of this huge crowd. It was only when we arrived back in the dressing room that I realised how I had been playing, as both players and officials came to me to congratulate me. Then the trainer presented me [with] the ball as a memento of the game, and I realised that my performance must had been satisfactory. I still have the ball and cherish it.'

'My next game was two days later, a charity game away to London club Millwall. It was not a pleasure at all as the field was bumpy, and with the club drawing its supporters from dock areas, it was a gloomy place to be. Several First Division teams have been beaten there, as were we (1-2).

'Playing against other Third Division teams Millwall are nothing special, but against First Division teams' sensitive players, often with better skills, are too easily scared by their robust play, which is far from elegant. Another handicap for visiting sides is the crowd, who have a certain knack of backing and cheering their own team and at the same time jeering at the away team.

'Incidentally, I was close to missing the game as my chauffeur got lost. However, I had been studying the route on a map the day before and was therefore able to show him the right way, which made me very proud as I had only been in London for two weeks. One way or another, for me it became a game to remember.'

Middelboe quickly proved himself indispensable, and as an amateur, with a job in a bank, he had to be kept sweet. 'To have football as a living with three times the salary I got from the bank was obviously a solution. But it was never a serious question for me as I was by no means mad about football. I took part in most of the games, which was more than enough, and with the pleasure of looking back on a successful career in English football staying as an amateur was more than enough for me.

'Of course, by saying that I am being derogatory towards the professional football game, but in England the circumstances are a little special, which I will explain later in another chapter.

'Chelsea's chairman, I can reveal, suggested in a very friendly way that I could play all the home games and choose which away games I played. It was a delightful arrangement for me, because the long trips from Friday afternoon to the night of Saturday were not a pleasure at all. But things were by no means so simple. Because the line-up had to change so often and I was anxious too whether resentment would arise among the professional players, especially with the player who would temporarily take my place only for the away games. Of course, he would have to play as he was on the pay roll, and it was the management who made the decisions about when and where he should play – but anyway.'

Middelboe's book offers a contemporary insight into how football faced up to the conflict that arose during his second season in London. 'It was then a big question if all or some parts of all league games in the season of 1914–15 should be cancelled,' he wrote, 'prompting a fierce debate in the press with strong words exchanged.

'The discussions concerned only the professional game as a very large number of the amateur players – up to 100,000 – reported as volunteers for the war, and a lot of the amateur games were therefore automatically cancelled.

'They thought it only reasonable that the professional player did exactly the same as the amateur; by "they" one means those people who were already hostile towards the professional player and who now found occasion to brand the sportsman as "a bad sport".

'Meanwhile, there were contrary views, and to stop the bad publicity the football authorities went to the War Cabinet. They responded that it was up to the FA to decide. For the time being the cabinet didn't find it necessary to call a halt – probably because of the large number of volunteers already signing-up early on – and at the same time they thanked all the big clubs for the very large amounts of money they had already presented, with the promise of more money for the hospitals and war funds if it was possible.

'At the same time, several clubs were turned into live shooting ranges, where the players could make exercise with rifles. That settled the matter and all parties involved calmed down. The season was played and finished without any problems, the scheduled fixture list being maintained.

'Only in one aspect did we feel any real effect of the abnormal conditions. I'm thinking here about the attendances, which were halved. Since clubs had promised war fund collections that were a very high percentage of the admission fee, they had to reduce the players' wages. This was accepted and they contributed in a way that helped the national tragedy.'

Later, Chelsea took to advertising their games in the *Daily News* under the banner, 'TO-DAY'S BEST MATCH'. In contrast, interest on the front remained undimmed. Servicemen wanted to hear more sport and less war news. Many a British soldier wrote home of how the Germans' massed attacks were reminiscent of football crowds leaving a stadium.

On 21 November 1914 recruitment drives – 'For the flag's sake' – were held at various football matches, including one at Stamford Bridge. Colonel Burn, MP, was among the speakers before 16,000 watched Chelsea beat Notts County 4-1. 'I believe in football,' he pleaded. 'I believe in your games being carried on as usual. I have come here to ask if there is any young man with no encumbrances to join the forces. I don't say come. I say, "Come, for God's sake. You are wanted."

'I have given my son. He enlisted at the start of the war. He is now dead.' It was not a survival ratio to brag about, especially as around a third of those present already wore khaki.

Not one new recruit came forward. It prompted a furious response from Evelyn Hubbard, influential chairman of Guardian Assurance, to *The Times*: 'An undue proportion of married men are leaving their wives and families in response to Lord Kitchener's appeal and coming forward to fill the spaces in the fighting line which ought to be filled by the thousands of able-bodied lads and single men whose devotion to football has overpowered their patriotism. The pitiable result of Colonel Burn's appeal at Stamford Bridge is nothing short of a national disgrace. Surely, sir, it is time that further League Cup football matches be stopped?'

Attendances reflected the guilt and poverty of action. At the time of the recruitment rally, November 1914, Chelsea's gate had dipped in common with other clubs, down from 35,000 to 15,000 on the corresponding weekend in 1913, a fall of 20,000, or nearly 60 per cent.

The campaign was stepped up outside the Chelsea v Arsenal game in December 1914. 'In these days,' wrote a reporter, 'the posters carried by a line of sandwich-men, walking up and down before the gates of the Chelsea football ground, ask the crowd such questions as: "Are you forgetting that there's a war on?", "Your Country Needs You", "Be Ready to Defend your Home and Women from the German Huns". So far as I could notice, little attention was given to these skeletons at the feast.'

By January 1915, however, it could be announced that more than 200 Londoners had been recruited into the so-called 'Footballers' Battalion' of the Middlesex Regiment. In November that year, the Footballers' Battalion paraded at Stamford Bridge en route to the front. As a gentleman amateur, Chelsea star Viv Woodward had received an officer's commission and rose to the rank of major.

Of medium height and slightly built, Woodward was a brilliant dribbler and had a great shot on him, which made him a prolific goalscorer. He once scored six goals for England against Holland and was rated one of his country's best ever centre-forwards, not to mention 'the living embodiment of the finest spirit of the game', as Labour MP and diplomat Philip Noel-Baker put it. Woodward, known to his friends as Jack, skippered England to victory in the 1912 Olympics and was credited with setting the standards of fair play that would forever be associated with the English game.

London born, he grew up in Clacton with a football-hating father. Woodward 'got some pastings' from opponents as a former colleague put it, but he would always shake it off, typically pointing out that there was a referee to deal with such matters. In the Second World War Woodward enlisted with the ARP. He died in an Ealing nursing home after a long illness in February 1954.

Back in 1915, while football carried on as normal, Woodward was given special leave from the front to play in Chelsea's first ever FA Cup final. He returned in time to play the match, at Old Trafford, but honourably insisted that Bob Thomson, who had played in every round, would have lost his place. Chelsea directors pressed Woodward to play, but he refused.

Another player who had done much to earn Chelsea this brilliant and always underrated achievement was local King's Road School boy Harry Ford. At 5 foot 7 he was still quite often one of the tallest in Chelsea's front line. He had scored the winner in the quarter-final replay against Newcastle at St James' Park.

Chelsea's oldest fan, Ethel Luland from Hampstead, made the trek up to Manchester for the final with her family. They were among the few Chelsea fans at the event. A scenario familiar to any away travellers today restricted the number of Chelsea fans at Old Trafford. Rail services operated under wartime restrictions and there were no cheap tickets.

It was a 'dark, dismal day' with 'yellowed, clinging mist and drizzle'. The crowd was largely in Sheffield United's favour. 'It included numbers of men in uniform,' wrote the *Manchester Guardian*. 'In the lower rows of the stand there was a group of wounded soldiers, accompanied by their nurses. Several of them had their feet in bandages and one, minus an arm, smoked his pipe and viewed the game in an air of perfect contentment. There was never a cup final played in such a depressing atmosphere. A sombre consciousness of war overhung the crowd, and the final touch was when the band started to play hymns.'

Calderhead must have longed for his team to reach a final, but not under these conditions. 'Chelsea only got in two really good shots,' continued the *Manchester Guardian*, 'and those came in the last few seconds of the first half. They were hard ground shots to the foot of the post and came so quickly that Gough had only just time to rush from the one post to the other.

'At the beginning of the second half the fog was so dense that spectators on the one side had only the haziest notion of what was happening on the other, and the ball was rarely seen except when it rose against the sky. There was a crowd of fifty thousand present.'

Old reliables had wilted in the mood. A poor clearance from Jack Harrow, a fumble from the keeper Jim Molyneux, an enfeebling injury to Ford. It ended 3-0 to the Blades.

Ford's daughter Gladys Hunt has a box of mementoes, and although his runners-up medal was pawned after he quit football and never bought back, there is one precious piece of memorabilia. 'We've got a programme made of silk from the 1915 final from when he was presented to King George V. Only the players and staff got it – you couldn't buy it.'

In July 1915 the Football League put all players on an amateur status, expenses only for tea and other refreshments, but gates were already collapsing. In September that year football became regional to reduce rail transport and unnecessary fuel use, and the London Combination League was born. The situation posed an interesting problem for Calderhead. Like other managers, he was able to call on soldiers based close by for matches, and that didn't preclude those registered to other clubs.

One London club manager had scouts out at all mainline railway stations on the look out for footballers on leave from the front. As usual, Chelsea's west London location was a boon. It was close to Aldershot, where many servicemen were based. Chelsea's wartime guests included Bolton's Corporal Ted Vizard and Bombardier Joe Smith, Charles Buchan (Sunderland) and Stewart Davidson (Middlesbrough). Buchan, who would make his name after his playing career by launching *Football Monthly* (a periodical briefly owned by Chelsea in the 1990s), was the Pensioners' joint top scorer with Thomson during the war. But it cut both ways. While the presence of Sheffield United's Stan Fazackerley (a scorer in the Khaki Cup final) was a bonus, Bridge legend Bob Whittingham was for a time banging them in up at Stoke.

By May 1917 the *News of the World* was happy enough with the camouflaged status quo to suggest, 'There was a mood to persist with the Combination format when the hostilities ceased because it guaranteed so many London clubs playing each other.' There was reduced travelling, it said, and a 'pleasant mix'. Chelsea chairman Claude Kirby was asked his view, and he was adamant: 'As far as Chelsea is concerned, we shall return to the English League when the war is over.'

Kirby's rationale must have been quite obvious to those looking at the often paltry attendances. Only 5,000 watched the April encounter between Chelsea and Arsenal, which the home team won 2-0. This was nothing unusual. Chelsea needed the likes of Manchester United to pull in a good crowd rather than yet another Arsenal rematch, even though Calderhead's team were playing some very good football with other people's players. In April 1918 Woodward scored as Chelsea, finishing with ten men, slaughtered Fulham 7-0. The 'incomparable' Joe Smith deserved a medal of sorts for scoring three in Chelsea's 4-1 thrashing of the Arsenal the same year.

Stamford Bridge was also regaining its reputation as London's leisure palace. On Independence Day, 4 July 1915, the King and Queen attended a baseball match there between US Navy and Army teams, and the following year a gymkhana was staged for the nascent British film industry, with celebrity jockeys competing in donkey derbies and the like. 'A club that can do no wrong in the field of enterprise' was how the *Daily News* saw it in December 1918. 'About half-past three in the yesterday,' it continued, 'when the sun was reddening towards evening, a terrific clatter of military canes on wooden benches, followed by round after round of applause, might have been heard at the ground of Chelsea FC at Stamford Bridge. The cause of the commotion was due to the fact that the giant forward of the Grenadier Guards had just scored the winning goal against the RFA from Charlton Park in the first round of the Bulldog Cup competition, and to Private Wilding belonged the honour.

'Private Wilding, who holds the Military Medal and a Bar, still carries shrapnel just under the heart, but the pluck he showed was characteristic of the whole 22.'

In 1919, Chelsea won the Victory Cup in front of 30,000 people at Highbury, beating Fulham 3-0. Neil, the father of John Harris, played for Fulham that day. Jack Rutherford of Newcastle scored two of Chelsea's goals. No one has won that trophy since. Calderhead was probably very fond of it indeed.

Four years of regional league competition and friendlies ended on the first day of September 1919. The Chelsea team showed five changes from April 1915 – perhaps less disruption than could reasonably have been hoped for given the ravages of the Great War.

The six who'd played in Chelsea's last official league match were stalwarts Walter Bettridge, Jack Harrow, Laurence Abrams, Harold Halse and keeper James Molyneux, now well into his 30s and under pressure from understudy Colin Hampton, a war hero who'd received the Military Medal for gallantry in Mesopotamia. His bravery and dependability on the less vital stage of association football saw him splitting custodial duties with the popular Moly in what would turn out to be an excellent year for the club.

On that opening weekend 35,000 people watched at Goodison Park as the slickers from the Big Smoke stunned Everton, reigning league champions from the last season before the war, with a 3-2 win, including a penalty from Bob Whittingham that extended his amazing wartime goalscoring sequence. What chimed with both sets of fans was that back in 1915 a 2-2 draw at the Bridge had confirmed the Toffeemen as champions. The peace dividend for Stamford Bridge playing staff proved short-lived, though, and personnel change was inevitable. The ageing Whittingham moved on and in his place arrived another Chelsea and England matinee idol, Jack Cock, from cash-strapped Huddersfield. The Cornishman would top-score for the Pensioners for the next three seasons and managed 21 in his first.

Calderhead laboured on for another 14 years, suffering relegation in 1924 and promotion in 1930, fielding teams of attractive, talented individuals under no discernible instruction. Middelboe's description of him is interesting. 'The manager [Calderhead], as I knew him 25 to 30 years ago, was rather impersonal in his dealings with the players,' observed the Dane. 'He only showed up in the dressing room a few times and didn't mix with the players very much, never more than necessary. Sometimes he viewed the training, which was handled by the trainer and only by the trainer. There were no tactical meetings with the manager – that was unknown at that time.

'Several clubs have now changed these conditions. First of all a modern manager now treats the players like human beings and not as in the past like "mercenaries". Nowadays he strives to understand the players' different mentalities, good and bad, so he can complete the machine, which is what a club is, and things will run smoothly.

'At the same time as he is the players' superior, a wise manager is the players' friend, someone they can talk with, even concerning private matters. Such a manager is, of course, always prepared to help, as he is sympathetic to the person, but he also knows that a player with private problems can never be at his best on the field.'

Middelboe returned to Denmark in 1936.

In 1951, to mark their 75th anniversary, KB invited a Chelsea team to play in Copenhagen, where 30,000 watched them beat the guests 1-0. Middelboe was KB's secretary at the time. He died in 1976 aged 88.

11

SHOOTING STARS

The 1930s is the forgotten decade in Chelsea's history. Promoted in 1930, the Pensioners remained in the top flight for the next 32 years – relief for a club that had spent ten of its first 25 years in the Second Division. Although several players of this period, including [Hughie] Gallacher, [Tommy] Law, [Reg] Weaver and [Vic] Woodley, are celebrated, it's often with a sense that what they achieved was nowhere near enough for the quality Chelsea was able to field on matchdays.

When governments need to divert minds from a domestic crisis, they invent one abroad. When football clubs want to cover up for failure, they buy big. So it was at Chelsea throughout the decade. Despite economic crises elsewhere, the club was prosperous, attractive and established. Record crowds flocked through the gates at Stamford Bridge despite the fact that the club finished no higher than eighth during the ten seasons of the 1930s. No matter how much money they seemed to spend, nor how glittering the squad, Chelsea never threatened to break out of the comfort zone, let alone properly break its silverware duck.

By the end of the decade, the proprietor of Harry's Dining Rooms on Chalk Farm Road, Camden, would feel confident enough to place a sign outside saying, 'I WILL GIVE A FREE MEAL TO ALL MY CUSTOMERS WHEN CHELSEA

WIN THE CUP'. And to invite the press round to snap him hanging it up in front of small, smirking crowd. This is the decade where the image of inconsistent, underachieving, lovable old losers Chelsea was established.

There are probably many reasons why the substantial investment seemed to go to waste. Luckily, we have two contemporary voices to help shed light on one or two of them.

In his book, *KB-Chelsea and Home Again*, Danish-born half-back Nils Middelboe was damning about some directors at Chelsea and elsewhere. 'You may ask yourself if it is necessary for a director to have some knowledge of football,' he mused. 'Absolutely not. Arsenal, for example, have for the past few years had a board of directors, well-known and powerful, among them two lords, who didn't have any knowledge of football, and didn't pretend they had. Of course, they were interested in sport but so is the entire English population. An idea, which has recently gained currency, suggests that it is important to have "names" who are good for the club's image, while the matters of sport are handed over to the manager.

'For the time being, though, most clubs still have the "old-fashioned" director. There are two kind of directors: those who have a very good knowledge of football and are therefore good for the club's sporting matters; and those who have a superficial knowledge of the game but still think they are experts. Within the latter category, which is the most widespread, you will find the most recognisable type of director. He is the one who watches the games from a special box, a big cigar in his mouth, wearing the club colours in his buttonhole. Occasionally he shouts at the referee or players, which often reveals how little he actually knows about football. He is something out of the ordinary – and is also a dangerous type who can do a lot of harm by interfering on the sporting side.

'In my time at Chelsea [1913–21] we had quite a few of this type of director. When they weren't attending games they were very pleasant people to be around and they sacrificed a lot of time and money for the club. Unfortunately they didn't understand that when they insisted on choosing the team, or picking which new players to sign, they did more harm than good.'

It doesn't take Sherlock Holmes to spot the likely suspects. Still on the board at the start of the 1930s were the last of the original 1905ers, J.T. Mears (habitually caricatured holding a cigar) and chairman Claude Kirby. They were joined by Mears's son Joe, Jack Budd, Colonel C.D. Crisp and

Charles Pratt senior. At this stage the board still liked to pick the team, even though they all had other business to attend to the rest of the week.

Throughout the 1930s Middelboe remained in London as a banker and maintained an interest in the club. He seems to have found businessmen fascinating and he wondered how Chelsea's directors, some of them powerful and successful men, could overlook basic principles when it came to football. He noted that the board rarely made selection changes in a winning team, but that they would spoil that by making individuals play out of their best position. 'The directors were also a big problem when it came to signing new players,' he argued, 'as they acted single-handedly, with the manager – the only person with any real knowledge of football – pushed into the background.

'As a result Chelsea managed some of the worst signings, if not the worst ever seen, in paying £25,000 in 1930 for Gallacher, Jackson and Cheyne. Obviously excellent players, but the personal qualities of these players were so poor, that the club just wanted to get rid of them a few years later. As they couldn't get any money for Jackson and Cheyne, they just let them go for nothing. Chelsea received only £3,000 for Gallacher.'

Middelboe was writing a good deal later. It would have taken a brave man to suggest such buys were mistakes at the time. Extravagant and ambitious, yes. But that was glamorous Chelsea for you. Hughie Gallacher was the outstanding centre-forward of his generation, a huge draw whose genius on the ball was often worth the admission price alone. He had been one of 1928's legendary 'Wembley Wizards' who took England apart 5-1 on their own turf. Winger Alex Jackson, the 'Gay Cavalier', was another from that famous win and again big box office – 51,000 turned up for his debut.

But the problems Middelboe referred to surfaced soon enough. Versatile forward Alec Cheyne found it hard to settle and spent some time in France before returning for another fruitless spell at the Bridge. Gallacher's indiscipline led to playing bans lasting months at a time. Jackson was in dispute with the board virtually from the start and in February 1933 left Chelsea to join Margate of the Kent League.

Already a Chelsea player back in 1928, Wembley Wizards' centre-back Tommy Law, famous for his sliding tackle, was now arguably past his best. Gallacher and Law entered into a divisive dispute over money with fellow countryman and manager of the club David Calderhead, which contributed in part to his enforced departure after 26 years in the spring of 1933. He had taken Chelsea to the FA Cup final in 1915 and won promotion twice, but the only other medal he owned was one awarded by the Football League for his 21 years' service as a club secretary.

Between them, the £25,000 worth of superstars he bought in 1930 played little more than 260 league games. These were potentially catastrophic failures. What had gone wrong? The board looked at the management and training. The newspapers of the day talked about Chelsea's artistry, but lack of direction. Glorious passing, but little penetration. And awful defending! The popular Jack Whitley was still training the players as he had since 1919. There was no working on set pieces, no discussion of tactics. Yet, despite everything, Whitley would survive till the outbreak of war in 1939.

Calderhead, the granite-faced Scotsman of so few words he was known as the Sphinx, was the man who took the rap at the end of March 1933. His team responded by thrashing Leeds 6-0 in the next home game. Chelsea's longest-serving boss suffered ill health and died in London in January 1938, aged 73. He was buried in Putney Vale Cemetery.

With the departure of the dominant football figure at Chelsea for 26 years came the opportunity for a fresh approach. It was a baton the board failed to pick up. New man Leslie Knighton was no dynamic replacement. He had managed Arsenal for six unsuccessful years and his stewardship ended with them 20th out of 22 in 1925. He also spent six uneventful years at Birmingham. But he was a wheeler-dealer in the transfer market and once again there was the sense that the money was available at Chelsea. But again it wasn't spent on the right personnel. In 1935–36, a few years into Knighton's tenure, Chelsea, who could still be described by one writer as 'the enfant terrible, whose conduct is unpredictable', finished eighth – and it was their best finish since promotion in 1930.

We are fortunate also to have the vivid testimony of a player who joined Chelsea at the midway point of the decade, albeit faithfully passed on through his son. Harry Burgess arrived after six seasons with Sheffield Wednesday during their golden age and was a title winner with them in 1928–29. There were no such highspots in his four seasons at Stamford Bridge, though they twice (in 1936 and 1938) finished in the top half of the First Division. But at least they remained in the top flight, which was good going for a club well used to tumbling down elephant traps.

Unlike some of his new colleagues, the two-footed inside-forward was a team player. He was 31, but even in the twilight of his career he held his own among the so-called stars. He was helped by his somewhat freakish physique – he was 5 foot 8 with a 33-inch inside-leg measurement. It meant that his stride ate up ground deceptively and he was able to hurdle heavy challenges with ease. Back then footballers referred to 'even time' – being able to run 100 yards in ten seconds. Burgess was able to hold his own over ten yards. And if someone got in his way, his powerful build allowed him to run them down.

He always talked fondly of his time at Chelsea, despite his frustration at what might have been achieved with the resources available. Burgess's old boss at Wednesday, Bob Brown, had to resign through ill health, and he knew Knighton, who asked him to do some scouting for Chelsea. 'My father met Brown on a railway station,' says son Martin, 'and he asked him what he was going to do. Father replied, "I'm approaching 31. If I don't get back in the first team here [Sheffield Wednesday] I don't want to play in the Combination." Brown said, "I'm scouting for Chelsea and I'll make a recommendation that they buy you straightaway." Well, Brown died before the transfer was completed in April 1935 but father still joined Chelsea.'

Mrs Burgess was livid with the timing, as it meant her husband missing out on an FA Cup-winner's medal and bonus with Wednesday, as well as a move south away from friends and family. But the move was worth it. 'It was the same then as it is now,' says son Martin. 'If you went to Chelsea and you were any good, you lived like a king. It was like a gentlemen's club. You didn't get the money, but it was all paid for.' With footballers' wages capped and other benefits severely scrutinised, boards competing for the best players were creative with alternative incentives. Chelsea's directors had more at their disposal than most. Ah, the Chelsea effect.

'Once,' says Martin Burgess, 'they sent father and Dickie Spence, who he knew from Barnsley, to Margate to stay in some fancy hotel, saying they looked a bit under the weather. And they gave them money for "tips" more than their wages.' Negotiations with the management for extras – legal and otherwise – were apparently handled by George Gibson, a dribbling Scots inside-forward who joined the club in 1933.

It could hardly be said that the Bridge had a holiday camp atmosphere, however. One matchday soon after he joined Chelsea, Burgess took a friend down to the ground early to play snooker in the billiard room adjacent to the stadium. During the game another player arrived and said 'Good morning' to Burgess. Burgess continued with his shot and made no response. His pal was flabbergasted and a little later said, 'You're a funny bunch, you footballers! He just said hello and you completely ignored him.'

'I'll be wasting enough breath on him this afternoon,' replied Burgess, 'without wasting more on him now.'

'Playing away and doing all right,' Harry told his son Martin, 'you'd score a goal and no sooner had you than there was one in the other end. Billy Mitchell's given away a penalty or free kick and there's the bonus gone!

'One that got up my father's nose was [Tommy] Law. He'd been around the club for ages and hardly ever played but he still got paid ... Bobby Gregg played 50 times for Chelsea, he'd been a colleague of father's in the 1928–29 championship season and the 1931 FA Cup at Wednesday but had moved on to Birmingham. He played in the same position as my father. He'd been with Leslie Knighton at Birmingham, and Knighton brought him down to London from there, along with Jimmy Argue in 1933. So when father turned up there two years later, he went up to him and said, "I suppose you've come to take my place again, you bugger." But Gregg barely featured again in Knighton's reconstructed frontline, with Burgess pre-eminent.

Burgess was to experience the timeless riddle of Chelsea. But even for a man who loved to do the bridge puzzles in the posh papers it was easier to state the problem rather than the solution. 'He said there was no proper strategy,' says son Martin. 'Like a lot of clubs do – even today – they would pay a load of money for players, buy stars to keep their fans quiet ... but they didn't always perform, and some were of the wrong age, but they were *always* forwards, even though they really wanted defenders. Father was a team player and probably the most successful in terms of pedigree of winning the league and in terms of effectiveness.'

If one man's view represents the skew of history, Harry Burgess's observations are interesting and plausible all the same. 'Father thought some of the players, with respect, were poor. George Barber he thought lacked quality and was more on the floor than on his feet, while Harry Miller was a fair player past his best. John O'Hare had a damaged left arm – the left-winger used to cut inside and he'd lose his balance ... Sam Weaver was a class player, very good going forward, but ill-disciplined, not in terms of fouls, but positionally. He didn't know whether he was a forward or a half-back, and he wasn't all that disposed to coming back once he was upfield. Father thought he played for himself a bit.

'Father thought the Northern Irishman Billy Mitchell had the possibility to be a top-class player, but he was a bit like Lee Bowyer is today. His temperament was suspect and for an old-style half-back that was a problem as you were always in the thick of it. If you upset Billy, the result was either a penalty or a free kick in a vulnerable area. Father used to say to him, "Look, if you're annoyed with someone, have it out in the last minute near the halfway line, not in a danger area."

'At centre-half was a Scottish player called [Allan] Craig who father thought wasn't bad at all. My father said, "The only time I saw him upset was when a player at Brentford called him a 'bastard'. He went berserk. He crashed into the opponents' dressing room and wanted to have it out with the player for disparaging his mother's name."

'Joe Payne had electric pace that put him up with Spence, but he had a bit of a fit and put his fist through a panel. The right-winger, Peter Buchanan, he thought was a bit of a crackpot – clever on the ball, but he would fall over it. There was Wilf Chitty too who was pacy and he quite liked him. And the keeper, Johnny Jackson, he felt must have taken a battering at some stage, because he seemed timid sometimes.'

There were others, of course. Jackson's rival Vic Woodley was the pin-up of the team for the entire decade, perhaps the only player who always justified his selection. He proudly patrolled between the England team's posts for 19 consecutive games until wartime.

Amateur centre-forward George Mills's goals had contributed greatly to promotion in 1930, and safety in 1934, and he was the first Chelsea player to achieve the magic one hundred. But with a conveyor belt of expensive strikers he was often overlooked in favour of the more glamorous Hughie Gallacher, Ireland international Joe Bambrick or Joe Payne.

Mills stayed around as 'A' team coach, and, having been overjoyed by the FA Cup success of 1970, died in July of that year aged 62. Northern Ireland international Bambrick joined fellow countryman Tom Priestley (the inside-forward who wore a brown skull cap to cover his bald pate) on the increasingly long Celtic underachievers list. He should have been a sensation at Chelsea. He had managed 94 goals for Linfield in one season and scored six of Northern Ireland's seven in one game against Wales (the Dunlop ball he did it with was actually laced by the father of the current Republic of Ireland manager Brian Kerr). But he lacked the thrust and power of Mills, to whom he was routinely preferred.

Amid all the anticlimax of this radiant decade of underperformance, it suddenly all looked to have come together on 23 October 1937, fittingly a day when even the weather couldn't make up its mind between sunshine and downpours. Chelsea beat Brentford 2-1 to go top of the table after 12 games. Mills was more prolific than ever, Burgess was banging them in, Mitchell was keeping most of his mischief for the right end of the pitch and former reserve Wilf Chitty was flying at outside-left.

But after the sunshine, the rain. In traditional fashion Chelsea proceeded to win just twice in the next 21 games, a run which began with a 5-5 performance at Bolton that belonged in a circus marquee. Bambrick played twice more after the Brentford win before joining Walsall.

'In father's last year, 1939,' says Martin Burgess, 'they bought a player – Alf Hanson – who looked promising, a great player, his brother or cousin played keeper for Liverpool.' Hanson was one of the driving forces in a near miss in the FA Cup, which ended dismally in a quarter-final defeat at home to Grimsby. That followed perhaps Burgess's finest hour, as he scored two goals in the Pensioners' 3-1 fourth round, second replay win at Highbury over Sheffield Wednesday, the club where he'd won his medals.

Then war intervened and even the Chelsea gravy train was commandeered for military duties. 'All my father was hanging on for was a benefit,' says Martin Burgess. 'There was a qualifying period of games, which he had played. But the contracts were all scrapped when war broke out. You got paid £2 per game in wartime – it was £8 normally.

'Looking back, my parents said, "We were always looked after very well." The overseas tours were like holidays for the players and directors. It was a different world to Sheffield Wednesday. Mother didn't want to go back up north – she thought it was the bloody Wild West after Chelsea!'

The board eventually agreed with the players' conclusion that with Knighton nothing would ever change. His meandering reign ended with his retirement in April 1939. He was replaced by another Scot, William Birrell, the secretary-manager of lower league Queens Park Rangers. With this unheralded arrival came a radical departure: Birrell pledged to overturn 35 years of Stamford Bridge orthodoxy, as the wallet of SW6 took a rest.

12
DOCHERTY'S LITTLE DIAMONDS

Even as Tommy Docherty succeeded Ted Drake in September 1962 relegation was draped around Stamford Bridge like funeral linen. But the following campaign, with a mixture of talented youth and seasoned pros such as Frank Upton and John Mortimore, Chelsea stormed out of Division Two, helped by Tommy Harmer's nether regions (providing the only goal of the game in the crucial win at Sunderland) and a 7-0 demolition of a Portsmouth side featuring Chelsea's later manager Bobby Campbell. First job done; now for the proper work.

Docherty was a new model Chelsea man for the 1960s: chirpy, mid-30s, sharp suit, crew cut, a little feral. He wanted to inject energy and pride into Chelsea's old, beaten-up carcass. 'Tommy Doc was like a whirlwind, difficult to pin down,' says Albert Sewell, whose duty it was to write the programmes. 'In a way, he couldn't leave well alone. I remember we used to go to press on a Wednesday night with the programme for the Saturday, and I'd ring Tommy Doc on Wednesday afternoon and say, "What team do you want printed?" And he'd say, "I'm giving it a bit more thought. Ring me this evening."

'I'd ring him in the evening. And one particular night I rang him and he went from numbers one to 11 and I said, "Hey, Tom, do you know what you've done? You've picked the same 11 you picked last week." And he said,

"Then I'll change the substitute!" Typical Tom, nothing could be the same for five minutes. A likeable man but a bit of a rogue with it.'

With the success of the European Cup, English football had debated the merits of a European league for the first time. Domestic success was no longer enough for the restless Doc. He was intoxicated with the idea of glory overseas and in 1964 he arranged a summer tour of the continent, playing teams entered for the European Cup and the Cup-Winners' Cup, such as Rapid Vienna, Munich 1860, Gothenburg and Swiss champions La Chaux-de-Fonds.

Looking for a definite break from the old regime, the club had also dispatched Docherty for a fortnight to study Miguel Muñoz's legendary 'Ye-Ye' Real Madrid team of the early 1960s. Their nickname was a reference to the Beatles, whose music penetrated even the oppressive Franco dictatorship – though when the mop-tops played in Spain, it was in all-seater bullrings with police jumping on anyone who went beyond tapping a toe.

Like Docherty at Chelsea, Muñoz was reconstructing an ageing side, putting the emphasis on youth and pace. 'Muñoz was of the school of "go out and enjoy yourself,"' says Guillem Balague, Sky television's Spanish football pundit and UK correspondent of *Marca*. 'He didn't work the players tactically, but made sure his teams had a couple of wingers and a decent striker to be on the end of crosses.'

One of the players Muñoz had to retire in order to give youth its head was his old friend and team-mate Alfredo Di Stefano. But this was the golden generation of Gento, Sanchís and Amancio, so people soon forgot. The vigorous new Real would blow away all before them and their secret was not lost on Tommy Doc. 'I watched their methods,' he said. 'I picked up their tactic of players overlapping in attack. At Real, it was only the forwards that did it. I extended it at Chelsea to the backs and half-backs.'

Other new methods contributed to the sum. He borrowed the chipping of close-in free kicks through the wall from Burnley and some tactical moves from West Ham. Docherty watched, listened and borrowed anything that would give him an edge. Even the innovative decision in 1964 to add numbers to Chelsea's shorts was at the suggestion of a supporter. In training the emphasis was on improving accuracy of passing, speed and endurance, two-touch games, running off the ball. On the field of play this meant a blend of strength and finesse, darting runs and passes to the spare man in attack and defence.

He was helped by the maturing of Chelsea's own first 'golden generation': Peter Bonetti, Terry Venables, Bobby Tambling, Barry Bridges, Ken Shellito, Bert Murray and Allan Harris – all home-grown players. Venables, in the centre of midfield, was the only man with a free role, but spontaneity was also encouraged in others. Mortimore was the oldest at 29; but by far the majority were graduates of the 1960 and 1961 Youth Cup winning-teams, aged between 17 and 23.

The fans, disappointed at the falling away since the club's sole title win in 1955, picked up on the new vibrancy. 'They could see the great times coming back again,' said the Doc recently. 'I mean I know they won the league, but other than Greavsie, since then the team wasn't exciting at all. And the only players we sold were the ones like Micky Harris and Micky Block, Mel Scott, the Silletts and people like that. So I thought, if we can get a few quid for them, it helps to pay for the youth policy. And the youth policy was even better than Man United's. They came off that conveyor belt like s**t off a shovel.'

Not all the youngsters were free. Docherty used an extensive scouting network, especially north of the border, and it was after a tip-off that he accidentally unearthed Eddie McCreadie, one of Chelsea's greatest ever left-backs. 'I went to see a boy called Gourlay from Arbroath. He played left side of midfield. I'd never seen him play but I got a phone call one day, "Good player," I was told. So I went to see him and they were playing East Stirling away. They gave me the teams and I was sitting at the back of the stand, and this left-back – I thought, "Why the hell are you playing here?" He was great in the air, he was quick, his control was magic. I didn't know if he was a left-back or an outside-left. I never spoke about Gourlay; I don't know if Gourlay was playing that day or not.

'Afterwards I met Jack Steedman. He said, "Hello Thomas, what are you doing here?" I said, "I'm looking at the boy Gourlay – he's not a bad player. But I wouldn't swap him for your left-back." "Och," he says, "now you're talking." He says, "I want a lot of money for him." I say, "How much do you want?" He says, "£8,000." I say, "Behave yourself', Jack, you can buy the whole of East Stirling for eight grand." Anyway, we bartered away and eventually we got him for five plus a friendly match at East Stirling. And Eddie was great. I said to him he'd be playing for Scotland within a year and he said, "Do you really think so?" And I said, "Aye." Anyway, he came in and he did ever so well, and he got Scottish caps.'

The team that had grown together won together. Having bagged the League Cup and narrowly lost in the FA Cup semi-final against eventual winners Liverpool, Docherty's 'Little Diamonds' as he called them had gone top of the league in April 1965, with four games to go. But the 'Blackpool incident', where eight players defied the manager's curfew for some after-hours drinking, led to players being sent home, and the dissected team was sponged 2–6 by Burnley. *The Times* mourned the fallen heroes, 'A sad ending to their eight months of ceaseless challenge in league and cup.'

Docherty was resolute, 'We can't be champions this year, but we want to prove that we are the great side some people predicted we would be. I still feel it will be three years before we reach our peak. But who knows what will happen next year.'

The 1965–66 side's style of play was skittish, with intricate little passing moves that often made for crescendos of interplay. But there was also a flimsiness in there, an automation, that could become ineffective and predictable – the same frailties that had dogged Chelsea for decades.

If Docherty needed reminding that he was in the entertainment game Joe Mears, son of the formidable businessman J.T., would have been pointing it out to him. As construction was completed on the first new grandstand at the Bridge for decades, an 'English Professional Football' survey was published showing that the public spent £122 million on enjoying football in 1964, more than twice that spent on cinema admissions, and a further £100 million was frittered away on the football pools. More naggingly for Mears, since the maximum wage had gone west, was that the average wage of a First Division footballer in 1955 was £800; ten years later it was £2,680.

And so Docherty began to build his next team. One that would challenge for honours again at home and abroad, and one that would entertain. The switch is encapsulated in one 'swap' – Terry Venables for Charlie Cooke; artisan for artist. Docherty made it clear Venables's time was up. 'In fairness to him,' he says, 'he was sorry to leave Chelsea. Because he was with the club more or less from when he was a lad – 17 or younger. I just couldn't see us winning anything with him. We had a lot of good players, but we had players who were never great players, like Barry Bridges.'

Docherty saw Charlie Cooke as a trade-up. 'I got eighty grand for Venables and paid seventy for Cookie. And what a buy he was! I knew what I was doing there. I knew what I was getting rid of and I knew what I was getting.'

The brilliant Inter-Cities Fairs Cup campaign of 1966, which ground to a halt with an ignominious 0-5 semi-final 'play-off' defeat in the Camp Nou to Barcelona, confirmed his thinking. Before that last match, Docherty always claimed that when he introduced Cooke to the team; Venables testily threw a football at the new boy. Cooke is supposed to have reacted with lightning speed, playing keepy-uppy, then catching the ball on his neck. 'It might in fact have happened,' said Cooke recently. 'I remember when I went on that trip. People said to me about taking Terry's place … it had never occurred to me, that's how naive I was. I was excited to be joining a big club. I had no idea whatever the cliques were or who was friendly with whom. I had no notion about the politics within the club. That may be hard to believe these days when people know everything about everybody in the club. But back then you didn't know nearly as much about what was going on.'

By the autumn a new, fluid Chelsea – the only unbeaten side in the division – topped the table with Bonetti, Ron Harris, Hinton, McCreadie, Boyle, Cooke, Houseman, Hollins, Osgood and, soon, Baldwin. Just Webb, Dempsey, Hutchinson and Hudson of the vintage 1969–70 set were missing. One event served to rob Docherty of the fun Dave Sexton was later to have playing with them. On 5 October 1966 at Blackpool, with little over half an hour gone, Osgood was challenged by left-back Emlyn Hughes and fell down with his right leg broken just above the ankle. Things went downhill from there.

One of the worst winters on record (at least in Chelsea households) had begun early. As in 1937, having just scaled it the climbers in blue fell halfway down the mountain. One league win in November and December followed. Then in January 1967 Southampton were beaten 4-1 and something clicked again. 'The wriggling, jinking Cooke … reduced the Southampton defence to confused submission,' wrote *The Times*, while 'the eager Baldwin … moved so astutely among the wreckage.'

The benefits were mostly felt in the FA Cup, though, and Chelsea reached the 1967 final only to lose to a Spurs side featuring Chelsea youth products Venables and Greaves. Yet just as Docherty looked to reap the patiently sown harvest, his own volatility began to undermine his position. In February 1967 he was severely reprimanded by the club for comments made to the media about the board of directors and was publicly warned as to his future conduct.

Things escalated in the summer. Lanky striker Tony Hateley had been bought for £100,000 in October 1966 but didn't have the expected impact, although it was his semi-final goal against Leeds that took Chelsea to that first FA Cup final. Docherty used to say that his passes were so bad they were labelled, 'To whom it may concern'.

He was soon trying to talk him up to prospective buyers, including an interested Bill Shankly. 'A hundred thousand wouldn't buy Hateley, Bill,' he told the Liverpool manager. 'Aye,' spat Shanks. 'And I'm one of the hundred thousand.' But Liverpool paid Chelsea £95,000 for Hateley in July 1967 when Osgood's recovery was certain.

That fee shed a different light on the dispute between John Hollins and the Doc that spilled over into the 1967–68 season, Docherty's last. Holly was holding out for £100 a week, whereas the Chelsea board would only stretch to £60 with or without the Hateley cash. Docherty was typically back-handed with his midfielder. 'He will never leave the club in my time,' said the manager. 'If I was a player of his ability I would ask the same, although it is doubtful whether economics would allow Chelsea to give it to him.'

Following another incident, on tour in Bermuda, when Docherty, according to the Bermudan FA, racially abused a local match official, the FA banned Docherty from the club for a month and he resigned in October 1967. For a while he looked set to take up a post at Panathinaikos but turned it down. 'I cannot go to Athens and leave my family without parental care,' he said.

Caretaker manager Ron Suart made way after a few weeks for Dave Sexton. Charlie Cooke welcomed the new man but recognised Docherty's contribution to building a team of indomitable spirit. 'Although for most of my time Dave [Sexton] was in charge,' said Cooke, 'I think a lot of it was started by Tommy Doc, his fast-talking, fast-thinking personality. And it rubbed off on the players.

'They were totally different personalities: Tommy Docherty was full of bounce, full of fun, always had a quick remark, always looking for a joke, real fun to be around. Dave was fun to be around in a different way: much more serious personality, much quieter, much more reserved. But when he started talking it was obvious that he was a deep thinker about the game.'

The end of Docherty's supremacy, followed swiftly by the club's most humiliating result at Leeds – 0-7 – prompted Chelsea's first public obituary, published in The Times's personal section of 11 October 1967: 'IN MEMORIAM. Chelsea Football Club which died 6 October 1967, after five proud and glorious years.'

13

TALES OF THE UNEXPECTED

'Dave Sexton wasn't happy in the spotlight,' says Albert Sewell of the man whose wisdom he had to tap to fill the matchday programmes every fortnight. 'He was happy with players, in the dressing rooms, but once he came out of the dressing room he found it hard work.'

Sexton was the chalk after Docherty's cheese. 'Dave was so inward, withdrawn,' says Sewell, 'and Tommy loved the media. Even now you could ring Tommy and he would talk all night. But Dave didn't have the media business. He was a brilliant coach but he was not comfortable talking to the press after games. It's the way people are, different characters. Ted Drake was the only manager to win the championship. Dave was the first Chelsea manager to win the Cup and for that, you know, they'll be indelible in the records as having done that.'

Long before his departure in the autumn of 1967, Tommy Docherty had begun the overhaul of his team, moving away from the high-energy 'concertina' style, as he called it, and bringing in masters of the more subtle arts, such as Cooke and Baldwin. As he puts it somewhat ruefully, 'They were the best crowd of players I ever had, even better than Man United. I left a great side to Dave Sexton.' On his accession, though, Sexton still saw frailties and in his first few years brought in the likes of Ian Hutchinson, David Webb,

John Dempsey. 'I got the players in that would stiffen the team up and make us better,' he says, 'and that worked out well. They were absolutely dependable players.' He also gave Alan Hudson his debut, at Southampton on 1 February 1969. Not only did the forceful, stylish midfielder almost immediately prove himself the very nearly mythical 'last piece in the jigsaw' for Chelsea, but he would come to epitomise the swagger of Swinging 60s Chelsea – its good and its bad points. In a quiet tragedy for Chelsea history, Huddy would miss the 1970 FA Cup final with a serious ankle injury. But he'd contributed as much as anyone in getting the club there and shaped up to be the closest thing Chelsea had to a Brazilian, so comfortable and influential was he on the ball.

Eddie McCreadie straddled the Docherty-Sexton changeover. 'I don't have a clear idea of which was the better team,' he said in 1996. 'They were different in many important ways. In Tommy's team, he was the general, really. The next team was severely different in terms of play and personnel. If you compare Bobby Tambling and Barry Bridges to Ian Hutchinson and Peter Osgood, people like Alan Hudson who were creative, outstanding, world class ... Bobby and Barry were obviously wonderful players, and proved it time and again. But there was something different, I always felt, about the Hudsons, the Osgoods, Charlie Cooke. These were, I felt, in a class by themselves. Ossie – I've never seen a guy of 6 foot 2 inches control the ball the way he did. He was so deft.

'So there were more individual players in the 70s team, but I personally felt that the team spirit in both sides was wonderful and, when I was on the field, there was never any question in my mind there we weren't all going for the same thing. That team spirit was the most incredible thing I experienced as a player, and through winning and having good players you went into every game not thinking about losing. And we didn't lose a lot of games for about ten years.'

One of the biggest beneficiaries of the Sexton plan was Peter Houseman. 'I have always had wingers,' says Sexton, 'and always wanted wingers and there was no problem with me and fortunately we had some good wingers there. I brought some good wingers in. He [Houseman] came to the club as a youngster so he came right from the bottom to the top.'

Sexton's memory isn't what it was, and he can't recall his mindset at the start of his tenure, but he is clear on one thing. 'I thought if we stuck to the task something would happen for us,' he says. 'I can't tell you what our positions were at the end of the season but I think if you looked them up we weren't far from the top.'

Chelsea finished sixth, fifth and third in consecutive seasons up to May 1970, when the FA Cup was secured. But the following season the improvement stopped and five years of decline ended, incredibly, in relegation in 1975.

On the hearts of supporters of a certain age is inscribed the words, 'Stoke City, 4 March 1972'. And it is written with the studs of George Eastham, the Potters' 35-year-old veteran, using the gloved hand of Gordon Banks, their legendary keeper. Chelsea did the double over the Midlands side in the league and finished way above them in the final rankings. But on the day, at a Wembley bathed in blue, despite the inspirational midfield work of Hudson and Cooke, they fell behind to their unlikely opponents, clawed back through Osgood and looked ascendant until Mulligan's injury forced a disruptive substitution. With the arrival of Baldwin and the switching of Houseman to left-back, the Blues lost their way. After Eastham tapped in Bonetti's save from Greenhoff, Banks kept Osgood's late header out and then dived at the feet of Garland after a poor touch from the otherwise uncompromising City defence. It was a mundane humbling. The old guard could not have known it then, but it would be their last proximity to major silverware, and Chelsea would not see its like for another 22 years.

There had been a bacchanalian mood at the Bridge after the cup wins of 1970 and 1971. Now unrest in the squad had started to emerge. The players showed open defiance of the manager. Although Sexton now says that, 'nothing unpleasant happened, I can't think of one unpleasant thing' that is not how the players saw it. There was intransigence on Sexton's side and childish, self-destructive behaviour from the squad. 'It's not a blame game,' says Charlie Cooke. 'I think we were all a bit churlish, immature about it. I think these days we would have been a bit better informed about what was going on in the world. The financial background was very discomfiting – you remember the ground was getting rebuilt, the team was being changed and results were pretty crappy. It was a pretty depressing time.'

Rolls-Royces were being replaced by Fords. 'Rolls-Royces,' snaps Cooke, 'that were not performing as well as they had. Let's face it, we weren't doing it as well as we had been doing it.' On one occasion the players attended a lunchtime book signing at Barbarella's, with plenty of drinks available. Dave Sexton sent two people round to collect them, recalls Dave Webb. 'Charlie and the rest had come back badly drunk – they'd drunk 30 bottles of Mateus Rosé or something – and it all went off between them and Dave. They were doing the same thing when he suspended Ossie and Huddy that time. We had to play QPR without them and I had to play centre-forward. And I said, "Can't you un-suspend them?" And he said no. He was really dogmatic on that. That was where there was a problem. If he'd been a bit more flexible that time, it wouldn't have happened, but it got too deep after that.'

Cooke now says he would have handled things differently himself. 'No question,' he insists. 'No question. That was just total stupidity. I've seen Dave many a time since. We never discuss it. It's a non-event, y'know? These things happen and they're just stupid. I'm sure Dave had no words for it. Just look at it and think that's just stupid. A lot of the guys, if we're really honest, have to say the same. A lot of the things were just a little out of control.'

'Of course,' says Albert Sewell, 'Dave couldn't cope with that side of things. That was the bust-up with Osgood and Hudson. And in the end they lost out because Dave went, didn't he? I think the club may have lost out on that.'

Things came to a head for the 70s team ahead of the New Year's Day 1974 match at Sheffield United. Osgood, Hudson and Bonetti were left out and Baldwin was named as sub. In a West Ham match previously, Hudson and Osgood were 'as elusive as last night's dream', as one observer put it. And that's how they were proving to Sexton and his assistant, Ron Suart.

After the fallout between Hudson, Osgood, Cooke and himself, it was often said that Sexton found the glamour side of Chelsea difficult, a charge he counters. 'I don't think I have ever been suspicious of glamorous or good players,' he says. 'The thing for a football manager to have is an eye for talent and there isn't anything better than that. So if you've got that you are a very lucky man.'

On the pitch though, Chelsea's luck was out.

Early March 1974 brought the dreaded chairman's vote of confidence, with Brian Mears denying Sexton had been sacked. The matter was 'not discussed' during a six-hour board meeting. 'Dave Sexton is still the manager of the club,' said Mears. 'There is no question of him being sacked or resigning. The club, from the chairman right down to the players, has one hundred per cent confidence in Dave Sexton. At today's meeting we discussed the problems that have faced the club over the last few weeks. They were both personal and internal.'

It had even been reported – incorrectly – that Sexton had left the club after a refusal to take Peter Osgood off the transfer list. Chelsea had slipped into

19th place after losing again to West Ham in March. But there had been little peace in the camp since he dropped the players for the New Year's Day game. The popular Ian Hutchinson had also been put on the transfer list and Osgood told to train alone, with Sexton's olive branch that, 'If he [Osgood] is prepared to knuckle down it may be possible to work with him again.'

By 30 September the following season, with no home league win since 16 March, 'full and frank discussions' were reported between Mears and Sexton. Elsewhere, Brian Clough had lasted just 44 days at Leeds before being sacked. When, on 3 October 1974, Sexton became football's fifth managerial casualty of the season in London, Norman Fox observed, 'Chelsea have made a forlorn start to the season and have been drawing crowds lower in number than required to make a profit and pay for the huge grandstand that the club hoped would act like a symbol of ambitious intent but is, temporarily, a lavish millstone.'

The chairman's statement was terse: 'It goes back over two years in which time we had very little success. You have to look beyond survival or a place in the middle of the table. The object is to win the championship and the board felt we had no chance of doing this.

'I admire Dave for what he has done in the past for Chelsea. Economic factors and the effect of the new stand have been blown up out of all proportion and were certainly not responsible for Dave leaving the club. The stand is no excuse for lack of success.'

Sexton accepted his fate meekly. 'I'm very sad,' he said, 'but I have no complaints. It's a blow to my pride, but it was in the best interests of the club and that's all right by me. If I had got a good result on Saturday [at home to Wolves, lost 0-1] I might still be here.' Although he denied 'player power' had ousted him he commented that, 'Everyone has got power, it's how you use it that's important.'

Webb, Osgood and Hudson had been sold; Hutchinson, Bill Garner and John Dempsey were discontented. Sexton's assistant Suart stepped in for a second time – he had held office for two weeks after Docherty's departure – declaring, 'It's going to be interesting. The players have to appreciate that results are important and we have to get good ones.'

Among those who turned down the Chelsea hot seat were 1955 legend Frank Blunstone, by then Division Two side Manchester United's youth team coach. Chelsea was seen as a basket case, with few options in its recruiting.

A 2-0 defeat at White Hart Lane was one of the final nails in Chelsea's coffin. Relegation, on top of financial difficulties and low gates, was a nightmare.

After six months, Suart's first team coach assumed control from him. Eddie McCreadie, the hardcore left-back and club captain who had retired through injury, had the tough task of ushering out the door old friends and relying on youth in cash-strapped times. Some of the youngsters – Ray 'Butch' Wilkins, Kenny Swain, John Sparrow – had been blooded by Suart. Other than the timely emergence of then £225,000 record signing David Hay as a figurehead, and the resilience of goalkeeper Peter Bonetti, McCreadie's bustling, push-and-run side would be built around Wilkins, Swain, Garry Stanley, Ian Britton, Steve Wicks, Gary Locke, Ray Lewington and Steve Finnieston.

'I was always ever so impressed by Butch Wilkins's performance,' says Cooke. 'Always loved his skills, technique and his finishing ability too. He set a great standard to all the guys around him. Unfortunately it also coincided with a time when it was very difficult to shine.'

Players' trust in McCreadie was so strong that he negotiated pay cuts with them to ease the finances. After two years in the lower reaches, McCreadie's intense motivation and focus on efficiency brought the joy of promotion in 1977. Then, as if Chelsea had not delivered enough unexpected disasters in recent years, a spat over a contract blew into an intractable row. The board blamed McCreadie's financial demands, McCreadie claimed it was contractual negotiations and he simply asked for the going rate, and posterity recorded the rumour that the whole thing came down to a company car.

'That was such nonsense,' says Albert Sewell, in the wings for another of Chelsea's great slapstick comedy moments. 'He got them promoted and then all this argument over a car or something. He stood out against them and that was the end of him. I would have loved to see what they would have done because he'd got a young team. He'd taken them up and you thought well, give it a go, what might he have been able to do with this?

'McCreadie's a complex character. Having taken them up in some style, out of a lot of young players, I thought he was entitled to see what he could do next and I think they threw it away there. It set them back again.'

At the time when a money crisis began to bring the entire future of the club into doubt; when the hugely talented Ray Wilkins might have expected careful nurturing; as crowds were plummeting; chaos was created by a succession of unconvincing managerial appointments. Poor Ken Shellito, ironically McCreadie's full-back partner of the early 1960s, found the step up from his brilliant work producing youth team graduates too great. Bizarrely, Chelsea then turned in November 1978 to former Spurs 'double' winner, contemplative *Sunday Express* journalist and Northern Ireland manager, 52-year-old Danny Blanchflower. 'He was bewildering,' remembers Albert Sewell. 'I don't think the players knew what he was on about half the time, in tactical stuff. A brilliant player and a brilliant tactician as a player, but I think he felt all the players should have been on his intellectual level, which they weren't by any means, and I was often convinced they didn't know what he was trying to do. He never really produced anything, did he?'

Wilkins, unsupported, was no longer the driving force he had been and was suffering under the stress. He had even been prescribed Valium.

Two wins from the first 22 league games – including 2-7 and 1-5 defeats away to Boro and Ipswich respectively – set up Chelsea's worst ever Division One performance – bottom of the table with just 20 points from 42 games and relegation for the second time in four years.

A month before the season had ended, Blanchflower pulled Wilkins to one side and told him he'd recommended him to be sold. In the summer Chelsea's golden boy was transferred to Manchester United, and Sexton, for £825,000.

In September 1979, in a hail of publicity, if not credibility, the board appointed the inexperienced boss Geoff Hurst, and his assistant Bobby Gould. Their start was superb: ten wins in 12 in the autumn of 1979, and despite a mixed follow-up, the Blues missed out on promotion on goal difference alone. Top at Christmas again in 1980, then came the horror: one win in 13 at the end of the 1980–81 season. Goalless in 16 of the last 20 games to the end of the season. An acrimonious sacking followed, 16 days after Mears had publicly asked that Hurst honour the final year of his three-year contract and a week before Dave Sexton was sacked by Manchester United for not providing entertaining football.

Who next? For the next few games, Chelsea were managerless. Tommy Docherty was even linked with an unlikely comeback. Then came 'one of the best managers', according to Ken Bates, who soon 'inherited' him. John Neal had overturned the dour legacy of Jack Charlton at Middlesbrough, and quit after a boardroom row there. Neal's unpromising start to his career at the Bridge, including a preposterous 6-0 defeat at the hands of mighty

Rotherham and culminating in a last-gasp avoidance of relegation to the Third Division in 1983, evolved into the brightest period at Chelsea for years.

'Without a doubt John Neal's greatest asset was that he could pick a good player,' says Nigel Spackman, perhaps including himself, a £40,000 signing from Bournemouth in June 1982, in that observation. 'You look at the players he signed in very difficult times, with little money, though backed by Ken Bates, and I bet if you examined them he didn't make a bad signing for the club: Eddie [Niedzwiecki, from Wrexham], big Joe [McLaughlin, Greenock Morton], Pat [Nevin, Clyde], Joey Jones, Speedo [David Speedie, Darlington], Mickey T [Thomas]. I think in today's market that's several million spent that they got on a shoestring. Except Kerry, who was another shrewd buy. John knew the way he wanted to play and he knew they were people who could do it for him.

'He also had the bottle to get rid of older players who had been around for years and years who he thought were dead wood. He wasn't a coach, he wasn't a talker, not a ranter and raver. But he had his way of doing things that was successful for him and it was successful for the club too. Ian McNeill was a great scout for him. John Hollins had come in as player-coach and was a great coach, and as a senior professional he was a great example to all the players John and Ian had brought together. Holly's sessions were always enjoyable and varied. Training was bright and competitive, whether it was sprints or ballwork, and we were happy doing it.'

The David Speedie-Kerry Dixon-Pat Nevin partnership, irresistible from 1983 to 1986, was assembled by McNeill and Neal for a total £350,000 and is remembered as one of the most effective attacks in the Bridge's history. With Nevin, the trickiest winger since the beloved Charlie Cooke, finding the goalscorers in the centre with intuitive accuracy, it was a case of two's company, three's a crowd-pleaser.

'Pat was sensational,' recalled Dixon, 'and gave the Chelsea fans something to marvel at. I admired what he did and remember him showboating in the 4-0 defeat of Newcastle. He beat five or six men from the halfway line, but the infuriating thing for me was he didn't cross it, he went back and beat them again, then crossed it.'

But this was not a mutual appreciation society. Like Abbot and Costello and other entertainment partnerships, hostility lurked beneath. Nevin was a left-wing, indie music-loving reader of depressing Russian literature who'd publicly attacked the Chelsea fans he loved for their abuse of Paul

Canoville. David Speedie wasn't. 'We hated each other,' laughs Nevin of his Scotland international team-mate. 'Absolutely despised each other. He was really volatile and I was very different – really quite laid back. But I didn't like his methods of trying to be in control of me and my play. And I knew why he was doing it, because he wanted the ball as often as possible – he wanted the ball more than Kerry!

'It went on for a long time, but what made it particularly difficult was that my understanding with David was probably better than with any other player in my life.'

The two finally settled on civil terms after the Scotland management put the two Chelsea boys together as room-mates. 'Well, we sat and we talked,' says Nevin. 'And we got to know where each other was coming from. And we finally clicked.'

The tension between Dixon and Speedie was no less acute. Colin Lee had been Speedo's strike partner before Dixon and he retained his place alongside Dixon with Speedie sniping from the bench until October 1983. The unresolved issue erupted in a post-match fight at the Bridge following a 1-0 defeat by Manchester City two months later in which both Speedie and Dixon missed good chances.

'I think you should always be able to air your views to your friends,' Dixon said later. 'If it came to blows so be it. I've always been like that and we haven't looked back since. Everyone knew Speedo had a short fuse, but people were all too quick to talk about that side of his game rather than the rest. He was superb at holding the ball up, was very aggressive and always let the centre-halves know he was about. He would put an elbow in or leave a foot in, which wasn't really my style. I was pacier than him and could get on the end of his flicks, so we complemented each other.'

In the seasons 1983–84, 1984–85 and 1985–86 the deliciously complementary trio produced 61, 59 and 57 goals between them. Dixon top-scored with 34 and 36 in all competitions in 1984 and 1985, putting him fourth and fifth in Chelsea's all-time returns in a season. The 1984 promotion campaign featured some of the least restrained and most flowing, attacking football for a generation. Few will forget the visit to Highbury for the first match back in Division One, when Dixon earned a draw and bragging rights for the rejuvenated Blues. Consecutive sixth-place finishes in the top tier confirmed the renaissance under new chairman Ken Bates.

But a heart problem eventually pushed John Neal upstairs as a director and his vital former coach John Hollins lost his way as the short-lived managerial replacement – a situation that pained those who had adored the leather-lunged midfielder as a player.

The trio of Dixon/Nevin/Speedie had been disgruntled and then dismembered. With Bobby Campbell installed as manager, Middlesbrough suddenly cropped up again, like the gatecrasher at your party that ends up headbutting your girlfriend. That's how it felt when, as a Second Division club Chelsea fans had all but forgotten about, they climbed through a hatch into the First Division relegation play-offs. Introduced in 1986–87, the short-lined system pitted the best (beneath the promoted sides) of the second tier against the least worst (above those relegated) of the First Division, with the winner gaining or retaining top-flight status. In 1988 that was the maelstrom Chelsea fell into after a freak goal from Charlton's Paul Miller had equalised the Gordon Durie penalty that would have condemned the Robins in the last match of the season.

Having impressed beating Blackburn 6-1 on aggregate in the first play-off, the old frailty returned at Ayresome Park. In front of 40,000 at the Bridge, Durie's spot-kick gave hope of turning round Middlesbrough's two-goal first-leg advantage, but the team that had finished six places below held out as Chelsea won 1-0 and were relegated for the sixth and last time.

Although Ken Bates can say that 'relegation was a blessing in disguise in retrospect' it still doesn't feel that way. The throwback crowd trouble at the second leg didn't help. 'We found out then who our friends were,' Bates maintains. 'All the fair-weather friends, all the corporates ... I'll give you one little story. One guy, he'd done a deal for years, he used to get 20 tickets and he used to paint all the dressing rooms and Bobby Campbell said, "We don't need this, an apprentice can do that."

'In those days they could, you see. And the guy went completely bloody apeshit. Well he'd been flogging the tickets for years. Next year he bought two! So much for loyalty.

'And then, of course, Bobby Campbell came in and said, "I want Dennis Wise and Andy Townsend," and we got them. We got Roberts, we got Nicholas, and that was the start of it.'

Having regained top-flight status at the first attempt in 1988–89 with a massive points haul, Campbell found it difficult to harness the undoubted

Above The Chelsea staff 1905–06: back row (left to right) J.T. Robertson (secretary-manager), H.A. 'Gus' Mears (director), Byrne, Frederick Parker (honorary financial secretary), McRoberts, Foulke, Copeland, Mackie, J. Miller (trainer), McEwan, Harry Ransom (trainer), Craigie, William Lewis (secretary), Jack White (assistant trainer); middle row Moran, Donaghy, T. Miller, J. Robertson, O'Hara, Windridge, Key, Kirwan; front row Dowland, Slater, Wolff, Watson. (Above right) The club's first chairman (1905–35), W. Claude Kirby.

An early tussle with Sheffield Wednesday (1908) as the Pensioners found their feet.

Above The stadium was a great community resource, used for all kinds of fund-raising and sports day events. (Above right) Outside the main gate 15 minutes before kick-off on a matchday in 1913. Police keep the crowds back while VIPs are dropped off in cabs.

From rolling down to the front to 'Roll yer sleeves up sonny.' After the bad days of the late 1960s to the mid-1980s, the crowd at Stamford Bridge has mostly returned to its friendly state of the 1950s.

Dynamic Lawton Big new signing Tommy gives the Russians a taste of English muscle, while an estimated 100,000 fans perch like starlings all around the Stamford Bridge stadium to catch a glimpse of the exotic Muscovite visitors.

In those days they did drink the champagne: Mickey Thomas, Kerry Dixon, Pat Nevin and John Hollins lead the dressing room promotion party at Grimsby in 1984. The suspended Joey Jones keeps his tattoos under wraps.

Something you won't find in the Mourinho methodology. This scene from the pioneering 1930 football film *The Great Game* shows Jack Cock (suited) in conversation with his manager and his trainer. Andy Wilson is among the Chelsea players pedalling imaginary upside-down bicycles in front of the old East Stand at the Bridge.

Take your pick, girls The King's Road swingers fly out of Heathrow for Salonika in Greece during the 1971 European Cup-Winners' Cup campaign. Marvin Hinton looks like he's just stepped out of a bookies, but so far only suave Alan Hudson looks like he's managed to hit the Duty Frees.

Right 'We can shine, all the time.' The Chelsea squad reached number five in the UK chart with 'Blue is the Colour' (Penny Farthing Records) in 1972. None of them has had a pop hit since.

Below Best in the world? Home-grown John Terry was voted PFA Player of the Year 2005. He is already Chelsea's most successful skipper, having won the Carling Cup as well as the League Championship.

Right The day Raquel got into Ossie's shorts: Chelsea fan Miss Welch shows half-decent technique on the set of the Western film *Hannie Caulder* in Spain, 1971. 'Tell them,' she said, 'Osgood is not forgotten on the plains of Almeria.' Class.

'Twenty stone of lusty manhood' How the *Guardian* greeted the sight of Willie Foulke at Edgeley Park in September 1905, Chelsea's first league match. He's the one in the middle of this early team photo, by the way.

Above Gallacher goes for it: Chelsea can boast a list of centre-forwards equal to any club's, and 'Wembley Wizard' Hughie Gallacher is right up there with the very best alongside youth product Jimmy Greaves (above right).

Right Charlie Cooke, Wizard of the dribble, in mesmerising form, sailing past future team-mate Steve Kember, whose arrival in 1971 heralded a change of policy at the club – from maestros to triers.

Below Chelsea's prodigal son: youthful skipper Wilkins was a Ray of hope in the poor mid-1970s sides, but lost his way and went to Manchester United in 1979. He returned to serve Chelsea on the coaching staff under manager Gianluca Vialli.

Above right Gianfranco Zola was voted the greatest Chelsea player of all time by Blues fans in 2003. 'As extraordinary a person off the field as he was a footballer on it.'

Above In January 1939, before the Pensioners met Arsenal in the FA Cup, Mr Rogers, proprietor of Harry's Dining Room on Chalk Farm Road, Camden, felt confident enough to put a sign up offering free meals when Chelsea won the Cup. They beat the Gunners 2-1 with goals from Jimmy Argue, but his offer went unclaimed for another 31 and a half years. They were still laughing at Chelsea in 1985 when Ken Bates (right) erected an electric fence as an anti-hooligan measure. It was never powered up.

Above Liverpudlian Fred Hanley became probably Chelsea's first black professional when he signed in 1938. He never played a first-team league game. Legendary Olympic footballer Nils Middelboe (right) was one of the first overseas players to make his mark in the Football League. He was with Chelsea from 1913 to 1921 and maintained a lifelong connection with the club even after returning to Denmark.

talents in the squad. A stunningly poor brace of semi-finals against Second Division Sheffield Wednesday in the 1990–91 League Cup hinted at deep-rooted problems, and Campbell was moved upstairs at the end of the season.

Another defeat to Boro, in the FA Cup in 1993, precipitated the removal of Campbell's successor, Ian Porterfield. Nigel Spackman, back at Chelsea in 1992 after spells with Liverpool and Rangers, had already spotted the danger signs. 'To come back after being at two big clubs that played in Europe,' he says, 'it was a bit of a shock how little they'd developed. By that I mean the club as a whole, the squad ... it had gone backwards.

'It was like a ship without a rudder. From the club which I had left [in 1987], which was a big one, competing, one of the top eight teams, I think they'd lost their focus and the lunatics were running the asylum. There's no doubt they had some good players, but you wondered who was running the team – the players or the manager?'

As managing director of the football club, Colin Hutchinson was also concerned about the status of the club generally. 'The thing that made me think that it's time we did something different,' he recalls, 'was the fact that after they got Porterfield [as manager], he and Ken Bates went to meet a player called Darryl Wassell, who was at Nottingham Forest, a defender. I'm sure it was Darryl. And Chelsea could not even attract him. He went somewhere else.'

Hutchinson considered Porterfield part of the problem and a drastic solution was needed. 'We were hovering very near relegation and David Webb came in,' he says, 'purely employed to do it for three months and he got the desired result by keeping us up.'

Webb, formerly boss of Southend, and trading in all sorts of goods, including mountain bikes, at the time, took over from Porterfield in February 1993. Spackman noticed an immediate change. 'When Dave Webb came in he took me to one side and said, "What's going on?"' says the former midfielder. 'I told him I was injured and he said, "Not you, the team. What's actually happening? Why are things going this way?"

'I told him what I thought was going on, as did others.' Spackman's concerns were that the dressing room had become unmanageable and cliquey. 'Webby's a really smart guy,' says Spackman. 'It didn't take long for him to sort it out. I think he did a great job. He really saved Chelsea from being relegated, which would been an utter disaster for the football club.'

'And then we obviously had to decide who we should bring in as the next manager,' says Hutchinson. 'My suggestion was Glenn Hoddle. I felt it was time to maybe go for a slightly more modernistic approach, because we'd tried it the other way. And I remember Ken saying to me ... now what was the expression? "I'm not sure he's strong enough."'

Bates relented and Hutchinson prevailed.

'The thing that really impressed me with him,' reveals Hutchinson, 'was the night I went over to his home in Ascot to sign the contract. His agent rang me up and said, "Can you delay it half an hour, he's been held up." So I did that and afterwards I realised that two directors from Tottenham had been there talking to him about the job there, and because the day before he'd given his word to me that he would come to Chelsea, he'd kept his word.'

Chelsea's era of the player-manager began with Hoddle, the first since J.T. Robertson nearly 90 years earlier. It was a symbolic rebirth. Again, Spackman, as a senior player, noticed an improvement of sorts. 'Little by little,' he says, 'he started what he wanted to do. What impressed me was that he had a formula, he knew how he wanted to play. He found it difficult, but then if you don't have the money to spend or the players at the time, you have to change the mentality to play more football, and it takes time to change. And that's what Glenn struggled with.

'Chelsea had been used to a rigid 4-4-2. He wanted to try 3-5-2. He had to change to a diamond midfield. Then, gradually, he was able to bring in Dan Petrescu, who was great for the system, Clarkey at centre-back or wing-back, where he was great, Terry Phelan did well, then of course, Ruud, Mark Hughes – quality players. It was a long hard road, setting Chelsea off to where they are today.'

A turning point was Christmas 1993, when Hoddle's Chelsea were floundering in the bottom three, with a visit to fellow strugglers Southampton. Striker Mark Stein was finding it difficult to reproduce his prolific scoring rate after arriving at the Bridge from Stoke for £1.5 million, and the pressure was on Hoddle. Things looked better at half-time with the score 1-1 thanks to a goal from Stein. But Chelsea lost 3-1 at the end. After the match a furious Dennis Wise overtook the team talk to berate his team-mates. It led to tension between the captain and his manager ever after lingering.

Hutchinson felt a show of support was in order. 'Ken was away for his usual Christmas break and I was on the way home and I rang Glenn to say,

"Don't worry, it's going to be all right, even if we're relegated you will still have your job.'"

But something had shifted and Mark Stein scored the only goal of the 1-0 win over Newcastle the following day, and went on a record run of nine goals in consecutive games. Gradually the FA Cup opened up to Chelsea, leading to a 4-0 defeat by Manchester United in the final, but, vitally, proper European football for the first time in 22 years.

There was a delightful Wembley moment in 1994, though it was not in the final. Sailing towards Bobby Tambling's all-time record of 202 goals, Kerry Dixon had suddenly found himself becalmed, ending his career nine short on 193. When he lined up as a Luton player in the semi-final, staged that year at the national stadium, he was serenaded by Blues fans – a fantastic moment for both parties.

Meanwhile Glenn Hoddle was helping take Chelsea out of the Edwardian era and into the new world of football, with Sky TV, separate newspaper pullouts, Fantasy Football and a new glamour. The training may not have been overly taxing, but the football was shaping up as the best seen at the Bridge for years. It just needed more players of a higher quality.

The most vital meeting in Chelsea history for 90 years then took place, the so-called Marriott Accord of 21 May 1995, at the Marriott Hotel, Langley, near Heathrow. 'There was Ken Bates, Matthew Harding, Glenn and myself,' relates Colin Hutchinson, 'and the major thing we talked about was the fact that Ruud Gullit was available. Glenn and I had already been out to Milan and met him.

'So we sat down to go through the philosophy of that and what it might do to the image and what it might achieve on starting to make Chelsea a bit better known Europe-wise. From that meeting it was decided that we should try and go out and get him and Paul Gascoigne. Well, obviously there was a deep intake of breath when I said what I believed it would cost. I mean, who was writing the cheques I think is confidential information. I did say we would never know for sure what the cost would be but if Matthew hadn't been around I'm not sure we would have embarked on that.

'The other thing that has to be recognised is the fact that we had Gullit who was a great magnet in attracting other players.' Who wouldn't want to play with Ruud Gullit?

Gazza was never considered a likely signing. 'We went to meet him in Rome,' says Hutchinson, 'the day before we went to see Gullit for the second time, and he listened to what Glenn had to say about football, he was his usual jocular self. I asked him directions to the toilet and realised I was about to walk into the kitchen. He was fine but it was always very clear to us that while he was joking and he was polite it was really sorted that he was going to Glasgow Rangers.'

But the Accord worked a dream. Apart from Gullit, Mark Hughes and Dan Petrescu arrived as a direct result of the Marriott Accord.

'I was the driving force,' says Hutchinson, then managing director, 'because I could see that football was changing dramatically. At that stage I didn't know how dramatic it would be with Bosman. With European competition, we'd had the taste of it and it was obvious that at that stage we were on the level of Crystal Palace and Queens Park Rangers. The ground was now secure, Matthew was now around, we were getting things together, we would probably never have that opportunity again and we had to grab it with both hands or really accept that we were going to be just a middle of the road club – *hoping* that we would stay in the Premier League, *hoping* that we might have the occasional cup run, but not really having any ambitions above that. Or we had the opportunity of trying to break in to that world.

'The press couldn't believe it. The day we launched Gullit all the press sat down to lunch and I went ... because I heard it was going to leak that we were in for Mark Hughes. We'd already basically agreed a deal, and I went to speak to Martin Edwards and said, "It's going to break, we've got a press conference on now with Gullit, can I put it out?" And he said yes so I went back and said ... "I've got a bit more news for you."'

Gullit, another player-manager, would become Chelsea's first democratically elected boss. The voting took place during the last match before Glenn Hoddle took over the England national team, at home to Blackburn on 5 May 1996. The electorate was the fans. And the voting format was in song. The chairman was told what to do with his widely reported favourite, 'You can stick George Graham up yer arse!' sang three sides of Stamford Bridge. And the people's choice was named, 'Rudi! Rudi!'

Gullit wisely chose youth team manager Graham Rix as his assistant.

Hutchinson's role now encompassed much of what a modern 'sporting director' does, especially in the area of finding players, which he performed expertly. But he was aware that Gullit was a novice and might need a day-to-day mentor. 'When Glenn said he was going,' reveals Hutchinson, 'I spoke to

Rudi and explained about a "dream ticket" with Sven Goran Eriksson and he was all up for that. I had various conversations with Sven and he thought about it. I would think the sort of money we were able to offer in those days wasn't a big incentive to him. In those days, you know, managers were very poorly paid compared to players.

'We never got so far as to how the nitty-gritty would work with him and Ruud but I think, knowing Sven and his background, he would basically also only have been a coach. Basically he comes from a background of working with sporting directors.

'So he decided to stay in Italy [with Gullit's former club Sampdoria] and we gave Ruud the job himself, but again really only as a coach. All the identifying of what players we wanted, asking him whether he wanted them, and if he said yes, going and trying to get them. Occasionally he would come up with a player he wanted checking out, same with Luca, but in the main it was the other way, pushing the players at them.'

The platform was laid and in 1997 Chelsea and Boro's paths crossed again and this time under utterly different circumstances – at Wembley in the FA Cup final. The north-easterners, having failed to field a team through illnesses in the winter, were facing a points deduction and relegation. Chelsea, with the almighty Gianfranco Zola having already proved his worth with moments of awesome skill, were in their pomp. When he had nutmegged Julian Dicks twice, then scored, in December 1996, team-mate Sparky Hughes suggested Zola had left the sprawling West Ham defender with 'twisted blood'. One of Zola's most sublime moments was against Wimbledon in the triumphant 1997 FA Cup semi-final at Highbury, when he picked up Di Matteo's deft pass in midfield, almost dislocated Dean Blackwell's hips with a disarming sideways flick and curled a stinger into the net from 25 yards.

Like striker Hughes and the iconic Gullit, there was a touch of the History Man about the elegant Italian Roberto Di Matteo, who arrived in July 1996 for just under £5 million, a sizeable wedge for Chelsea at the time. 'I'm very excited,' he conceded before only his second major final, 'because everybody is talking about this game, excited about it. I like the big stage. To play in front of 70 or 80,000 people is a great moment.'

Three days later he showed he was the man for the big occasion too, picking up the Man of the Match award, having scored that wicked dipping

25-yarder on a mere 43 seconds. Only he, Steve Clarke and Dennis Wise of the Chelsea boys had even touched the ball. 'I thought to myself maybe I will shoot,' he nonchalantly told the press corps assembled in the tunnel after the match. 'So I did. I was very lucky because when I hit the ball it went first up and then down behind the goalkeeper.'

On a hot and humid afternoon, the Middlesbrough players gave him so much space it was an invitation to unleash a typical long-ranger. 'Maybe they didn't think I would shoot,' he grinned. He had never heard of the previous fastest goalscorer in an FA Cup final, 'Wor' Jackie Milburn.

'So I am in history?'

'Yes – how does that feel?'

A pause. 'Not too bad.'

In the stand was his blind 23-year-old sister. Their father was next to her, describing the action, but Di Matteo felt he wouldn't have needed to spell out what big brother had done. 'I think she would have heard the Chelsea supporters for herself,' he said. Even Bryan Robson was impressed. 'Well, you look at something like that and you wonder, "Well, is it going to be our day?" But it was a great goal.'

Home-grown midfielder Eddie Newton scored the second from a delightful Zola flick. It was deliverance for him from the nightmare of the 1994 final, when Manchester United had been marginally outplayed in the first half but, thanks to spot-kicks conceded by himself and best mate Frank Sinclair, ended up runaway 4-0 winners. 'Let me tell you all about last time,' said Newton. 'Last time was the worst moment in my life, especially with Frank's penalty as well. I've put away the memories of giving away the penalty in 1994. I'd put them away anyway, I'm a strong character, but for me now, this is even better: I've sealed it, they're never getting out again. I've scored a goal in the FA Cup final. That's it.'

Even though the opposition at Wembley in 1997 were threatened with relegation, defeat in the 1994 final and in the semi-final in 1996, also against Manchester United, meant that among the supporters, at least, confidence was not overflowing. Tony Banks often said that football is the only form of paid entertainment where, as soon as your team goes ahead, you want it to finish as soon as possible.

'All I knew was in 1997 it was the be-all and end-all really,' says Karim Kassam, whose Chelsea-loving cousin took him under his wing in the mid-

1960s when he arrived from Kinshasa, Zaire (now Congo) – birthplace of Claude Makelele. 'My expectation was different from the 1970s finals. My attitude was probably different. But when we got to 97, I mean, it was the FA Cup, I really felt that it was a redemption moment. Had what's happened to us since not happened, I would have gone to my grave relatively happy having won the FA Cup in 1997. Now I think everybody who was there, who went on and on with those celebrations after the match, would probably say the same thing.'

At the final whistle lifelong fan and Chelsea masseur Terry Byrne turned to manager Ruud Gullit and said, 'You don't really realise what it means to Chelsea fans to win a trophy.'

Gullit admitted, 'No, I don't think so.'

'I'm just happy as a person,' Gullit said, having gathered his thoughts for the press conference, 'happy as a coach also, and happy for the fans and all the people that helped me, for our chairman Mr Bates, and, of course, Matthew Harding who passed away. I think we did it also for him. It's great. It's like a dream come true. I think that every cup is important to win. I think this cup is as important to me as the first cup I won in Barcelona with Milan for the Champions League.'

It was the first proof that under proper management on and off the field the good times had returned to Stamford Bridge. 'It was a new sensation, a new feeling for me,' says Rix. 'I'd never worked with senior players at that level before. Me and Rudi had never worked together before. So everything was new. And to be fair, I think it took me and Rudi two months, three months, to suss out what we could do, what we couldn't do and what was expected of us and the players. I think certainly towards the end of the season, we were very much together, very much. I thoroughly enjoyed it anyway, but winning the Cup was the icing on the cake.'

Steve Clarke graduated from being Gullit's team-mate in 1995 to his assistant manager at Newcastle in 1998. 'When he came into the side, along with Mark Hughes, he was one of the first big steps forward,' he says, 'bringing in class players to make the club better. As a player he had a great presence: a great athlete, very strong, dominating. Arrogant, if you like, but in a good way, because all the good players are arrogant.'

Yet as a manager that arrogance sometimes made him appear aloof and not bothered with detail. Clarke thinks that impression was deceiving.

'He was always more concerned about his own group,' he says. 'He didn't bother too much about the opposition. His philosophy was that if we had the ball then the opposition could do what they liked because they would be chasing it. And when he took over as manager, it worked well because we had a good team. He got some good players in, we played very good football at that time; maybe a little too pure – we didn't really have that nasty side where we could close up a game and win without playing very well. If we played well, we won; if we didn't quite hit it off on the day then we normally got beat. That wasn't great but it made us a cup team, which was why we won the FA Cup. We had a team which could produce against anybody on our day. Ruud was a good man.'

As a man who trod his own path, Gullit looked increasingly isolated when his judgment on team selections and substitutions went awry in January 1998. In the press conference at Goodison Park after a dispiriting 3-1 defeat to Everton, Gullit's eyes betrayed the signs that he was losing his grip on the team. There were rumours that Ken Bates had tried several times, unsuccessfully, to arrange a dinner and a chat. There was undoubtedly concern that the management contract, which appeared a formality eight months earlier when the cup had been won, was stalling on money – 'netto' entering the English language as Gullit's huge tax-free opening demands were publicised – as well as his insistence on retaining a playing contract. Gullit claims he was merely setting out a negotiating position, but the board lost patience.

At Everton he had omitted Wise and Zola completely and brought himself on as a late and ineffectual sub. 'He needed help,' observes Clarke, 'and he needed time. He wasn't given either. He'd been taken from Ruud the player – because of the demands of the crowd really – and been made Ruud the manager. He didn't ask for the job, he didn't really want the job, but he took it because it was there and he thought it was a logical step in his career. And everything went OK for him to start with. He got a few players in and the team responded and then, as happens with all managers, the players got upset and started having a snipe at the manager and not quite doing what they should be doing. And he just didn't have the experience to deal with it.'

Almost out of the blue, Chelsea sacked Gullit and installed Gianluca Vialli. He was yet another inexperienced player-manager, the third in a row. 'It was important, because the ball was rolling, that we didn't do something that disrupted things so we appointed someone from within,' explains Hutchinson. 'And the fact that first Rudi and then Luca came in meant we weren't taking one step forward and five back. If you bring somebody in from the outside they want to get rid of half your players, bring new players in and we could not have kept the momentum going. We'll never know if a lack of experience cost us winning the league. But we didn't do bad. We qualified for the Champions League.'

'I think it was a fantastic transition,' says fan Andy Jacobs, 'from Glenn Hoddle coming in and taking over this moribund club where we all got off on Vinnie Jones. And here's Hoddle, a man who has his critics, but I think he did a great job for Chelsea. It's not an original observation, but he changed the way we thought about the club. He changed the way the club thought about itself and so we had that period from the 1994 FA Cup final, which was incredibly disappointing, we get to the final in 1997, we've got a fantastic team, we've got Ruud Gullit as the manager. That was a great side. That side should have gone on to win the championship in 1999. It should have done.'

Vialli's early period as manager was also great. He toasted his new role with champagne before the inspired demolition of Arsenal at the Bridge in the League Cup semi-final, a competition his team was to win, tediously enough, against Middlesbrough in 1998. The successful European Cup-Winners' Cup campaign, concluded a few months later, was extraordinary. And, of course, he brought the Super Cup to Chelsea for the first time later the same year after beating Real Madrid in Monaco.

But the fissures of the Gullit era, like the incredible talent in the dressing room, were taken, untouched, into the popular Italian's reign. It is strange to consider that there was friction between Gullit and Vialli, where Vialli did not feel he was treated correctly, and yet the same thing seemed to happen with Zola, Di Matteo and Leboeuf. In truth Vialli found handling the players – especially some of the well-known internationals – awkward and trying. In return some people at the club found him difficult to deal with.

Inexperience at dealing with the pressures of the job may have been at the heart of such problems, and was possibly the decisive factor in why the brilliant league challenges became near misses. In particular 1998–99's, when a painful loss at home to West Ham was followed shortly by three damaging draws with Boro, Leicester and Sheffield Wednesday.

Hoddle, Gullit and Vialli were fine players with many medals, but none of them held diplomas in man-management. None of them had a senior figure to advise and support them. 'It is only in the last, say, six or seven years that Chelsea were ever in a position to go after the big names,' says Hutchinson, 'and particularly in the English market. We've been criticised for not signing enough British players throughout.

'One of the problems we had with our Accord masterplan was that if a top English player became available, we were well down the queue of clubs that he might select to go to. It would be Manchester United, Liverpool, Arsenal and so on. And the other thing was that we didn't have the capital to invest in the 24- and 25-year-olds, whether they were British or from abroad.'

In April 2000 one such possibility arose. 'We had an opportunity on van Nistelrooy,' says Hutchinson. 'We were in the ring at the same time as Manchester United.' This was when Nistelrooy failed the United medical. 'It wasn't a major injury and he was out of action and we got permission to talk to him. We had permission through his agent and PSV to see whether he would like to come to us and we had a fair idea of what the fee might be.' For whatever reason, Vialli chose not to pursue Chelsea's interest in the then 23-year-old goalscorer. Other near things over the years included Latin stars Marcelo Salas and Gabriel Batistuta.

Even though Vialli's team managed to win a dull 2000 FA Cup final against Villa 1-0, it could not conceal the need for fresh blood. Vialli made his requirements clear immediately after the match, the last played at the old Wembley. 'Luca pulled Tore Andre Flo and Zola to one side,' reveals Hutchinson, 'and said that if he could move them on and get somebody better in the summer he wanted to do that. It was the morning after. And during the summer he was on holiday in Sardinia and Zola was at his place there and because relations were a bit strained between the two of them I had to go out there on a peace mission. Fortunately, everybody was grown up about it – I think! – and I resolved the situation.

'Most of the managers, if they had problems with players, they sent them to me so they didn't fall out with them and have problems in the relationships. Over the years, some of them have been cowards, but that is another story.'

At the last home match of the previous season, chairman Bates appeared to make a statement by escorting Vialli round the pitch on a lap of appreciation, his arm around the Italian's shoulder. It was a symbolic gesture of support for a manager said to be having difficulties.

The 2-0 Charity Shield win over Man Utd brought a stay of execution. But morale was low. By mid-September, having won just a single match in the opening five and with his team lying ninth, Vialli was sacked. It was, said Bates, the 'most difficult and distressing' of many dismissals. Vialli publicly blamed an unnamed, scheming 'Mr Nice Guy', as yet unidentified, for his downfall.

When Vialli's brief golden age came to an abrupt end, the Marriott Accord died with it. Graham Rix assumed temporary control, but Hutchinson knew a clean break with the recent past was needed. He soon recruited the Italian Claudio Ranieri, late of troubled Atlético Madrid, where he resigned before the club was relegated in 2000, and Valencia, where he was fondly remembered as the man who had built the Mestalla's great team of 1997–2001 for Hector Cuper. He had won national cups in Italy with Fiorentina and in Spain with Valencia. 'I brought him in,' says Hutchinson, 'because he was experienced and it was also obvious that a lot of the players were getting older together and some changes had to be made. It was really time for rebuilding. He was a coach with experience of team-building. He is a great person. Once he got grips with English his charm came through.'

Hutchinson had proclaimed at the time, to some derision in the British press, that Chelsea was 'a continental club, playing in England'. It was actually an observation that could stand for any decade since 1905. The trick would have been to convert the club's celebrated cosmopolitanism into a title win for the first time in more than four decades.

'We'd had league aspirations, without saying it publicly, with the players we'd assembled, certainly towards the end of Ruud's era and in Luca's spell, and it hadn't quite happened,' acknowledges Hutchinson. 'We knew after Luca went that there was going to have to be a short period of treading water while the squad was rebuilt. I don't think there was any question about that – any fair-minded supporter would've accepted that as well. In fairness to Ranieri, in his last season, despite immense pressure, he came very close.'

Having been the architect of the 'continental' player-manager era at Chelsea, Hutchinson left Chelsea in May 2002 to join the Proactive agency as a consultant. 'I went to Chelsea in 1987 and a year later the club was relegated,' he reflects. 'I thought I was a jinx. I look back on the 15 years with pride. I would've liked to have won the title while I was there but it wasn't to be. But if I reflect on the position we started from and where we got to in basically a decade from when we started the Marriott Accord, then there is some satisfaction. In football you can never be complacent. One of the great things is no matter how much success you have in a season you should always try and put that little bit more into the team for the following season. That's why I've always been opposed to PLCs – the philosophy of a football club is that the profits you make should be ploughed back in.'

Hutchinson remains a football man and a Chelsea follower. He keeps in touch with several old players, including Zola, Jimmy Floyd Hasselbaink and Boudewijn Zenden, who contributed to the foundations that were in place when Roman Abramovich arrived. He smiles broadly and sincerely when the 2005 title win is mentioned. 'I saw the Bolton match,' he beams. 'I was absolutely delighted for them.'

He recognised that the three-part harmony of board, players and manager, something he strove for during all his ups and downs at the Bridge, had produced that ultimate, longed-for conclusion.

EMPIRE BUILDING

Playing **abroad**,
1929 to 2005

14
SOUTH AMERICAN WAY

In keeping with its Bohemian neighbours, Chelsea never lacked a taste for exploring exotic, faraway locations. A club established by wealthy entrepreneurs would always enjoy its jollies.

Even in May 1906, at the end of the club's very first season, a tour was undertaken of Denmark, Vienna and Budapest – 'fin de siècle' Danube was simply the place to be, darling. Copenhagen were trounced 6-2, while on 22 May 1906 the illustrious Hungarian league winners Ferencváros were beaten 3-1. They played three matches in the Austrian capital, overcoming Cricket Vienna (now Austria Wien) 3-1, First Vienna 3-0 and a Wiener [Sport-Club] XI by a whopping 6-0.

It must have set the next hundred years of jaunts up superbly.

However, not all jaunts were successful. One thinks of Chelsea arriving in Mozambique for two games in May 1969 – three months after the Portuguese secret service had assassinated Frelimo rebel leader Eduardo Mondlane with a bomb disguised as a book. Nice. Or El Salvador in 1971, when a civil war raged, Honduras had been engaged in conflict and shots were fired outside the team hotel. Then there was the little jolly to Baghdad to play the Iraqi national team, a celebration courtesy of Chelsea's first shirt sponsors Gulf Air, in March 1986. That's right, in the middle of the Iran-Iraq war.

It doesn't rank in Pat Nevin's top five getaway-from-it-all locations. 'It was a nightmare,' he remembers, 'quite a strain, to be honest. I would write these Hunter S. Thompson-esque letters to people. John [Millar] and I were followed in Baghdad because we went for a walk around the bazaar and got lost.' Nevin sought solace in his books – a dangerous occupation there in other times. It puts certain people's jibes about Chelsea always fearing visits to the grim north into perspective.

No trip, though, has the aura of adventure, of romance, of aspiration quite like Chelsea's massive tour of South America in 1929. Over three months, pretty much the entire close season, the staff and players travelled to the great cities of Argentina, Uruguay and Brazil, in a landmark tour, playing clubs that would become household names worldwide. Oddly, it has rarely been discussed in the context of Chelsea's history. The story is told in full here for the first time.

The tour took place a year before the inaugural World Cup was to be held in Uruguay, to which no British and few continental teams would travel, protesting at the distance, the heat and anything that wasn't European and sophisticated. Long before the World Cup, Britain's sniffy attitude was that international events such as the Olympics were a lot of fuss about nothing. 'Other nations (which have no Henley, Lord's, Wimbledon, Hurlingham and so forth),' wrote *The Times* in 1913, 'think much more highly of the Games than we do.'

Chelsea's board, and especially enthusiastic directors Lieutenant-Colonel C.D. Crisp, chairman Claude Kirby and former player Vivian Woodward thought differently. We cannot be sure whose idea this was, but Woodward had missed out on a similar trip 20 years earlier as an amateur player with Spurs, shortly before he joined Chelsea. He would have known the impact Spurs and various amateur clubs had made in the region, and having joined the Chelsea board in 1922, may well have known that the time was right for another English visit. South America's booming football scene was on the brink of turning professional and Uruguay had won the football gold at the 1928 Olympics. Kirby and J.T. Mears, on the other hand, may well have been enticed by the substantial financial lure on offer as well as the opportunity to obscure some of the annual accounts.

In early May 1929 the gossip column of *All Sports Weekly* had reported that, 'It is hardly a secret that Chelsea had a good deal of trouble to persuade their players to go to South America,' and 'at one time it looked as if the tour would have to fall through.' Remuneration was the issue. The club was effectively wiping out the players' entire summer break and stood to make a tidy sum in appearance fees from the tour. Traditionally, the players' wages were a third lower in summer as well, because they weren't playing. In 1931, even a superstar such as Hughie Gallacher earned £6 a week between late August and late May, and £4 at all other times. The FA's wage ceiling was supposed to apply whether games were played in England or overseas.

Eventually a gentlemen's compromise was reached to clear the way across the Atlantic. Unofficial bonuses were paid to every player taking part in the tour, with the burghers of English football turning a blind eye.

It was the Royal Mail ship *Asturias* that initiated one of Chelsea's *gran turismo*. In its dotage, RMS *Asturias*'s port side was used as the *Titanic*'s 'body-double' for lifeboat-lowering scenes in the 1957 Rank film *A Night To Remember*. Happily, Chelsea avoided anything remotely akin to that legendary 1912 sea disaster. The trip, though fraught with logistical challenges from beginning to end, left a positive legacy for both tourists and hosts – but for very different reasons.

If there hadn't been unanimity at the club about the tour, once it started the squad made the most of it, and there would have been much excitement at the time about visiting the land of steamy tangos, the swarthy gaucho cowboy and corned beef (Fray Bentos is an Argentinian port, by the way, not simply a brand).

Given some of their flagrant lifestyles in London, the players might have enjoyed time off to sample the already world-renowned carnival in Rio, about which *The Times* of the day glowed, 'dancing reigns supreme and masked balls are the order of the day'. But carnival is in February and the *Asturias* docked in smouldering June.

On board the ship, something of a novelty itself since it was the first of its type to be fitted with diesel engines, the players kept fit and entertained fellow passengers with extended sessions of keepy-uppy and head tennis on the wooden deck. A few leather balls were lost over the rails into the ocean on what, by modern standards, was a gruelling expedition.

Today, you can fly from Heathrow to Brazil in under 19 hours. The journey from Stamford Bridge to South America took three and a half weeks by sea and land each way, so almost two months were spent in transit overall.

Once they were there, though, indelible impressions would be left, including the barbed-wire fences around the pitches, which failed miserably to stop crowds invading the pitch to 'hug and kiss' goalscorers; the vast gulf between the luxury of some club facilities and the destitution of others; the massive crowds and warm response of football fans in Brazil, Uruguay and Argentina outside the more reckless Buenos Aires; and the pace, fluency and skill of the South American players.

It was a visit that intrigued South America too, giving the local amateur footballers a chance to pit their skills against European opposition. Details of the tour appeared in newspapers in Argentina, Uruguay and Brazil in the first week of April 1929. There was special interest in São Paulo, home, then as now, to Palmeiras, Santos, Corinthians and São Paulo themselves. No British professional club had previously visited the football-mad city.

Perhaps the greatest excitement was in Uruguay, which was then riding the crest of an incredible wave of Olympic football success.

In Argentina, though, where the bulk of the matches were played, there was a confidence bordering on arrogance. The Gaucho Trail had already been blazed by a motley collection of visiting teams, including Southampton (1904), Nottingham Forest (1905), Spurs (1909), Swindon Town (1912), Exeter City (1914), Plymouth Argyle (1924) and Motherwell (1928). After Chelsea, amazingly, no British club made the journey until Sheffield United in May 1967.

Chelsea's games were all played against local amateur teams. A look at what professional league teams were like was one of the allures of their matches. Professionalism didn't come to South American football until the early 1930s.

Back in 1929 observers felt that the locals' experience of such visitors would give them an edge. Some Argentinians predicted Chelsea, five years marooned in the English Second Division, would not win a single match. The ripples were felt all the way back in Blighty, with concern about Britain's good name in world sport being battered, especially among the sizeable population of ex-pats over there. *All Sports Weekly*, in its 18 May 1929 issue, published two days after Chelsea reached the Americas, forewarned, 'Chelsea's progress will be watched with deep interest, for their success is vitally necessary in republics where British football has always gone through the melting pot.'

Later, *Athletic News*, the London-based weekly paper covering virtually every sport in detail, published an ominous piece under the headline 'A Public Warning to Chelsea' on 17 June, midway through the tour. 'The suggestion is being made in various quarters that the defeats of British soccer teams overseas do not damage our prestige. This is sheer ignorance and folly.' An open letter published in the *Buenos Aires Standard* (an English-language newspaper still going strong) by a former international as Chelsea arrived in South America warned, 'The British community looks to you to raise the prestige of British soccer in the eyes of South American enthusiasts in general. The Motherwell FC last year gave us poor exhibitions. There are teams here – I do not exaggerate – that could worthily compete in First League football at home.'

Athletic News also gave the tourists some cultural tips about how to get on with the locals. Argentinian crowds of '40,000 upwards' were all 'tremendously proud' and 'most excitable'. 'The slightest shoulder-to-shoulder charge is immediately penalized,' it warned. 'The most casual "hands" causes the whistle to be heard. The former ruling is inexplicable. The latter is due, perhaps, to the fact that the Argentines are up to all the tricks of the trade, and know just as much about stealing a march on the referees, not to mention heel-tapping, as you know yourselves.

'The Argentines have nothing to learn. They require no more teaching from the nation that actually did teach them. Football is the national Argentine game; it is played in the smallest little village in this vast republic.'

Among the squad, coached by trainer Jack Whitley and managed by David Calderhead, there were few names of international repute at the start, save the famous Scots, striker Andy Wilson and 'sliding tackle' exponent Tommy Law. Another innovator, long-throw expert Sam Weaver, was in the party; along with fellow England star Sid Bishop. There was Ireland international wing-half Sam Irving too, but for most of the rest, even including flat-capped keeper Sam Millington, popularity extended barely beyond North End Road, let alone the English Channel. In the course of the tour trainer Whitley would serve as an emergency keeper and his have-a-go colleague Jack Harrow as a makeshift forward. The squad was: Millington, goalkeeper; G. Smith, Law, Odell, Irving, Townrow, Bishop, W. Russell, Roger, W. Ferguson, backs; Thain, Meredith, C. Ferguson, Elliott, Wilson, W. Jackson, J. Crawford, Weaver, H. Miller, G. Pearson, forwards; David Calderhead, manager.

Having finished the 1928–29 season on 27 April by beating Reading 2-1 at the Bridge, Chelsea had cruised into Rio de Janeiro's breathtaking harbour on 16 May. If they gazed up at the top of the Corcovado Mountain, they would have seen the wooden scaffolding where workmen were constructing the outstretched arms of the statue of Christ the Redeemer. From Rio the Chelsea entourage travelled on by train and bus to Argentina – in those days a trek of nearly a week.

Chelsea director Lieutenant-Colonel C.D. Crisp accompanied the players everywhere and wrote regularly of the Chelsea perspective on the unique experience. He was alternately amused and amazed. 'Matches timed for 2.30 start about 3 p.m.,' he noted in one of his early jottings, 'and "it does not matter" seems a prevalent reply when you ask why this unpunctuality. Although the Argentine players have nothing much to learn from us in the way of playing football, the arrangements for entering and leaving the ground could be improved if a thousand of our Metropolitan or Sussex Constabulary were loaned to this city for six months.'

Chelsea played 16 matches in all, won five, lost eight and drew three. What follows is a run-down of the games Chelsea played accompanied by eyewitness reports.

The first games were played against representative XIs drawn from Buenos Aires and its surrounding provinces. There was almost unprecedented interest in the English team among the public and the media. The incredible welcome extended to the heavens, an overnight thunderstorm over the capital giving Chelsea a taste of home on an unusually boggy pitch at the San Lorenzo de Almagro stadium. So het up were the local media it was reported that in the press box for the opening game on 25 May the hacks became hyper, 'one gentleman who was engaged in transmitting details by radio almost swallowing the apparatus in excitement'.

In that opening game played in front of 32,000 people, and the two games that followed, patterns would be set on and off the field of play. It was Chelsea's 'nippy and clever methods allied to superior teamwork and greater accuracy in heading' that eventually won the day.

Goalie Sam Millington's 'thoroughly sound' keeping met approval. 'He does not attempt anything of the showy or gallery type but reveals discreet anticipation, agility and confidence in his interventions and clears strongly.' Reg Weaver's performance came under the spotlight as the transfer fee

Chelsea paid for him had caused 'a minor sensation'. He was summed up as 'a good footballer possessing dash and skill', although 'his qualities as an opportunist were not in evidence yesterday'. Harry Miller was judged to be the best of the inside trio, while what John Crawford and George Pearson lack in stature 'they make up for in determination and effort'.

The Almagro team had emerged from a *barrio* gang in 1908. As Chelsea would discover, its supporters didn't form the most disciplined of audiences, and the stadiums were designed accordingly. 'The grandstands are built at a most perilously acute angle, and there is no roofing,' Crisp observed. 'The London County Council would not pass the structures. The spectators all stand, and when their players do anything good they whistle, cheer and wave white handkerchiefs.'

He was amazed by the barbed-wire barricades designed to deter pitch invasions – little knowing that one of his successors on Chelsea's board would infamously install even more fearsome fences topped with electrified wire half a century later. 'The pitch is surrounded by a 10ft high wire netting,' he scorned, 'with a high barbed-wire-top about nine yards behind the front arrangement. I understand they are erected to prevent spectators running on the field. Many of them did so, however, in order to embrace and kiss goalscorers.' This habit led to some unsavoury scenes later on the tour.

There was also one major visual innovation in football, with the teams wearing numbers on their backs – ten years before the English Football League would vote them in at home. The Chelsea team earned a rather fine nickname, 'Los Numerados', as a result.

A Buenos Aires newspaper reported that to help spectators recognise the visitors, 'each player will carry a number'. It then listed the Chelsea line-up – without numbers. The innovation reportedly provoked 'some amusement' in the crowd. (Later, though, Chelsea could be forgiven for wondering if it wasn't just their shirts, but their days that were numbered in Argentina.)

In that first match Chelsea beat an all-star team from the capital 3-2 and the locals, aware of how far away Blighty was, gave them the thumbs-up. 'Three weeks on board and the same number of days on land prior to Saturday's game hardly constitutes an ideal preparation for a hard contest,' noted one reporter, 'but the customary early handicaps of bright, light, rock-like ground and lively ball gave way to the conditions resembling those frequently prevailing at home, possibly the latter features may have influenced events in some measure but we opine that upon their initial appearance Chelsea created a favourable impression in a fast and even duel, contested in good spirit.'

The lessons of the first game were not lost on the hosts, who laid on a lavish reception that evening. Chelsea director Crisp appreciated the Argentinian FA's hospitality. 'They have been kindness personified,' he glowed. History doesn't record how extensive the hospitality had been at the banquet, but Chelsea lost 4-0 the following afternoon – a Sunday – to a *gauchos* or 'country boys' XI at the home of Racing Club, the Avellaneda. There was something familiar about the press comment that 'there was harmony and skill that has always been a feature of Chelsea's play, but unfortunately does not always produce goals.'

In other words, the same old Chelsea of the 1920s.

In that second game, a strong wind caused the ball 'to be pranky'. In fact, perhaps tipped off beforehand, the visitors had brought and insisted on using their own footballs, which were bigger and lighter than the local cannonballs. A feature of the early games, until Chelsea ran out of balls, would be the Argentinians appealing to the ref for the matchball to be replaced. The *Herald* reported, 'A new ball of a different type was rolled out when the teams reappeared, but after a brief discussion it was decided to continue with the original pill, further diversion being created when the ball landed amongst the spectators who thought it correct to retain it for a few minutes, a foolish attitude.'

By half-time in the third game, the Argentinians had had enough. The English ball was deemed to be underweight and, remarkably, spent the interval immersed in a large bucket of water to gain a few ounces. Crisp was irritated. 'I only hope our Argentine friends will standardise the match ball and alter their methods in regard to other adaptations connected with the laws of the game,' he wrote in *Athletic News*. 'The ball used here is a heavy one of a size adopted by the schoolboys in our country.'

It was a foreign ball, by jingo. The *Buenos Aires Standard* tried to make an issue of it, suggesting gamesmanship on Chelsea's part. In response, Crisp noted, 'Spectators, believing the ball to be at fault, showed their chagrin in no uncertain manner, and on four or five occasions not only refused to return the ball, but kept it. Ultimately, the smaller and heavier Argentine type of ball was introduced ... but this went the way of the others.'

One thing the Chelsea director could appreciate was the local style of forward play, comparable Crisp thought with the awesome Wembley Wizards of 1928. 'The combination of the Argentines was excellent,' he wrote, 'the passing at times reminding me of the Corinthians' balmy days. The fairest praise I can award the players of this Provincia XI is that they were almost up to the classic form of Scotland when that country beat England last year at Wembley. They possess great players out here. Bossio, for example, is a peach of a goalkeeper.'

By the third game, another Chelsea victory watched by 50,000 at the River Plate ground, the patterns of play after the first game had become set templates on either side. 'The defence of Chelsea was far superior to the local defence,' noted the *Buenos Aires Herald*, 'while the local forwards were head and shoulders above the visiting five.'

But the physical side of the English game wasn't going down well, Chelsea's backs being continually pulled up for charging. The visitors' frustration at whistle-happy referees led to frightening scenes at the Boca Juniors stadium in Buenos Aires on 2 June. *The Times* told part of the story: 'The Chelsea Football Club was this afternoon beaten by an Argentinian team by three goals to two. After an alleged foul on the part of one of the Chelsea players, the spectators rushed into the field, apparently with the intention of attacking the visitors, but the police intervened in time.'

There was slightly more to it than that. The 40,000 crowd was boisterous and had breached the 10-foot barbed wire-topped fencing round the pitch whenever their heroes scored. Perhaps fed up with all the encroachment, Wilson went in hard on goalscorer Kuko and left him writhing on the floor. Spectators invaded again, bringing play to a halt, and one of them, wearing a postman's uniform, ran up to Wilson and punched him in the face. How's that for special delivery? He was led away by police.

It got worse. Skipper Monti, seething about what he perceived to be an unfair challenge on a team-mate, ran up to George Roger (who, presuming the game to be over, held out his hand). Instead of a shake, Monti delivered a fist to Roger's chin, laying the Chelsea midfielder out cold. He then gave him a hard boot in the groin as he lay on the ground. Monti's team-mates hustled their captain away before the police could arrest him.

All hell broke loose in the chaos. 'Various fights and arguments were started all over the field,' reported the *Buenos Aires Standard*, 'whereupon the referee, finding the situation beyond his control, immediately suspended the game and literally made good his escape.' Another eyewitness saw the ref, Señor C. Cidrigliano, give one of the pitch invaders 'a sweet upper-cut' on his way to the dressing room. The game was abandoned with three minutes to go.

Substitute Sam Irving was on the touchline when he was struck by a piece of fruit. 'Although oranges are very plentiful here, they are not too kind a missile to receive in the face,' wrote *Athletic News* in London, under the heading 'Savage Attack on Chelsea FC Players'. 'Irving, though, gained a point when, having been struck by one, he calmly proceeded to peel it and consume it at intervals.' It paints a stiff upper lip scene reminiscent of the banquet at the end of *Carry On Up the Khyber*.

All in all, the British emerged with great credit. Wilson, for example, 'wisely stood perfectly still' after being thumped by the postie, though he later told an English acquaintance that he had been 'thoroughly disgusted' with the spectator's lack of sportsmanship.

Through the melee police tried to clear a path so the Chelsea team could leave the field, but the crowd continued to pelt them with missiles – including a huge jagged-edged stone which one Chelsea player picked up, took back to the hotel and eventually brought back to Stamford Bridge as a souvenir. The locals took their own mementos, including the tyres from the visiting team's coach. It took them an hour to get on the road.

Local papers exploded in condemnation of their fellow countrymen. In particular Monti's kicking of the prone Roger was condemned as 'savage and cowardly' by the papers the following day. Spectators who had chanted 'Muy bien, Monti' were also slated.

The *Buenos Aires Herald*, describing the spectators as 'the dregs of the population', wrote, 'When Roger fainted and was carried off the field, the public cheered. In the same way their forefathers cheered when a Roman gladiator's bowels were ripped out on the arena. That Roger had played the game he played every week of his life was no concern of theirs. I venture the hope that no more English teams will come here until the Argentine footballer has learnt to conduct himself like a sportsman.'

Cartoonists enjoyed themselves. A whimsical strip in the *Herald* pictured Chelsea 'throwing their weight around', before spectators 'threw stones about', Kuko was accidentally kicked, Wilson was hit by 'an enthusiastic spectator', then the Argentine captain 'tested his boxing skill on Roger'. Another spectator 'did a little infighting with the referee' before the police cleared the field – 'or should we call it ring?'

The *Standard*'s verdict was, 'Scrap the leagues and football matches and, before teaching the teams to play football, teach those who watch them to be sportsmen.'

Back in London, *All Sports Weekly* reported that, 'Chelsea's stock has gone up tremendously in the foreign parts owing to the way they accepted the outburst against them when they played a game in which fisticuffs came into action.' The article wondered whether Chelsea's experiment of numbering its players was to enable them to count them when they came back in 'to see if they are all there'.

Today's Boca Stadium – where former star Diego Maradona owns one of the private boxes – has fences nearly 30 feet high.

Surprisingly, Monti returned for Chelsea's next game, their first against a club side, but Roger was understandably absent. A slick and inspired Chelsea beat an insipid San Lorenzo 2-0 in front of just 8,000 people but with a notably sporting attitude on the pitch. It was the only way Argentina could say sorry.

That night, the Chelsea entourage caught the night ferry from Buenos Aires for the eight-hour, 130-mile cruise across the mouth of the River Plate to Montevideo, capital of Uruguay, no doubt with some relief.

No one could describe this tour as a holiday for the players. The day they arrived they had to perform in front of a noisy full-house at the tight Pocitos stadium behind the main station against Peñarol, league champions and the heartbeat of the national side that had won Olympic gold and would soon be crowned the world's best.

There was a festive air in the soccer-mad capital, one year ahead of its staging of the first FIFA World Cup. And Peñarol, like many overseas clubs, had a strong English influence. It had been set up by railroad workers as the Central Uruguay Railway Cricket Club but became Peñarol in 1913. It is still one of the country's most successful clubs and today's Chelsea may have more than we think in common with them; locally they are known as 'Bolsiludos' or 'moneybags'. Back then, in contrast, as with all Chelsea's South American opposition, it was an amateur side.

The national daily *El Dia* pronounced the match a complete success.

Everyone had already picked up on the 'Numerados' nickname and there was great curiosity about seeing a British team. The date chosen for the match was also deeply significant to locals: the fifth anniversary of the Uruguayan football team's first Olympic gold triumph, in France in 1924. There was a tribute in memory of the late Beccar Varela, a South American delegate in FIFA who had been decisive in having Uruguay chosen as the seat for the first World Cup in 1930. Oddly, the minute's silence came 20 minutes into the first half.

Despite the interruption Townrow opened the scoring for the Pensioners in the second half but a penalty levelled the score and a late winner handed Chelsea a creditable 2-1 defeat.

The English tourists headed straight back across the River Plate and would not return until the end of the month, en route to Brazil. In the meantime, hostilities were resumed with the Argentines.

If the Chelsea staff and players hoped for the slate to be wiped clean, they were mistaken. It all began so well: the tourists' directors, manager and players made a $1,000 donation to the Mendoza Catastrophe Fund, set up after the earthquake which had struck the capital of the westerly wine-producing region at the end of May. But during a crazy itinerary of three games in two days the sabres were rattling again. The first match was a 1-1 draw with Independiente, but things erupted when 'Crawford was pulled up for fouling Martinez, the latter shaping up to kick the Chelsea forward when he was on the ground. The incident was terminated by the intervention of the players. Another little scene followed when Lalin was injured in a collision with Roger, play being suspended for a space of two minutes while the crowd gave vent to uncomplimentary epithets. Theatrical gestures by the referee towards Roger evidently indicated displeasure. The concluding moments were uninteresting, the locals obtaining a fruitless corner and Perez distinguishing himself by striking Roger.'

Not so jolly Roger, then – smacked twice in a fortnight.

The next two games the following day – 'Super Sunday?' – were even in different cities and seem to have been squeezed in at the last minute. For the first, against Santa Fe, Chelsea indicated their seriousness by fielding trainers Jack Whitley and Jack Harrow in goal and up front respectively. They were probably none too concerned with a 0-5 defeat before heading to

Argentina's third city. In the busy port of Rosario, 90 miles to the south along the Paraña River on the edge of the country's *pampa*, they fielded an entirely different, much stronger XI, and still lost.

After that it was back to the capital and there were the usual observations about the over-dramatising and inconsistent referees, the crowd disruptions and Chelsea's lack of sting. 'It becomes monotonous and almost unpleasant,' said the *Buenos Aires Herald*, 'to regularly criticise the lack of scoring power of the Chelsea forwards. Up to now, of the bunch only Wilson has shown anything like class form.' However, the press were hugely impressed by Chelsea's defensive organisation and strength: 'No club that has visited us has had a better defence. Millington has done splendidly; his mistakes have been very few. Law, Smith and Odell are class backs and all six halves are well above the average.'

In a heartening valedictory the Pensioners saw off a young but promising Estudiantil Porteño team 3-2 at River Plate's ground, Willie Russell scoring the winner after Estudiantil had clawed back a 2-0 deficit. But the end of the match summed up the Buenos Aires legs of the tour, 'Play deteriorated to the extent of becoming farcical,' the *Herald* complained, 'not one really bright or clever interlude was forthcoming, and fouls by both sides did not improve matters.

'Going for the man instead of the ball was a common occurrence in proceedings that did not enhance the rivals' reputations and had one or two players been ordered to quit the arena, no injustice would have been done.

'Chelsea appeared content to preserve their lead and during the concluding ten minutes they resorted to touch-finding, sometimes of a deliberate nature, that was certainly not warranted when those responsible had ample time and space.'

Needless to say the frustration of the local players and crowd gave way to violence. 'When the final whistle sounded,' the *Herald* reported, 'two players were shaping for a bout of fisticuffs, and as the teams retired a section of the crowd gave Chelsea a farewell in the shape of a shower of stone, two or three of the team sustaining injuries as an outcome of this cowardly demonstration.'

Athletics Weekly's correspondent was adamant: 'I hope no further English teams will go to the Argentine until the Argentine footballer has learned to conduct himself as a sport. He must learn to lose as well as to win. In that lies the essence of what football means. Any player can win gracefully; it takes a better man to lose gracefully. In Argentine, they lose disgracefully.'

Montevideo welcomed Chelsea back warmly for a game against Wanderers at Parque Central, one of the venues for the World Cup the following year. Unfortunately, according to *El Dia*, the poor display of the home side, whose pacy attacks foundered chiefly on Smith and Millington, coupled with 'the hard work of the triangle of Townrow, Miller, Meredith and Pearson', subdued the expectant crowd. Chelsea's organisation was impressive though it wasn't great to watch, and star man Harry Miller's goal brought victory by *el minimo* – 1-0. 'The triumph of the English,' it decided, 'was justified.'

And so to Rio de Janeiro for the final leg, where 45,000 fans turned up at the Rua Guanabara stadium, home of Fluminense, to see Chelsea draw 1-1 with a team of Carioca all-stars. If the players thought they might enjoy some late nights in the city of carnival and 24-hour parties they were right, but it wasn't what they'd expected. The kick-off time was 10 p.m., and so 28 June 1929 became the first time any Chelsea team had played under 'electric light'. The stadium, with its recently installed floodlighting, was described by Chelsea officials as 'one of the finest and best equipped in the world'.

The local paper *Folha da Manhã* warned its readers to expect a team 'playing their football like a game of chess – slow and calculated, using their physical superiority to good advantage.'

The game kicked off half an hour late and after a wary period Chelsea opened the scoring through Jackson and dominated for a long period. Eventually, though, with ten minutes remaining Ripper equalised from a cross by Nascimento. Left-sided forward Nilo missed the chance to snatch victory at the death.

A member of the Londoners' party painted a wonderful picture of their Brazilian experience for *Athletic News*: 'Chelsea drew 1-1 after a brilliantly contested game. Can your readers picture a cloudless sky all day, with the thermometer at 90 degrees in the shade, then darkness at 6 p.m. and this wonderful city illuminated with millions of lights. We were all entranced and our drive to the ground was full of interest.

'The home team were fine players; the goalkeeper performing excellently (all these South American custodians are as good as the very best in England) and their left wing gave a splendid exhibition. The whole team, in fact, were speedy, controlled and trapped the ball magnificently, and took up positions admirably. Their fault was precisely that of our own side – the forwards dribbled and manoeuvred in front of goal until they were robbed.

'The crowd was most sportsmanlike, cheering us to the echo – quite a novel experience for us on this trip – and they let off rockets, squibs and detonators when the play pleased them. Everyone seemed pleased with the result.'

Except the reporter from *Folha da Manhã*, who described the 'cold and mathematical' Chelsea as 'a team lacking in method, precision and above all loyalty' – as in devotion to the principles of good sportsmanship. The best that could be said was that they were fit, keen and displayed good ball control.

O Estado de São Paulo felt that Motherwell – who had played in Brazil the previous summer – were 'much more impressive as they definitely displayed a quality of football that was more interesting, neater and more combined'.

Because of the late start, staff at *O Globo*, the Rio newspaper, worked all night to get their report out the next day, and it was far more complimentary, 'The first match of the English professionals resulted in a 1-1 draw in the international game yesterday night between Chelsea of London and the scratch Carioca team.

'The Fluminense stadium, fairy-like lit, was yesterday full of football aficionados anxious to watch the premiere of the famous professional players from Chelsea, the great English club, visiting on the initiative of the Tricolour Cariocas.

'There were few gaps in the crowd and everyone there greeted the home players and the team from London with enthusiasm.

'The Cariocas, captained by Lagarto and wearing white strip, stepped onto the pitch carrying a beautiful basket of flowers. There was uniform applause and the team took their positions.

'Then came the English team dressed in blue shirts and black shorts. They formed a circle in the centre of the pitch and greeted the Cariocas, then took their positions.

'[Chelsea] is capable of great moves. Its defence is secure. The front line is difficult to mark with its tightness and precision in the way the ball is passed from one player to another. In spite of these qualities they failed with almost all of their powerful shots as they lacked accuracy.

'Millington, the goalkeeper, is an outstanding figure in the team. He made thrilling saves in last night's match. Our team put on a bad exhibition.'

Chelsea played the same Rio all-stars team two days later and lost 2-1, but having appreciated the flowers they presented each of their opponents with a small England flag before the game. 'The English team were received with applause,' noted *O Globo*. 'They were elegant in their blue/black strip.'

At the first match observers had thought the Pensioners were tired after their 1,130-mile voyage from Montevideo. Now they concluded that, 'Their professional game is very much inferior to that of our amateur Cariocas.'

'It's true that their players possess some qualities, but they always prefer the pass to dribbling. They didn't fail to score and always worked hard in moments of danger. There was a certain harmony between the halves and the forwards, harmony that deserves eulogy. But their players simply don't have our agility.

'The Rio public weren't impressed with the English team's show, because better games are seen here every Sunday in the inter-city championships.'

On the last part of this exhausting tour, taking the night train from Rio, the Chelsea players found themselves spending a few days with Rio's 'ugly sister', São Paulo.

The first game was against the team named after the famous English amateurs Corinthian Casuals, previous visitors there. Brazil's now legendary Corinthians have since produced players such as Sócrates, Rivelino and Gilmar. In 1929 they were already known as the team of the masses. After this famous 'seesaw' encounter with Chelsea at Palmeiras's stadium on 4 July, they earned a new sobriquet: the 'team of the turn'.

An extraordinary eight-minute spell inspired by Sid Elliott put Chelsea 3-0 up. Elliott set up Jackson for the first, then scored the third himself; Wilson scored direct from a free kick in between.

But after a shot deflected in off Tommy Law, Chelsea started to wobble and concede free kicks. One led directly to a goal, and then Gambinha equalised as the game disintegrated with 'Chelsea displaying inferior technique, in a sporting and social sense', according to one reporter. 'The shouting and booing of the spectators and the violence of the game made it look like a bullfight,' said *Estado de São Paulo*.

The Corinthians winger De Maria made up for a glaring miss in front of goal by putting his team ahead, before Elliott's long shot again levelled for 4-4. There were near misses in a lively finish, but it stayed all square. 'Those present were subjected to one of the greatest sporting deceptions in living memory in São Paulo.' It was all a far cry from the 4-4 with Sheffield Wednesday at Hillsborough in 1985.

The final game of Chelsea's epic tour should have been against Santos (later the club of Pele), but they faced a combined São Paulo (Paulista) team instead and lost 3-1. (Santos corrected the oversight by playing Chelsea in Jamaica in 1971.) Before a ball had even been kicked there was a bizarre exhibition of Brazilian people power. São Paulo had recently been defeated by visiting Hungarians Ferencváros, and when their centre-forward Petronilho came on to the pitch, the fans disagreed with his inclusion and made their feelings all too clear by booing him. With everyone in position before kick-off, the Paulista selectors took off Petronilho and replaced him with Araken of Santos.

The homesick blues were playing up one last time and spent most of the first half camped outside the São Paulo box. 'The second half began at high speed which was kept up throughout,' marvelled the *São Paulo Times*, 'clearly showing that in spite of all rumours the Chelsea men were in very good training and if anything had the extra turn of speed for they almost invariably managed to be first on the ball.' (Rumours? In Rio? Perhaps the boys had finally been able to let their hair down.)

In this match, as on the whole tour, it was Chelsea's finishing that let them down and it finished 3-1 to the Brazilians.

'Chelsea were defeated thanks to the solidity of our defence, chiefly in the second half,' *Gazeta Esportiva* concluded, 'when the Numerados doubled their attacks in search of an equaliser. Chelsea did not resort to any form of brutality, and left the referee in peace. Their sportsmanlike spirit undid the bad impression that was left last Thursday [against Corinthians].'

A few hours after that final game, Chelsea were given a rousing send-off from the Luz train station in São Paulo as they headed back to Rio where, later that week, they caught the steamer back home to Blighty.

It had been an astonishing adventure, full of controversy, and with lessons to be learned for the club and for English football. Chairman Claude Kirby admitted that the South Americans generally were 'true masters in tactical play', and that the Chelsea board had marvelled at the style and ball control they saw.

In contrast Mr F.O. Radford, who had attended some of the Chelsea games in Argentina, wrote from Buenos Aires to *Athletic News* concerning the stilted nature of English league football: 'When any player on the home side tries to scheme or dribble, there are immediate howls and shrieks to "part with it", "get rid of it" or "sling it about". It is really astonishing to me why good clubs allow this style of play to dominate their game. Why do they not encourage the dribbler and artist, and endeavour to develop the old-fashioned, true football again?'

That was a lesson not lost on Chelsea. Amazingly, despite the lack of 'the brick-hard grounds and the broiling heat of the Argentine', the club started off well on their return home with a 2-0 win over Forest with goals from the presumably well-tanned Weaver and Elliott, then ended six seasons in Division Two with promotion the following April.

Immediately, the Chelsea board was inspired to embark on a spending spree, starting with the closest thing to Argentina's ball-playing forwards they could find – Gallacher and Cheyne of the original Wembley Wizards.

15

GERMANY CALLING

Another little-known and perhaps more surprising overseas tour took place in 1932. It was to Germany, of all places, of all times. In his column of 11 August 1950 in *Newcastle's Weekly Chronicle*, Hughie Gallacher wrote about it, 'My most vivid memories are concerned with the conditions in the country rather than the football.

'I remember that after the match in Munich [16 May 1932] we Chelsea players were sitting in the hotel lounge discussing what we had seen, good and bad, of the early effects of the Hitler regime. As a matter of fact our general impressions were not unfavourable, for there is no doubt at this time a lot of good work was being done to improve conditions in Germany. Naturally Hitler's name was mentioned pretty frequently during our conversation until one of the waiters came and whispered a warning in perfect English. The waiter, who, it turned out, was a Londoner, told us that it was dangerous to talk about Hitler in public, whether the Führer was being praised or criticised.'

In actual fact Hughie's wires were crossed – President Hindenberg and centrist Chancellor Bruening were in power at the time of Chelsea's bemused arrival. The truth was that when poor old Chelsea were there, Germany was in utter social chaos and on the road to Valhalla, not Utopia, national socialist or otherwise. It's true that the Nazis – their 400,000-strong SA brownshirts a part of daily street violence – were a major political force by 1929, but the SA and SS were actually banned by Bruening in April 1932. This explains the waiter's advice to the Chelsea players.

The team played Preussen Munster (lost 0-2), Bayern Munich (won 2-1), a Germany XI, in Liepzig (won 7-3 – how's that for Tommy getting in an early how's-yer-father, eh?) and SV Stuttgarter Kickers (won 2-0). At no stage were the players asked to perform a Nazi salute.

Within days of Chelsea leaving Germany the road to hell was laid with the resignation of Chancellor Bruening. On 4 June, the Reichstag was dissolved for a July election and the Nazi organizations were unbanned. The rest is on the History Channel.

Surprisingly, Chelsea did return to the 'Fatherland', but in late May 1936 (after Gallacher's departure), and only for breakfast on Friedrichstrasse in Berlin, en route to a ferry from Hook of Holland on the way back from a tour of the Netherlands, Sweden and Poland. In several ways it seems an extremely odd choice of dining venue – were the cured meats, smoked cheeses and heavy breads any better there? – but it is geographically well placed, so we must assume it wasn't some propaganda exercise cooked up by one of the right-wing directors on the board.

Later, the France and England national soccer teams, and many other national and club sides, generated surprisingly little criticism at the time for saluting Hitler. It even earned praise from the contemporary British press for making 'a good impression'. This despite it being public knowledge by then how vile the Third Reich was. The Chelsea players themselves were surrounded by examples. The headquarters of Oswald Mosley's British Union of Fascists in the early 1930s was just up the road from Stamford Bridge at the symbolically named Whitelands College on the King's Road. Blackshirts paraded outside and attended the gymnasium or lecture theatre inside and Fascists were attacked on the streets of Chelsea and Fulham with sticks.

In 1938 the Granville Theatre, Walham Green, staged a contemporary version of Shakespeare's *Julius Caesar* drawing clear analogies between the Roman megalomaniac and his modern reincarnation in Berlin.

A young German girl who came over in December 1935, interviewed before watching a team from her Nazi homeland play at White Hart Lane (of all places) knew only three English words, picked up through conversations at home. One of them was 'Gallacher'.

There were protests at the game and graffiti outside the ground, with 'Stop the Nazi match!' leaflets circulating before police intervened to confiscate them, so as not to disturb the 10,000 crowd. 'There was otherwise no expression of anything other than goodwill towards the Germans,' said *The Times*. 'The two teams went on to the field together amid enthusiastic cheering. The reception given to the German side was, if anything, even more robust than that given to the English side. The band played the German national anthem and the German visitors, players and spectators alike, gave the Nazi salute. The Union Jack and a flag bearing the Swastika emblem flew on each side of the standard at half-mast.' The German players wore shirts embossed with a picture of an eagle holding a swastika in its claws.

Incredibly, after the game people lined the nearby streets to cheer the visiting players and team coaches. Four years later they would be on opposite sides of the world's most destructive war.

Research in Germany now suggests that it was never actually made compulsory by Hitler for visiting sportsmen and women to salute in the Nazi fashion. It was a matter of choice, though many players protested afterwards that they had been coerced by the Football Association. Nevertheless the fact is that in Munich, 1938, before a friendly match between Germany and England, Chelsea keeper Vic Woodley and future Blue Len Goulden stood alongside the likes of Stanley Matthews and Cliff Bastin and raised their arms as the Führer would have liked it.

There was little controversial about Chelsea's post-war return to Germany except its nature and timing, just ahead of the 1966 World Cup in England. A Scottish manager of an English club, whose chairman also runs the FA, agreeing to assist the Germany national side? Surely some mistake! There were collaborators in pockets of Europe who were still being hunted down for less. 'It was the way we played,' Tommy Docherty told me in 1995. 'We were invited to play the German national team twice; we beat them once and drew the other time. What a compliment that was for us.'

The chief reason for the invitation was that Chelsea had become one of the first English teams to use overlapping full-backs – the closest thing to one of Germany's main rivals, Brazil. 'It was 1965, just before the World Cup,' says Docherty. 'And I asked Helmut Schön [then German national team manager] why he picked us. And he said, "You play like a South American team. You don't play like an English team at all. Your full-backs are like wingers. We haven't seen this before."

'And he said to me, "Could you help? In the World Cup next year, Uwe Seeler, our centre-forward, will be given a chance ... he's just recovering from an Achilles tendon injury; can you ask Harris to mark him close?" I says, "Helmut, you're taking a bit of a chance there. With the late Chopper Harris." He says, "Why – is he dead?" I says, "No, he's just late all the time."

'He said, "Can you tell him to mark closely?" I said, "Yeah." "Not tackle, just mark." I said, "Well, it's a bit difficult telling Chopper Harris not to tackle."

'Anyway, I spoke to Chopper and he was as good as gold. And they were delighted. At that time they gave us about ten thousand quid a game, to play the two friendlies – two games, twenty thousand quid. And we murdered them in the first game: I think we beat them 3-1. And the second game I think it was three apiece. And I'm talking about Beckenbauer and all of them, and Uwe Seeler and Berti Vogts. It was some team. They were all young – 21, 22 – and the stadium was packed: there were fifty-odd thousand there. And we came out, we were blue shirts, blue pants and white socks, and we were flying. Eddie [McCreadie] was like an outside left. He said to me, "I want some ideas how to beat the right-back." Great side. Great days.'

Sir Alf Ramsey would obviously have agreed.

16

OUR MEN IN SOFIA

Previously classified and strictly confidential, correspondence regarding another controversial tour in Chelsea's history was released under the Freedom of Information Act and can be presented for the first time here. It sheds light on how clubs had to deal with the sometimes forceful diplomacy of the Cold War when all they wanted to do was play a game of football. The occasion was Chelsea's August 1958 trip to Sofia in Bulgaria, then a Communist satellite state of the Soviet Union. If ever friendlies deserved a more appropriate name, it was then. As it turned out, though, in contrast to the riotous scenes of South America in 1929, the biggest issue for the club in Eastern Europe was boredom.

To club secretary John Battersby and the board any trips abroad were handy for financial reasons. Even behind the Iron Curtain visiting teams received an appearance fee from their hosts, but that wasn't the most significant purpose. 'We didn't make a hell of a lot of money,' says Battersby, 'because there were all sorts of "repayments" that were due on tours. So we used to go everywhere in cabs as far as the officials knew. I never walked anywhere, I always went in taxis!

'The Bulgarians paid us in dollars if I remember right. On overseas trips my arrangements used to be that I'd want a certain amount of money in local

245

currency, so I could dish it out. The players were on £2 a day or whatever it was, as spending money. They would want that in local currency so they could buy bits and pieces and have a few drinks and whatever, and the bulk of it we wanted in dollars. We didn't want the lev, which was the currency in Bulgaria.'

The 'repayments' may have been a way of using up money that was acquired through means common to all clubs but not approved by the FA. There was a widespread rumour that one big northern club had a slush fund into which all the staff would place any money made for spending abroad on tours like this. In April 1957, Sunderland FC had been fined £5,000 by the Football League and four of its directors suspended – two of them permanently – for financial irregularities. The club accounts had revealed that local contractors connected to one of the board members had submitted invoices for amounts way in excess of the work done and that when the money had been paid, the difference had been 'refunded' to the club. 'No entry appears in the club books of the amounts so refunded,' said the report. The manager admitted to having made an illegal payment to an unnamed third party. In the world of football there were always talent scouts, promising young players' parents and all sorts of bonuses to be paid.

As secretary Battersby was the man who signed the staff contracts and he was aware of all the tricks. 'I had one player that came to me saying that Ted Drake had promised someone a car,' he said. '[Chairman] Joe Mears being a Ford dealer, Ted had promised this player a motorcar.

'I forget who he was, quite a well-known senior player transferred from another club. "I'm promised a motor car," so he said. But I said, "We can't give you that, we're not supposed to give you the money either, that's completely contrary to Football League rules."

'It's all very well for managers to promise all sorts of things; it was up to the secretary of the team to get round it somehow. That's why we went on foreign tours in the summer, where there was a lot of money flying about!

'Anyway, with this player, we rented a house which was actually owned by another club in South London somewhere, and they wanted to sell it. Our player was in it, you see, and I said to him, "Look, we will sell you this house" – he didn't know it belonged to another club – "for what we get for it with you as a sitting tenant," which reduces the value of a house immensely.

'And I said, "If we sell it to you at that price, you arrange to go and live somewhere else, then you can sell it the same day without a sitting tenant, and you can make yourself a few thousand quid, which is equivalent to the cost of the car which you haven't got. He did it.'

In 1972 Tottenham's chairman Sydney Wale, presiding over a bank balance £223,000 to the good, publicly confessed, 'Unfortunately Spurs made a considerable profit last season mainly because we went through the financial year without buying a player. If we don't do that or improve the ground, the tax people get more out of our profit than we do.'

Little wonder that clubs looked to offset some of that surplus on foreign trips. However, the background to a tour of the Eastern Bloc in the post-war period was tense to a degree unimaginable now. Bulgaria had been one of the staunchest allies of the USSR and a one-party state since 1946. The Bulgarian secret police was a branch of Russia's KGB and its network of spies was active all over the Western world.

The journey would never have happened if the FA had listened to the British Embassy in Sofia, and especially their enthusiastic Cold War warrior Mr R.L. Speaight.

In a confidential scrambled telegram to the Foreign Office dated 1 August 1958, and copied to the Moscow embassy, he urged pressure be put on the Blues, through the FA, to cancel the visit:

'1. Chelsea Football Club are due to play here on 10 and 17 August. They may also visit Varna but we have no details of their tour, which has been arranged direct with the Bulgarian Football authorities.

'2. I am not happy about this visit in the present strained situation, with the regime trying to create a war atmosphere and anti-British feeling.

'3. The Bulgarian authorities are unlikely to cancel it since they will wish to show that their quarrel is with "imperialists" and not with sportsmen, but I do not see why we should play their game, and hope that Chelsea will themselves decide to postpone their tour. They could tell the Bulgarians that reports of a current anti-British campaign, war preparations, and restrictions on movements of foreigners had shown them that they could no longer expect a friendly visit without a risk of incidents.

'4. I suggest the position should be explained urgently to the Football Association, preferably to Sir Stanley Rous personally. It is, of course, important that Chelsea should appear to act on their own initiative and not under Foreign Office pressure.'

J.F. Wearing at the Foreign Office casually replied that 'our experience of

Rous indicates that any intervention by us would be regarded, and represented, as Foreign Office pressure ... We are, therefore, taking no action.'

But Speaight wasn't giving up that easily. He thought the fiendish Bulgars had 'previous' and he had made the details known to Rous at the FA.

In March, ahead of CDNA (more familiarly CSKA) Sofia's game at Stamford Bridge, he wrote to Rous at the FA advising that the Bulgarians had falsified documents in order to field ineligible players in a previous Under-23 international match. He also suggested that CDNA, the army team, was packing players from other crack Bulgarian sides so as to put on a show that would be good for propaganda in London.

'One knows, of course, that all the Communist countries are pretty unscrupulous in the selection of teams for international events,' Speaight persisted, 'but this is the first time we in Sofia have had actual proof of cheating. If they realise that you know about their tricks, they may be more careful in future.'

The FA had replied, glibly, that 'Sir Stanley Rous does not require this information urgently.'

If he couldn't be John Le Carré, Speaight had then tried to emulate Charles Buchan with some pithy tactical observations. His fallback position was to provide a scouting report, including a probable CDNA line-up, presumably to be passed on to Chelsea: 'Team captain and most experienced member of the team is Bojkov (47 caps). The team trained with Milev (Master of Sport), and the whole team except Diev are international players. Strong in defence and midfield, weak in front of goal.' That's the spirit, Speaighters. Following several other behind-the-scenes attempts to scupper Chelsea's August trip to Sofia, Speaight's embassy in Bulgaria received a final hint to get over it. 'I cannot recall a request for advice from the Football Association,' wrote Wearing of the Foreign Office in London, 'but if there was one I should undoubtedly, as Mr Joy says, have said that there was no reason to change any plans that had been made because of the international situation. I think we can let this rest.'

Battersby cannot remember any discussions or correspondence with the Foreign Office about this at all. Chelsea's tour went ahead and they played two games on a seemingly trouble-free trip.

Jimmy Greaves remembered it as the worst trip he went on in his career. Nothing to do, even less to eat or drink. Club secretary John Battersby was more amused by the experience than anything. 'They looked after us very well, as best they could,' he says. 'It was a brand new hotel with hardly anybody in it. Bulgaria then, there wasn't much in the place at all.'

'They had a policeman standing on a rostrum in the middle of the crossroads, but there was no traffic. If you saw a car approaching he got really excited and waved his arms about and gesticulated – "Come on!" – and waved them as if he was in the middle of Piccadilly Circus! After Chelsea's tour had finished Speaight wrote in the tone of unconcealed glee reserved for those snatching at any tiny form of vindication: 'When Col. Edwards called he mentioned the visit and said it had gone well. The footballers' eyes were still further opened by the fact that they observed (from the balcony of their hotel) the incident in which the Bulgarian security police drove their car deliberately at the French and Italian military attachés.

'In the event all went well. Chelsea lost their first match against the Bulgarian Army team [CDNA/CSKA Sofia] 1-2, but won the second 2-0 against the leading Bulgarian civilian club [Levski]. Both games were reasonably clean; there were no unpleasant incidents such as marred last year's match between the English and Bulgarian Under 23s, and the crowd in the stadium behaved well.

'Chelsea spent the time between the two Sunday matches training and resting at Varna, where they were the guests of the Bulgarians at one of the best hotels. I had them all in to drinks after the last match (without any Bulgarians) and they made a good impression on all who met them. The management and most of the team seemed to have been well briefed by someone (? by our department) about the realities of life in Bulgaria and had not been unduly taken in by the VIP treatment accorded them.

'They had no complaints except about the food (even the best Bulgarian hotel food is pretty disgusting) but there seems to have been little fraternisation; no formal banquet was organised after the matches and none of my staff were invited to attend any social function by the Bulgarians as we were after the Under 23s match last year.

'This was, of course, all to the good.

'Incidentally the team nearly decided to cancel the visit off their own bat, mainly, I gathered, because of financial difficulties but partly also through concern at the international situation. I was rather surprised to learn from the Club Secretary that they had consulted the FO through the Football Association and been informed that there was no political difficulty whatever over their visit. This was presumably before you received my telegram.

'Yours ever,

Richard Speaight'

17

DON'T BLAME THE OYSTERS

There were echoes of the fallout from South America 1929 and Uruguay 1930 in the reaction to an invitation that fell on the Stamford Bridge mat in 1955 following the title win. *France Football* magazine had devised a tournament bringing together champions from across Europe in a season-long tournament, and Chelsea had a mind to accept.

The club had played in a prototype tournament at Paris's 'Tournoi International de l'Expo Universelle' in May and June 1937, beating Marseille (on the toss of a coin) and FK Austria, before going down 1-4 to Bologna in what the Italian side's president lovingly described as a 'great victory for Fascism'.

The world might have seemed smaller in the post-war jet age, but the Cold War had made it a more threatening place too. Britain's ambition to rebuild Europe had not extended to international soccer competitions such as the inaugural European Cup. Nor was there much of a wind of change blowing through football's microclimate. Commentators who observed the paucity of English talent, who dwelt on the recent, high profile defeats of England at the hands of the USA, and Arsenal to Dinamo and Spartak, were not heard in the corridors of power. English football was seen by some as lacking the intelligence, athleticism and the technical skill of continental –

even Soviet – teams. Some progressives had even floated the idea of English teams joining a European league to improve. England may have given football to the world, but now England was finding the world devilishly hard to tackle back.

As champions Chelsea were in an immensely strong position to lead British clubs into Europe. But it was not to be and Chelsea backed down. What they didn't know was that they were not only giving up a slot in the inaugural year of what is now the world's greatest club competition; but also surrendering a reserved seat at the top table of European football just as the superpowers of the continent began to be established.

Gabriel Hanot of French sports magazine *L'Equipe* was the driving force behind the European Champions Clubs' Cup, and Chelsea were the only English team to attend meetings, along with 17 other clubs, including what remains a who's who of football: Anderlecht, KB Copenhagen, Real Madrid, Sporting, AC Milan, Sparta Prague, Dinamo Moscow and Partizan Belgrade.

'I received an invitation at the club to send a representative to Paris to discuss the idea of this new European competition which emanated from *L'Equipe*, the French newspaper,' explains John Battersby, club secretary at the time. 'I rang the chairman and told him I had this long letter from *L'Equipe* asking would we be interested in sending a representative to a hotel on Boulevard Haussmann. He said, "What do you think John?" And I said, "With the advent of flying (which really came from the improvement of aeroplanes during the war), it won't be long before European competition is quite feasible. International football will expand at national and at club level. In my mind it could have been similar to the Football League being formed and putting the Football Combination in as a reserve competition, the European competition would knock the stuffing out of the Football League as far as championships were concerned. It would become more important. He said, "Go over."

'So I took my wife and we went over to this hotel on the Boulevard Haussmann. This fellow called Jacques Godet was the *L'Equipe* man who ran the meeting and we all assembled there. There were people from all over Europe, but I was the only one from the UK – that's the odd thing about it.

'Although they sent invitations to Scotland, Wales, and other English clubs, I was the only one who went. I sat there, and I can get by on French not too bad, and they were running the meeting in French and it was quite interesting. We went through the morning session and they finished, and in typical French fashion we meandered through the streets led by the chairman to a café. We had a wonderful lunch set up there and the first item on the menu was half a dozen oysters. Now I used to eat oysters pretty regularly in my time at Chelsea, particularly on my way home on a Friday night, I'd call in to a pub in Notting Hill gate. Anyway, I had a bad oyster one Friday night and I went home and I was taken violently ill and I was sick for two or three days, and I had so many pills I rattled!

'I'd never had them again until I'd met them in Paris. This menu had "first course: oysters" and I thought what do I do? I felt I didn't want to make a fuss – I was sitting next to Jacques Godet, the chairman, and I suppose that was an honour because I was the only one from the UK.

'I thought I'd chance it, so I ate my oysters and then we had duck á l'orange – I always remember because I saw it later! We meandered back and carried on the afternoon session and then gradually I started to feel pretty queasy. Eventually I thought, oh no, and I got up and I made my way along past the chairs of the other delegates and I whispered in the ear of the chap from Northern Europe, I knew he spoke English. I said, "Please convey my apologies to the chairman, but I don't feel very well."'

Battersby hurried up to his hotel room before nature took its course.

'Unfortunately,' he laughs, 'I used the bidet instead of the toilet! Then my wife came in and found me in a state of collapse and I was trying to get undressed and she ran out shrieking for a doctor. Eventually she got me one. I'd changed into my pyjamas and then I said to her, "I'll have to go to the toilet," and she said, "Don't lock the door."

'So I went to the toilet, which was separate from the bathroom, and I went in and I didn't lock the door and I sat down, because I'd been vomiting then I got pressure to go the other way.

'Anyway, I started to feel faint, and my wife told me this afterwards. I started to fall forward off the seat as she came in, and she caught me with her arms under my shoulders and leaned me back. And at the back was the cistern with a button on it. It was a press-button flush and as I went back, my weight flushed the toilet and it went woosh. My wife said she nearly passed out because she thought that was my insides dropping out!

'I was ill for two or three days actually in Paris. What better place to be! I don't know what else went on at the meeting, I didn't hear. The committee members came up that evening to tell me in my absence I'd been elected onto the committee.'

Others elected included the president of Real Madrid, Santiago Bernabéu (the first vice-president), Ernest Bedrignans of France and Gusztav Sebes from Hungary.

Chelsea won the league and the invitation to join a meeting of Europe's elite was fulfilled. 'We had one or two meetings of this committee after Paris,' reveals Battersby. 'We met in Madrid, where Bernabéu really looked after us. We had even decided on a name for the committee – I know we were toying with the name of Rodolphe Seeldrayers. He was FIFA president. But then FIFA stepped in and said you lot aren't technically empowered to run an international competition and so they took it over. I was upset because I was enjoying swanning around Europe, all expenses paid and the best hotels, taking my wife with me and so on. I was a bit upset when we were ruled out of it.'

The Euro bubble was soon popped though. Not by dodgy oysters, but by the Football League's Alan Hardaker. Battersby was incensed. 'The Football League had a rule, if you studied the handbooks at that time, whereby they had power to authorise – or not – participation by clubs with other nationals, and they used that clause to stop us.

'They wouldn't give us permission and Joe Mears was in a difficult position. The Football League management committee decided Chelsea couldn't do it and they used the same rule the following year when Man United became champions. Man United put up a couple of fingers to them, said "Stuff you, we're going to take part, whether you agree or not."

'Joe Mears was a member of the management committee. I suppose it was a bit difficult for him to say, "We're going to do it this way, what do you say?"'

The governing bodies' usual concerns over fixtures 'congestion' and loss of status for the domestic league, along with Mears's official status, denied Chelsea a place in the cup, on the fledgling committee and, most likely, an invitation to join the G-14 of Europe's elite.

Brian Mears maintains that his father Joe, chairman of the FA at the time, was in favour of Chelsea participating in that first European Cup. It would have brought honour and status to the club, and extended its traditions for innovation and cosmopolitanism. Mears voted accordingly, but was outgunned. Without Mears's difficult position Chelsea might have ignored the Football League's decision – as Matt Busby's Manchester United did the following season.

But propriety and tradition won the day. Britannia ruled the playing field.

Strangely, in these days where the Champions League has become arguably the most important tournament and certainly the most glamorous, back in the pre-Common Market days Chelsea's decision was greeted largely with apathy among supporters. 'I wasn't terribly worried about not entering the European Cup,' says Peter Ralph, a season ticket holder at the time. 'I don't remember other fans being too bothered about it either. Back then it was just an embryonic tournament against foreign teams.'

There was no problem in Scotland for Hibernian, who had actually finished fifth in the league but progressed to the semi-finals of the fledgling competition where they lost to Reims.

Perhaps it's simply a fact that the English take sport less seriously than other countries. In 1987, for example, hostage Roger Auque's Islamist captor was sensitive to the impact of what he was about tell the Frenchman. 'I have some very bad news for you,' he said. 'Platini has just retired.' You can't imagine them thinking Terry Waite should be told about Chris Waddle's penalty against the Germans.

Ironically, Joe Mears got his own back by managing several Chelsea players in a London XI entered for the inaugural Industrial Fairs Inter City Cup in April 1955, a quirky competition open to cities that had held a trade fair. If you think the Champions League has been unwieldy, this one had a group stage, spurious seedings, variable squads, and took three years to complete. The Chelsea chairman actually managed the capital's team, which included the likes of Peter Sillett, Jimmy Greaves and Jim Lewis of Chelsea and Danny Blanchflower, Jack Kelsey and Noel Cantwell from their London rivals. They even played their home games at Stamford Bridge and drew a crowd of more than 45,000 for the 2-2 home leg of the final against Barcelona. With a hint of things to come for Chelsea at the Nou Camp, the Catalans ran out 6-0 winners in the away leg.

Chelsea's first competitive European games came in the more streamlined version of the competition the following season, beginning with Frem of Copenhagen, the home leg of which was played under floodlights at the Bridge. The aggregate score was a healthy 7-2 but Chelsea were outclassed by Belgrade the following spring. There was barely any coverage of this European novelty. Even Real Madrid's second successive European Cup victory warranted just a few lines.

By 1965–66, Chelsea took Europe seriously enough not to defend the less important League Cup. 'I think that even today if you go and watch a match at Chelsea, there's always a special atmosphere if it is a European tie,' says Ron Harris. 'The same thing applied years ago. We played AC Milan, some fantastic household name clubs. We played a couple of good German [and Austrian] clubs and from my point of view, it was an experience because you were playing against some of the best players in Europe .

'But anybody involved in football will tell you that even in my time, European nights were special. It was fantastic. I've been down there more recently to some of the games with 40,000 but you imagine going to Chelsea years ago when the capacity was more. It is different nowadays too, because in my time if you got beaten by someone you were out [of] the competition. The spectators got a bit more adrenalin going.'

Stress hormones were not lacking for the visit of AS Roma in September 1965. In what became known as the 'Battle of the Bridge', Roma niggled, Chelsea retaliated and, 'Together they proceeded to kick the match half dead, rifle its pockets and scatter the loot of a dreadful game into the night air,' noted *The Times*. McCreadie was sent off before half-time for decking Carponetti with a perfect right hook. Venables, Chelsea's 'calm, complete commander-in-chief as he moved the pins on the map' needed treatment after a horror tackle by Barison, but the three-card-trick of a free-kick in his hat-trick soon passed into legend. While the Italian line of defence assembled, he complained and theatrically strode out ten paces, infiltrating the wall before suddenly receiving the ball from Bridges at his feet and turning to strike home. The match is not remembered for that though.

'At one time, as the first half developed,' sneered one reporter, 'I felt there would be nothing but a police report or a dispatch from the battlefront when the time was over. The fact is that for almost three-quarters of an hour the match developed into nothing better than a Roman orgy, the roars for blood of the Stamford Bridge Coliseum in one's ears.'

'Eddie got sent-off,' recalls Harris, 'and Tommy Doc was manager, and he was supposed to have either passed a comment or made a sign at their officials on the touchline. I suppose it got built up into a thing come the return leg.'

In Rome's ferocious atmosphere, Docherty deployed Boyle as a roving extra defender, with the aim of stifling and frustrating the home side. Leonardi punched Hinton following a heavy tackle. Carlo Cudicini's father played in goal for Roma in the second leg and tipped away a decent shot from Bert Murray.

Joe Mears condemned the 'disgusting scenes' after the final whistle had confirmed Chelsea's progress and mobs attacked the Chelsea entourage. 'I've travelled all over the world watching football and never seen a crowd so hostile,' he said.

'It was a frightening experience over there to come away with all the coach smashed up,' says Harris, 'and players hiding under the seats at the back with glass flying about. No one got hurt, they were just hanging about under the seats hoping a brick never come on their head. But we qualified and that was the most important thing.'

Later in the tournament, 33 years before another famous visit, came the mighty Milan. 'Giovanni Rivera ... I remember marking a Brazilian fella on the left side who was a bit useful [Amarildo] and Maldini. There were a few useful names that people know about but the golden boy was Rivera. He looked useful against us,' continues Harris. 'To go over to the San Siro is a fantastic experience and I have been over there two or three times since to see Chelsea play and even sitting there and watching it brings back memories of us losing there, coming back to Chelsea and winning and I think we drew over there again and I won on a toss of a coin.'

In actual fact, after drawing impressively over two legs with Milan match skipper Ron Harris lost the first toss – to decide the play-off venue – but chose right when it came to the one after that match had also ended in a draw. 'They go to penalties now obviously,' remembers Harris. 'It was a daunting experience going out on the pitch again. I remember Tommy Docherty and the players waiting up by the tunnel at the far end where the players come out. It was against Paolo Maldini's father Cesare and I can't remember whether I called heads or tails [it was heads] but it came down on our side and the lads knew straightaway because Tommy Docherty grabbed me and punched the air.

'It is a poor way to decide a European game, but George Graham scored over in Milan and we came back to Chelsea and in the end I think we deserved to go through.'

As the song goes, 'Barcelona – it was the first time that we met ... How can I forget? ... You took my breath away ... And if God is willing ... we will meet again... some day.' In the Fairs Cup semi-final that year Chelsea had the first of several astounding Catalonian experiences.

Deluges have figured strongly in Chelsea history, one of which was self-inflicted. Docherty claims to have ordered the fire brigade in to Stamford Bridge to flood the pitch for a postponement so that the home leg arrived last.

'The first game there ended 2-0 and, to be truthful, I don't think we got out of our penalty area, we were absolutely hammered,' recalls Harris. 'We came back to Chelsea after that and won 2-0, and if you look back at that game, I scored a goal about ten minutes from time that would have put us 3-0 in front but it was disallowed because someone was offside.'

It finished 2-2 on aggregate, so another play-off draw was required. 'I heard Brian Mears [mourning the recent loss of father and chairman Joe] drew the straws to see if we played home or away and got the short one,' says Harris, who didn't witness things personally. But programme editor Albert Sewell remembers it being a little better organised. He recalls the referee going up into the old East Stand offices and pulling two blank envelopes from his pocket, each containing the name of one of the two clubs. Then in a method surely better suited to Oscar ceremonies, he opened one of them, which was found to contain the name 'Barcelona'.

'We went over there and got beaten 5-0,' says Harris, 'which should have been the score in the first game really. They were a good side then, Barcelona, and they would have beaten anybody to be truthful.'

'The one thing I remember about that trip,' said new-boy Charlie Cooke, who had just signed for the club, 'is arriving at the airport, flying out to Barcelona. I came down on the train with Tommy Doc, and when we got to the airport, there were a lot of guys hanging around in the waiting area, and I remember Barry Bridges talking with Tommy Doc and Barry left, didn't travel on that trip, but I didn't associate it with some big political upheaval in the club. That's maybe how naive I was. But I don't remember any long faces or ugly faces.

'It's not something that's come up very often as a topic of conversation, but afterwards people talked about the break-up of the team as something that was instigated solely by Tommy Doc, and I would say that it was probably a

50:50 thing. Once the players had dug their heels in about what their beef was with Tommy, it seemed to me it was as much their doing as Tommy's. If there was guilt involved, everyone was guilty. Both sides had drawn the line.'

The Barcelona debacle signalled the demolition of the treble-chasers of 1965. Bridges and Venables were soon out, but Europe would be very much back in fashion a few years later.

The Cup-Winners' Cup tie with Bruges in 1971 was another minor epic. After winning the Belgian leg, Coach Frank de Munck exuded confidence: 'In London, Chelsea may beat us, but we will make one goal for sure and go through.' The Chelsea programme cover that evening sported a wonderful photograph of the away supporters at the De Klokke ground. Inside, as well as chastising the highly visible '*l'hooligan* element' among its fans, the talk was of the fantastic atmosphere in Bruges's tight little stadium, and calls for Stamford Bridge to equal it for noise and passion. They were not to be disappointed.

In the Bruges line-up was an old adversary, the excellent winger Pieter 'Rob' Rensenbrink, who had played for DWS Amsterdam in the 1968–69 Fairs Cup when Chelsea lost on a toss of the coin. His colleagues back then included a masseur, a PE teacher and a café owner.

But this was to be a night for professionalism. Chelsea surprisingly ditched the time-honoured pass-and-move style for a direct approach targeting the heads of Baldwin and Osgood, returning from his unprecedented eight-week FA suspension for indiscipline. Stamford Bridge throbbed every bit as much as the De Klokke, and in equal or greater magnitude to the visit of the same team in 1995, or Vicenza in 1997, or Barca in 2005. Houseman, man of the match, scored the opener and Osgood equalised the aggregate with eight minutes to go before jumping onto the greyhound track. Bruges rallied briefly before the end of normal time, but with Houseman outstanding the extra period was Chelsea's, and Osgood and Baldwin vindicated Sexton's policy as they won 4-0 on the night and 4-2 on aggregate.

The semi-final, as in 2004–05 with Liverpool, pitched Chelsea against English opposition in Manchester City. Two players performed vital cameos. Ephemeral South African striker Derek Smethurst scored the goal that returned a 1-0 victory for the Blues at Stamford Bridge. While Keith Weller hit an indirect free-kick that City's unfortunate keeper Ron Healey flapped off the post into his own net in the return.

It capped another famous night in a rainy city, almost a year to the day after the FA Cup win. It set up perfectly the natural complement in the trophy cabinet, the European Cup-Winners' Cup. But the side that Chelsea faced in the final in Greece was Real Madrid, the don of European football teams.

The first game was drawn after Dempsey's late uncharacteristic defensive lapse. It was okay for the officials, who merely put the table away and removed the blue and white ribbons, and the players, whose job it was to stay for the few days before the replay. But for fans with jobs to return to it was a dilemma. The reaction of teenage Karim Kassam's cousin was quite normal, 'I don't think we played particularly well in the first game,' remembers Kassam, 'but it was just one of those things and my cousin just said, "Right, that's it, we're staying." And we did.'

Ahead of the replay Madrid's Spanish international striker Amancio told the press, 'If we stop Cooke, we will win.' 'I'm delighted you brought that up,' said Cooke in 2004, 'because I'd never heard it. You didn't read the newspapers, especially foreign ones, except the headlines, because it's just more stuff, more baggage. But I'm proud if that is what he actually said. I remember the game itself. It was even-stevens for most of it but we deserved to win. I think we wore them down. And it was a bizarre ending to it all because we hadn't expected a second match.'

'The lovely thing about Charlie,' said Peter Osgood, 'was if you were winning 1-0 with ten minutes to go, you'd give it to him, he'd take it away for five minutes and they couldn't get it off him. A great dribbler, great runner, terrific player and a great character.'

Cookie was excellent in the replay, but Ossie stole the show.

'It wasn't a great Real side we played,' said Osgood later. 'They were rebuilding a bit, but were still a force to be reckoned with. We fancied ourselves against them, as we knew we had plenty of grit and the flair as well. In the replay John Dempsey scored a goal early on and the second came from a dummy by Tommy Baldwin. He was screaming at me, and the two players went with him and gave me the chance. I curled it in the corner with my left foot. It was a terrific goal. Again it was a team goal, but a great goal to score in the final. That was the main thing. I had a knack of doing that.'

Of course, the second most famous 'bunking off' session in Chelsea history being abroad (the most notorious being those who truanted to see the Moscow Dynamos game at the Bridge in 1945) offered unexpected leisure opportunities. When Chelsea were in Rome to play Lazio in 2003, for instance, it brought a sight of enduring quaintness: several hundred people sitting and standing around inside the Colosseum, almost all wearing Chelsea replica shirts, and mingling with people dressed as gladiators. Back in 1971, however, before Spain and Greece had shaken off their dictators, football tourism was a genuine novelty. 'It was amazing,' recalls Alan Tomkins. 'There were about 40 or 50 of us and it was £70 for the ten-day trip to Loutraki. In those days you didn't have the package tours, you just had local Greek hotels.'

A German holiday camp called Poseidon caught their eye. 'It was just like you're in Skegness in a hotel and you see Butlins and you just want to go in and see what it's like. And we said, "Can we come in?" They said, "Oh no, no English hooligans."

'We convinced them that we weren't there for trouble but for the football and they let us in. And we had a great time, playing the Germans at table football and everything like that.'

The pioneer tourists went to look at the sights of Athens, including the Acropolis, and caused quite a stir. 'Amazing place ... huge,' Tomkins remembers. 'We came out and the Greeks were complaining because all the American tourists were coming up and photographing all the Chelsea supporters – not the Acropolis. "You must go, you're causing a blockage."

'We left the Acropolis and ended up in Constitution Square, where the royal palace is, with little cafés and all that. There was nothing like that in England at all at the time, that outdoor, coffee culture. It was totally alien and we had a fantastic time.'

The draw and the number who spontaneously decided to stick around for the replay made for hasty measures. 'We must have smuggled another 30 onto our coach,' says Tomkins. 'We bunged the driver loads of drachma to take them. We took them back to Loutraki, went to the hotel owners, who were brilliant, and said, "These kids, can they stay?"

'"Yeah, no problem," they said, "as long as they pay for food we can feed them." Ah, the Greeks were brilliant.

'We had this big Chelsea banner, everybody signed it, and we presented it to the family who ran the hotel. They pinned it on the wall and they gave us a Greek night with the bazoukis and everything. One of our guys went back to

Loutraki in about 1985, and he says the banner we gave them back in 1971 is still on the wall. I love the Greeks.'

The following season came a disappointing defence of the trophy, losing 1-1 on the away goals rule at home to Swedish semi-pros Atvidaberg. It was a damp squib after the sensational two-leg splicing of Jeunesse Hautcharage. The 8-0 and 13-0 (21-0 aggregate) scores broke many records: the 13 beat Manchester United's 1956–57 10-0 against Anderlecht; Osgood's eight beat the British two-leg record; 21 exceeded Sporting's 18-1 demolition of Nicosia in 1962–63 in the same competition. But if Atvidaberg were part-timers, Hautcharage should have been claiming benefit.

Ron Harris was the first skipper to raise a continental trophy for Chelsea and he is aware perspectives on Europe have changed since his day. 'Winning the FA Cup was the major one and winning a European competition was second,' he says. 'I think if you are a footballer today it is the European Cup that has all the glamour. I just feel that without naming any managers, the FA Cup has been devalued, like the Carling Cup. This year you look at the Arsenal that won it, they played Sheffield United and put out a reserve side. Every football club at the moment is clamouring to get into Europe.'

It would be a long time before Chelsea could compete against the continent's best again. It is a shame that the Chelsea of the late 1980s could not have done so even if they had qualified because of the post-Heysel ban.

The great gleaming silver lining to the storm clouds of the 4-0 defeat at Wembley 1994 was the European Cup-Winners' Cup entry, earned because United won the League and FA Cup. Unfortunately, on 28 February 1995, a return to Belgium prompted the last hurrah of the thugs, out for revenge for the Cup-Winners' Cup ambush nearly a quarter of a century earlier. It was not without its comical side, mind.

Being one of the thousand who'd made the perilous journey out there, it was easy to imagine what a gathering of the clans would have been like when some heads needed bashing in the Highlands. There were fans of every club: Huddersfield, Tottenham, West Ham ... To my personal surprise, there was also a delightful journalist friend from the *Face* magazine, Gavin Hills – a Man United fan. He had written several pieces about terrace casuals and cool violence and knew acid DJ and 'Junior Boys Own' legend Terry Farley, a renowned Chelsea fan. He said he was there because it was the biggest match in years and he wanted to be part of it.

Getting there was the toughest part. A no-match ticket, no-travel policy had been applied on all borders. There were rumours, too, of forged tickets on the market. At Ostend immigration, some passengers on the SeaCat had come prepared for the heavy security. If you looked like you were holidaying for two weeks in Holland rather than going on the lash in Bruges you might get through, with or without tattoos, cropped hair and alcoholic breath that could melt flock wallpaper.

One skinny young lad in a Fred Perry carried a huge old-fashioned suitcase, as big as a chest of drawers, apparently packed for a long break. An old Belgian copper sauntered over to him and asked if he had a match ticket. 'No, I'm here on holiday for a fortnight.' The copper's reply was inaudible, but the English lad took umbrage, and began gesticulating, 'What you on about? I ... am ... going ... on ... holiday! Look at all the clothes I've packed!'

Unfortunately, the mention of packing only drew attention to the suitcase, which had been wafting around all over the place with every wave of the arms. The copper nodded at the suitcase. 'Why should I open it?' More officers closed in. 'All right, all right ...' The case was placed on a table, opened up, and it contained ... absolutely nothing. 'Jeesus! Who nicked all my stuff!' shouted the lad half-heartedly. Laughing, red in the face, he turned on his heels and sauntered over towards the next SeaCat home.

Inside the compact Olympic stadium it was Belgian fairyland. The crowd swayed and sang along to a medley of oompah and folk songs played over the PA, and the noise at kick-off from an 18,000 crowd was extraordinary.

Outside, though, innocent package travellers had felt the squeeze of the Belgian mangle. Around 500 Chelsea supporters were rounded up and herded into a giant warehouse outside Bruges by police before the match. Inside, they were pushed into pens, handcuffed, sprayed with water cannons, and denied food or drink and bathroom facilities for up to nine hours. They were deported, some in cuffs, at dawn the following day. All had missed the game.

Some had been grabbed just before kick-off, chucked into a police van and attacked with a baton. Belgian police claimed their tickets were forgeries and tore them up in their faces. A Miss McDonnell from north London watched a sinister development. She said, 'I watched from a bar window as Belgian police hit out at people for merely walking along the street. These scenes were later shown on *News at Ten* and *Sky News*.'

The media wanted scenes of English fans rioting ahead of Euro 96 and the police seemingly did their best to provoke them. Inevitably the press suggested a Combat 18 [a far-right organisation known for racial violence] /BNP association with the trouble. The police, though, confirmed there was no evidence of Combat 18 involvement among the supporters of Chelsea, although 'some of those who associate with the supporters may have sympathies with this group'.

Almost as bad as the treatment of some Blues fans in Bruges was that dished out to many who travelled away to Real Zaragoza two months later in the same campaign. Trouble kicked off in the overcrowded lower section housing Chelsea fans and police charged after Zaragoza's third (and, as it proved, fatal) goal. Outside, they clubbed visiting fans randomly.

Nothing approaching these levels of official brutality, not even the blank incivility some experienced at the Moscow stadium in 2004, has happened since, thank God.

The 1994–95 campaign was, however, made pleasurable in the recollection by one truly magnificent performance, the 1-0 win at Austria Memphis. 'I was in the process of reading the SAS book *Bravo Two Zero* at the time,' said the game's hero John Spencer later. 'And it was totally an impulse to have Fiona Hitchcock [wife of Kevin] give me a number three haircut. She was, like, "Oh, I can't do it!" So she asked my wife, and she went into a huff. But it ended up that Fiona did it for me. I put a cap on the next day going to the airport and nobody thought anything of it. So I was sitting near the front of the plane, and stood up in my seat and took my hat off – some of the boys' faces were like "f**king hell!!" because I'd gone from having long hair down the back of my neck to looking like a psycho.'

'And I said to the lads, "This is *Bravo Two Zero*, I'm going in to do a job and get out." It was tongue in cheek, but I think the gaffer got hold of it and he said it to the pressmen and all of a sudden, the next day, all this stuff. People reading it must have thought I was an absolute lunatic! It got a bit embarrassing towards the end, but not to worry.'

His goal will live long in the memory of every Chelsea fan who watched it. 'It will with me as well,' he said. 'I would say that is the goal that turned my career around. I came back, I was out again for four weeks after the Leicester game, and it was my first game back. I had a 12-minute run on the Monday, trained Tuesday at the stadium, and trained Wednesday morning, the morning of the match. And I remember I was useless in the shooting in training before the match. I was spooning them all over the place, and I thought, "Oh for God's sake!"'

Chelsea had struggled throughout the tournament with the UEFA rule allowing only three 'foreigners' – as a Scotsman Spencer counted as foreign. Café Crème-smoking youth team manager Graham Rix had to turn out several times to make up numbers. It often meant playing out of position. 'Then the gaffer pulled me and said, "Listen, I'm going to play you, and I want you to play as a left-sided midfielder,"' said Spencer. 'I think he put me on the left side beside Andy Myers, because he's a whippet: if anybody gets by this lazy so-and-so, Andy Myers'll be able to run after him!

'So I was, like, "Yeah, I'll play there, give it a go." And Neil Shipperley played alone up front and I was supposed to get to him – I don't think I did too often, right enough. I was trying to link up but we had our backs to the wall. It was an impossible job to defend and get up to support Neil.'

Then negligence by Memphis at a corner kick left Spencer with a free – but 80-yard-long – run at goal. 'As I received the ball,' he recalled, 'I looked about, took two touches from the box and I was over the halfway line. I just knocked it forward and tried to get into my stride as quickly as possible. I was worried about the hamstring, but I looked around me and saw there was nobody anywhere near me, and there was no need to go any quicker.

'And there was these big mad Austrian plodders running after me, going "Rooarrrrrrrr!" like six Erland Johnsen's with black hair. And I just remember as I was running seeing, I think it was a black hand, out of the corner of my eye – and it was Eddie Newton's. I looked round and he's galloping like a madman. I thought, "Jeezus, he's crackers!" And I was saying, "C'mon, keep up with me, keep going." And the keeper's seen me looking, and I've faked the shot and he went one way and I put it into the net.

'And I said, "Thanks very much Ed, you're a great decoy." He made a 70-yard decoy run there! Very important player for the team, Eddie Newton! I said to him if I'd have given it to you, we'd be out of the cup!

'It was just one of those things – it wasn't as if I had to beat four players or anything. Afterwards I was sick on the park. I ran back and gave the fist to the bench, and the gaffer's gone "Well done!" And suddenly: *mnnk, mnnk* – I'd thrown up all this water I'd drunk before the match. After the game my legs just went.'

The Austrians equalised but Chelsea needed just to hang on to go through on the away goals rule. 'Myself and Dennis Wise were shadowing the ball in their half, just trying to keep the ball.' says Spencer. 'The final whistle went and I just fell on my backside. I couldn't believe it. Then the Chelsea fans were going mental, it was a different class. I threw my shirt into the crowd that night. I remember the guy who got it came up to me a few weeks afterwards and said I was a smelly bastard – no, I'm joking, he asked me to autograph the shirt. A week later, I was in the Scotland squad to play Russia – I got that much publicity, and I think Craig Brown saw it and decided to give me a chance.'

Three years after the Zaragoza defeat, following the 1997 FA Cup win, it was a confident and experienced Chelsea that enjoyed another memorable Cup-Winners' Cup spree. 'We want to win it,' said Ruud Gullit's assistant manager Graham Rix at the start of it. 'We want to win everything, but a European trophy is something special not only for Chelsea, but for the Premiership in general. It gives a good standing in Europe. It's important. But if we won the Cup-Winners' Cup and finished seventh in the Premiership, I'd be very pissed off. I think the quality we have in the squad, the experience and the knowledge now, there's no reason why we shouldn't go from strength to strength.'

In May, following a campaign of celebrated nights, especially the defeat of Betis in Seville in which Flo starred, and one of the great floodlit European nights at the Bridge, the 3-1 defeat of Vicenza, Chelsea faced Felix Magath's Stuttgart in the final at the Rasunda Stadium in Stockholm.

Chelsea fans arriving in Sweden by plane were taken through a bizarre security check in a double-decker bus on the airport tarmac. It was a lovely day and the squares and bars of the city were decked in blue and white; the fans were in for the long haul.

Gianfranco Zola had flown abroad in a desperate bid to overcome an injury that looked certain to rule out any 'Zola power' in the Rasunda Stadium. He was dismayed when, having worked so hard to declare himself fit, Luca Vialli named him only on the bench and started himself with the deserving Flo. 'I'd been his guardian angel for about three or four weeks before,' recalls Gary Staker, 'and I heard a lot of what he was going through mentally. In the hotel, when I knew he was sub, he came over to me and he couldn't believe it. I said, rightly or wrongly, "I think today you're going to come on and score."'

In truth the match was a dour encounter. After 70 minutes the fans rose to applaud Zola as he stripped for action, replacing Flo. Almost immediately, Dennis Wise saw his darting run and popped the ball into his path, as he did effectively so many times. 'I thought, "This is the moment, Franco, take it,"' Zola recalled of that split second. 'And fortunately everything went right because I hit the ball perfectly and it went where I wanted it to go. It was absolutely magnificent.'

Five minutes before the end Dan Petrescu was confusingly sent off for perhaps the only hard tackle he ever made. But Chelsea held out to win 1-0.

As fans filed out of the stadium, speculative locals were already offering T-shirts with the final score printed on them. Even a three-hour queue of coaches to the chaotic Stockholm airport, where anyone was getting on any flight to London, couldn't dampen spirits. As in 1971, this crowned the glory of a great team. Everyone glowed, especially Rix. Chelsea had finished fourth in the league too – progress, just as he and Gullit had demanded.

Chelsea's defence of the title was a comparatively dull affair, with three Scandinavian sides – Helsingborgs, Copenhagen and Valerenga – comprising the opposition as far as the quarter-finals. The away match in Copenhagen featured a winner from Chelsea winger Brian Laudrup, a rare contribution from the much-heralded but disappointing Dane, who soon moved back there from London. A 2-1 aggregate loss in the semi-final to pacy but unfashionable Real Mallorca was a blow, tempered a little by the colour and pageantry of flag-waving Spanish supporters on a warm night. Blues supporters left the holiday island craving more European jaunts.

Changes to entry criteria benefited Chelsea. In 1997–98 UEFA had allowed championship runners-up to compete in the Champions League. In 1999–2000 this was expanded to include four clubs from the top four nations, and a trio of clubs from the next three most successful leagues, and Chelsea qualified by finishing third in the Premiership – 44 years since the club was first invited.

The Champions League campaign that year was the real return to the class of 1971, and in excess of it. The trouble-free 5-0 win in Galatasaray, where banners at the airport said, 'Welcome to Hell!', was the biggest ever away win in the Champions League. As so often in Europe, Tore Andre Flo was unplayable that night.

With De Goey, Ferrer, Desailly, Leboeuf, Le Saux, Di Matteo, Deschamps, Wise, Poyet and Zola also available it was a fantastic team that showed itself on a par with Italy's finest, including Milan in the first group stage and Lazio in the second, where the ultras endeared themselves to travelling fans by unravelling a complicated sequence of long banners that ended with an expression of hatred for Arsenal.

'As soon as the groups were announced everyone just landed on AC Milan for the big one, the European trip to savour, and so it proved,' says season ticket holder Damien French. 'A group of us did the Da Vinci museum of science and technology, which was amazing. And every time we all met up again in a restaurant or bar someone was carrying Prada bags or whatever. Sunderland away didn't quite compare!'

The San Siro was throbbing and for Chelsea fans there was a sense of arrival, fulfilment of what should have been in 1955–56. It was also a great game of tactical, technical and tense football. 'One funny thing was that the tickets we had were in a mixed end and we were behind two young Milan geezers who were quite obviously smoking a joint. We had a nice little chat about each other's players – my uncle's Italian and I know one or two bits of the lingo – and then when Oliver Bierhoff scored with about 15 minutes to go, one of the geezers turns round with a smile and passes me and my mate Giles a joint, supposedly to soften the pain. Three minutes later Wisey scores, and Giles taps him on the shoulder and hands the spliff back! They had to laugh. It was a great atmosphere and a landmark match for the new Chelsea.'

The draw virtually assured Chelsea of progressing to the next stage. Everyone connected with the club instantly recognised its importance. 'The crowd that night was the most intimidating I've ever seen,' says MTV presenter Trevor Nelson. 'The Milan fans were really quiet until they took the lead, and then it was as if someone just turned the volume up. It was incredible. When Dennis Wise equalised it was amazing, all the Chelsea fans went mad. We were kept in the stadium for over an hour after the match but no one cared because it was just like a massive party.'

'I heard "Oh Dennis Wise, scored a f**cking great goal, at the San Siro, with 10 minutes to go," sung at the next game,' says French, 'and it's great for Dennis that his goal is immortal now.'

Chairman Ken Bates reckoned the prize money from UEFA and gate revenues was worth about £5 million to Chelsea. 'I'm pleased for Dennis Wise,' he said. 'He loves the club. But, mind you, he probably needed it because he's going on holiday for a month.' Wise began a four-match domestic ban straightaway.

Chelsea's progress on the club's debut in the club football's biggest competition sparkled with the joy that comes from exceeded expectations. No one expected Vialli's men to win it, but a quarter-final against a Barcelona side that had sometimes looked vulnerable brought as much hope as glamour.

The home leg was as great a night as can have been experienced at the Bridge. The full flair and effectiveness of Wise and Deschamps, Zola and Flo was wrought on the Catalans, a devastating eight-minute spell setting Chelsea up 3-0. But Barca, and particularly Luis Figo, gathered themselves, the Portuguese winger marking a virtuoso second half display with a great goal to stir doubts in Chelsea minds.

The performance of the Nou Camp stadium for the return was even better than its team's. Before the game brilliantly orchestrated card displays in the main stand showed the English and Catalonian flags side by side, then the badges of the respective clubs, and finally the required scoreline, '2-0'. It was a great example of groupthink.

With Graham Rix unavailable because of the scandal involving a 16-year-old girl, Vialli looked to his other assistant, Chelsea legend Ray Wilkins. Many observers felt the best way to beat Barcelona was to attack their defensive heart, noted for its feeble pulse. Vialli's tactic, though, was to sit back. Years later Graham Rix suggested that the players had actually been too attacking in the game for him. At half-time, the card scoreline had been realised and Chelsea looked unusually insipid. Then a mistake by the Barca keeper Hesp allowed Flo to grab a goal potentially even more vital than Figo's at the Bridge. From then on, though, wave after wave of attacks battered the Chelsea backline and each one seemed to produce a free kick, a corner or a chance.

Even though De Goey, Desailly et al held out until seven minutes from the referee's whistle that would have brought an undreamt-of semi-final, it was always frantic and out of control. Dani missed chances before scoring the goal that set up extra time. Rivaldo missed a late penalty that would have saved us the sad spectacle of extra time and watching our heroes battered like washed up heavyweights. Nevertheless it was an incredible experience; the night, the tournament, everything.

Claudio Ranieri's second match as manager of the Blues in September 2000 was away to lowly St Gallen of Zurich. Pursuit of the UEFA Cup ended on a cold, damp night amid the sound of cowbells and oompah music, and in the presence of celebrity supporter Martina Hingis. It was Swiss misses of a different kind though – and three damaging 'hits' – that occupied the thoughts that evening.

Muller levelled the aggregate score on the night, and soon the stellar career of Roberto Di Matteo – ironically one of the casualties of the Vialli reign – would come to an end with a multiple leg-break as he alone drove forward for the equaliser. St Gallen's second in a spiritless second half brought ejection from the tournament at the first stage and utter disappointment.

The financial setback was equally damaging, but there would be more Euro-dismay in the ensuing two UEFA Cups. In 2001, following the assassination of an Israeli minister, security fears led six star players to pull out of the trip to Tel Aviv to play Hapoel: Emmanuel Petit, Graeme Le Saux, Marcel Desailly, Eidur Gudjohnsen, Albert Ferrer and William Gallas. Gudjohnsen and Petit cited their respective partners' pregnancies, while Desailly was suffering toothache and an Achilles injury. Mario Melchiot was sent off and an inexperienced, scratch side lost 0-2. It prompted Leeds fans at the next match to twist a well-known Chelsea anthem, 'Five men wouldn't go,' they crowed, 'wouldn't go to Israel.'

The lacklustre home leg was a poor 1-1 draw, reminiscent of Atvidaberg 30 years earlier.

The following year Viking Stavanger cancelled our holiday plans. Chelsea went in a goal to the good from the home game but away, just past the half-hour, Viking had cancelled that out. The only good news was John Terry returned from injury to score one of his six goals that season, but Chelsea were dumped out of the European pool, 4-2 on aggregate, by one of football's 'minnows' for the third consecutive season.

Nevertheless, Chelsea qualified on league merit for the Champions League qualifying rounds in 2003–04 and easily beat Zilina to make the group stage, to be set up against Lazio, Besiktas and Sparta Prague. As we know, the arrival of Roman Abramovich brought a massive influx of personnel. It may have been useful to coaches that UEFA's benches could now seat seven substitutes, but that was no consolation to last season's stalwarts Terry, Lampard and Gudjohnsen, who sat there glumly, perhaps pondering their futures, throughout a poor first half in Prague in the opening game.

The new solidity of Chelsea was becoming evident, however, and occasional opportunist William Gallas capitalised on indecision to knock in a vital winner from close range with five minutes to go. The group was now set up nicely for the Blues and when they inflicted a 4-0 defeat on Lazio in Rome, which equalled the heaviest away defeat by any foreign side on Italian soil – Mihailovic's bigotry and stupidity exposed and punished with a red card – there was genuine belief in winning the trophy.

In the quarter-finals, Chelsea were paired with perennial continental underachievers Arsenal. One side would reach the semi-finals of the competition for the first time – and it wouldn't be Arsenal. The Gunners made the mistake of not pressing their slight advantage once Pires had equalised Gudjohnsen's opener and Desailly had been sent off late on in the first leg. The drama of the 2-1 (3-2 aggregate) win at Highbury and Wayne Bridge's goal might never be surpassed for some fans.

Of the possible semi-final opponents, Chelsea might have chosen Monaco, managed by old boy Didier Deschamps, over Deportivo or José Mourinho's Porto. But the away leg of their clash, on a terrible pitch in a Lego stadium, was a disaster for Chelsea and Ranieri. Carrying poor league form into the biggest match in the club's history to date, and missing the talismanic Damien Duff and vital Carlo Cudicini, the Blues managed to cancel Dado Prso's disappointing early goal through Hernan Crespo midway through the first half.

Things went wrong when Chelsea earned the numerical advantage just after the break. The small but vociferous Monancians knew Claude Makelele had (untypically) overreacted to Zikos's challenge to get him sent off, and in the moments following whipped up a storm that drove their incensed heroes on.

Chelsea failed to respond, and a series of spontaneous and ambitious substitutions, for which Ranieri was panned, disrupted the visitors' structure. Ranieri was already under media pressure, with other managers' names already linked to his job. If he could have heard what exasperated Chelsea fans in the stands were saying about his judgment, he might have resigned there and then.

When Jimmy Floyd Hasselbaink somehow failed to convert Wayne Bridge's great through ball, the Monaco keeper set up free-running winger Ludovic Giuly, who held off Desailly, feeding Fernando Morientes. The on-loan Real Madrid striker easily beat Marco Ambrosio. Monaco's almost ridiculously fired-up sub Shabani Nonda then beat Ambrosio's poor attempt to save; 3-1. It meant a long, long night in the world's most expensive bars.

'We are very angry,' said Crespo afterwards, 'we are very disappointed. But now it's clear in all our minds, I think about the second leg. I think this team has the attributes to change things. Second half we don't play like the first half. We mistake and we pay. When you play at a high level, it's normal, when you mistake, you pay.

'Now we want to change these things. It will be a great battle, but we want to restart. We want to stay in this Champions League. We want to write history now. With our crowd and our stadium.'

Brave words, and there was genuine hope in a turnaround during the home leg when Gronkjaer and Lampard reached the target 2-0 scoreline in 44 minutes. It must have had the yachts on the Cote d'Azur bobbing nervously. But a minute later, despite the look of handball, Ibarra beat Cudicini and stuck a sword through Chelsea's faith. It ended 2-2, 3-5 on aggregate.

'I think back to then,' says John Terry, remembering the first leg, 'and everyone talks about tactical changes and stuff, but I think it was down to the players, and we didn't perform. It was our first really big game together and maybe it got to us a little bit, because there's no doubt in my mind that we're better than Monaco. We were better than them and we should have gone all the way.

'But you know we just didn't have that ... maybe that experience together. That experience of winning, that driving mentality, and it didn't happen. It's frustrating because I think Chelsea, over the last ten or 20 years, have always been that *nearly* club and going into that we wanted to change things. We wanted to start winning trophies for Chelsea and after that people were saying "Same old Chelsea, got there, but not good enough."'

There was to be more semi-final disappointment to put crystals in the blood when Chelsea met Liverpool in the semi-final in 2005, but first there was Barcelona.

'And I was fed up with that and you know the new manager coming in and installing great confidence in the lads, he bought some great players in and something from day one last year felt right, it felt special. And from that moment the manager was in charge, we knew,' explains Terry.

Seemingly the only challenge to José Mourinho being in charge came from the authorities. Something snapped at the Champions League 'last 16' match at the Nou Camp in February 2005.

Leading through a delightful Belletti own goal, under pressure from Didier Drogba, after 33 minutes and with his team playing better than any previous Chelsea one at the famous old Barcelona stadium, Mourinho was still concerned. 'During the first half of the game,' he says, 'Rijkaard was very aggressive to the fourth referee. Before the end of the first half, I'm always the first one to go to the dressing room, because I have my notebook, and I have to organise the information, but I talked to my assistants, "You wait here and you go only when the ref goes. Just wait, just wait to see."

'And I went to the dressing room and I did my speech at the half-time, and my assistants, they were not there. And in the end of the speech, they come and Steve [Clarke] told me, "I saw this, this, this and this."'

'"Okay, if you saw, you saw. Okay, let's go for the second half." In the second half what happened, happened.'

He is referring, of course, to the performance of referee Anders Frisk in twice harshly booking the hard-working Drogba, who was sent off in the 56th minute. Mourinho's mind went back to what Clarke had just witnessed at half-time. 'I told the fourth official, "My people saw it, they told me, and in the end of the game I will tell this to UEFA. You don't go home without this."'

Ten-man Chelsea lost the game 2-1. The dilemma for the Chelsea manager and officials was how to handle the complaint and the imminent press conference. 'In the end of the game the decision was, do we say now publicly or do we do it properly and we do a written information to UEFA,' says Mourinho. 'And we decided in our opinion, in the best way for the game, instead of saying publicly in the press conference, "this happened, and this and this," we did it properly, we wait, we wrote the information, and after that is what you know happens.' Chelsea's decision to read a statement rather than have the manager and players face the media was a breach of UEFA rules that allowed their media team to launch an attack on the club and its staff, especially in the ill-advised outbursts of UEFA's director of communications William Gaillard, even before Chelsea had presented their written evidence. Once they had, the club and named individuals were charged with making false statements.

Chelsea's case was that Barca boss Frank Rijkaard had breached UEFA regulations by talking to the match referee at half-time. They further suggested that this conversation had taken place in the referee's room. The fact that this was incorrect can be explained by the special layout at the Nou Camp and does not affect the main charge that Rijkaard may have attempted to influence the Swedish official.

In the Nou Camp, the tunnel off the pitch leads upstairs to a junction of glass doors, with the separate dressing rooms in very distinct directions. Straight ahead, through double glass doors, leads only to the officials' rest room. Chelsea's claim was that Rijkaard had pursued Frisk through the doors towards his room and inside it. In retrospect, it may have inferred complicity on Frisk's part, whereas Chelsea's problem was with Rijkaard's conversation with him.

Gaillard claimed, 'There is a contradiction between what Mourinho says and what Chelsea say in their report. The truth is that none of the three [men charged] were in a position where they could have seen that [alleged meeting between Frisk and Rijkaard] taking place. We are talking about incidents that brought the game into disrepute over a two-week period, a conspiracy to put pressure on match officials. It obviously poisons the atmosphere and can lead to violent acts by supporters, a totally unnecessary situation. Chelsea have been using lies as a pre-match tactic. They were trying to qualify for the next round by putting pressure on referees. They were ready to use disloyal methods. There is no place in football for this type of behaviour.'

Or, you might think, there is no place at an impartial football authority for such spouting off. He also suggested that expulsion from the tournament was a possibility and he wasn't even on the inquiry panel. 'I thought the comments by Gaillard were totally inappropriate,' says Bruce Buck, Chelsea chairman. 'If the objective was to do what's best for football, he didn't. We had to respond to those kinds of comment.'

The issue had been clouded by the sudden resignation of respected ref Anders Frisk for alleged 'death threats' from 'Chelsea fans'. While not making light of any such emails, texts or whatever, if they actually happened, aren't such 'I'm gonna kill you' outbursts a part of everyone's lives from cradle to grave in the digital age, where communication has become compulsion? Mourinho himself has received threats from 'Porto fans' but carries on.

All emails are ultimately traceable. Chelsea publicly made it clear to UEFA that the club would take action against any of its supporters responsible for such threats, and they requested the evidence be passed on to them. None ever was.

Frisk's regrettable decision nevertheless pressurised Chelsea further. In fact, on the night of the game, Rijkaard admitted to the press that he had tried to discuss 'something which happened in the first half'. This was overlooked.

Rijkaard utterly denied any wrongdoing, however, saying Chelsea were 'exaggerating' the issue. As the hearing approached, it had the mark of the old comedy line, 'the punishment's hanging, now what's the crime?'

The whiff from Nyon, in Switzerland, home of UEFA, had reached Canary Wharf. British journalists started to examine UEFA's probity. How fair would the inquiry be? Martin Samuel found it 'a little disconcerting that the head of the UEFA disciplinary committee, Josep Lluís Vilaseca Guasch, is from Barcelona. Not that UEFA would confirm that yesterday. Having been fired by truth on Monday, yesterday it was the voice of vagueness that fielded questions about Guasch's hometown. "He's from Spain," it said. "You would have to ask them."

'Eventually, a nice chap at the Tribunal Español de Arbitraje Deportivo (the Spanish Council of Sports Arbitration), where Guasch is president, confirmed, "He is based mainly in Barcelona." Later, Guasch stood down from the Chelsea hearing, although by then the damage was done.'

When the judgment of the panel was announced, it was a surprise. Chelsea's version of events was corroborated by witnesses, save for the detail of the conversation taking place in the referee's room.

Here's what UEFA's report actually says about Rijkaard talking to Frisk in the tunnel, '... The latter [Frisk] reported that he could not understand what the Barcelona coach was saying. It appears that in the tunnel a member of the Chelsea technical staff, i.e. the goalkeeping coach Silvino [Lauro], tried to pull the Barcelona assistant coach Henrik ten Cate away from the referee, causing a further gathering of representatives from the two sides. At the top of the stairs [at the end of the tunnel] Anders Frisk and his assistants went through the left glass door and turned left for gaining their dressing rooms that were locked. Frank Rijkaard and his staff went through the right glass door and it appears that Frank Rijkaard tried to address some words to Anders Frisk at the end of the reception area [i.e. outside the referee's locked room]. However, the referee told him to gain his dressing room, and Frank Rijkaard did so immediately ... '

Three witnesses said Rijkaard didn't enter Frisk's room, contradicting the two Chelsea technical staff who thought he had.

'Nevertheless,' continues the statement, 'it can be inferred from the witness statements at hand that Frank Rijkaard addressed some words to the referee behind the glass wall, notably in the reception area.'

The statement of Pascal Fratellia, UEFA's venue director, confirms that Rijkaard wished to 'try to talk with him [Frisk] while climbing the stairs' and that this continued all the way to the referee's door. The Barca manager was told that, 'it was not the moment or the place to speak about any match situation'.

It seems Chelsea were vindicated except for a small but damaging technicality, yet were found guilty nonetheless. Rijkaard was clearly trying to have a word with the referee at half-time, but has never been censured.

To Mourinho the outcome was 'a big surprise. A big surprise. I think in football, in these kind of things, there are not big players, small players, big managers and small managers. If a player elbows another one, it can be Shevchenko or it can be a player from Fourth Division, is the same thing. Is red card, is red card. Handball is a penalty, Okay? Is the same for everybody, and for me it was a big surprise that Steve Clarke was saying, "I saw this, this, this and this," and Rikjaard was saying, "It doesn't happen." And I never understood what's the difference between Frank Rikjaard and Steve Clarke. As a man, as a football man, what's the difference? In that moment, in that space, what's the difference? Why the truth is there and the truth is not there. Why?'

No lesson is ever lost on the Chelsea boss, though.

'They admit everything after,' he notes. 'The lesson is that you are in their hands. You can do nothing to prove you are right. Nothing. You can do nothing.

'I think in that moment it is not important the truth. It is important what they want to be the truth and you can do nothing. But what I will do in the future if it happens again, I'll speak again! And suspended again! And pay money again! And criticised again! But I know no power for the truth to win, no power for that.'

'A lot of people say, "Chelsea are arrogant, they have too much money, they don't care about the rules, they just do what they want,"' sighs Buck. 'That is absolutely not true. It's a feeling within some people in football, but we really want to be a good citizen. If you went through a lot of the off-field problems, a lot of them were insignificant.

'We saw an inappropriate situation. We got the guilty parties wrong. The ref, followed by Rijkaard went through the glass doors then went left – the only thing left was the referee's room.Not until the day before the hearing did we see testimony from Anders Frisk that said, "I told Rijkaard that it was inappropriate to talk about match events." We saw something, we made a mistake, but the whole situation was blown out of proportion.

'There was no formal apology to Frisk. But after the hearing I think we made it clear we thought he was a man of integrity. But that's all behind us. When you're number one, people always want to knock you down. We just have to deal with that.'

As bad as Barcelona was in 2000, and again at that away leg in 2005, it was magnificent at home in 2005. In one of the Bridge's greatest ever nights, after 20 minutes the 1-2 deficit had been dramatically overturned. During a spellbinding 11-minute spell – perhaps the best in the club's history, given the level – the dynamic Gudjohnsen, Lampard and Duff put Chelsea three up. Then, shockingly, the Brazilian Ronaldinho struck twice, once through a penalty and next with a piece of inspiration – a samba sway and a toe-punch into the net – that even Chelsea fans marvelled at. (Incidentally, Spaniards have only contributed two of the last ten goals the Catalans have scored against Chelsea.)

With the game poised at 3-2, 4-4 overall, by half-time the Blues were losing on away goals. But Mourinho's men showed the power of patience in the face of adversity and controlled the second half. With less than 15 minutes to go, John Terry scored what would prove the winner and sent the fans home throbbing. 'I don't know what was going through my head,' Terry smiles at the memory. 'I just remember signalling to Duffa that I was going to make my run near post. So I made my run far, and checked back to the near post, and I just remember maybe being too far out. I tried to ... not even to go for goal – I just glanced it back across towards the far post and I just remember looking up thinking, "I got good contact on that," and seeing it go in, it was like slow motion.'

The wily Ricardo Carvalho, near the line, diverted the attention of those who might have stopped it.

'After it went in, I just remember running away. It wasn't much of a celebration. I run back up the pitch rather than towards the fans and Coley grabbed me, said, "Stay here, let's stay here for a little bit," and, you know, "Stay with the lads, together, waste a bit of time." And we were saying, "Let's f**king keep it tight," and things like that.

'But it wasn't till after that I got home and saw it and thought, "Oh, f**king hell, what a goal!" I was buzzing at scoring against such a great team and especially to get the winner.'

THE WORST OF TIMES

Chelsea **tragedies**, from Ben Warren
to Matthew Harding

18

THERE'S ONLY ONE MATTHEW HARDING

Chelsea has been relatively free of the tragedies that have shaped the reputations of other football clubs. As fans we cannot embroider 'Justice' on banners nor wear armbands with the number '96'. No uncomfortable marble plaque in our museum commemorates the dead from rival terraces. There is no clock outside our stadium frozen in time, nor a list of names of those who died watching their team. But there was a moment for the club when, as with Hillsborough, Heysel, Munich, Ibrox or Bradford before, the compassion of the football world found an unforgettable focus.

On the night of Tuesday 22 October 1996, a twin-engine French Aerospatiale AS 355F1 Squirrel helicopter plummeted to earth in farmland near Middlewich in Cheshire. Passengers Raymond Deane and Tony Burridge, both businessmen, and *Telegraph Magazine* editor, Bolton fan and Bob Dylan anthologist John Bauldie, died instantly from multiple injuries, along with pilot Michael Goss. Four terrible family tragedies.

It was the presence of another, though, that would send shockwaves through the whole of football. Matthew Harding, director, sometime vice-chairman and benefactor of Chelsea FC perished along with his friends on the way back from the club's 1-2 Coca-Cola Cup defeat at Bolton's Burnden Park.

A lifelong supporter who had made a fortune from reinsurance, Harding began to make important investments in Chelsea after being introduced to Ken Bates by Janet Rainbow, an executive of Chelsea Pitch Owners. Harding had teased Bates that he was rather wealthier than the chairman, a boast that led to greater things. Harding's money had helped build the new North Stand, possibly sign some major players and secured the freehold of Stamford Bridge. For a time he was announced by Bates as a putative successor, but the two men fell out badly as a power struggle ensued. A while before the fatal accident, Bates had actually banned him from the directors' box. But even he suspended his war of words temporarily following the crash.

The inquest jury was told that the man at the controls, Michael Goss, a 38-year-old ex-serviceman with limited helicopter experience, had probably become disorientated and confused. Soon after take-off Goss had asked air traffic control if he might abort and return to Manchester airport. But he carried on, flying at an altitude below the safe minimum to avoid thick cloud and on a tricky route over high ground and obstacles that a weather forecaster had suggested he avoid. For a man of Goss's limited experience, the chief accident investigator concluded, this was 'more than was achievable', flying alone at night with no autopilot while trying to read a map and talk to air traffic control.

The aircraft went into a nose-up position after Goss tried to climb steeply. Terrifyingly, they would at this point have been flying 'blind', relying solely on Goss's instrument reading skills – for which he had no qualifications. Then the helicopter spiralled to the ground. Although tests showed that the passengers had been drinking, the amounts were not sufficient to have produced 'irrational or unrestrained behaviour'. Harding had booked the pilot for seven trips. This was the first and last.

'I was on the executive coach coming back from Bolton,' remembers Colin Hutchinson. 'And I got a call from the team coach to say that a helicopter had gone down and there was a fear it might be Matthew and his party. Then when we got back, my wife Linda was with me and she was very close to Matthew's wife. It's all a blur now, but we were making calls through the night. There was no confirmation, but it was becoming more and more apparent what had happened.'

The wreckage burned for 90 minutes, making the forensic task difficult. There was an agonising wait for confirmation of the victims' identities. The mood on the players' coach was sombre. 'We'd just arrived at Harlington and the players had just got off,' recalled fitness coach Ade Mafe. 'I was sitting across the table from [assistant manager] Graham Rix, who received the phone call on the coach in the early hours. He whispered over to the other side to Ruud Gullit. I overheard what he said. It was just pure shock. We didn't know any details. You just knew straightaway that something bad had happened. When I got home I checked Ceefax and saw the story about the crash. Then it was confirmed the following morning that Mr Harding was killed in it.'

For Hutchinson, a close confidant of Harding's who often travelled with him to games, there was an added element of the macabre. 'The most eerie thing,' he remembers, 'was there were journalists actually ringing me the next morning, really just checking whether I was still around.'

Neil Barnett, editor of the programme and *Onside* at the time, arrived home from the game at 3 a.m. and scoured TV text for updates. 'Matthew's death was confirmed about 8 a.m. the day after the helicopter crash,' he recalls. 'There had been strong hints in the media because they kept reporting that bits of the Bolton v Chelsea programme had been found on the scene. I remember Capital Radio phoning me up at 6 a.m. and just asking me if I could confirm it was him. It was a good job I already thought that it must be or it would have been a complete shock.

'Within hours hundreds of fans had gone down to Stamford Bridge and created a memorial wall by leaving flowers, shirts, scarves, all sorts of mementoes, and the emotion was extraordinary. The outbreak of grief was a bit like Princess Di's death, it was just overwhelming. There were soon tributes from fans of other clubs and the "wall" just grew and grew.'

The crash had long-term impacts. Following the inquest, new rules were introduced by the Civil Aviation Authority governing pilots who fly by visual means only. More poignantly, it had provoked that rare experience in football – communal lamentation, that moment when Britain surprises itself with a spontaneous outburst of emotion and unity. This was, remember, the aftermath of Euro 96, the de-brutalising of English football, the new flowering of fandom. Chelsea received cards, flowers and scarves from supporters of hundreds of different clubs, many of whom usually maintained a hatred of the Blues. Over the days before the next home match, Stamford Bridge became a shrine to Harding and what he stood for.

The view usually expressed in those cards, on websites, in bars and on terraces was that 'every fan would love a Matthew Harding at their club'. They had watched, fascinated as this millionaire, Guinness-supping, terrace-chanting, Ossie-loving benefactor had invested substantially in the club he loved, to give it a long-overdue chance to lasso the moon. 'He was the forerunner to Roman Abramovich,' says Neil Barnett. 'He flashed his cash, loved his football. But he was quite willing to be highlighted in the media and a lot of fans identified with him.'

The mood in the game at the time was for more fan representation on the board – here was the board member who represented the fans. As the floral tributes grew it became clear that what Harding actually stood for, in the minds of supporters up and down the country at least, was pure faith; hope and charity. He was the Everyman Fan; given the chance, who would not do what he did for the club they loved?

'Ken Bates and Matthew were getting on better at the time,' recalls Barnett, 'so on the [Wednesday] afternoon Chelsea held a press conference and announced the new North Stand would be renamed the Matthew Harding Stand. Colin Hutchinson was very close to Matthew and was determined his contribution wouldn't be forgotten. He was at the conference as well, so was Ruud Gullit.'

On the day of Chelsea's next home match Ade Mafe mentioned the sombre air he'd noticed at the training ground the previous few days, '... not many people saying very much, knowing we'd all got a job to do and had to keep doing it, but obviously full of sadness at the loss. Hopefully, today we know he would have been cheering and shouting along with the rest of the fans and let's hope the game really becomes a tribute to him and what he's done for the club.'

Of all fixtures, the match that followed four days after Harding's death brought Tottenham to Stamford Bridge, the team with whose fans there was often a nasty, sometimes shameful edge. There were ill-judged fears that a few Spurs fans might disrupt the solemn occasion. As it was, the visiting fans' tears flowed along with the hosts', and there were rare moments of bonding as Chelsea fans applauded their impeccable behaviour. Before the pristine minute's silence the players, led by skipper Dennis Wise, Kevin Hitchcock and Gianfranco Zola, laid on the centre circle their own tribute – a Cockney funeral-style wreath spelling out 'MATTHEW R.I.P.'

Harding's widow Ruth, wooed by him as a teenager with pizza and a match ticket in 1970, sat with dignified emotion at the front of the directors' box while his children and friends took their places in the new stand his money had built. Harding's girlfriend Vicky Jaramillo was also present. Chelsea won 3-1.

'The game that Saturday was unique,' says Neil Barnett. 'Tottenham fans were fantastic, completely respectful of the occasion. Rudi [Gullit] started his first game of the season and scored the first goal, then went crazy at Kevin Hitchcock for gifting them the equaliser. Poor Hitchy had been one of the players crying real tears in the silence.'

Immediately after the match Mafe felt Harding and his friends had received a fitting send-off. 'The team winning today is a very good way of sending Matthew off in the best fashion,' he said. 'We had to win today. I don't think the lads or the fans would have accepted anything else. And I think that's our tribute to Matthew and the others.'

Chelsea FC, so often supplying the first-minute open goal opportunity for satirists, found itself in the rare role of victim. There was 'Only one Matthew Harding'. Chelsea fans reminded everyone of that fact on the tortuous road to long-awaited success at Wembley in the 1997 FA Cup final.

To his boardroom ally Hutchinson, Harding's absence was hard to bear. 'There was the shock of somebody so vibrant,' he says, 'gone just like that. I remember the last conversation I had with him in the boardroom at Bolton. We'd gone out of the League Cup and in his half-serious, half-joking way, he said, "Chelsea out of another cup ... " And I said to him, "Well, we're going to have to try to win the FA Cup aren't we?" He said, "Yeah, we're bloody going to do it!"' And the fans acknowledged Harding even as the players collected their medals, as if he was somewhere high in Wembley's recesses, out of sight but not out of mind.

The glory sat more comfortably on chairman Ken Bates's shoulders than the sympathy, although his bowing to popular appeal in naming the North Stand after his adversary was a selfless and magnanimous gesture. Bates was never happy coming second in a popularity poll with the Chelsea fans. His subsequent public remarks about Harding being 'evil' perhaps present a truer story of his feelings about the man.

Bates doesn't like to comment on Harding these days. He's saving that for his own book. But he was keen to tell one final story. 'You know he [Harding] always used to put himself round as a man of the people,' says Bates. 'He spent a lot of time buying you lots of drinks and pubbing it down at the Imperial Arms – which, by the way he adopted as his pub after I took him; he'd never been in there before. He'd never eaten oysters before I took him there either.

'I always used to invite two fans to be my guests at home games. Well, I used to put him next to them, because next to me I normally had the vice-chairman or the chairman of the visiting club. And Matthew hated it. "You put those f**king people ... blah blah blah."

'He gave me a mouthful one home game, in the boardroom: "F**king w**kers, I don't want them near me." And in the end, he finished up on three occasions insisting on having cheese sandwiches in the boardroom, rather than going down to sit next to the fans. Which, of course, amused me somewhat.'

Harding is not here to defend himself, of course, and the positive memories outweigh the negative. Writing shortly after Harding's death, the *Daily Telegraph*'s Henry Winter looked back with affection at the man he once observed whistling 'Who the f**k are Man United' while standing next to the Old Trafford chairman Martin Edwards.

Winter continued, '"What about Gullit's goal?" he would say, the schoolboy smile widening. And off the conversation would go, a rollercoaster ride through the life at Chelsea. It could have been any committed Blues fan talking.

'It was impossible to finish any conversation with Harding without a smile. His enthusiasm was infectious. He would rattle on about Gullit, Glenn Hoddle, and the greats of days gone by, of Bobby Tambling, Terry Venables, Charlie Cooke, Alan Hudson and above all Peter Osgood, whose picture used to adorn his wall.

'Along with reminiscing about Ossie, Harding loved telling jokes. A year ago, he used to recount that Chelsea fans like him were obsessed with "the three Hs": Hoddle, Hughes and Gullit.

'That other "H", Harding himself, will be terribly missed.'

How life would have differed at the Bridge had his relationship with Bates not curdled so completely and had the one-time vice-chairman become successor to the man who came to detest him, we will never know.

Though there were attempts to beatify him, Harding was human, with the usual frailties. Anyone who passed any time with him, in the Imperial or elsewhere, knew that he was not the panacea to be prescribed for all Chelsea's ills. He probably drank too much before games, could be boorish, may well have agreed with the high level of admission prices, and was heard – perhaps in jest – to suggest that a woman's place was not in a football ground.

He might also have fostered a highly unlikely comeback.

Brian Mears had spent 16 years chipping away with a pen, through books and interviews, at the edifice of his reputation as the chairman who undermined the old family estate at Stamford Bridge. He was a pariah at Chelsea in Bates's era, but Harding's arrival offered possible rehabilitation. 'I rang him,' says Mears, 'and I said, "I need to speak to you because I like the way you're doing things and your financing ..." [the Matthew Harding Stand, as it turned out to be]. He said, "Come on, let's go for it," and I met him four times at a hotel and we had a bottle of champagne.

'We got on like a house on fire. "It's great to meet you," he told me. And he said, "Would you think of coming back?" I said, "No, no, my era is finished."

'I thought he was a lovely man. He said he thought that the fans were exaggerating that I was useless as chairman and I was useless at this and that. I don't think the fans thought much of me.

'And I said, "But there you are. In my reign we won the FA Cup and Cup-Winners' Cup which had never been done before in the history of the club, so I'm proud of that." He said, "Well, I'll tell you what, I'll ring you later on and we'll get together at Chelsea, I'll leave a couple of tickets on the gate." And then, what, two months later, he was dead.

'I wonder what would have happened if he was still alive. It would have been incredible, wouldn't it? He was determined that he was going to take over Chelsea. He wanted to put me on the board. I am convinced of that. And how can a man be evil who loves the club, who has invested a lot of money in that wonderful North Stand?'

Neil Barnett puts the tragedy neatly into perspective. 'The crowd kept singing Matthew's name against Tottenham,' he says, 'and would do so at the FA Cup final the following May – and even at Bolton for the Championship in 2005 over eight years later. It was more about what he stood for than who he was: this rich guy who just wanted to be on the old terraces having a singsong. In the end, crowd support would have stuck with Ken Bates in their battles, but the grief was real enough and it was undoubtedly the biggest outpouring over a Chelsea loss in the last 50 years. There'll never be another game like the Tottenham one.'

19

IMPERFECT SYMPATHY

One of the saddest tales of a Chelsea player is that of popular England international Ben Warren and his descent into sickness and depression. Warren joined Chelsea from Derby County in 1908 aged 28 and in his prime, and was until 1912 the regular goalscoring right-half for club and country. Recognised for his stylish play and rare consistency, he starred for England alongside other Chelsea-related players such as George Hilsdon and Vivian Woodward and became a popular player for his 'kindliness, courage and clean, sportsmanlike play,' according to the Chelsea handbook.

Warren was born into a large family of publicans in 1880, at Newhall, near Burton, Derbyshire. His father, Harry, an occasional boilermaker and repairer at the Warren Brothers' family smithy, ran the Thorn Tree Inn on Bretby Road. Ben's wife Minnie was the daughter of Mr and Mrs Staley, of the Bear Inn at Swadlincote, a mile away.

The story of his signing to County was related by their secretary-manager Harry Newbould. 'One Saturday afternoon a friend and I went to Burton-on-Trent to see a local cup final,' he said. 'Rain interfered, so we went over to Swadlincote to watch a medal competition in the hope of picking up a good junior – and we succeeded. Warren was signed on a few weeks later without costing our club a penny.'

The deal was concluded in an unnamed wayside inn and Newbould refers to the rage of the landlord, who had confidently anticipated that Warren would be signed up by his own pet local club, Newhall Swifts. Perhaps it was one of Warren's relatives behind the bar.

The polished, dedicated half-back scored eight goals in seven matches during the Rams' run to the FA Cup semi-finals in 1902. He'd earned six of his 22 England caps six years later before signing for Chelsea, where his impact became the stuff of cigarette card writer's dreams. 'The best wing-half in the kingdom,' suggested one journalist, and 'worth three men to his side.' Off the field he was equally professional and well groomed, with a finely tuned moustache and a resolute gaze.

In December 1909, following a kick in the abdomen (from which a cyst developed and was removed) and a bash on the head, Warren became one of the many casualties that prompted Chelsea to try – unsuccessfully – to spend their way out of relegation.

Warren starred again in the Second Division, but in October 1911, during Chelsea's victorious promotion campaign, the half-back damaged his knee. The injury and loss of earnings played on his mind. A footballer's lot was not as it is now – even that of a glamorous England star. As in other walks of life of the day, absence from work meant no pay, which was hardly conducive to recovery for an athlete just into his 30s with a family of four young children to support. Suddenly, it was as if the control for which he was renowned on the field snapped in his private life. He would never play football again.

Within two months Warren became 'very strange and at times violent'. On 15 December he was admitted to a private clinic in Nottingham, the Coppice, suffering from 'acute mania', 'delusions that he was being poisoned' and 'hallucinations of hearing and vision'. Dr W.B. Tate of the Coppice wrote of the persistent difficulty in getting him to eat anything and noted, 'His language is most filthy. He is a rather celebrated (international) footballer and uses his feet as freely as his hands.' It transpired that there was a history of mental illness in the family.

In February 1912 Warren was admitted to the unfortunately named Derby County Lunatic Asylum at Mickleover, now a set of luxury apartments. His case notes from what turned out to be a five-year stay there catalogue a devastating decline. He is at various times described as incoherent, restless, destructive, 'stuporose', and 'a danger to himself'.

It was a mark of the respect in which he was held that a North v South match was organised for 27 April 1914, and played at Stamford Bridge 'for the benefit of the wife and children'. It attracted a crowd of nearly 12,000 – well below the usual 30-40,000, but honourable nonetheless. The crowd were royally entertained in the spring sunshine by a stellar display of skill from his old club and country colleague, Viv Woodward.

In 1916, while on the suicide monitoring list at Mickleover, Warren attempted to kill himself with shredded pieces of his shirt, saying he was 'no use to anybody and ought to be out of the way'.

A year earlier, the ominous symptom 'dry cough' had been noted. Two months after this suicide attempt, in October 1916, the unmistakeable signs of tuberculosis were noted and his enfeebled body rapidly succumbed. At 11.30 pm on 15 January 1917, international footballer Ben Warren was found dead by a night attendant. He was 37 and when they buried him the records described him as a 'pauper.'

Earlier still, the fate of another popular figure brought the best out of the football community and established a lifelong association in the process. Chelsea's well-known Scottish trainer Jimmy Miller died suddenly at Christmas, midway through the 1906–07 season. Miller had been capped at international level while with Glasgow Rangers, scoring in both his games against England in 1897 and 1899, but spent most of his 14-year career at Sunderland. He had turned out for Chelsea's reserves in 1905–06. At his death the comedian George Robey organised and played inside-left in a benefit match early in 1907, between Chelsea and a London All-Star XI, to help the widow. His best intentions inadvertently led to links with Music Hall comedy that the club has struggled to shake off ever since.

Premature death struck too in the boardroom when Gus Mears, the founder and 'father of the club', died in February 1912 of blood poisoning, caused by chronic kidney failure, at his home at 390 Upper Richmond Road. He is buried in Brompton Cemetery, within earshot of Stamford Bridge's cheers and jeers. The *Chelsea Chronicle* bid him a fond farewell, noting that his abrupt, unruffled exterior masked a good heart and passion for the club.

Two years later came the war that was supposed to end all wars. It is a sad irony that the only known fatality amongst the Chelsea squad in the Great War was nicknamed 'Pom-Pom' after a military weapon. Bob Whiting had stepped into the considerable shadow of departed Willie Foulke between the sticks in 1906. At 14 stone he was no featherweight himself, and the Maxim Machine Gun, first converted for light artillery use in the Boer War (1899–1902), weighed 70lb. The gun's moniker was applied to Whiting chiefly because his enormous upfield kicks reminded people of the arc created by the Maxim's rapid-fire 1lb percussion-fused shells, as they bombarded enemy emplacements and fortifications. It serves to remind us how commonplace thoughts of war were in Chelsea's early days.

Signed from Tunbridge Wells Rangers – where he lived on Albion Street up to the time of his death – Whiting missed just one match in the Pensioners' successful promotion campaign from Division Two in 1906–07, conceding just 34 goals in 38 games.

The following season Whiting lost his place to Jack Whitley, later to become Chelsea's long-serving trainer, and moved on to Brighton and Hove Albion, earning a Southern League championship medal with them in 1909–10. In those days, that meant a Charity Shield play-off with the Football League champions, so on 5 September 1910 the former Chelsea custodian found himself back at Stamford Bridge in front of 15,000 people, keeping Aston Villa at bay. Brighton won 1-0.

Whiting later signed up to the army's 'Football Battalion', the 17th Middlesex Regiment, as a private and was killed in the middle of the rapacious Arras offensive on 28 April 1917, near Pas de Calais, where he is buried in the Arras Memorial cemetery. He was 34.

There were other casualties of battle in the Chelsea 'family', notably Harry Wilding, who played after the war with shrapnel beneath his heart; later acquisition Andy Wilson's arm was permanently damaged by shell fragments and his wounds caused him problems for many years. In the late 1920s he was X-rayed after a training ground injury and found still to have a piece in there requiring an operation. Others achieved honour in combat and survived pretty much unscathed. But the static parade of terribly injured veterans in their 'invalid tricycles' around the Stamford Bridge pitch on matchdays were for many years a reminder that the sacrifice had been universal.

Later, when a brilliant young flame of English talent was snuffed out in his prime, the sympathy of the football world was directed at Chelsea. Tommy Meehan died in St George's Hospital on 18 August 1924 aged just 28. The cause was encephalitis lethargica, a rare inflammation of the brain caused by viral infection, also known as 'sleeping sickness' but not to be confused with the African parasitic disease carried by tsetse flies. Its symptoms, physical and mental degeneration similar to the latter stages of Parkinson's disease, must have contrasted dramatically and terribly with the previously fit young footballer in his prime. There was a worldwide epidemic of the condition between 1917 and 1928, possibly as a result of the huge troop and refugee movements resulting from the First World War.

On the field of play Meehan was a clever, stylish, tenacious but constructive left midfielder, or wing-half, with responsibility for penalties. He was a good influence off it too, being teetotal and a non-smoker, neither of which were rampant virtues in the world of football at the time. During the 1914–18 conflict the young Meehan had played for Rochdale. Chelsea had paid a substantial £3,300 to Manchester United in December 1920 for his services and in 1921 he had formed, along with the likes of Nils Middelboe, David Cameron, John Priestley, Harry Wilding and occasionally Stephen Smith, what was rated as good a midfield line as any in the country.

In 1922, a young men's periodical, *Jack's Paper*, celebrated the coming man of football with a glowing profile. The *FHM* of its day carried gripping yarns and handy lifestyle hints: 'If your teeth are discoloured through smoking you can't do better than brush them with powdered charcoal' or 'Do you suffer from hiccoughs? You can stop it easily by pressing your finger firmly on your upper lip for a few moments.' And its advice page, headed 'Thanks for your letter, Old Chap', carried gift ideas for a girlfriend: 'I should give her something useful, like a pair of gloves or some handkerchiefs'; guidance on how to keep Christmas poultry – 'the tiniest thing will disturb the geese – a ladder leaning against a stack, or a pup walking through the yard'; and a consideration as to whether Charles in Crewe should carry out his crazy plan to grow a moustache – it would help him get a job but he'd better square it with his fiancée first. Through this quirky world of innocence it introduced 'Tommy the Terrier'.

Meehan was, it gushed, a 'mighty atom' worth his weight in gold.

'They call Tommy a terrier – some forwards have used stronger language. He's a full 90-minute man, on the go from whistle to whistle, and there's nothing he likes more than to see two big, hefty forwards standing in the opposite line-up. He worries 'em, confuses 'em, until their nerves and skill are torn to shreds.'

Readers may hear an echo of one of the club's more recent middleman, Dennis Wise, in all this, though for various reasons the appreciation of Wisey was not universal as it was with Meehan. There was certainly a difference in personality; Meehan had been initiated in the spirit of football by Catholic priests. 'For such a little fellow,' continued *Jack's Paper*, 'he is wonderfully clever with his head, and the crowd roars with laughter when they see the atom popping up from behind a stalwart forward.'

Meehan was 'quite the outstanding player on the Chelsea side', according to an observer of the October 1922 match with Sunderland. 'He seemed to be everywhere, and nipped in to get the ball at the most unexpected times.' He helped form a formidable first line of defence. The problem was that the second and third lines were more hyphenated. When he and Cameron were injured against Cardiff that same season, the nine-man Pensioners collapsed 1-6.

His spot-kicks also proved valuable with a forward line, even featuring the pacy and skilful Bob McNeil, Harry Ford and Jack Cock, that couldn't often convert the chances he regularly created. Andy Wilson's arrival in November 1923 from Middlesbrough was only a partial remedy, but at least he took over responsibility for penalty kicks. Before then it was joked that Chelsea's best forwards were its half-backs. Chelsea were relegated in April 1924 in a tight scrap between the teams at the bottom of the league – and the illness had already afflicted Meehan during the closing weeks of the campaign.

Meehan had previously impressed suitably enough to earn English League representative XI call-ups. In October 1923, he had earned a full England international cap, playing in the Home Internationals against Northern Ireland at Windsor Park.

Now, after agonising months of deterioration over the summer 'Tommy the Terrier' was dead. His wages had been used to sustain three generations in his family – from grandparents to children – and the loss touched people throughout football. Two thousand people turned out for his funeral in Wandsworth in the pouring rain. Exactly a year after his England debut, on 20 October 1924, a benefit match against a Football League XI raised funds for his widow and other dependants.

But Chelsea were not always the victims in tragedies that involved the club. On 5 February 1936, James Horatio 'Jimmy' Thorpe, 22, Sunderland's goalkeeper, died a few days after a match at Roker Park in which he appeared to be buffeted by Chelsea forwards. He had been taking insulin for diabetes and had spent time in hospital. The jury at his inquest found that death was due to diabetes, accelerated by the rough usage he received, and that the referee was very lax in his control of the game. They even went so far as to 'urge the board of management of the FA to instruct all referees that they must exercise stricter controls over the players so as to eliminate as far as possible any future accidents'.

The coroner, Mr J.C. Morton, declared himself in agreement with one eyewitness that the ill-tempered game had been 'a disgrace'. 'We find players in first-class football,' he said, 'who resort to methods that are far from what is to be desired, and they do not really help their clubs or the game.'

Passions were always likely to be intense because there was a lot at stake for both teams. Chelsea had gone into the game two points away from the First Division's relegation zone; Sunderland were runaway leaders. In the incident that evidently contributed to his death, the goalie pounced on a loose ball in his area and drew it up to shield it from the forwards between his knees and body. Four Chelsea players followed up and proceeded to kick at the ball regardless of Thorpe's grip on it. Sunderland's players reacted with fury and the crowd was bawling at his apparent mistreatment by the London visitors. It's not clear which of the Chelsea players were involved, but the records show that the famously hot-headed midfielder Mitchell was sent off in the game. George Gibson, Chelsea's inside-forward on the day, was very badly affected by the damning inquest and missed several games after the announcement of its findings.

A watching policeman agreed that football could be a rough game, but that he had never 'seen kicking like this' and reckoned Bolton referee, R.S. Warr, to be 'very slack' in his handling of the incident. Warr was not at the inquest to hear the criticism.

Thorpe's father described seeing his son in a kneeling position in the goalmouth amid the pushing and scrambling. When the whistle blew to break up the melee, his son sprawled out on his own and placed the ball over the touchline. After a moment or two Thorpe continued, refusing treatment and playing out the rest of the game, despite making mistakes to allow Joe Bambrick to score twice and draw the game. However, he'd already been badly at fault for Gibson's earlier goal.

Thorpe felt well enough to go home by bus, but complained bitterly that he'd received three kicks to his side and one to his head. The pathologist concluded that the roughing-up might well have precipitated a diabetic coma in the keeper, who collapsed and died in hospital four days after the game, from diabetes and heart failure.

Naturally the public image of Chelsea was tarnished by the publicity surrounding this tragic and unusual episode. It happened to coincide with an extended period of mourning at Stamford Bridge during 1935–36, over the deaths of founder directors J.T. Mears, vice-chairman, and Claude Kirby, chairman, as well as Kirby's replacement, C.J. Pratt.

Despite the vicious criticism of him, the referee was cleared of negligence at the inquest and absolved of any blame by an FA commission two months later. Within weeks Sunderland went on to win the league. Thorpe's widow Elizabeth was presented with the championship medal earned by his replacement, Johnny Mapson, but her husband was buried in an unmarked grave. His lasting legacy was a change in the laws of football to prohibit any forward raising a foot to the ball when the keeper has it in his hands.

20

CHELSEA BARRACKS

Before calamity befell Matthew Harding, a tragic car crash provoked mixed emotions of despair tinged with regret amongst Chelsea's fans. In December 1977, Bartholomew Smith, 22, of White Waltham, Berkshire, was found guilty of causing death by dangerous driving on 20 March that year, when he had lost control of his sports car at between 80 and 100 miles per hour – at least 30 above the limit. On his way back from a dinner party, he turned broadside across the A40 near Oxford, crashing into the Hillman Avenger driven by Janice Gilham, carrying her husband Alan and their close friends Peter Houseman, 30, and his wife Sally, 29. The Avenger split in two on impact and both couples were killed outright, instantly creating six orphans, three in each family. The Housemans' oldest child, Matthew, was just seven years old.

Smith had owned his 160 mph Maserati for just a month before the crash and was said by the judge to have been driving 'with maniacal fury' at the time. Acquitted of being under the influence of alcohol, despite observations from a doctor who was 'in no doubt that he was completely intoxicated'. Smith was, amazingly, only fined £4,000 and banned from driving for ten years. Judge Anwyl-Davies, QC, pronounced the driver 'totally incompetent' to handle the car he'd bought and revealed his appalling history behind the wheel.

Home and away testimonial matches between the two clubs in Peter Houseman's career, Oxford United and Chelsea, were convened, benefiting the orphans.

The reason for the regret was that the home-grown winger had become the latest in a line of wingers to have fallen victim to the boo-boys at Stamford Bridge. Football was changing at the end of the 1960s, already on the march towards the physical approach of the late 70s. 'Shift the emphasis from the destroyers and stoppers back to the stylists and goalscorers,' begged Albert Sewell, editor of the programme, pleading with the authorities. It wasn't the best environment for a slow but graceful player like Peter Houseman.

Fans wrote to the club after the Jeunesse Hautcharage game in September 1971, angry at the 'treatment handed out to Peter Houseman all too frequently by large sections of the crowd', as J. Powell put it. The singling out of the winger made Powell wonder if the crowd really understood football at all. Fellow fan Dennis Ottrey pointed out that 'barracking in this way can do nothing but undermine a man's confidence'. He cited Houseman's critical contributions at key moments – including his scudded fluke in the 1970 FA Cup final against Leeds. He also recalled the treatment of Eric Parsons, Ted Drake's winger from 1950 to 1956, who was harangued by fans until 'the crowd were forced to eat humble pie when we won the championship', as Ottrey put it.

In fact, on the day Bentley and Drake addressed the triumphant fans from the old East Stand for the first time as title winners, supporters hollered for Parsons with chants of his nickname: 'Ra-bbit! Ra-bbit!' When he came forward he received rapturous acclaim – the voices of the silent majority perhaps. There was never quite the same unconditional moment of 'closure' for the man known as 'Nobby'.

'The problem with Houseman developed acutely towards the end of the 1960s,' says Neil Barnett, a regular on the terraces in those days. 'For a start he looked stuck back in the 1950s with his short hair and wide side parting, and he played on the wing but lacked pace. There was no glory to his game. He didn't take right-backs on and stuck to the touchline rather than roaming. He'd get the ball, make a bit of space and cross. Sometimes the crosses were rubbish and sometimes they were excellent – although once Ian Hutchinson joined Peter Osgood in the centre almost any cross that got into the area was made into an excellent one.

'But we were supposed to be a "glory" team, and where Manchester United had George Best, Manchester City had Mike Summerbee and later Arsenal got Peter Marinello, Nobby Houseman looked like a middle-aged bank clerk. He was never in the papers going out to nightclubs or with a woman on his arm or being drunk, being a King's Road boy. Plus there were always rumours that Best wanted to come to London and to us. The booing of Houseman just grew and got worse and worse. Sometimes it was all round the ground. At Wembley in 1970, however, the crowd sang his name before kick-off along with the others and when he waved he got a special cheer, which was a rarity and a lovely moment.

'The Best rumours climaxed in late 1971 around the time we slaughtered Jeunesse Hautcharage at home in the European Cup-Winners' Cup. Nobby didn't have a great night and put a couple of crosses behind the goal when attacking the north end. The crowd in the West Stand was getting on his back and booing more and more, but he never hid and he finally got one cross on the spot – Osgood's head. Goal! Nobby turned to the West Stand and put two fingers up in a gesture. It would get him suspended today. A hell of a lot of the West Stand applauded him for that. Others booed. Alan Hudson made a point then of running to him from Osgood and giving him a special cuddle in front of the West Stand ... Funnily enough, Hudson was never the darling of much of the crowd either. Because of his long hair and flowery shirts the skinheads never took to him, so there was some booing of him too! Next day Peter Bonetti came out in the newspapers defending Houseman and saying how much the players valued his work rate.

'When he and his wife died, less than two years after he left, there was a genuine sense of shock. You can't say there was a sense of guilt, but it did feel like that at the benefit game. There was genuine concern over his three children and for several Christmases there were collections at games in December for them.

'At the time of the benefit game Eddie McCreadie was manager and the 1970s side played the current side. After the minute's silence, which was very emotional, Peter Osgood ran and grabbed the white corner flag and offered it to McCreadie who was playing left-back for the 1970s team. Everyone knew he was short-sighted and he held it like a stick for the blind. It wasn't just a funny moment, it was a tension-breaker and it was a typical reflection of those teams. It was very un-Peter Houseman-like though.

'It was just such a shame he never knew in life how much he came to be valued after death, that night and from thereon.'

Because of his great contributions in the community, Peter Houseman has a youth football league in the Basingstoke area named after him, as well as recreation grounds in Oakley, where in 1967 he lived and founded a football team of the same name. Ironically, it means that his legacy might be more public and permanent than many of his more glamorous team-mates.

Back in the 1980s a friend once claimed that his fellow Brighton fans were the worst moaners in the country. 'I was there the other day,' he said, 'and they booed the kick-off.' The jeering at Chelsea has usually been less general, more individual. There have been notable targets other than Parsons and Houseman over time. The Chelsea barracks, it seems, wasn't just a home for the Foot Guards; it was the hobby of terrace regulars for many decades. And if we have loved our flankers at Chelsea, from Kirwan and Ford through to Duff and Robben, we've dug out a few too.

Chelsea Pensioner Joe Cusselle, who has been going to games since the 1920s, recalls a winger bought from Wolves in 1934 who copped it worst than most. 'Standing on the terracing along the west side of the ground,' he says, 'you tend to remember the wingers and full backs that played directly in front of you. One poor player I remember was William Barraclough, who played at outside-left. I'd like to say it was because of his skill as a footballer but it's more because of the way he was barracked by the crowd. I learnt some very colourful language thanks to William Barraclough.'

Barraclough was on Chelsea's books for three years, playing 29 league games in his first, 15 in his second and, well, the fans had their way after that.

It was one thing to be picked on for missing sitters or slicing crosses. The worst days at Stamford Bridge, though, came when players were abused not for the their skills but for the colour of their skin. On Monday 12 April 1982 came a moment that will resound ignominiously in Chelsea history. On the grass, Clive Walker's header from Gary Chivers's cross brought a second London derby win in three days (the first being over QPR on the Saturday). On the terraces for Palace's largest crowd of the season, however, Chelsea's support lost it.

It had looked likely for a while that Hillingdon-born Paul Canoville would become the first black man to play in a competitive first-team match for the Blues. So those who objected to the breakthrough were well prepared, as he looked set to come on as sub. They'd warmed up by ritually hooting at Palace's stylish midfielder Vince Hilaire as usual.

'It wasn't the booing that upset me,' recalled a Crystal Palace fan there at the time. 'That was just a fact of life for black players. It was what the Chelsea fans were singing. Canoville was standing on the touchline about to come on, when the chant started, "We don't need the nigger, we don't need the nigger! La, la, la, la!" And because the Chelsea were in all four areas of the ground it became a wall of sound. For the ten minutes or so that Canoville had to play, every time he touched the ball the Chelsea were booing their own player. Now being a mixed race boy in my early teens this was very scary indeed. It didn't put me off though.'

It didn't *seem* to affect the victim of the abuse either – at least, he always played his best, never gestured to the crowd, and, eventually, actually chipped away at the number of abusers with some vital goals and stellar performances.

Nigel Spackman played alongside Canoville from 1983 until the latter's departure to Reading in 1986. 'At that time,' he recalls, 'we had a terrible disease in our country and in our football of black players being abused. The vast majority has gone away, but some of our black players still get abused overseas and playing for their country.

'Chelsea had a reputation of having a troublesome support. But it was fantastic support in many other ways, some of the best away supporters. And for Canners, being the first black player when there weren't that many in football, it was a very tough time, but worse for him at a club with that reputation.'

Canoville was a tall, pacy, powerful winger with great skills and a distinctive straight-backed running style. He could be direct and incisive, but then tortuous and clumsy. There was frustration that he couldn't un-bottle the genie of his talent. So there were reasons justifying criticism him, but his colour wasn't one of them.

'You'd come in at half-time and there'd been monkey chants and you'd go over to him and say, "Don't listen to it, Canners, you're playing really well." And he really was a confidence player. On top of his game with his skill and pace he could murder any defender. He could be a great player. It was what was going on in his life outside of the dressing room that you didn't know about.'

Canoville has had some tough times since being forced to quit football through injury. It has been said that he never recovered from the barracking his own fans gave him. 'As a white English person, you don't know what it's like,' says former team-mate Spackman. 'Unless you're in that situation you don't know if you'd handle it. Sometimes you find people put up a very good front, try and be funny or aggressive, but behind that it they are finding it very tough. With Canners, along came Keith Jones and Keith Dublin [both black players at Chelsea] suffering the same thing and – I don't mean to make it sound better – but you've got other players who can share the problem. Keith Jones was quiet, just got on with it. Dubbers could get aggressive sometimes about it. With Paul, he was on the edge of it; is he handling it or is he not? He liked to have a laugh with everyone, turn up in his beaten up old BMW, and always liked to have a good time.'

Spackman and others have lost touch with him. 'The majority of fans will always remember him for putting in some excellent performances in the 1980s,' he says. In posterity, it is certain he will be an icon of perseverance in. almost intolerable circumstances.

Not many people are aware that Chelsea almost had to face the same issues nearly 50 years earlier. The story came to light after the chance finding in an archive of a photograph of Frederick Hanley, dated 5 August 1938. Although there may have been black or mixed-race players at Stamford Bridge in the past, Hanley was almost certainly the first black professional on Chelsea's books. In the photo a thin young man stands proud, smiling, bolt upright, his hair in a fashionably smart side parting.

A relative was traced in the form of his niece and what emerged is a story that says a lot about the times in which he lived. Fast-forward to Liverpool in the mid-1990s and a distant relative of Hanley's, who worked in the building trade, was knocking down old council houses – known colloquially as 'corpy' – as part of the city's regeneration. In one of the lofts about to be demolished was a pile of belongings and in amongst the junk was an old cardboard box containing personal belongings such as photos, letters and official documents, which seemed vaguely familiar. The box was mentioned to an older relative, and, at the name Frederick Hanley, a connection was made – it was the maiden name of a woman who'd married into the family at the end of the 19th century.

The box was brought home and found to contain pictures of other family members. The box was sent to the widow of Fred's brother and found to be a treasure trove. 'It contained lots of letters (mostly from women), photos of Freddie – with more women,' says his niece, Joan Andrews. 'There were photos of Freddie in his service days, photos of Freddie and my dad, postcards from around the world, mostly sent to his mother, my grandma.

'He played for Skelmersdale and the contract he signed in 1938 at Stamford Bridge is in the box. It also tells him how to get by train and bus to Stamford Bridge.'

Hanley was signed from Skelmersdale and put on wages of £1.6s per week and an extra week's pay if he scored a goal. Although he never played a league match, he turned out regularly for the second string and scored a respectable ten goals. Then came the war and Hanley's chance of becoming the first black player to make a league debut was dashed. He moved from Chelsea to Clapton Orient and then to Scotland, where he settled down and married. Joan's father always proudly told his children stories about uncle Freddie's football career, especially with such a big club as Chelsea.

But Freddie lost touch with the rest of the family after a row in the late-1950s and he was never seen again. 'My mum tried to find Freddie in the late 1970s but she failed to trace him,' says Joan. It's not clear whether he or any descendants are still alive.

Hanley was born in Liverpool to Margaret Hayes, née Hanley, the result of an affair with a Jamaican man after her husband had died. Joan's father was several years older – and white – but the boys grew up together like siblings until Joan's father joined the navy and Freddie's football career took off.

He was given his mother's maiden name so that he could be passed off as the son of a relative. It was a way of countering the 'shame' of a white, widowed woman having a 'half-caste' baby in the late 1910s.

How the history of Chelsea and the experience of the likes of Canoville, Dublin and Jones might have been different had there been an earlier pioneer such as Hanley in the first team. As it is, he has never been mentioned in any Chelsea history books and we know little of his experience at the club.

Twenty years after Walter Tull blazed a trail at Spurs, and twenty years before Albert Johanneson's crushing experience at Leeds, what prevented

Hanley from making his debut? After all, Chelsea finished 20th in the First Division during his one and only season, 1938–39, with goals not easy to come by outside of the reliable Joe Payne and George Mills, despite great efforts from winger Dickie Foss. Hanley's ten goals for the reserves must have tempted Billy Birrell and Jack Whitley to throw him in at some stage.

Perhaps, like Jack Leslie, Plymouth Argyle's top-scoring striker of the late 1920s and early 30s, the selectors were intimidated by his ethnicity. Leslie was called up for England for his impressive statistics but overlooked for his skin colour. He told the *Daily Mail* in 1978, 'They found out I was a darkie and I suppose that was like finding out I was foreign.'

It would not have been easy for Hanley, as one of only a handful of black professionals at that time. Leslie remembered, 'I used to get a lot of abuse in matches, "Here darkie, I'm gonna break your leg," they'd shout.' There was nothing wicked about it – they were just trying to get under my skin.' It may sound a strange attitude to adopt, but it was not unique to ethnic pioneers on the pitch, nor off it. If you want something enough, sheer strength of character is needed to overcome adversity.

Trevor Phillips, chairman of the UK's Commission for Racial Equality, was the seventh son of Guyanan immigrants and was born in Finsbury Park in 1953. He recently explained to writer Simon Kuper that he'd been a Chelsea supporter since the early 1960s, sometimes despite the club and its fans. 'There was a long period where I couldn't go because I'd be the only black person in the Shed,' he said, indicating the type of physical threat ethnic minorities often faced at the Bridge. 'There was a time when dart throwing was one of the great sports in the Shed. "Excuse me, here I am," – bullseye!'

Thankfully, Phillips stuck with the club. 'Now I can take my daughters,' he said. 'That makes a huge difference. And being able to support a football club is in itself an integrationist factor. I belong to something which doesn't define me by my colour.'

Jamaican-born Chelsea season ticket holder Wes Taylor started supporting the Blues from his adopted Birmingham home in the 1960s. His two brothers favoured Manchester United. 'Being of immigrant parents we shared a house with a number of other families,' he says. 'One of the other kids had spent some time in London and supported Chelsea. Whenever we played footy in the garden I had to be on his side and it was always Chelsea v Man U.

'Coming from Brum my early days of seeing Chelsea were against the likes of West Brom, Villa and City. I remember being absolutely amazed at how green the pitch was. In those days we had a black and white TV and somehow I guess it didn't register until I saw it in real life how different it would be.

'I didn't regularly go to the Bridge until I moved to London as a student, in 1984, and it was around this time that I nearly gave up supporting them because of what was going on around me in the Shed End. At that time people would be standing right next to you calling all the black players [Chelsea's as well as the opposition] all the names under the sun plus all the monkey chanting. I used to wonder why I wanted to have any association with these people. Also at that time the majority of the Shed End joined in – it was like the Spain v England game the other day. Amazingly, and this is what I couldn't get my head around, as soon as we scored these same numbskulls would be grabbing me and hugging me, jumping up and down cheering.'

Some black fans withdrew at that stage. Like Trevor Phillips and others, Wes endured, and Blues-mad son Louis has sat next to him in the stands for the last few years. He remembers when he began to feel more comfortable about being black at the Bridge. 'For me the big change came with Glenn Hoddle,' he says. 'That's when we seemed to have quite a few black players come through. And, of course, the biggest change occurred when Gullit became manager.'

Karim Kassam and his season-ticket-holding cousin attended both final legs of the FA Cup final in 1970 and the Cup-Winners' Cup final the following season. He has been a Chelsea regular ever since and his young children now go with him to games. But he's also a Muslim of Afro-Asian origin, and for some of his fellow fans, that has made him a target for ill treatment.

'When I started going regularly in the late 60s,' he says, 'I never really had the perception of being slightly different, or looking different to anyone else. Having said that I didn't see other Asian fans though, and I have to say looking back over the last 35 years, it's not till the last decade or so that I've noticed a reasonable number of Asian supporters dotted around, even though London is one of the most cosmopolitan cities in the world.

'I can't remember too many coloured people generally, not just Asians, but West Indian, Afro-Caribbean fans coming either. Later on it was something I was more conscious of, and there was more racism manifesting itself in football. I can remember very clearly, around 1986 or 87, going to Everton and hearing them chanting something about "Pakis" and the whole of the Chelsea away end at the time getting up and singing, "I'd rather be a Paki than a Scouse." I was virtually the only one not singing it.

'It depends how personally you take it, which sounds a bit of cop-out, but I took it as being part of ... not football banter, but almost acceptable, which is obviously wrong. Then when we played Newcastle about the same time I was standing in the Shed, with a group of mates that I still sit with now. In the Shed there were always quite a few quips, a lot of banter between groups, and it was quite a good place to stand. And there was one guy who was fairly tough-looking who made some sort of comment at a Newcastle player, such as, "You f**king black c**t!" Then he turned round to me and said, "Sorry mate – no offence" and carried on saying the same thing throughout the game.

'It's a bit confusing in a way, 'cause you don't really know what to do or what to say. You're really offended, but you think it's ignorant and almost comical really ... He wasn't the sort of bloke I would have liked to argue with. And I don't think he was in a minority of one either at the time at Chelsea.

'In the late 1970s, early 80s I didn't feel the club tried to combat the racism at all. It wasn't a big issue. Racism was really just an added risk to all the hooliganism that was going on at the time. Just isolated incidents. I don't remember there being any special arrangements or protection for non-white Chelsea fans coming from the club.'

The official line often appeared to be apathy. The atmosphere around Stamford Bridge at the time did little to project a positive image of Chelsea to the outside world. When I took my future wife to Stamford Bridge for the first time in 1981 the first thing that hit her (after the smell of horse manure and burger onions) was the sight of people openly selling the National Front magazine *Bulldog* outside the main gates. The Front was a violent far-right political organisation for people sharing anti-Semitic and anti-immigrant views. And my then girlfriend was Jewish. The idea that the bigots felt confident enough to use my club as a recruiting ground made me sick.

A Danish Chelsea fan, Kenneth Quisgaard, witnessed some of the racially inspired harassment that went on inside the ground in that period. 'It was 1985, the Chelsea v Man United game, and it was overcrowded in the Shed

End,' Quisgaard relates. 'An Asian man and his son walked in to the Shed, and suddenly a big crowd of idiots were shouting, "Squeeze the Pakis". Lots of others joined in, having a big laugh at this man and his son. Thankfully they were not hurt or harmed, except by the shouting, which, of course, was very humiliating.'

Karim Kassam remembers rushing for a train at St Pancras for a match at Luton and finding himself in the 'wrong' carriage. 'I turned round to find it was basically full of a load of National Front Chelsea fans, handing out *Bulldog*. These were the same people I used to walk past on my way into Stamford Bridge. If I'd seen them first I would have got into another carriage. I had a Chelsea scarf on me and even though there were a lot of spare seats I remember thinking, "I'm not sitting down. I'm just gonna stand here and basically pray for 35 minutes."

'In the end I saw a few of them look at me and make a few comments, but they left me alone really, didn't think I was worth bothering about. I was at least expecting someone to come up and hassle me, shove me around a bit, call me names or spit in my face. But that never happened ... It was the one experience where I was on my own in a nasty situation. I think the Chelsea scarf was my safety belt, if you like. It made me one of them even if they didn't like it.

'I take my children to games now,' says Kassam. 'I don't even consider that they might get racially abused or hear racially abusive chants as we did back then. The good news to me is that a combination of social awareness and change in the make-up of our fan base (like that of most other top flight clubs) has helped to contain it to a minority, with some decent effort from the clubs and fans themselves of course. Having a more cosmopolitan band of players over the last quarter of a century also helps.

'Like any right-thinking person I was and am appalled by what Canoville had to put with. I think that perhaps as this was one of the first public instances of racial abuse by some fans towards their own players, coupled with our high profile for "hooliganism" at the time, it made more headlines than what was going on generally at the time. That didn't help, in that it misled people into thinking that this was an isolated Chelsea attitude. Of course it wasn't.'

It was, though, the beginning of Chelsea having to confront its personal problem. Credit Ken Bates for making very public shows of support for

Chelsea's black playing staff and, of course, for hiring Ruud Gullit in 1995 – the first black manager to win a piece of top English silverware, the FA Cup in 1997.

It was a gradual healing process with many involved. The creation of the *Chelsea Independent* fanzine in 1987 was important. Its liberal editorial position may not exactly have convinced committed racists to take up social work, but it helped create an environment where opponents of bigotry had the confidence to speak out and maintained pressure on the club to deal with the problem.

All of which was too late for the pilloried pioneer, Paul Canoville.

His fellow midfielder Nigel Spackman, who moved on to play for Liverpool and Rangers, is no longer a player or manager, but having witnessed race-hate in football at close quarters, he is sure that vigilance is still required. 'I'm sure in some cases some players still do get abused,' he says. 'At Liverpool I used to talk to John Barnes about what he used to suffer. When Mark Walters was being abused at Rangers, their other supporters reported the abusers.

'As a fan you're here to support your players whatever colour skin, whatever nationality. It's a multicultural game now. It wasn't the same in the early to mid-1980s. You might expect abuse from opposition fans, but not your own.'

GREAT RIVALS

Arsenal, Leeds and the joys of *Schadenfreude*

21
LITTLE LOCAL DIFFICULTIES

For a rivalry to have real meaning, it must be reciprocated. There has to be an eye for an eye, a ding for a dong, and a win for a win. It is also better if the two clubs squaring up are of equal standing. It is even better still if there is longevity, so that old, obscure triumphs can be disinterred and tacked on the end of a grudgingly congratulatory email the day after a game.

And it helps if the games have some intrinsic significance. That's why, despite the battle for west London supremacy with Queens Park Rangers in the 1980s, the tight games with Brentford before and during the Second World War, or the recent gentlemen's excuse-mes with Fulham, those teams don't really count. Yes, the third round of the Milk Cup in November 1985, won 1-0 by the SW6 Blues, is noteworthy as Eddie Niedzwiecki's greatest ever game for the club. But it's the friendliest of enmities. There is only one team in Fulham – and it's not them.

If Chelsea, Fulham and QPR had ever all been in the top flight simultaneously, we might have got something cooking. As it is, Chelsea fans' opinion can be summed up by the 1980 consultancy report prepared for QPR, which concluded that up to 15 per cent of its fans were 'floaters'.

With some teams the rivalry can be quite intense but transient. There needs to be a frisson at the mention of the name for it to matter – between

1905 and 1912 tiny Gainsborough Trinity regularly turned us over, but it hasn't made us sworn enemies.

In 1921 the supporters of Swindon could be forgiven for dreading their name coming out of the FA Cup hat alongside Chelsea's again. Four times before then, from 1910–11, they met the swanky west Londoners and lost out. Three of these were at Stamford Bridge, and the M4 wasn't really stitched together until half a century later in 1971.

But Swindon means nothing now other than 'carrot crunchers' to Chelsea fans. Chelsea might as well wish to play the 'Sops again: Glossop, beaten 9-2 in Division Two in 1906–07 and Worksop edged 9-1 in the 1908 FA Cup. But it wouldn't be any fun – too one-sided.

We might include the other teams that vehemently hate Chelsea, especially West Ham, Charlton and Crystal Palace. Lord knows, in the early 1980s the mutual pastings between Chelsea and Newcastle might have taken on extra meaning, but never did, even after the Blues' FA Cup semi-final victory in 2000.

Either – like Frank Sinclair's puddle-finder back-pass at Selhurst Park in January 1993 – nothing has really hurt that much, or the *schadenfreude* has not been great enough. It has to be visceral. Not everyone will agree that the following are our greatest rivals, of course, but hopefully it represents a fair selection of figures of hate and fun.

ARSE

The oldest and frequently most bitter London rivalry on the league football calendar first appeared on 9 November 1907 at Stamford Bridge – the first ever top flight London derby. Chelsea, just promoted, won 2-1.

Back then Woolwich Arsenal played at the Manor Ground, off suburban Plumstead's High Street. Their offices and part of the playing field, on Griffin Manor Way, are now quite appropriately buried under Belmarsh Prison – a purpose-built detention centre for the world's most fiendish villains.

By the time they had moved to Highbury it was the dawn of war. From Chelsea's perspective it is a shame that the results of the temporary regional London Combination during the conflict remain 'unofficial'. Amongst the pick-outs were the January 1915 6-0 win at Highbury in which Fulham-born Harry Ford got a hat-trick and a guest, Sunderland star Charlie Buchan, scored two; and the ludicrously overlooked April 1916 match where the mighty one-eyed striker Bob Thomson put five past the Arsenal keeper and Buchan four. That's 9-0. Against Arsenal. At Highbury!

Even then derby results had the power to heal. In November 1917 Chelsea met Woolwich Arsenal at Stamford Bridge in a 4-3 humdinger of a match. One Chelsea supporter present was a distressed soldier who had lost the power of speech during trench combat, had been discharged from the army and had been unable to speak since. As the ball crossed the Woolwich Arsenal line for the winner, he finally found his voice again, shouting 'Goal!' at the top of his voice. From then on, it was reported, he was able to speak quite normally.

Fast-forward to January 1947's three-game encounter in the FA Cup and we have the beginnings of the type of Chelsea-Arsenal derby familiar to many fans over the years. Chelsea, with the Tommys Lawton and Walker, having all the possession and flair, dogged Arsenal the lucky escapes and occasional incisiveness. Cultured Chelsea, scientific Arsenal. Even the heavy rain that has marked several notable encounters made an appearance in the first game at the Bridge.

In the second replay at White Hart Lane, Chelsea went ahead in the tie through Lawton for the first time after two 1-1 draws. Arsenal had missed a penalty and belief sapped away from Mercer, Compton et al. 'Arsenal seemed conscious of battling against their fate,' said *The Times*. Swiss full-back Willi Steffen and forward Len Goulden were outstanding, but it was Lawton who scored again to make it 2-0.

It was a different outcome in 1950. Chelsea fan Peter Ralph was at White Hart Lane again, this time for the FA Cup semi-final. 'Roy Bentley scored twice to give Chelsea a 2-0 lead,' he remembers. 'It was a terrible, wet, windy day and just before half-time Arsenal got a corner. Freddy Cox took it and the ball swung out away from the Chelsea goal. Bill Hughes, Chelsea's Welsh international full-back who was standing on the line, saw the ball going away from goal, so he moved off, only for the wind to carry the ball back towards the Chelsea net, leaving goalie Harry Medhurst helpless. Arsenal's equaliser also came from a corner 13 minutes from the end, taken by Denis Compton and headed into the net by his brother Leslie.

'For the replay me and my work colleagues managed to smuggle a radio into the office so we could find out the result – 0-1 unfortunately.'

Towards the end of the century there have been too many great tussles to feature them all here. Indeed, when Arsenal reserves lost 5-0 at home to Chelsea reserves in the fourth round of the 1997–98 League Cup it was greeted with a Gallic shrug of indifference, but it was highly enjoyable all the same.

But nothing can compare to the transcendent game of 6 April 2004, when Wayne Bridge won the quarter-final of the European Champions League at a Highbury that had been drenched the night before and was slippery under foot. 'This was a classic of a Cup contest,' wrote the *Daily Telegraph*'s Henry Winter, 'a feast for the watching millions around the globe marvelling at a real ding-dong London derby played with European touch and technique, pace and panache in equal, thrilling measure. It was impossible to take the eye off the unfolding drama.'

Arsenal had sealed a 1-1 draw in the first leg, but were aware, even after Reyes had scored against the run of play in the first half of the second leg, that a Chelsea reply would spell trouble. Fans in the Clock End were similarly well versed. Straight after the goal, Chelsea fans everywhere reassured their neighbours, 'It doesn't matter. It doesn't make any difference. We just have to score now.'

There was not a weakness in the Chelsea team – even the questionable pedigree of accident-prone keeper Marco Ambrosio stood examination and came through. Terry and Gallas were imperious at the back, Lampard and Makelele won the midfield duel against an always-combative Vieira, and upfront Gudjohnsen and Duff were focused and inventive.

A Makelele shot is enough of a rarity to warrant inclusion in a diary, but it often yields something greater. That night, the instinctive 25-yarder hammered back off Lehmann's chest to be side-footed home by Lampard, who was soon roaring over to the Chelsea fans with his team-mates. Highbury was stunned in an instant. Fans started leaving. It seemed as if the old stadium's shoulders actually slumped in despair. Once again, 'Arsenal seemed conscious of battling against their fate.' In the Chelsea end there was absolute mayhem. Two friends disappeared down in the celebrating tumult, then reappeared 15 yards away, as if momentarily lost in a snowdrift.

There was now a collective sense that nothing could stop Chelsea beating Arsenal – the away goal was enough to take us through. But when Wayne Bridge played a one-two with Gudjohnsen and picked up the ball in the penalty area the fans at the Chelsea end stood up simultaneously. 'We were directly in line with the Bridge shot,' says season ticket holder Damien French. 'As soon as it left his boot I shouted "Gooaal!" and grabbed the nearest person on the shoulder and shook them, quite violently, probably, until it hit the net. People were jumping around everywhere in sheer ecstasy. Some nutters were standing on the backs of seats and just jumping anywhere, just for joy. It was mad. It was nice both goals were at our end; this team and the fans really bonded that evening.'

Afterwards there were few Arsenal fans to be seen anywhere. French, a north Londoner, strolled back across Highbury Fields cheering into his mobile at the top of his voice like everyone else. 'Then we went to the Medicine Bar on Upper Street, got champagne and cigars and sang loads of songs. Someone went off to find a pub showing the highlights, and took us to a bar full of little posh Gooners who had watched it on the telly.

'My mate Tim Rich and I had an idea and quietly told the others with us about it. So when they showed the Reyes goal again, the Arsenal fans were amazed to see us all applaud and nod sportingly! Their faces ... But of course, we all went loopy again when they showed our two goals. After so many annoying defeats to lucky old Arsenal, it was nice to gloat a bit.'

They are the team we have played more than any other and this was the best of them all.

POOR OLD SPURS

There has always been more of a political side to the enmity with Tottenham. But they started it, sir! In 1905 the Spurs board waged a successful campaign to prevent Chelsea joining the Southern League. A few years later they had the cheek to jump ship to the Football League, and in 1909 a goal scored by former Blue Percy Humphreys for Spurs sent Chelsea back down to the Second Division. It was not the best way to play with a new friend.

Much later, in April 1960, Chelsea enjoyed retribution of sorts. If Spurs were to beat Chelsea and Man City they would win the league. They lost 1-0 to Chelsea, whose new keeper, 18-year-old Peter Bonetti, had an outstanding game. At the end of the game Spurs's Danny Blanchflower ran up to him and warmly shook his hand. Others would have preferred his throat.

A rare hubbub has always surrounded these clashes, even if the business has often been of private interest only. Spurs's visit for the FA Cup third round replay in January 1964 attracted 70,123 fans – still a record for a floodlit game at the Bridge and then-record gate receipts of £11,426. Thirteen months later when the teams met in the fifth round of the same competition in SW6, 63,205 supporters brought a return of £19,606. Even in November 1970, 61,277 strolled down the Fulham Road to watch the two capital rivals play in the league.

Since the first all-London FA Cup final in 1967 was a massive disappointment to the Blues, the more so because old boys Venables and Greaves were in lilywhite, it's surely better to concentrate on the last quarter of the century. The glorious unbeaten run against them was broken once, with the 1-5 semi-final second-leg defeat in the League Cup in 2002, when yet another old boy, the great former Chelsea hero Gustavo Poyet, blotted his fabulous copybook in some fans' eyes.

His crime was to whip up Spurs fans as he was being subbed late on. But their ire might be directed at referee Mark Halsey, who sent off sharpshooter Jimmy Floyd Hasselbaink when it was actually defender Mario Melchiot who had slapped Teddy Sheringham.

Eidur Gudjohnsen has played in more Tottenham games than most of the title-winning team. 'I played in the 5-1 defeat, and I scored two in the 4-0 FA Cup win there after that,' he says. 'In moments like that I feel like a proper Chelsea fan, without a doubt. The 5-1 defeat is the worst day I've had at Chelsea by far. But the consolation is that it wasn't in the league but the Carling Cup, or Worthington Cup, or whatever it was called at the time. Not the biggest trophy in the world, and not the league record, which we're very proud of. The fact that we put it right in the FA Cup does help you forget about things.'

And in that 4-0 cup win came one of the all-time great songs from the Chelsea terraces: 'Normal service has resumed!' 'Ha ha!' Gudjohnsen laughs at the memory. 'That was good. We all realised it was just a blip and hopefully this record may continue for a long, long time.'

The infallible streak in the league has now stretched to 30 games: Won 20, Drawn 11, Lost 0; For 61, Against 22.

But there is an issue at the heart of the fans' rivalry that makes it more divisive, and that concerns the 'Yiddo' chants that emanate from both sets of fans, having originally emerged from the stands at Highbury. The Tottenham fans themselves sing 'Yid army!' adopting the term as a badge of honour and deflecting the venom. But does that eliminate the idea that its use is the last vestige of racism amongst Chelsea followers?

Like the racist abuse directed at black players in Blue, anti-Semitism was at its most prevalent on the terraces in the early 1980s. Andy Jacobs and other Jewish fans decided to give up on games for a while in disgust. 'The time I got turned off,' he says, 'was Chelsea versus Tottenham in 1982. In general you kind of turned a blind eye to it, because everyone knows it's just football banter. It's that thing that individually if you spoke to people you wouldn't come across it. These days it's completely and utterly unacceptable.

'My father-in-law started coming. He was already a football fan, but when my boys started coming, he came with me and he's quite an old-school Jewish bloke and I think suddenly there I got really aware of it. I'd kind of got used to it, but he found the "Yiddo" cries, and "Spurs are on their way to Auschwitz" and all that stuff, incredibly unpleasant and just not necessary.'

To Jacobs it's a by-product of hardcore racism. 'I remember an old boy when we were in the family section,' he says. 'A bloke tackled Mark Stein and he said, "Leave him alone, you nigger!" I said to him, "What? What about our niggers? Do you think they might be upset by that? Do you think that's a good thing to say?" He was old school and I know from my upbringing that casual racism was very much a part of that generation.'

Perhaps it has actually been in the atmosphere of SW6 for generations, what with the Blackshirts' HQ being on the King's Road, and the ruling class and the Chelsea Bohemians both displaying a fascination with 'Herr Hitler' in the 1930s. C.B. Fry, the famous sportsman, socialite and Chelsea vice-chairman, was besotted enough with the Third Reich to visit Hitler in 1934.

As early as 1911, with Chelsea misfiring in front of goal, the extraordinary front cover of the *Chelsea Chronicle* had featured a cartoon depicting a stereotypical Jewish cobbler called Cohen addressing a Chelsea Pensioner, 'Vat, you vant to try some more of mine boots? Vell, just vait until your friend Gainsboro' has been served.' Gainsborough Trinity has just beaten Chelsea 3-1 and this was the type of scapegoating for every ill in which Mr Goebbels would later specialise.

During the war George Orwell noted the rise of anti-Semitism and gave many personal examples of irrational statements he'd heard in recent months from a variety of social classes. 'There is more anti-Semitism in England than we care to admit,' he said, tied inexorably to English nationalism, with the idea of the 'Chosen Race' being at odds with visions of God's own Albion. Can the arrival in 2003 of a rich Russian Jew in the heart of the Chelsea establishment, respected and even idolised by so many supporters, maybe change the climate? It has given some supporters confidence. 'I'm very proud to be Jewish,' says Andy Jacobs. 'I'm very proud that Roman Abramovich has come in with the club. I'm very proud that he is Jewish.'

One might expect one of the original right-wing North Stand hooligans, like post-war teenager Garrison, who wore SS badges on his jacket in the 1960s, to take issue, and at least object to the club he loves having a Jewish owner. His answer is surprising. 'I'm half Jewish,' he says, 'so Abramovich taking over doesn't bother me at all. You know, great. I mean to me the only people that can handle money are Jews anyway. If ever I've got a business I always get a Jewish accountant.'

But the 'Yiddo' banter doesn't upset him either; it's a matter of knowing the code. 'What people don't realise is that there's football banter and there's anti-Semitism,' he says. 'I've actually got thrown out of Tottenham for smacking a Chelsea supporter for making a hissing sound. Because to me the hissing isn't banter.' The mimicking of gas going into Nazi extermination chambers is a step beyond the pale to even the likes of Garrison. 'I said to the stewards, "He's making the hissing sound." "Don't care, you hit him, just be thankful you're not arrested." For f**k's sake!

'But with calling them Yids, they're the ones that gave them that name. Now nobody moans at Arsenal being called the Gooners. You know, "It's unfair to Gooners." Nobody cares about West Ham being called the Hammers or the Irons, but because Tottenham decided to call themselves the Yid Army and all the songs are like "Yiddo", it's treated different. It's nothing to do with anti-Semitism. It's nothing to do with Jews. It's like the Washington Redskins, they're called the Redskins but it's not derogatory to Red Indians. They actually got that name as respect for the Red Indians, you know, but you get all these left-wing loonies who want to make a name for themselves, "Oh you can't say that because it's this and that" – political correctness.'

In football, how things seem is often more important than how they actually are. Chelsea's sensible official stance is that 'Yid' chants are anti-Semitic and unacceptable, but does that apply to visiting Spurs fans? The day White Hart Lane stops resounding to the chants of 'Yid army!' it will bring clarity to a sensitive matter.

22

THE NORTH-SOUTH DIVIDE

There is no love lost between the north's mill and mining town clubs, and those of the cosmopolitan capital city. To northerners, no club personifies the clichés of London more than swanky Chelsea. But it's a Scottish manager who most regularly refers to the differences. As his team struggled to keep up with Chelsea's 2004–05 title charge, Sir Alex Ferguson muttered darkly that Chelsea 'still had to come up north'. It was the latest suggestion that Stamford Bridge is like some huge confectionary box: a continental selection filled with soft centres.

Mourinho's team actually dropped four league points during the championship season away to northern teams; Manchester United shipped 15 at home alone – in the grim north.

Most supporters above the Watford Gap find Chelsea a great place to visit but a difficult club to like. But no long-distance rivalry is quite as hostile as that between Leeds and Chelsea.

DIRTY LEEDS
It always rears its ugly head, even when we're nowhere near them. As predictably as the late plod of Corporal Jones's foot, when Leeds fans gather in any stand, they will sing their song about their Cockney rivals. 'Fetch your

father's gun and shoot the Chelsea scum'. Chelsea fans still sometimes reciprocate with an elegy to the hatred of Leeds over the tune of 'The Dambusters March'. We know that the 1970 FA Cup final was dirtier than Paris Hilton's home video collection, but the unmitigated mutual hatred between Leeds and Chelsea started before that.

Perhaps we should blame the M1. The extension from Aston to Leeds was completed in July 1967 and it was almost as if the new infrastructure made loathing, as well as other goods, easier to transport. Three months before that was the match that may have ignited the whole thing. But by then there had already been several bouts in the classic Yorkshire grit versus flash Cockney encounter.

There was a fifth round cup epic in 1952, settled at Villa Park with a Monday afternoon kick off at 2.30 p.m. Boisterous youth product Bobby Smith was 'a lively spearhead' and gave celebrated Welsh centre-half John Charles a nightmare game. Charles twice slipped up for Smith, wearing borrowed boots, to capitalise. It ended 5-1 but the ferocious tackling of the first replay at Stamford Bridge had forced Chelsea into seven changes for the subsequent league game. Nearly 150,000 fans watched the three games – and winced.

Early in World Cup year, 1966, the fourth round draw brought the two foes together again. *The Times* enthused, 'Chelsea and Leeds are two of the most fancied teams for Wembley. Heaven help those who live in the Fulham area who own a motorcar; heaven help those who wish for a ticket on 12 February. It should be a taut match. The winner should reach Wembley, and the winner may well be Chelsea.'

The winner definitely wasn't going to be football.

There were chaotic scenes outside Stamford Bridge before the game with a 57,000 crowd there to see the previous year's beaten finalists lose 1-0 to a Tambling strike. The police dealt with it harshly. 'One will hope,' said *The Times*, 'that the expression "cross swords" will prove groundless in the sense of bared sheaths.'

The game was actually seen beforehand as Osgood's chance to outdo Bobby Charlton and claim a World Cup place. At times Chelsea were left 'spinning like a top' by Leeds's fluid formation, Madeley acting as a deep-lying centre-forward to cover Osgood – who 'drifts about as silently and elusively as a smoke ring'. Boyle and Bremner were booked. Bonetti made three or four world class saves. The template was established.

Ay ay ay! A rare action shot of Chelsea's amazing 1929 tour of South America. This shot is from the controversial Argentinian leg, often marred by rioting and stone throwing by the crowds, despite the high fences.

Above 'Los Numerados' line up for their first game in Argentina. Chelsea caused a sensation in Buenos Aires by wearing numbers on their shirts. For some reason they also wore black shorts. (Many thanks to Richard Coburn for the photograph.) (Above right) Bowled over by the reception in the United States? Didier Drogba and John Terry enjoyed the short tour of America in 2005, playing Milan twice and winning new fans for global brand Chelsea.

Above 'There was never a Cup Final played in such a depressing atmosphere. A sombre consciousness of war overhung the crowd, and the final touch was when the band started to play hymns.' Chelsea's first FA Cup final; lost 3-0 to Sheffield United at Old Trafford in 1915. (Above right) Chelsea returned to the venue in 1970 and made amends. Peter Houseman (in action against Leeds), tragically killed in a car accident in 1977, scored at Wembley against Leeds.

A goal of inestimable value Clive Walker, Burnden Park, 7 March 1983. His 25-yard strike helped stop Chelsea drop to the third tier for the first time in its history.

A picture of dejection Wembley 1994: 'John Spencer threw his medal away,' said Gavin Peacock. 'I gave mine to my dad.' Steve Clarke, Dennis Wise, Eddie Newton, Frank Sinclair and Graham Rix found redemption in 1997.

Doldrums Mighty Carlisle won 2-0 at Chelsea on the opening day of the dreadful 1974–75 season. Bill Garner was among those unable to score. Chelsea were relegated third from bottom. Carlisle did the double over Chelsea and finished last.

Docherty the diamond geezer
The Doc prescribes a game of Subbuteo for coach Dave Sexton, some of his recently promoted players, and local children in sunny Huxley Lane, Ewell, July 1963. His brilliant, controversial management spanned five great years at Chelsea.

In the late 1970s and 80s, incidents at Derby and Brighton, and against Sunderland and Middlesbrough, made Chelsea fans public enemy number one.

August 1974 and the grandiose, long-delayed East Stand makes its inauspicious debut, Chelsea losing 2-0 to lowly Carlisle. Next door is the absurd-looking North Stand that quaked as trains passed.

Me and my shadow At the time of his death in 1996, millionaire director Matthew Harding's relationship with chairman Ken Bates had soured, very publicly. Nevertheless the club made progress.

Dismissed Referee Anders Frisk's fateful brandishing of a second yellow card at Didier Drogba in Barcelona sparked a furious row between UEFA and Chelsea. The referee had been approached at half-time by Barça boss Frank Rijkaard.

Above 'They always seemed to be whingeing, moaning round the referees.' Chelsea's hatred of Leeds runs very deep.

Above right Mark Hughes celebrates the goal that turned the tie. With Chelsea 2-0 down at half-time, Sparky came off the bench and battered Liverpool to pieces, scoring this first goal as the Blues ran out 4-2 winners.

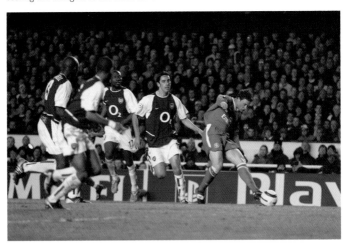

Silencing the Library Wayne Bridge ends a 17-match run without a win against the Gunners in glorious fashion to score the winner in a 2-1 victory in the quarter-final of the European Cup on 6 April 2004.

The greatest game? The midfield tussle between Frank Lampard and Ronaldinho was just one of the aspects of a breathtaking night at Stamford Bridge as Chelsea overwhelmed Barcelona 4-2 on 8 March 2005 to reach a second successive European Cup semi-final.

The changing faces of Chelsea Roman Abramovich's (below, left) takeover heralded the end for Claudio Ranieri (right), and the arrival of perhaps Chelsea's greatest manager of all time, José Mourinho (below right, with chief executive Peter Kenyon). Football's biggest ever experiment is well under way.

Lifelong yearning Joe Cusselle was a fan in the 1920s, survived the Japanese PoW camps, and returned to the terraces first as a supporter, then as one of the famous Chelsea Pensioners. He helps Chelsea's community education projects and was in the 2005 title-winners' guard of honour.

The following year, the humour of the FA Cup draw became vindictive. Leeds and Chelsea met in the 1967 semi-final at Villa Park with 62,378 in attendance. With major semi-final wins proving elusive, the game was billed as manager Docherty's 'triumph of mind over matter, of will-power over the perpetual inertia that once reigned at Stamford Bridge'. On the day he sacrificed brilliance for backbone and changed the forward line, exploiting the absence of broken toe victim Jackie Charlton. Now came the compellingly disappointing Hateley's greatest triumph: his headed winner from Cooke's run and cross.

There were other little skirmishes. McCreadie snapped at Giles's heels. 'The tackling throughout was frighteningly ruthless,' thought one reporter, 'and too often retaliation was penalised while provocation escaped unseen. Shirts, elbows and studs were used and abused; to be caught in possession was like standing in the path of a stampede.'

Then came a controversy that, unhealed, would erupt at Wembley 1970. As Chelsea tired, Leeds laid siege to Bonetti's goal and twice put the ball over the line in melees. The first was undoubtedly offside, but it came as a great relief to Chelsea when the second, a thunderbolt from the hammer boot of Lorimer, did not stand. The referee ordered a retake, because he had been directing Chelsea's wall back the full ten yards when it was taken, to the fury of Leeds' players. The Blues then held out and, at the end, Docherty danced a provocative jig of joy.

'They say third time lucky and we proved that,' says Ron Harris, skipper that day. 'People say Peter Lorimer scored a goal that was disallowed with the last kick of the game from a free-kick, but I don't think anyone could begrudge us getting to the final having played the semi-final the last three years.

'After that the 1967 FA Cup final was a real let down because we were very poor on the day against Spurs. It was a very disappointing game all round.

'One of the things when you got to a cup final was the players were allowed to buy a hundred tickets. That was a noted thing. We had a chairman at the time called [Bill] Pratt, and he insisted that there would only be 12 tickets each. I remember Tom [Docherty] phoning from the hotel and saying, "If these lads don't get their tickets, they will not be part of the game." But it was all sorted out and we got our tickets at the finish. It didn't affect our performance on the day.'

There were no such hiccups three years later. In fact, other than the Wembley pitch being ruined by an equestrian event beforehand, the preparation was perfect. 'We used to go down to Brighton before every cup tie,' reveals Harris, 'because people were superstitious and we used to go to a Chinese restaurant, but I don't remember anybody eating that much.'

'It was not long after my 15th birthday,' remembers Karim Kassam. 'I remember Leeds were such a massive team then and basically invincible. I think we'd lost a league game 5-2 to them and we were 2-1 up at half time and I remember that really clearly. And so when I went along I remember two things about it. I remember thinking firstly that we'd never be able to beat them, you know, however many times we'd played them. And secondly, I remember on the BBC they used to have the teleprinter prediction and it came out at 3-2 to Leeds and it said that Ian Hutchinson would score both our goals or something, so although he didn't score both our goals, when it went to 2-2 I was absolutely petrified that we were going to lose 3-2.'

If the *X-Factor* panel had been auditioning the teams, it is unlikely that Leeds would have been there at all. 'If you remember,' says David Webb, 'the best final would have been Chelsea v Man United, but about three replays they had, with Leeds. If you looked all round the country, nobody liked Leeds. They always seemed to be whingeing, moaning round the referees. And so it wasn't so much that Chelsea was the team that everyone liked, it was more of the fact that we were the last chance to stop Leeds.'

But in May 1970 'DJ', the first Chelsea player to score a match-winner in an FA Cup final, felt the weight of expectancy not just of long-suffering Blues fans, but of the footballing public beyond 'God's Own Country' bearing down on his hefty shoulders.

The load appeared too much even for the £60,000 Action Man in the Wembley game. Like a stuck bull tormented by the matador-like Eddie Gray, Webby had a nightmare. Later the same evening, the full-back met actor and Chelsea fanatic Michael Crawford for the first time. 'He came up and shook my hand,' says Webby. 'I said, "Phoor, shake my hand after that?" He said, "No, I've never seen anyone show so much balls in all my life."'

Webby believes he approached Wembley in the wrong frame of mind. 'I must admit I'd never been there, and I didn't go there focused – I got caught up in the occasion. I could have just as easily gone on the terracing. And Eddie Gray kept trying to take me on, almost like a personal vendetta. In a way it worked, because if you looked at all the dangerous stuff, it came from people like Lorimer. But that day, I looked round and there was no help; Ron Harris shouldn't have played, he wasn't fit. He played centre-half, and what happened? I was here, and he was there [he motions a long distance]. I had never ever felt so knackered in all my life.' On a dreadful sandy pitch, coming back from behind twice was as much as Chelsea deserved. But the thuggery on the pitch set the handprints of our hatred into football's wet concrete.

The replay at Old Trafford was different. 'I was telling myself I've got my bovver boots on for the second game,' said Webby. 'I made up my mind, there was no way anyone was going to do anything there, and I went out and didn't give a monkey's.'

With a fitter Ron Harris deputed to look after Eddie Gray, Webby returned to his usual all-action role – at one stage deflecting a Johnny Giles shot just over his own bar. 'I thought if ever there's a God up there he looked down on me because he made sure that ball went over the net. It could have easily ricocheted and gone in the net.' That apart, Webby rose (quite literally, as it turned out) to the occasion.

'I liked the Old Trafford game,' says Charlie Cooke, 'just because it was going to be tough, exciting. There was a much more intimate atmosphere than Wembley. There was a lot at stake too. They were our arch-rivals for quite a few years. There was no love lost. It was a cutthroat contest. I thought our worst enemy on their team was this constant whining at referees they did, the referee baiting. That gamesmanship used to ruffle our feathers.'

Once more Leeds drew first blood, but once Ossie had dived to convert Charlie Cooke's intuitive cross, the initiative switched. 'I can't remember it clearly – and it may be a total lie! – but I remember feeling that the game was kind of drifting, we were going nowhere, we needed to "crack something open" – that was on my mind, "Let's get something happening here." And when I picked up the ball, it was pretty far out, just over the middle, and I was just trying to force something to happen, take a chance.

'It was a beautiful cross – Ossie always makes the most of these things!'

Leeds collectively blinked. The Blues took control.

'We had a kind of a feeling there,' smiles Webby. 'When the chips were down, you could hear the teeth grinding.' His winner came from a Hutchinson long throw flicked on by Jackie Charlton under pressure from Ossie, and the villain of the first game was transformed into hero, rising at the far post to bash the ball in off his cheek past David Harvey. He didn't know where it had gone until he saw the ball nestling in the net:

'Charlie Cooke was my big hero,' says Karim Kassam – and he wasn't alone. 'His fantastic through-ball and Ossie's diving header, it just sort of summed us up really. Peter Bonetti was basically playing with one leg and he was phenomenal. I've got very fond memories of that team generally and obviously that was their finest hour.'

Fittingly, while the rest of the team collected cup and medals at the end, Webby claimed his trophy – Eddie Gray's shirt – and ran off round the pitch with Alan Hudson – ruled out of the final through inury – to milk the applause. 'It was,' says Webb, 'the most fantastic atmosphere, the feeling there.'

It was left to Brian Clough to fetch DJ his medal from a back room at the Manchester United ground. 'Well done son,' he said as he handed it over. And Clough always hated Chelsea.

'The only disappointing thing about that win,' says Harris, 'was, with no disrespect to Manchester United, the replay was played at Old Trafford and that did take a little bit of the gloss off walking up the steps to get the trophy.

'We had to go back to the hotel straight after the game and have a quick drink with the chairman Brian Mears. Then we just went into town and some nightclubs and I think some of the players just come straight from there to catch the train the next morning.'

The celebrations continued while the train took the strain.

'By the time of the bus one or two of them were a bit too merry. Some of them were used to it anyway! But it was a fantastic feeling to get into Euston and get the open-topped bus and drive where there were mobs and mobs of people up the King's Road and up to the town hall by Fulham Broadway station. It was fantastic, it was the best feeling I think any footballer can get and I will treasure it for a long, long time.'

For Webb, the glory remained unique for too long. 'It's funny, the European thing the next year was equally important yet it never had the same impact as the FA Cup. I think it was because it had been such a long time.

'It's the same now.' He was talking in 1996. 'It's gone from 1955 to there and from then to now. It's a sadness really, when you think about it. It's a lot longer now – and it's about time someone else got a winner.'

Harris enjoyed the rivalry with Leeds and explains it in terms of two great teams of equal quality and aggression squaring up and not backing down. 'I know a lot of sides who went up there and wouldn't kick a ball as soon as they got on the pitch,' he says, 'because they were frightened out their lives.

But we could look after ourselves and that was why there was great rivalry over a period of time. It went on into the semi-final when they thought they'd scored from that free-kick and even up to two or three years ago when they were in the Premiership, there has always been a bit of rivalry.

'A lot of it was to do with Don Revie because he used to antagonise teams the way he went around and did certain things. Leeds were a very good side and they had the likes of Eddie Gray, Billy Bremner, John Giles that pulled all the strings. People who could play and people who were very aggressive – Norman Hunter and Jack Charlton – and we were the same. We had Ossie, Huddy, Charlie Cooke and people like myself, Webby, John Dempsey, who could look after themselves and we were never intimidated by Leeds.'

But the aggression was, claims Harris, confined to the pitch. 'After you had finished the game we used to have a little lounge at Chelsea,' he says, 'just for the players and the away team and I've never seen anything, even when we played at Leeds or anywhere, I've never seen players take their vendettas off the field or anything like that. The Leeds players would still turn up for a drink.'

Not so the two sets of fans. The baiting between them reached its nadir at Stamford Bridge in October 1982. Vast numbers on each side were like caged animals desperate to have a go at each other. During the game they taunted each other with chants about their respective misogynistic psychopaths – the Yorkshire Ripper and Jack The Ripper. A smoke bomb went off during scuffles in the first half, with a Chelsea 'steward' spotted kicking Yorkshire fans through the fencing.

The only thing that unified the mad hordes was subjecting black Chelsea player Paul Canoville to racial abuse as he ran down the wing. At the end of the game, the pitch became a battleground, a thin line of police, some on horseback, failing to maintain the segregation. Manager John Neal was distressed: 'There are a lot of people here today who watched the match in comfort, enjoyed it and went away without causing any trouble. It is only a small minority that causes the trouble, and that hurts.'

Of all the rivalries, this is perhaps the most irrational, class-ridden and deep-lying. There is something Sicilian about it. It's the kind of hatred that made the Peloponnese build fortified tower houses with no windows so that you can fire at each other from a distance, and never cast eyes on your enemy again.

That's why a lot of fans especially enjoyed the last league match of the 1999 campaign, when Gus Poyet's goal sealed the possibility of Champions League football and its financial rewards for Chelsea, and just as importantly, denied it of Leeds.

That's proper *Schadenfreude*.

MANCS

Throughout its hundred-year history, one of the biggest attractions in English football has been the meeting of the fashionable west Londoners with the 'cock of the north', Manchester United.

It was a measure of the slant-eyed focus on each other that Chelsea's stated ambition under Ken Bates was to become 'the Manchester United of the south'. When the balance of power appeared to shift in 2003, naturally, the focus was ambitiously switched to United being 'the Chelsea of the north'. For long periods, especially in the 1960s and 70s, there was a great empathy between the teams' players that was wholly absent from the terraces.

It is fair to say that all in all the Mancunians have had the upper hand, but there is a delicious quirk in that they do rather well at Stamford Bridge and Chelsea perform quite outstandingly at Old Trafford. In the four decades since 1965 Chelsea have lost just four times in the league away to United: in 1987, 1993, 2000 and 2003. Amongst 11 wins are famous formbook-scrapping victories, including September 1977, when the harrier-like Bill Garner scored a legendary early header that won the day for the newly-promoted Blues; or spring 1994, when Peacock brilliantly completed his duet of single-goal winners against the eventual double-winners.

Ever since Chelsea was formed in 1905, though, this has been a fixture to draw the gaze and the money of the footballing public. The first visit of Manchester United (renamed from Newton Heath two years earlier) to Stamford Bridge in the Second Division in April 1906 brought the stadium's first 60,000 crowd. In fact, an incredible 67,000 was the official attendance – among them Ethel Tomkins and her family from Hampstead. She remembers with awe the size of the crowd and the atmosphere around the ground. The match ended 1-1, inside-forward James Robertson getting Chelsea's goal.

The throng that day dwarfed that which had turned out earlier in Chelsea's debut season on Monday 25 December 1905. United's stadium, then on Bank Street, Clayton, hosted 35,000, still a substantial number, and by far their biggest crowd of the season so far. The buzz surrounding the new London club created what sounds like an atmosphere to savour for a long time.

'For Christmas Day in Manchester there was one of the most interesting events on the Clayton programme, the meeting of United and Chelsea,' enthused the *Manchester Guardian*. 'When the fixtures were arranged Chelsea were, of course, a club of unknown strength. Their team has proved brilliantly successful, and they came to Manchester yesterday having been beaten only three times in 17 matches and having had fewer goals scored against them than any team in the whole league.

'Such visitors proved an irresistible draw, and the United ground has very seldom been so thronged as Chelsea made it. The usual open spaces between the grandstand and the slope were quite filled, and once inside the gates you could barely jostle your way out again. But only people with very pressing "other engagements" wanted to get out before the end.'

Remember those words the next time you hear Old Trafford reverberate to 'You've only come to see United.'

'The match was a glorious and memorable struggle,' continued the *Guardian*'s correspondent, 'and its spectators were on the tiptoe of expectation from the first whistle to the last. Chelsea retired unbeaten once more, and with no further addition to their wonderful "goals against" record, for not a goal was scored by either side.'

The deadlock was not for the first time a result of Foulke's goalkeeping. A few minutes before the end 'amid a yell that must have shaken the chimney towers that circle the ground' the referee gave a penalty. Yes, it even used to happen at Clayton. The task of eluding the one-man solar eclipse that was Foulke fell to full-back Robert Bonthron. Over-compensating for Foulke's reach, he sent the spot-kick wide.

'A draw was a just result,' summed up the *Guardian*. 'Chelsea were the more artistic, the more polished and the more accurate side – no eleven of finer "class" had been to Manchester this season – while United, with swift, headlong wide-passing onsets, in which trickery and finesse were scorned, seemed on the whole as an attacking force the more dangerous, not withstanding that they had the ball less often near Foulke than Chelsea had it near Moger.

'Every man in both elevens played like a hero, as indeed, among an almost deafening tumult of incitement he could not choose but do. After seeing

Chelsea's calibre the vast gathering dispersed with little disappointment. One point against such opponents would be a good enough record for any side.'

The duels between the two sides from 1965 to 1973 were frequently sparkling, and they would have been images of each other had a mirror been placed across the country between Stroud and Grimsby.

Unlike with Leeds, Chelsea and United's players were friends. George Best always maintained he would have loved to play for the King's Road swingers, and haunted the bars and shops of the area. Paddy Crerand almost joined Chelsea.

The Blues's finest game in that period was a 4-0 win in Manchester in August 1968, United's heaviest defeat for six years. It might have been like Henry VIII's Field of the Cloth of Gold, so much potential flair was available to either side. Crerand, Kidd, Sadler, Best and Charlton for the home team, McCreadie, Webb, Hollins, Osgood, Tambling, Birchenall and Baldwin for the visitors. But Cooke was injured and Chelsea went for effort and grind over ostentation and Bonetti kept out everything. Stepney, it was said, was quiet for 85 minutes and spent the other five fishing the ball out of his net. Baldwin scored after 40 seconds and added another wonderful side-footed flick in the second half. Tambling and Birch completed the scoring.

That scoreline obviously brings us to the debacle of Wembley 1994, when hope sprang a leak. 'That rain didn't help!' says Gavin Peacock. He's right. Many of us still have clothes drying on radiators 11 years on.

Single goals from Peacock had beaten United home and away in the league, but the FA Cup was a different challenge, wholly new to a young and inexperienced Chelsea side who at least kept things blank in the first 45 minutes. 'You get a feeling about things as a player,' he says, 'and I felt we were holding our own out there against them. They were arguing amongst themselves a bit and you sense that "We're doing all right here" against a team that on paper was stronger than us.'

Famously, Peacock had a great shot from distance that looped over Schmeichel. It might have been as famous as Di Matteo's five years later. 'I picked that ball up,' he remembers, 'just hit it instinctively. It popped down, I whacked it and I thought, "Here we go again, he's beat." Schmeichel, it's going over his head, crack against the crossbar, a split second later they are down the other end and the game goes on.

'If we'd gone 1-0 up there then we'd do what we did in the league games.

We become a bit tighter, everything changes, they probably would have had a lot of possession and tried to break us down. Now they may have been able to do that, I don't know, but I just feel we may have been able to nick that goal. It would have been different.'

Mark Hughes, playing for the Reds that day, admitted after joining Chelsea that he and his team-mates were aware they'd found it hard to break teams down when behind. But it was not to be. 'We gave the penalty away,' continues Peacock. 'The first was a penalty but the second one was a killer. It wasn't a penalty, I believe. Then we are chasing the game and they hit us on the break, but it was a little bit of a false scoreline. It stands, though, and that was it.

'If the Chelsea team under Mourinho had gone a goal down, they wouldn't go like we did. We went off our shape a bit and we were flying all over trying to get it back and then we got caught. Now, they would have worked their way into it, got the first goal back and then if it meant equalising in the 92nd minute, they would have done that and got back that way. We got a spanking because we didn't know any other way to do it and they did us.

'I've watched my shot on video and each time I think that ball is going in but it hits the crossbar. I was able to take a lot from the day and I enjoyed playing in an FA Cup final. Rixy came in the dressing room before and said, "Boys, it will go like a flash, try and enjoy it." I remember thinking I am going to do that, even though we lost and it was bitterly disappointing.'

Not everyone was capable of doing so. 'John Spencer threw his medal away. I gave mine to my dad as one of the things I wanted him to have as an achievement of playing in an FA Cup final, even though we lost. It was certainly an experience I would have loved to have repeated and been on a winning team.'

Revenge for 1994 is waiting round some corner, some time. But in 2005 it was a nice touch of Sir Alex Ferguson's to tell his players to form an admittedly reluctant guard of honour before kick-off to applaud the title winners onto the pitch. Chelsea had done the same to United in the past, and the last time the Blues won the Championship, with Old Trafford the next port of call, Matt Busby had made his players do the honours. Ferguson had also promised 'no cheap Portuguese plonk in the manager's office tonight, but fine wine deserving of a champion'. He praised José Mourinho's 'formidable achievement'. They get on well. The league win at Old Trafford in 2005 established a new record Premiership points total of 94, beating United's previous tally of 92. It also topped the hosts' record of 28 wins in a 38-game season. Many United fans even applauded Chelsea's team off the pitch.

And here's the thing with the United manager. I have attended more than a dozen post-match press conferences at which he's talked about Chelsea, and there have been very few of the mealy-mouthed cheap shots with which Chelsea fans always associate him. He has almost always been respectful; which is more than you can say about Arsenal.

SCOUSERS

There is one match for which Chelsea fans will always thank Ian Porterfield, and it is that 4-5-1 match at Anfield in February 1992, when ex-Wimbledon players Dennis Wise and Vinnie Jones prowled the Blues's midfield. Both scored in a memorable 2-1 win – the first time we had won there since December 1935. The local papers roared 'Mugged by Crazy Gang' when it emerged that Jones had stuck a disrespectful note on the usually sacrosanct 'This Is Anfield' tunnel sign which said 'We're bothered'. And that's the attitude they showed on the pitch.

It was a standout episode in the long-running soap opera between the Scouse Reds and the London Blues that was launched with Chelsea's first ever game at Stamford Bridge, the friendly of 4 September 1905. Chelsea set the tone then with a 4-0 win. To a great degree it has been a case of 'no place like home' for both sides ever since. Chelsea only won nine times and drew 13 times at Anfield in 100 years; Liverpool's record at Stamford Bridge was lost 16, drawn 14. Between October 1919 and October 1971, when Bonetti played in a 0-0 draw, no Chelsea keeper had managed to keep a clean sheet in the league at Anfield.

Against Arsenal or Manchester United, there is nothing like that relative consistency through thick and thin. Even when Chelsea have been rubbish Liverpool have often been the Blues's FA Cup bunny, as in the glorious 4-2 of 1978 and 2-0 in 1982, when the home-growns made the bookies happy. There have been big scores too. Chelsea's record win was in August 1937, a 6-1 thrashing featuring a Mills hat-trick and a brilliant lob by Mitchell. Burgess and Argue also scored in a rare moment when pricey forwards paid their way.

Then, on 7 September 1946, the day Chelsea brought inside-right and 'Ace of Hearts' Tommy Walker down from Tynecastle to sign for them, his new team-mates lost 7-4 to the eventual First Division champions on Merseyside – Liverpool's record win against Chelsea. During Liverpool's lean Christmas spell, though, Billy Birrell's men turned the tables in London with a 3-1 win earned by Goulden and Lawton's goals and Walker's finesse.

It was in the 1960s though that the rivalry reached boiling point.

Docherty's Diamonds reached five semi-finals, three without progressing. The most hurtful of those defeats was in March 1965 against Liverpool, who had played a European away match three days earlier. The fitness of Docherty's Chelsea was renowned, the Blues were flying in the league, and few gave the Reds a chance at Villa Park. But then, most punters fancied the Man Utd of Best, Charlton and Law to prevail over Leeds in the other semi-final. Football gets the finals it deserves, not the ones it wants, and it would be Liverpool versus Leeds at Wembley that year.

'Chelsea wore the mantle of physical and mental fatigue,' it was observed in one newspaper and the usual waves of attack and movement were missing, other than in Bert Murray's and Barry Bridges' solo runs. Their tactic appeared to be to sit back. John Mortimore's first-half goal was ruled out – wrongly, in Chelsea eyes – and tempers frayed as the game progressed. Liverpool endured and sneaked two goals without reply, one a penalty resulting from the feud between Ron Harris and Ian St John.

The revenge a year later in the third round was a dish served warm but no less tasty for that. 'They were the holders, but we were up for it after how the semi-final had gone for us,' says Bobby Tambling, 'and we played them off the park.' His goal in that famous 2-1 win at Anfield remains a favourite amongst his record-breaking 202 for Chelsea. 'They got an early goal that set us back a bit, but if you remember Ossie put us back on level terms. My goal came in the second half and what was especially satisfying was that it was the winner, but also that it was a sweeping move involving all of our forwards. George [Graham] sent the cross over from the right and I looped a header over their goalie.' Amongst that 202, there weren't too many headers. Unfortunately the Blues lost to Sheffield Wednesday in the semi-final, again at Villa Park.

In 1978 it was speedy young winger Clive Walker's day. It was as if the former youth player knew that he had to impress on the big stage, and he scored two of Chelsea's four. 'On paper we had no chance,' Walker said later. 'It was like beating the team of the decade.' It was live on TV – a novelty for unfashionable Chelsea at the time. The atmosphere of surprise and joy on the terraces of a club whose First Division status and economic viability were in doubt, toppling the classic Liverpool team 4-2 in the FA Cup third round, still provokes goosebumps even now. The fact that it was all part of the club's traditional ability to raise its game for the occasion didn't matter.

The upset in the fifth round of the same competition in 1982 was as near as dammit to All Fool's Day, and was watched by nearly 41,500 people, though the Blues were then in Division Two. It was a measure of the long-distance enmity that this was the biggest Bridge attendance since that famous 1978 game. Chelsea won 2-0 with Rhoades-Brown's early wonder strike and a finish from Colin Lee. The cultured but lethargic Mickey Fillery controlled midfield like a master. Micky Droy towered over Dalglish, in football as much as height, and centre-back Colin Pates excelled as a holding midfielder to stifle Graeme Souness.

It was a performance that helped the youngsters to gain confidence and promotion was achieved quite brilliantly in 1984. When Liverpool arrived on 1 December that year, Liverpool had lost their last four games in London. The match pitched the champions of Division Two against their First Division equivalent. David Speedie was awesome, harassing Alan Hansen and Mark Lawrenson (who was booked for persistently fouling him) into what the two *Match of the Day* summarisers would no doubt call 'schoolboy errors'. Kerry Dixon, discovering his irresistible power, brushed aside Hansen for the opener. Molby notched his first for the Reds before Bruce Grobbelaar, who had acted the giddy goat on two Chelsea corners, utterly misjudged Paul Canoville's cross, which hit the back of Blues defender Joey McLaughlin's head, bounced twice and crossed the line. Speedo, about to serve one of his regular three-match bans (Gordon Davies was bought from Fulham specifically as cover), capped a fine show with an excellent third.

With John Neal unwell, it was left to his assistant Ian MacNeill to pronounce that 'beating them makes us feel that we have arrived'. It meant that Chelsea hadn't lost at home to Liverpool for a decade.

But the most memorable of all these great matches came in the fourth round in 1997. It is hailed by many of those who took part as the moment the revolution took hold and belief surged through the club. 'You know,' says Colin Hutchinson, the club's then managing director, 'maybe it was written on the cards because if you remember we were 2-0 down and McManaman should've scored a third before half-time. It would definitely have been over.

And then we came back to win 4-2 in the end. I reflect on that as one of Chelsea's most significant matches of that era. If we hadn't won the [FA] Cup final that year we wouldn't have been in the Cup-Winners' Cup the year after and our progress would have been stifled by at least a year, probably more.'

Fowler and Collymore had scored the Reds's goals as they surprisingly swept Chelsea aside. A catalyst for perhaps the most significant comeback in the club's history was manager Ruud Gullit's half-time correction of an error, bringing on the player he'd left on the bench, the player that Liverpool feared, the talismanic Mark Hughes. The other factor was the tactical shift to a 3-3-1-3 formation, pushing Roberto Di Matteo on to stifle the influential John Barnes. The midfielder was sold by Liverpool in the summer.

From Hughes's first shuddering challenge it was clear this was a different game in the second half. With the subtlety of a mechanical digger he carved out a chance among a gaggle of terrified Liverpool players and shot home after five minutes. From then on, and especially after his sliding stab that set up Zola for the second, the course of Blue history was changed forever.

'Hughes's feisty, distracting presence also liberated Gianluca Vialli and Gianfranco Zola, two Italians who showed their qualities and finishing with the remaining goals,' wrote Henry Winter. 'Zola was terrific, making runs, making plans and making dashes back to thwart Liverpool incursions. Chelsea's victory was a triumph for teamwork from exceptional individuals.'

It was the first time since the 1960s that Liverpool had lost after being two goals ahead. Alan Hansen was conspicuous in the box housing the BBC TV commentary team. 'Hansen, Hansen, what's the score?' came the chant. The same Hansen of 1984. This time, there was a sense of ships passing in the night. Chelsea was becoming the bigger club now. The look of utter powerlessness on defender Mark Wright's face after the fourth goal, his mouth agape like a soldier stunned by the horrors of war, will live long in the memory.

Chelsea, playing 'sexy football', went on to Wembley and won their first major piece of silverware in 26 years, launching the most successful period ever in terms of trophies won.

There have been four big matches between the two sides since then. The most vital as far as Chelsea were concerned, for a number of reasons, was the final game of the 2002–03 season, 11 May, because it decided who would finish in the fourth Champions League slot. It was, the tabloids announced, 'the richest match in history', so much was riding on it monetarily.

'There were a couple of matches during the year that were important,' says Trevor Birch, 'but the one that just stands out above all else was the final game against Liverpool. Early in the season I looked at the fixtures and thought it could be an interesting game because obviously both were challenging for the European place. And as it got closer, for it then to be worth over £20 million to the winner was incredible. I think it meant everything to the club to win that game – who knows whether Mr A [Abramovich] would have been as interested if we hadn't have been in Europe, if we hadn't had that extra money.'

The stakes were high enough to worry Birch long before kick-off. 'I think it obviously meant such a lot to the club, the additional income that would have been available from the Champions League,' he says. 'It starts to play on your mind and was keeping me awake. So one night I got up and put down a few words. I mean, I come out in a cold sweat when I think about it now – why I did what I did – but you feel an overwhelming compulsion to try and do your bit.'

What Birch was writing was a pre-match speech to rally the players.

'They know it's a big game for them,' he is prepared to concede, 'but I just thought, in my misguided way, whether it would inspire them for me to say a few words. And Claudio [Ranieri] very kindly allowed me to address them, in the dressing room actually, yeah. So, you know, some sort of Martin Luther King type test of character speech which – as I say, I'm sweating now as I'm talking about it – I just felt I had to do.'

Here's part of what Birch said to the players in the dressing room before arguably the most important game in Chelsea's history, 'There are only a few times in life that your character is really tested. This is one of them. This could be the difference between staying at the top table of football or drifting into oblivion. Now is the time, boys, to step forward and prove your worth.'

Birch, a former pro at Liverpool, was aware he was taking a chance laying so much on the line and that it might paralyse some players. 'I'm sure,' he laughs, 'as soon as I left the dressing room they thought "What a w**ker!"'

The odds on the day were stacked in the Blues's favour, whether or not Birch's speech would work: not just home advantage, where history weighed heavy, but in points. Liverpool required a win; Chelsea needed just to draw on a wet surface in front of the biggest Stamford Bridge crowd for nine years.

Sami Hyypia put Liverpool one up on 11 minutes but the lead only lasted three minutes before Marcel Desailly, to whom prestige in Europe meant more than anyone, equalised. Even though Jesper Gronkjaer's spectacular second settled nerves and won the game, it was the Rock's goal that changed Chelsea forever.

'And when Jesper scored the goal you think ... unbelievable,' smiles Birch, still looking as relieved today. 'That's probably what a few people in the stadium thought!' But ask Birch what he was thinking at 0-1 and his face freezes. 'Yeah,' he winces. 'To say I was concerned was an understatement. If we had lost it would have been more difficult, that's for sure. The cash gave us just that bit more leverage and ability to deal with the issues we had.'

There were big payments to be made on various loans around that time. 'It wasn't as acute as people were talking about,' Birch notes, calmly, 'it was under control, but it certainly made a huge difference by getting that Champions League place.' It was manager Claudio Ranieri's lasting achievement and he began fittingly by praising the talismanic Franco Zola – it would be the Italian's last competitive match for Chelsea. 'Look at the last 20 minutes today,' said his manager. 'He's fantastic, wonderful.'

Then Ranieri revealed the secret of his success had been squad stability. 'We have the same team,' he said, 'but this year we have done a little bit better. Last season we finished with 64 points, this year we are three points better with 67. From tomorrow I will start to think about the next squad. If we can improve with one or two players, then okay, but change for change's sake, I don't like. I like this group of players. I respect this group. I am confident we can fight against the best in Europe. I think we have learned the hard lesson from our UEFA Cup matches.'

That summer, of course, came the influx of money and players under Abramovich's aegis. The expensively acquired squad had not won anything when it arrived at the Millennium Stadium in February 2005 for the Carling Cup final. As a club Chelsea had not won any silverware since almost complacently beating Aston Villa in the FA Cup final in 2000. But this was José Mourinho's squad, a different animal. Liverpool took a shock lead inside a minute through slack marking of John-Arne Riise and it took an age for a Blue breakthrough. 'After their early goal we basically dominated the game,' remembers Frank Lampard. 'We were getting stronger and stronger, but it was a question of, "Are we going to score?" Once it was 1-1 there was a mental control.'

The equaliser was an own-goal by well-known Chelsea transfer-target Gerrard. 'He's scored his first goal for Chelsea,' sang the fans in blue under the closed roof. After that Chelsea ran out 3-2 winners, the tireless Drogba and Kezman enjoying their day out. It was the first trophy for the Roman Empire and, to Frank Lampard, it was 'very important indeed. Basically even though it's a competition that's talked down, for us as a group of players I'd say it was massive because it was the start of winning things. We'd done a lot of talking, but until you actually get one in the bank there's no reality to it.'

Inexorably, the two teams were drawn together again in the Champions League semi-final the same season. The 1-0 aggregate defeat delivered the only telling disappointment in Mourinho's first season, but they were massive occasions. The goal that decided the tie, though patently cleared off the line by the athletic Gallas, went unanswered by a Chelsea team that had just won the league title. The atmosphere at Anfield would rank amongst the most extraordinary of any Chelsea game. The following morning I received a call from a Liverpool season ticket holder friend offering commiseration. 'My ears!' he marvelled. 'I feel like I've been to a Status Quo gig!' It was true – my ears were ringing too. 'You know what,' says Frank Lampard, 'the atmosphere at Anfield was unbelievable, something special. The noise before kick-off, and when they scored ... All credit to their fans for creating that.'

He has a sense that destiny took its course in the tie, what with Chelsea having already pocketed the Premiership and Carling Cup. 'We lost basically because we didn't play as well as were capable, but a lot of it was ... there was sense in the grand scheme of things that maybe you can't win everything this year. Of course, Eidur might have tucked that [chance] away in the last few minutes and it might have been a different story, but it's nice to have something still to aim at in the future.'

There was one final sting in the Scousers' tails following that loss. At the last match of that season, away to Newcastle, the Chelsea school of 2005 surpassed the record meanness of Liverpool's 1979 defence – Clemence, Hansen, Thompson et al. Graeme Souness had been establishing himself in the Reds's midfield side that season. As the St James' Park press conference dissolved, the Newcastle manager privately pondered Chelsea's achievement. 'What I do know,' he said, 'is that it's not just about the defenders and the goalkeeper. The defending starts further up the field. You need people who can protect the back four and restrict the number of chances. And in Makelele Chelsea have what I believe is the best in the business today.'

He paused a second. 'Did they really beat the record today?' 'Yes,' I told him. 'Unbelievable ... '

FOREVER BLUE

Supporting **Chelsea**
– a **life** sentence

23

THE GAME OF TWO FACES

One of the most gratifying stories of the modern Chelsea is that of someone who joined the club after years of standing on the terraces, worked his way up through the underrated quality of usefulness, and became a priceless member of the squad. But he's not a player.

Gary Staker became a part-time member of the informal security team at the Harlington training ground after Glenn Hoddle became manager in 1994. A long-term fan and matchday steward since the late 1970s, Staker was also known to away rail travellers in the 80s as one of those who handled catering on Chelsea 'specials'. 'Myself and Geoff Buck and another steward approached Ken Bates and said, "Look, why aren't you running refreshments?"' he recalls. 'And he said, "Well, we weren't making a profit." I said, "You've got to be making a profit on food!"

'So the club gave us money as a float and with people like Brian Waghorn, in our own cars and vans, we used to go to a cash-and-carry on a Friday night, buy Mars bars, Cokes, crisps, and sell them on the trains, giving the profit to Chelsea.'

Ten years on, as part of Hoddle's team, other assets came to prominence. Staker's mother was Italian, originally from the northern city of Trieste, and his grasp of her mother tongue was sufficient for him to strike up conversations with Ruud Gullit, newly arrived at Chelsea, in the language the player was used to at Milan and Sampdoria.

His language skills provided a solution to football problems that had not previously existed to the same degree – the language barrier between players and management and handling the culture shock of London.

Staker proved himself a discreet, respectful and helpful 'buddy' to those settling in. Despite remaining a fervent fan, he was unruffled when dealing with the superstars then arriving at Chelsea. 'My attitude is they're normal people,' he says. 'When I was young I had my favourites: Bobby Tambling, Johnny Hollins. But then you get to see that they're just normal people. And yes, you understand the adulation that they get and why they get it, but to me it was no different than a normal person in the street.'

When Gullit took over from Hoddle as manager in 1996, Staker received a phone call from Chelsea saying, 'We'll need you in the summer.' He was still working for the BBC on security at the time. Since a day can be a long time at Chelsea, he sensibly told them to get back to him when it was confirmed.

'Then I was at work one Friday and I got a phone call from a physio saying, "I'll see you in an hour." I said, "See me where?" "Well, we've got a player coming in, and I've been told that you've been told about it."

'So I rang Colin Hutchinson and he said, "Yeah, yeah, yeah, he's coming in today, we need you." "Well I'm at the BBC, I'm working. Let's see if I can get an afternoon off."' Luckily his boss was agreeable. The physio picked Staker up outside Television Centre in Wood Lane, drove him down to Harlington, and Gwyn Williams brought Gianluca Vialli into the room. 'Gianluca spoke very little English,' says Staker, 'but he said he knew a lot about Chelsea. And we went through a medical process with him, did the tests and then took him up to Stamford Bridge to meet Colin Hutchinson and Ken Bates and everything. At the end of the day I said to Gianluca, in Italian, "If you need any help, you can give me a call." At that time, none of us had mobiles. "Yeah, okay, thank you".'

Vialli was an extrovert who threw himself into overcoming the language barrier. Dennis Wise and the 'chaps' – as Vialli soon called them – began drawing up a list of phrases Vialli liked the sound of – mostly obscene – and pinned it on the dressing room wall. Vialli, with Chelsea-supporting masseur Terry Byrne's help, also made a collection of English clichés. Sometimes they came out slightly mangled, such as his famous press conference comment on 'when the fish [as opposed to chips] are down.'

Two weeks after Vialli's arrival Colin Hutchinson offered Staker the role of 'personal assistant-cum-driver'. It was part-time at first, but as the likes of Roberto Di Matteo joined the Ruud revolution, more overseas players would find a use for his time – there were always electricity bills that needed interpreting, TV licences that needed sorting. Staker became the buffer between the footballers and the world. It was Vialli, though, who was closest to him at the time.

'In Italy it's a completely different culture,' says Staker. 'Gianluca was living in a hotel and looking for a property, and because of who he was, a lot of our time was spent walking round estate agent windows at eight or nine o'clock at night looking for properties and me ringing up the next day and saying, "I'm looking for a property costing x amount." I wouldn't tell them it was for Gianluca.

'I used to finish work, travel back into London, meet Vialli. One of my vivid memories with Gianluca was when he did find a property; he invited me to his house to watch the 1997 European Cup final. The year before joining Chelsea, he'd won it with Juve, and now here he was in London, sitting watching it in a house on his own. All the chat was about him, last year's final, with him lifting the cup, and all the adulation. And I thought, that's football. One year ago the world's at your feet and now you're sitting there, no friends, nobody else, just you and me watching the European Cup final.'

At the time Vialli was feeling isolated and sorry for himself on the pitch too. Things had been looking positive back in January when he scored twice in the incredible 4-2 FA Cup fourth round fightback against Liverpool, when Mark Hughes had come on at half-time to form a three-pronged attack with Vialli and Gianfranco Zola.

The following week, however, a practice match was specifically set up so that Gullit might experiment with formations to accommodate his three forwards. But nothing seemed to click so he fell back on the customary 3-5-2 and Vialli was the one who lost out. Vialli reacted badly. After the next match, a 2-1 win at White Hart Lane in which Vialli played no part, he sat smoking a cigarette by the side of the pitch. This in itself was a familiar occurrence. But the appearance of photographs in the papers the next day increased the tension. The Zola-Hughes partnership had been unstoppable on the road to Wembley that year, and Vialli was a last minute, almost honorary substitute in the final.

'I knew a lot of what he was going through,' says Staker. 'After the cup final he was on the bus on the celebration parade. He thought at the time he had said goodbye to the fans at Wembley. We discussed it: said things might happen, might not happen, but I said, "You're a part of Chelsea history now."

'And as we're going along the Fulham Road, as we pulled up outside the town hall, he said to me, "Make sure I have a photograph with all the people in the background so I have a photograph of the fans." I said, "You will be here next season, you will stay here."

'I think he went away on holiday and realised he wanted to make a success of it in England. By that time he'd learnt a lot of English, because he'd studied English three or four hours a day. He changed and became more English. Being wealthy, being a well-paid footballer, he loved good quality, and coming from an aristocratic family, he obviously knew the finer things of life.

'He was fascinated by English culture. We were walking in Sloane Square and he said to me, "Gary, how do you get on these buses, what do you do?" I said, "You just pay and get on." He said, "Come on then." So we went on, it was 80p or 60p at the time, a number 19 or something. We went upstairs and sat down and he was like a kid. We went from Sloane Street all the way to Piccadilly. He'd never been on public transport before.'

Through helpfulness and flexibility former 'specials' refreshment man Staker had made himself one of the most trusted people at the club, a confidant who only wanted the best for the club he supported, and an eyewitness to most of the key moments in recent Chelsea history.

'It was funny,' he recounts, 'because I was walking round the backstreets of Chelsea with Luca, around midnight, looking at these properties. And I got a phone call from Colin Hutchinson saying they were about to sign Zola. And Gianluca's telling me all about Zola and everything.

'When Zola came over, by that time I'd worked out what to do, and Chelsea said, "Can you come to the press conference for Gianfranco Zola?" Just like that, in November 1996 Staker landed his first public engagement as an official Chelsea FC interpreter. 'I met Franco for the first time,' he says, 'and he'll love me for saying it, but he looked a *right* state in his little brown jumper and his little black hat. I thought, what the hell is this here?

'And he looked at me and started talking to me. His wife Franca was very nervous and he said, "It's very strange, and we've been to places in London today and we don't really like it." I was able to say, "You'll get to like it. Luca likes it, Roberto Di Matteo likes it, Rudi loves it. Because here, you're not classified as a superstar, you can walk around and live your life." I think from there we just got friendly.'

Staker's friendship with the magical Sardinian holds firm to this day but it was sealed, unusually, with a flat-pack furniture bonding session. 'The first game that he played was Blackburn away, when we came back he rang me and asked, "Can you come round next week?" I had helped him sort himself out with phone bills, electric bills and various other domestic things. So I went round on the Friday, the night before we played Newcastle and he said, "I've just bought a load of flat-pack stuff for my kids. Can you help me with the instructions that are in English?" So we spent the entire Friday evening constructing children's bedroom furniture.

'Franco said, "I cannot believe it, Gary. I'm playing my first home game, it's very, very late in the night and I'm up with you making furniture for the kids." And we managed to fix the stuff and his wife was laughing. He said, "I've never done anything like this." I told him, "But that's what it's like in England. Tomorrow you'll be playing football, but tonight you can do what you like."'

On the back of the influx of overseas players, Staker went full-time at Chelsea in early 1997. He found himself spending most time with Zola, the player who was rapidly bringing the magic back to Chelsea and wowing fans. Zola's impact was felt on his home debut, even if his first goal – a whipped-in cross that eluded Newcastle's Srnicek – was claimed by Vialli. Before going for a celebratory meal after that game, Zola was mobbed outside the ground. 'I can't believe these fans,' he said. 'Well,' said Gary Staker, 'they've not seen nothing like you before.' Even when you'd go out privately with him he'd love the way the British people just respected him. He'd go out and walk about where he lived in London, or just outside of London, and he was the same to the highest people in the land as he was to the lowest person in the land. He was the same person. Always had time to speak to everybody.'

He enjoyed the professional adulation and a four-year love affair resulted in Blues fans voting him the greatest Chelsea player of all time. In his opening season he also became Chelsea's first ever Football Writers' Player of the Year. If the board ever decided to build a statue or some other memorial, the Sardinian would be everyone's first choice for its subject.

'Franco just loved to play football for the joy of it,' says Staker. 'He was not interested in any of the periphery. He just loved to play football ... to train, to play. He was always the first to come to Harlington. He loved to show things to the youth players or any of the senior players. He'd always sign autographs and he just loved being round the little children and the way kids looked up to him. He thought he was still a kid – maybe because of his size! He was as extraordinary a person off the field as he was a footballer on it.'

When Claudio Ranieri was appointed, Staker acted as a chaperone for him too, and became, without any training, his translator, alongside Alex Leith, the Italian-speaking editor of the official *Chelsea* magazine. 'Claudio came over and didn't speak a word of English,' he shrugs, 'so at the time there was people like Gus Poyet and Franco and myself helping to translate for the team and everyone. And the club, Colin Hutchinson and Ken Bates at the time, said they wanted somebody that they could trust.

'I spoke Italian, not having translation qualifications, but I could say things and look after Claudio and be by his side if he needed any help. We went to Old Trafford. Straight afterwards they wanted an interview. They had nobody to translate, so I was thrust into it, without even time to ask him what he thought of the game, where Claudio made a tactical change and we came from behind to draw 3-3.'

Elements of the media were soon scathing about the stern-faced Ranieri anyway – the fans had provided the ammunition by chanting Vialli's name at matches. Chelsea's usually unsophisticated press conferences became even less coherent with the Italian's lack of English. The brilliant but eccentric Brian Glanville didn't help with his spontaneous outbursts of private dialogue with the Chelsea manager in his mother tongue. Friendly UK-based Italian journalists such as Giancarlo Galavotti of *Gazzetta dello Sport* sometimes had to step in with a correcting word or two. Ranieri took to avoiding the awkward moments altogether.

The deteriorating relationship between the press and Chelsea's teetering Tower of Babel reached a nadir with a piece in the *Standard* by Kate Battersby that caricatured Staker, who is physically disabled, as a polyglot 'gnome'. Zola was captured on film interpreting lengthy instructions to team-mate Jon Harley as 'play better'. Later, on the day of a match, one Chelsea player refused to pass on the manager's message to another that he was dropped. He was promptly removed from the team line-up. The player stood in front of everyone and speculated about whether he had been dropped for his translating, or his football.

If Chelsea wanted professionalism, they could have forked out for a full-time, qualified translator. But at the time trust was more important. 'The one that everybody remembers is the old football cliché,' says Staker. 'Ranieri was saying, "It was a game of two faces," which in England you wouldn't say – you'd say it was "a game of two halves," which is what I said. And everybody thought it was funny because it sounded like he'd said a lot more than that.

'People want to write what they want to write. That's okay because the people that mattered to me, Claudio, Colin and Ken Bates, didn't say bad things to me. Lots of the players and people in football not involved with Chelsea, some I knew and some I didn't know, wrote to me apologising. I had lots of chances to reply but that's just not me.'

Ranieri was taking English lessons, but his closest staff were Italian and it was not easy for him to learn. As he left for the summer break the under-fire manager worried, 'By the time I come back I'll have forgotten what English I know.'

But he returned, picked it again, decided to conduct the conferences in quirky English and suddenly his impish sense of humour was revealed. The media view of him softened; he switched from buffoon to loveable charmer. Now they could get the stories they wanted.

'It became a laughing stock because of his English,' says Staker, 'but towards the end the journalists loved him. He'd turned it round because he'd come out with his quotes in English, which if you said at the start, you'd wonder who this man was?

'It's like any translation – whether it's a politician, a footballer, a pop star, a poet, anything – you cannot translate the same way as the person who's trying to express it. The person who's trying to express it in his own language has got the full force of his venom or his pleasure. And you translating, whether you're a professional translator or whether you're a person that's helping out in various ways, you're just translating as seen.'

The media coverage of Claudio Ranieri's period as manager is instructive. It was constructed for its own ends: to sell papers or increase viewing figures. That it only paid lip service to the feelings of those on the terraces is natural: journalists like the people that give them stories and dislike those who don't because communication is the lifeblood of their profession.

When a relationship is struggling, counsellors advise talking. Ranieri, whose grasp of English had stepped up from faltering to comedic over the summer of 2001, began increasingly to avoid press conferences altogether as the goals dried up and speculation over his future festered towards the end of the season. In the football press, as with so much else in life, evil fills a vacuum. His absence from post-match chats was greeted with exasperation and malevolence in pressrooms. No good could come of it.

In place of an interrogation of the good value Italian, a few selective quotes from Chelsea players were sometimes read out, which often heightened the issue. The occasional playing back of an exclusive interview for Chelsea's travelling media over a hand-held cassette player didn't help. The resentment of a generation of hacks was compounded in this period. It was the club, not the manager that bore the brunt of this, which made the transition in their treatment of Ranieri easier. His coverage slipped from 'comic cut' to the 'death of a thousand cuts' at the hands of the wicked new Roman Empire once Abramovich took over.

The theme was enhanced when one of the first press 'briefings' by Peter Kenyon, the new chief executive at Stamford Bridge, appeared to suggest that Ranieri might not be a long-term solution.

After a 2003–04 season in which the media successfully strung out the Ranieri-as-victim story – culminating with his dignity in tears after the European Cup win at Highbury in 2004 – Chelsea at last established a communications department. The first director was Simon Greenberg, a former *Evening Standard* sports editor and football fan, and press events, while not always harmonious in a season of controversies, were suddenly far slicker and more professional.

Gary Staker remains as much an installation at the Cobham training ground as he was in the days of Vialli, Poyet and Zola at drafty Harlington, helping new players come to terms with English bureaucracy and oiling the wheels of the Chelsea bandwagon. He's just not translating any more – at least not in public. It's reassuring to see a little of the old Chelsea still at the heart of the new. He's still just being himself. He doesn't think he does anything special. 'I think you make contributions through everything you do with a football club,' says Staker. 'Everybody. Whether you're a supporter or whether you work inside. A football player, manager, chairman, chief exec are just passing through, and their jobs are for a company. Yes, you're in a privileged position working inside, and you get to see the other side of the coin, but a fan is always a fan.'

24

A CHELSEA LIFE

'My name is Joe Cusselle. I was born in Lambeth, south London, in 1920 and was first taken to Stamford Bridge by my dad when I was eight years old. Dad, my brother and I would always stand in the same place on the huge bank of terracing on the west side of the ground. We always used the same turnstile at the Britannia entrance to get in and soon got to know the turnstile operator that worked there. He would let my dad pay a shilling and then let my brother and I sneak under the turnstile without paying.

'It is difficult to remember much about individual players from those first few seasons that I saw. It was more about the people I saw there every week and the atmosphere among the crowd. There really was a sense of community about our small section of the terraces, so much so, that if my dad or my brother were missing for any game, people would ask after them.

'We used to count the steps up from the front so that we always took up position in the same place every game. This was about half way up the west terrace bank directly opposite the tunnel. We liked it here because we could see the players emerge from the tunnel before the match from the grandstand opposite. This is over 70 years ago now but I can still visualise the blue of the Chelsea players emerging against the grey backdrop of the crowd. People didn't really wear bright colours then and that's why I suppose they and the Chelsea Pensioners in the grandstand stood out.

'I can still remember as a child my first sightings of those Chelsea Pensioners. It's strange to think that I'm one of them myself now, but back then they were part of the attraction of coming to Chelsea over going to other clubs. They made us stand out as a club, made us a little bit different. They would sit in the south-east corner of the ground in front of the grandstand. This was the area that also used to accommodate the invalids who arrived from that corner of the ground in their three-wheeler buggies. Many of these men were First World War veterans and amputees. Their buggies had a set of levers, which they used to push themselves along with. I think they must have come from the Oswald Stoll Foundation homes, which were very near to the ground by Walham Green tube station. As a child I used to believe that the Oswald Stoll Foundation building was the Royal Hospital and that was where all the Chelsea Pensioners lived!

'One occasion I can remember vividly from my childhood days is the day we played Arsenal after we won promotion to Division One in 1930. I was about ten and there was a huge crowd squeezed into the ground. Although we had taken up our place early on the terrace, by the time kick-off approached I couldn't see a thing. However, before I knew it a man next to me had lifted me up and swung me on top of the heads of the crowd. I then rolled on top of the crowd all the way down to the front and was allowed to stand on the edge of the pitch on the greyhound track. Many away fans used to put down Stamford Bridge as a venue for football because of that track, but when the really big games came along it came into its own.

'My memories of Chelsea are much clearer in the seasons just before the war. I think this must be because I started going more regularly once I started work. You left school at 14 in those days and I saved hard to buy myself a Hercules pushbike for just under £3. That was quite a bit of money then and that bike was my pride and joy. Instead of having to get two buses to get to Stamford Bridge, now I could cycle directly there. In those days quite a few people cycled and the people living around the ground would do very nicely by charging them to leave their bikes in their front or back yards. I always left my prized bike with a lady who lived directly opposite the main gates in a little terraced house near to where the old Chelsea railway station used to be. It would cost me 3d and she must have done very well out it. I'm surprised she could have moved in her house by the time kick-off came; not only did she rent out her front and back yards, but she had bikes inside along her hallway too!

'It's always small details about the players that stand out and make you recall them. The first player I really took notice of was our keeper from the 1930 promotion season Sam Millington. He was a really reliable keeper and I remember he always wore a really large flat cap.

'Another player I remember was a tall Cockney named George Barber who played full-back. He was a really cultured player in many respects but he was also hard as nails. He was one player who could get the crowd going just through making a tackle. His slide tackles were legendary for their ferocity. The Chelsea crowd will forgive anything if they think a player is 100 per cent committed to the cause and George, like Ron Harris years later, was one of those players. Today I expect he wouldn't last five minutes on the pitch tackling like that and more's the pity for it. I think we've lost something by taking the art of tackling out of the game.

'Another player with a similarity to one of the great players of the 1970s was Sam Weaver. He was our left-half just before the war and stood out because of the tremendous long throw he used to have. He could throw the ball right to the far post, a tactic almost unheard of in those days. He really was the forerunner of Ian Hutchinson and it was such a shame that his career was cut short by the war.

'We had some great forwards both before and straight after the war. My favourite before the war was George Mills. The fans loved him because he remained loyal to the club even when he was dropped, often unfairly, for the likes of Irishman Joe Bambrick. Fans always appreciate a player being loyal and George certainly was.

'At Stamford Bridge we have always loved our forwards and we had some great ones in those days. Hughie Gallagher on his day was a world-beater and after the war Tommy Lawton really stood out. What a great header of a ball. I don't think I've seen anyone better, before or since.

'Chelsea have always had some great Scottish players and Jimmy Argue was one of them. I can close my eyes and picture him now because of his shock of bright red hair. It's funny how things like that stick in your memory. Another player with bright red hair like him was one of Chelsea's great opponents over the years, Charlton goalkeeper Sam Bartram.

He brings back memories of one of the funniest things I have ever seen at the Bridge.

'I came to the ground on Christmas Day 1937 for a match against Charlton. In those days games were frequently called off because of dense fog [we know now that it was caused by the smog created from all the coal-burning fires and chimneys in London]. It was just about playable at kick-off time but as the game went on it became obvious to us that it wouldn't finish, as we couldn't see the Charlton goal from where we were standing and it must have been equally as bad for the players. Soon enough the ref blew his whistle and took the players off. I was making my way up to the exits as the crowds tried to leave the ground when I heard a roar of laughter from fans behind me. Looking around as the fog cleared briefly I could make out the bright red hair of Charlton goalkeeper Sam Bartram. Nobody had bothered to tell him that the game had finished some minutes before and he was still guarding his goal from non-existent Chelsea attacks. It just goes to show some of the extreme conditions which were tolerated as normal in those days. Football has changed in so many ways since then.

'Back then the players certainly seemed closer to us as individuals. Certainly their wages were! They were ordinary working-class blokes like we were and not surprisingly you would often find half the playing squad in the pub, over the road from Stamford Bridge, once training had finished in the week. Even during the 1960s nothing much had changed. I often saw the likes of Peter Osgood and company in the World's End pub after I'd been to the dogs at Stamford Bridge.

'The players are certainly more professional nowadays. I think the reason why Chelsea remained the great underachievers for so many years was because of the distractions to be had close at hand. If it wasn't the drink then it was the dogs. Footballers are often big gamblers but back then they couldn't really afford it and it became a distraction.

'My family still train and run greyhounds today and back then I remember staying on after seeing Chelsea play for the evening greyhound meeting at the Bridge. It would always fascinate me as a kid to watch them start preparing the ground for the greyhounds almost as soon as the final whistle had gone. They would start swinging out the track lights that were stored at the side of the pitch to place them over the track as soon as the players had left the pitch.

'If Dad couldn't make the evening meeting himself he would often leave me with money to put a bet on for him. This left me with a lifelong passion for the dogs that has never left me. I even used to have some of my own dogs in the kennels, behind the old North Stand, when I was older. That North Stand was a real eyesore but I suppose, like the Shed itself, it wasn't really designed for football but for greyhound racing.

'Like so many fans of my age, my days at the Bridge were cut short by the outbreak of the Second World War. I joined the forces on 12 October 1940. After three months training as a gunner I set sail for the Far East. It took us about 64 days to reach Singapore. I arrived on 24 July 1941 as a 21-year-old gunner with the 11th Battery, 7th Coast Regiment, Royal Artillery. My life was never to be the same again.

'On 15 February 1942 we received word that the British had surrendered. We were stunned and surprised at the news. It took some time for it to sink in. We all felt let down; so here we were, prisoners-of-war. It was a very strange feeling. We had not seen a Japanese all through the war. We did not know what to expect next. Looking back now we should have been prepared to expect the worst. For the next four years I was worked, nearly until the point of death, building the infamous Burma railway and the bridge over the River Kwai.

'I managed to keep a packet of photographs with me to remind me of home but I never thought I would see my family back in London again. One day I got a bamboo splinter in the leg. It turned poisonous and in just a few days I had an ulcer as big as my fist. I could not walk. It was very painful. I was operated on by two Australian majors. They cut the ulcer right out off my leg. They told me that if it had been a few days later, I might have lost a part of my leg. I was most grateful for what they did. I was lucky.

'Every day at least eight people died. I saw them taken past my hut with a Union Jack flag draped over their bodies. This went on for days. There must have been many men who died in this camp and this was only one hospital.

'News soon began to filter through about the Japs not doing so well in the war. Then we heard about this atomic bomb that was dropped on Japan and then another bomb a couple of days later. The next morning, we woke up to find that all the Japs had disappeared into thin air!

'Then a lorry arrived from the Royal Navy ships which had arrived in Keppel Docks. It was loaded with freshly baked rolls. The sailors started throwing the rolls to us. What a wonderful sight it was.

'After that it was not long before we were told to get ready to leave. When we arrived at the docks we boarded the Aussie ship SS *Monowai* and within a few hours we were on our way home.

'When I arrived back in London there were flags and bunting hanging over the front door. I was home! I can never explain to anyone just how wonderful that felt. When I lay in that hospital, close to death, it was thoughts of my family and London that helped to give me the strength to go on.

'That was October 1945. I was still in quite a bad way, mentally as well as physically. The army offered to allow me time to recover before being demobbed, but my dad insisted that I start work as soon as I could, because he said that there would be thousands of soldiers looking for work soon and I should take what I could get whilst I still had the chance.

'In November 1945, while I was waiting to be demobbed, I went with my dad and my brother to see the Chelsea v Moscow Dynamos game. I expect many men that day, who had returned home from the war, longed to be at Stamford Bridge to get back to how things were before the war: to stand with friends again and not have to worry if death was just around the next corner.

'I remember how exotic the Russian players seemed to us back then. I expect that's why so many people tried to get into the ground. Tommy Lawton was making one of his first appearances for the Blues and it was great to be there to witness that too. I don't remember much about the game itself, except I lost my dad and brother on the way out of the ground. It didn't really matter. There was such a friendly feeling of comradeship among the crowd that day. So many different uniforms, so many men lost in the simple pleasure of going to a football match with their mates again.

'To go to football and the dogs at Stamford Bridge was something I really needed to help me blot out what had happened to me over the previous four years. I received a gratuity of £69 for my Army service on being demobbed and had spent it within a month going to the dogs at Stamford Bridge. That seems quite a reckless thing to do now, but I needed to let off steam. Looking back, I needed more time to try and get over what had happened to me but back then you just got on with it.

'I'm 85 now and have been a Chelsea Pensioner for nine years. I remember being interviewed by the adjutant on arriving and being asked whether I liked football. On hearing I was a diehard Chelsea fan he said that I should put my name down for one of the free tickets that the club provide for each home game. It took me some time until I got the chance to go but once this happened I soon became a regular.

'As a pensioner, I've also been involved with the club's Education Through Football scheme over the past two years, which has allowed me to give something back to the club. I really enjoy working with the children that come to the Bridge and am really looking forward to the events that are planned on the project for the centenary season.

'Most of the men are really appreciative of the opportunity of going to see games but I'm the only one who has always been a Blues fan. That's why it was such a special moment for me on 7 May 2005, when I formed part of the guard of honour for the players when they received the Premiership trophy after the game. I'll never forget the roar of the crowd as we came out behind Roy Bentley and Stan Willemse, who were carrying the trophy up to the podium. I was just one of the crowd in 1955 when these two great players brought us the championship for the first time and now I was walking out with them to crown the new champions 50 years on.

'It's difficult to describe how proud I was that day. I just stood there, lost in my memories, and thinking back to when I first came to the Bridge with my dad and brother, as a kid, all those years ago.'

EPILOGUE

Back-to-back
Champions 2006

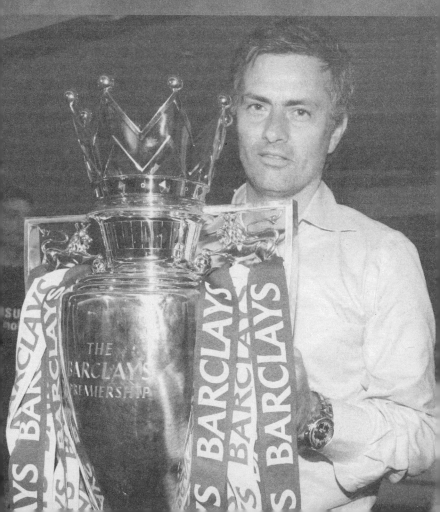

25

RAISING THE BAR

We can never entirely know the private ambition of the Mears brothers, the Janes family, Fred Parker and the rest of the Chelsea hierarchy back on that Sunday afternoon in February 1905 when the Chelsea Football Club was born from their investments. We know they intended to create a popular attraction at Stamford Bridge capable of competing with the best Edwardian London leisure could offer. And that in the new professional era of football they wanted to break the north-west domination of the sport. But did they ever consider Chelsea might become the biggest football club in the world? Perhaps they did.

The fascination of looking back on a season when English football's biggest prize was comfortably secured for a second consecutive season, while the greatest players in the world are being secured for the future, is that the present Chelsea – always a rich man's plaything to some – is in fact a fulfilment of the 1905 prototype.

That it took 100 years to achieve is all part of the inscrutability of the club. In 1907 George Hilsdon became Chelsea's first England international, followed shortly by Jimmy Windridge and Vivian Woodward, to provide three of the national team's forwards. In 2006 Chelsea sent four Englishmen to the World Cup – the most ever for the club. In 1907 Gus Mears's board forked out £1,000 for the first time (officially, though rumours dispute it) on Everton's Fred Rouse. In May 2006, Peter Kenyon negotiated the arrival of Michael Ballack from Bayern Munich. The German club's general manager, Uli Hoeness, commented that there was one club in the world Bayern could not fight to keep their star, 'and that's Chelsea.' The same month the planet's greatest striker, Andriy Shevchenko, arrived to negotiate terms despite the clamour of Milan's fans, players and board ringing in his ears for him to stay. It is all a long way from being knocked back by targets such as Neil Warnock or Darryl Wassell for being too small a club.

So what value do we now place on Marcel Desailly's equaliser against Liverpool in 2003, the goal that secured Champions League football and made feasible the arrival of the ambitious new owner from Chukotka? In a way, Abramovich returned the club to normality. Apart from the period between 1974 and 1994 the club has always invested heavily in its playing staff. The difference is that whereas the money was too often used to fund expensive, sometimes underperforming strikers in cavalier sides designed to delight massive crowds, today's squad, under Chelsea's greatest manager, José Mourinho, has the efficiency of the New Model Army.

In April 2004 Arsenal's Patrick Vieira had advised, 'If you want to be successful and you look at Manchester United in the 1990s or Liverpool in the 1970s and 1980s, they won the title two, three or four times in a row and that makes you a great team.' Arsène Wenger suggested the same in 2005. His words have been thrown back at him in style.

On the way to back-to-back title wins that still have fans pinching themselves, the squad set new standards. Having outmuscled Arsenal to win the Community Shield, Mourinho's men stormed ahead in the Premiership, establishing an all-time record of 10 straight wins. No team even scored a league goal against John Terry et al until Luke Moore's opener for Aston Villa at Stamford Bridge on 24 September. By 2 January Chelsea were 14 points clear of Manchester United and 25 ahead of Arsenal. They would concede just two points at home all season – a record equalled only by Newcastle, 99 years earlier. For the first time in 99 years of London derbies Chelsea also achieved league doubles over both senior rivals: Tottenham and Arsenal. Mourinho masterminded the beating of every Premiership club at least once.

Perhaps the manager's crowning glory that autumn was the transformation to a world class player of Joe Cole, architect of the Blues' definitive 4-1 win at Anfield in October.

Old personalities were redrawn in this new light, especially when Chelsea's spring stumbles appeared to let rivals get a sniff of the silverware. Soccer pundits on TV, radio and in the press openly hoped for Chelsea to fail 'for the good of football'. It seemed nearly everyone felt threatened by Chelsea's supposed 'dominance' – a dominance that had not yet lasted even two seasons.

The persistent criticism made the media required non-viewing for anyone with a Chelsea affiliation. Some supporters did find the change from glamorous also-rans to ruthlessly efficient winners difficult. Certainty reduced the drama. And many took the critics' words about 'grinding relentlessly' to a successive title win to heart, making the back-to-back achievement an oddly joyless one for them.

At first it seemed all about the money. In 1910 the papers delighted in 'moneybags' Chelsea's doomed attempt to avert relegation by forking out on a host of players during the most severe injury crisis in its history. In 2005 Wenger was able to describe Abramovich's Chelsea as 'financially doped' with impunity. Chelsea were 'buying the title'. But, since many clubs had tried but failed in this regard, and Blackburn's Jack Walker-funded 1995 champions dropped off to seventh the following season, we seem to have got something right.

One broadsheet journalist made loathing of Chelsea his specialist subject for the season. In one almost Biblical column headed, 'Ruthlessness and efficiency guarantee Mourinho trophies but not lasting glory... He is the reason for both their success and their now raging unpopularity,' he made a valiant attempt to dictate history for all time.

As José Mourinho, feted as the Special One a year earlier, laconically observed, 'Football is a box of surprises and you never know what might happen.' The manager had a series of run-ins with the media throughout the season. He objected to the persistent replaying of a Michael Essien challenge on Dietmar Hamann in the Champions League by *Sky Sports News*, helping prompt UEFA's surprising retrospective two-match ban (originally three, but reduced) that ruled the important midfielder out from both legs of the tie against Barcelona. He was surprised at how the verbal spat with Arsène

Wenger – during which Mourinho suggested his Arsenal counterpart was like a 'voyeur' because he seemed obsessed with the goings-on at Stamford Bridge – escalated into a duel. He was dismayed by the singling out of Didier Drogba over 'diving' and handballs.

As a result of these and other annoyances, Mourinho withheld from the media the 'golden egg' – his eminently quotable press conferences. The vacuum was predictably filled by at first irritable, and later angry attacks on him and his club. But behind this he had forged a playing side so powerful that even the likes of Arsenal and Manchester United adapted their tactics to take on the champions, even on their respective home patches. In this and other ways the football community itself at least was paying respect. It came from some unlikely corners.

Having organised a 'guard of honour' for the champions at Old Trafford in May 2005, then watched Chelsea's easy 3-1 win, Sir Alex Ferguson had confessed that 'in winning the Premiership so handsomely they have raised the bar for the rest of us. There was no catching them, as I'm sure Arsène Wenger will agree, and a new challenge has arrived for the rest of us.'

By December 2005, as the elusive bar rose even higher, the United manager was all but conceding the title, mid-season. 'You have to give a lot of credit to them for their defensive qualities,' he said. 'We are all jealous of it. The margin for error is getting less.'

And after watching his side taken apart 3-0 in the title decider in April 2006, he added, with genuine respect, that Chelsea had deserved to win the title back-to-back. 'Their home record is sensational,' he enthused. As Mourinho had predicted, using a classic Portuguese metaphor that stumped many at the time, United 'died on the beach' at Stamford Bridge that day.

So it is fitting to close this period of Chelsea history with the views of the man who, more than any other, wrote it: José Mourinho.

'In 2005–06 I think we had a great initial period and a very good end,' he said. 'And when I say end, I'm not speaking about matches after we're champions; I'm not speaking about Blackburn or Newcastle [both games lost after the title was won]. I'm speaking about West Ham, Bolton, Man United. The first period of the season makes me very, very happy because we establish a level where other people couldn't compete with us. We won a lot of consecutive matches and we put ourselves in a very comfortable position where September, October... people were already saying Chelsea would be champions again.

'After that, the middle of the season was up and down: better, worse; playing well, playing bad; winning, drawing, losing. And when people tried to put pressure on us in that period where Man United was winning consecutive matches, I'm very happy with the answer, the personality, with the power.

'I would say the game against West Ham [in April] at home was the one that makes me say, "It's over, no chance." Losing 1-0, playing with ten men, change the result, win 4-1, play fantastic, and after that go to Bolton, very difficult place to win, win 2-0. So you need a draw to be champions, you beat Man United 3-0: you are champions at home. This last period was brilliant.'

At the start of the campaign, mindful of the potential for distraction of Germany 2006, Mourinho had privately warned his players they risked being dropped if they talked about the World Cup. He knew the demands sponsors, managers and the media might make on his squad of internationals. 'It's very difficult,' he admitted. 'It mainly depends on national coaches and depends on players as individuals. National coaches act differently. One, he say to the players, "It doesn't matter what you do in your club, you are my choice, you will be in the World Cup," and it leaves the player with a lot of freedom. Another one can say exactly the opposite, "If you don't play, I don't select you. You have to think about the move. In December if you are not playing, you have to move, you have to go on loan, you have to change your club; if not, you are not coming." But the other way, some managers are worried about leaving the players free and some are always behind them. "If you're injured, you don't play. If you feel a little bit tired I will be careful with you. You have to think about the World Cup. If you feel something in your ankle, don't play because you can do it worse." And there is a lot of different kind of influence on the players.

'I have to say that, in that respect England is very good because there's no pressure on the players, easy communication direct with me and not with the players, the players they know the manager trusts them, they don't have a medical department always chasing them and trying to create ghosts in their mind. And in that respect English players are privileged. But some other countries it's not the same picture and it's quite difficult to cope with it.'

Mourinho had feared complacency all season. 'That, I think, was not just about the World Cup. I think it was also about, for example, because we didn't progress in Champions League. You can be comfortable and have no motivation in the Premiership – because you won it already – but if you are involved in Champions League, you keep the standard high, you keep training at the high level, at the high intensity.'

In the second half of the season, along with the traumatic defeat to Barcelona in March, Chelsea surprisingly dropped points to Charlton, Aston Villa, Middlesbrough and Fulham. On the day of the Charlton match at home – the only points dropped at the Bridge all season – on 22 January, Chelsea had been 16 points ahead of United. As usual, though, it was the reaction, not the event itself that the manager was examining. 'My players are the players of the first period and the players of the last period,' he said. 'That's what I want to believe. And that's what I do believe, because if they are not that kind of player and not that kind of man they cannot react the way they did. So for me that was not a surprise. For me the surprise was during the season, during that couple of months, February, March, up and down, not so committed, not the same level of motivation and *I'm* in that group. I'm not saying I was the perfect professional and they were not good. I'm in the same group. We all felt it's over, but it was not over.

'When you are out of the Champions League and at the same time you feel like champions of England you have nothing else behind your brain to push you for high standards, so you let the season fly, you let the season go, because you know in one more week, two more weeks, three more weeks, you are champions. And you know it's incorrect but it's very difficult to fight the situation, so only when we felt they are seven – not 20 any more – they are only seven points behind you, it's then that you feel you wake up to the reality. And if you are good you react the way the team did and you win it. If you are not good, you can collapse. You can collapse under that pressure, but the answer was magnificent.'

As Chelsea's sureness lessened, the media resurrected the image of the United thoroughbred, whipped along by Ferguson – the same wily old jockey who had chased and overtaken Kevin Keegan's runaway Newcastle a decade earlier – catching the Blues. It was instructive to the Portuguese about the psyche of his host country. He produced a story from his homeland in response, in which two men are in a boat a mile out to sea. They jump into the water and race to the beach, but one is a better swimmer and gets ahead. The one chasing struggles with all his might to catch up, and while the first one arrives on the beach in comfort, the second collapses from a heart attack. 'We call it "Dying on the Beach",' Mourinho told reporters, smiling. 'He shouldn't chase me! He should say, "Please take my boat a bit closer first!" He's so enthusiastic chasing me, but he has a heart attack.' The inference, albeit to a man who had endured heart problems of which Mourinho was presumably unaware, was that United might undo themselves trying to catch Chelsea.

'The English have "Devon Loch",' mused Mourinho months later. 'And we have Dying on the Beach. It is the exact opposite. It is better being in the Devon Loch position. How many times does Devon Loch collapse? Once. Normally the guy in front has more chances to win and that's what the Portuguese metaphor I try to bring to football is about. If you are in front, people used to say, "Ah! You are under pressure, under pressure." Under pressure is the one in second position, because the second one is behind me – even if he's one point behind. I never accept the pressure is in the first side.

'In England, people go a lot for the history and they remember Newcastle when Man United did it, and they remember Man United when they are second in December, they finish first. But history is to be changed, and I think Chelsea in these two years have proved that. Because of the second title, we are not a Blackburn that was champion once, isolated, and after that is miles and miles away from it. Chelsea is not any more an isolated situation. It's back-to-back. And if, in the next five years, we can be three or four times champion, definitely that's an era where Chelsea has become very powerful.'

In this period of unprecedented progress Mourinho cites Roman Abramovich's influence as stronger than ever. 'He is always present,' he said. 'Players cannot complain about him being just in the bright moment and not in the dark moment. Always respectful, always supportive and I only can say positive things about him.'

And yet the Champions League, the tournament that inspired Roman Abramovich to enter the football world, eluded Chelsea again. After the controversy of the previous season's win over Barcelona, it was inevitable that football's mischievous sprite would pair the respective champions of England and Spain again when the knockout ties were drawn in December 2005. The prospect of these matches cast a shadow over the season until they were over, but Mourinho was sanguine about the outcome – even the disputed sending-off of Asier Del Horno for a lunge on Leo Messi that swung the tie inexorably in Barça's favour. 'You know,' he said, 'I think, if you can say it not in a negative way, Barcelona was "the chosen one". I think they are a great team. They have great players. They play very attractive football and they are an amazing club and they have, in their history, only one Champions League and they couldn't do it for decades. And, in the last two years, everybody was feeling they were the chosen one. Last season was a big kick in their overall ambitions when Chelsea beat them. This season, you know, they played against Chelsea with ten men. Against Benfica there was a clear penalty for Benfica in the last minute: not given. Against Milan [in the semi-final], Shevchenko scored a beautiful goal. Nobody knows why it's not a goal! Against Arsenal [in the final] was what was.

'So I think you can say they were the chosen one. Everything was in their favour. Everything was supporting them and they had great conditions for that, so when we played them, the point was not just Chelsea against Barcelona, it was more than that. Again, they are a great team and they can beat us, but we also can beat them and we played against them not in difficult circumstances. So it was not a good draw because we know the general tendencies.'

He is not concerned that the two clubs could meet again in the future. 'I think next season could be different because they are already European Champions,' he said. 'I think it will be a competition where everybody starts with the same possibilities of winning.'

One aspect of the matches with Barcelona and the other dramatic defeat – the disappointing FA Cup semi-final against Liverpool at Old Trafford – was that for once Mourinho's strategy and tactics were criticised. For a manager who has frequently gambled shrewdly and won, and who successfully introduced a diamond midfield at the end of the season to win games, this was a novelty. 'Well, first of all, I'm happy with the critics,' Mourinho said. 'I won so many times and people routinely see my team win and win, and when we lose they have to go for something and I'm happy they go for my strategy. They don't remember how many matches we won this season with tactical changes. They don't remember how many times during the game I change and I change and I finish some matches playing with two defenders and winning matches. They don't remember these kind of things. They remember because you lose against this or you lose against that. We lose against Liverpool. I only ask who had the first chance to score? And that was Chelsea.

Drogba had an open goal in his face and he didn't score. How did Liverpool score first with a free kick that is not a free kick. Why the John Terry goal is not allowed because was a clear goal? How the game finished – Joe Cole missing a chance with an open goal. Against Barcelona, we played at home, we played with ten men, we were winning 1-0. John Terry score in his own goal. We played brilliant. The crowd was magnificent with the team because the team played so well with ten players. We went to Barcelona, very difficult circumstances, opponent is good, the crowd, 100,000, behind them, supporting them, and very difficult to do better. But I'm very happy with that because, you know, when I lose my first game with Chelsea at home for the Premiership, I will be under criticism and it will be after how many matches? I don't know! So I'm very happy with that.'

His response to the media attacks was equally defiant. 'That is as always,' he smiled. 'I feel it as a motivation. I'm quite happy with being at a club where you fight the establishment. Because of that establishment, the day Chelsea was champion, you know, I couldn't see it mentioned in the press because it was "Rooney, Rooney injury, Rooney plays World Cup, doesn't play"... "Chelsea champion" in a little corner.

'On the day of our champions parade, it was all Liverpool and Liverpool parade, and a Chelsea photo in the corner of page 34 or 28. It's absolutely amazing. It's absolutely amazing. So I think we are fighting the establishment and I am quite happy with it. I always used to say that the media can manipulate the people... That's obvious. Media goes to your house every day through television, through newspapers, through the Internet, through public opinion.

'I think Chelsea, with the effort of the last years... Roman bought the club, changed the club, brought Peter Kenyon, changed the manager, changed players, does a lot for English football, does a lot for kids, does a lot for society, does a lot for charity, does a lot in many, many different areas, I think Chelsea deserves much more than it gets. Another club would be already on the moon, and Chelsea is still far from being on the moon.'

And so the first hundred years concludes with a brash, successful Chelsea struggling to be properly appreciated by a threatened football establishment. Nothing much has changed. Not quite yet, but the manager sees definite movement in the right direction. 'I think I saw it in the champions parade,' he said. 'I think it was a parade without the real emotion, because parades, all over the world, are usually on the same day or the day after you win the title. So when you have to do a parade one month later it means 10 per cent of the reality. You can imagine: Chelsea beat Man United 3-0 and after the game – parade! There would have been maybe 500,000 people there.

'That's what happened to me in Porto or in any place. But even in that parade that lost a lot, I saw a lot of kids. I think that the kids will be the ones for the next step because the reality is like that. The people of my generation in Portugal, everyone support Benfica. Everybody Benfica. And the people of this generation, everybody's Porto, because Porto won Champions League, won UEFA Cup, won titles and titles and titles. Everybody supports them. Doesn't matter north or south, because everybody used to say, "Oh, people in the south is Benfica, people in the north..." It's not true now.

'And in England, if Chelsea keep winning, even in the north, or even kids with parents supporting Arsenal or Man United or this or that, if you are a kid and I am a kid, I go to the school with a Chelsea shirt because Chelsea is winning and winning. "You are from Arsenal? Ah, you want a blue shirt!" You want a blue shirt; you hide your Arsenal shirt. It's true. So I think if we keep winning that is what can make the Chelsea family bigger and bigger and bigger and be stronger.

'In our side of the world, in my Latin side, we used to say, "In football, the memory is very short." But I also say that when you do very important things, that short memory cannot fight against that. You know, it's history forever. You can destroy every record, papers, photos, everything, my grandson will know his grandfather won the Champions League with Porto. Some things you cannot erase.

'So we go for the worst picture: next season, relegated; John Terry, the worst player in the Premiership; Frank Lampard, killed 20 people behind the goal, never hits the net; Mourinho, only bad decisions. You know, you can imagine the worst picture possible, you cannot erase the history. Fifty years later, Chelsea was champion, the champions were him and him and him.

'I always think about the future, you know. I mean I'm in the history. I'm very proud to be in that history, but I want more things: more things for me, more things for Chelsea and one day more things for me not in Chelsea. Because one day you have to stop because I want or because Chelsea wants, but I am happy, I'm looking forward to the challenges. I want to repeat what we have won. I want to win what we didn't.

'And I think sometimes you feel like, "Ah, I don't want this for my life." But other times you feel enjoyable, this strange feeling around Chelsea and myself, and so I'm not a man to... I thought during the season that I expressed my feeling, I thought, "Ah! Why? I don't need that in my career now!"

'But maybe I need it! Maybe I need. I'm ready.'

In early March the loss of 1970s legend Peter Osgood, whom Mourinho met and liked, was commemorated at West Bromwich by a display of portraits held aloft, expertly organised by the away fans themselves. Despite the title glory, it was this emotional moment that finally bonded the long-suffering fans with the new, stellar Chelsea. Mourinho is aware of the passion the fans have for the greats, and his own place in the Blues' history. 'A few things is unforgettable,' he said. 'It's not about the club; it's the respect that people deserve. I can imagine, I hope it happens in 20 years' time, I come back to London and to Stamford Bridge to see a game and I have to believe, with what I see, that people will respect me and will cheer me in this kind of situation. Or one day I hope in 60 years' time – so I hope I go to 100 – when I'm dead, Chelsea supporters will remember this guy was the coach. So I understand that.'

What will the legacy of Chelsea's finest manager be? Should a statue be erected to his memory? 'No, no, no,' he laughed. 'I don't think so, and especially because I believe in 60 years' time being champions at Chelsea cannot be an extraordinary thing. It can be something just natural. Just natural. So the objective is exactly that. It's to make victories in this club something normal, something that you are waiting for, and nothing extraordinary. It's the routine. I think what Chelsea has to find now is the culture of victory. Chelsea won the title twice consecutively. Victory is normal. When you don't win, it's not normal. You know, so the statue must be for the guys that lose the championship!'

How Gus Mears and his board of dreamers would be inspired by that.

CHELSEA RECORDS

facts and figures
1905–2006

All statistics are correct to the end of the 2005–06 season.

In 1992–93 League Division One became known as the FA Premier League and Division Two became Division One. In 2004–05 Division One was renamed the Championship. References to Divisions One and Two prior to the 1992–93 season use the leagues' original names.

The Football League was suspended during the First and Second World Wars and league and cup football played during that period was regionalised. Teams fielded during those years often featured guest players from other clubs. These games do not count in the official records.

References to the Football League Cup include the Milk Cup, the Littlewoods Cup, the Rumbelows League Cup, the Coca-Cola Cup, the Worthington Cup and the Carling Cup and references to the Full Members Cup include the Simod Cup and the Zenith Data Systems Cup.

KEY

FAPL = FA Premier League
PO = Play-offs
FAC = FA Cup
LC = League Cup

UCL = UEFA Champions League
UC = UEFA Cup
ECWC = European Cup-Winners' Cup
SC = UEFA Super Cup
FC = Inter-Cities Fairs Cup

CS = FA Charity/Community Shield
FMC = Full Members Cup

Eur = Europe
Rd = Round
P Rd = Preliminary round
QF = Quarter–final
SF = Semi–final
WIN = Winners
RU = Runners-up

og = own goal
aet = after extra time
In lists of appearances, substitute appearances are given after the + symbol
In lists of results, Chelsea's score is always given first

HONOURS

DIVISION ONE/FA PREMIER LEAGUE
Champions 1955, 2005, 2006
Runners-up 2004

DIVISION TWO
Champions 1984, 1989
Runners-up 1907, 1912, 1930, 1963, 1977

FA CUP
Winners 1970, 1997, 2000
Runners-up 1915, 1967, 1994, 2002

LEAGUE CUP
Winners 1965, 1998, 2005
Runners-up 1972

EUROPEAN CUP-WINNERS' CUP
Winners 1971, 1998

UEFA SUPER CUP
Winners 1998

FA CHARITY/COMMUNITY SHIELD
Winners 1955, 2000, 2005
Runners-up 1970, 1997

FULL MEMBERS CUP
Winners 1986, 1990

FA YOUTH CUP
Winners 1960, 1961
Runners-up 1958

MAJOR AWARDS

CHELSEA PLAYER OF THE YEAR

1967	Peter Bonetti
1968	Charlie Cooke
1969	David Webb
1970	John Hollins
1971	John Hollins
1972	David Webb
1973	Peter Osgood
1974	Gary Locke
1975	Charlie Cooke
1976	Ray Wilkins
1977	Ray Wilkins
1978	Micky Droy
1979	Tommy Langley
1980	Clive Walker
1981	Petar Borota
1982	Mike Fillery
1983	Joey Jones
1984	Pat Nevin
1985	David Speedie
1986	Eddie Niedzwiecki
1987	Pat Nevin
1988	Tony Dorigo
1989	Graham Roberts
1990	Ken Monkou
1991	Andy Townsend
1992	Paul Elliott
1993	Frank Sinclair
1994	Steve Clarke
1995	Erland Johnsen
1996	Ruud Gullit
1997	Mark Hughes
1998	Dennis Wise
1999	Gianfranco Zola
2000	Dennis Wise
2001	John Terry
2002	Carlo Cudicini
2003	Gianfranco Zola
2004	Frank Lampard
2005	Frank Lampard
2006	John Terry

CHELSEA YOUNG PLAYER OF THE YEAR

1983	Keith Dublin
1984	Robert Isaac
1985	Gareth Hall
1986	Micky Bodley
1987	Jason Cundy
1988	Eddie Cunnington
1989	No award
1990	No award
1991	Andy Myers
1992	Zeke Rowe
1993	Neil Shipperley
1994	Mark Nicholls
1995	Chris McCann
1996	Jody Morris
1997	Nick Crittenden
1998	John Terry
1999	Sam Dalla Bona
2000	Rhys Evans
2001	Leon Knight
2002	Carlton Cole
2003	Robert Huth
2004	Robert Huth
2005	Robert Huth
2006	Lassana Diarra

FOOTBALL WRITERS' ASSOCIATION FOOTBALLER OF THE YEAR

Winners	
1997	Gianfranco Zola
2005	Frank Lampard

Runners-up	
1970	Peter Bonetti
1996	Ruud Gullit
2004	Frank Lampard
2005	John Terry
2006	John Terry

PROFESSIONAL FOOTBALLERS' ASSOCIATION PLAYER OF THE YEAR

Winners	
2005	John Terry

Runners-up	
2004	Frank Lampard
2005	Frank Lampard
2006	Frank Lampard

Short-listed	
1997	Gianfranco Zola
2002	Jimmy Floyd Hasselbaink
2003	Gianfranco Zola
2005	Petr Cech
2006	Joe Cole, John Terry

PFA DIVISIONAL TEAM OF THE YEAR

1984	Kerry Dixon, Joey Jones
1985	Kerry Dixon
1989	Gordon Durie, Tony Dorigo, Graham Roberts
1991	Andy Townsend
1992	Andy Townsend
1996	Ruud Gullit
2003	William Gallas
2004	Frank Lampard, John Terry
2005	Petr Cech, Frank Lampard, Arjen Robben, John Terry
2006	Joe Cole, William Gallas, Frank Lampard, John Terry

PFA YOUNG PLAYER OF THE YEAR

Winners	
2004	Scott Parker

Short-listed	
2002	John Terry
2004	Glen Johnson, John Terry
2005	Arjen Robben (3rd)

BARCLAYS PREMIERSHIP PLAYER OF THE YEAR

2005	Frank Lampard

BARCLAYS PREMIERSHIP MANAGER OF THE YEAR

2005	José Mourinho
2006	José Mourinho

FIFA WORLD PLAYER OF THE YEAR

Runner-up	
2005	Frank Lampard

BALLON D'OR EUROPEAN PLAYER OF THE YEAR

Runner-up	
2005	Frank Lampard

FIFPRO WORLD TEAM OF THE YEAR

2005	Frank Lampard, Claude Makelele, John Terry

CAF AFRICAN PLAYER OF THE YEAR

Runner-up	
2005	Didier Drogba

Short-listed	
2004	Didier Drogba
2005	Michael Essien (3rd)

DIVISION ONE/FA PREMIER LEAGUE CHAMPIONSHIPS

1954–55 FOOTBALL LEAGUE DIVISION ONE CHAMPIONS
Manager: Ted Drake; Captain: Roy Bentley

League Table

		P	W	D	L	F	A	Gd	Pts
1	Chelsea	42	20	12	10	81	57	+24	52
2	Wolves	42	19	10	13	89	70	+19	48
3	Portsmouth	42	18	12	12	74	62	+12	48
4	Sunderland	42	15	18	9	64	54	+10	48
5	Man Utd	42	20	7	15	84	74	+10	47
6	Aston Villa	42	20	7	15	72	73	-1	47
7	Man City	42	18	10	14	76	69	+7	46
8	Newcastle Utd	42	17	9	16	89	77	+12	43
9	Arsenal	42	17	9	16	69	63	+6	43
10	Burnley	42	17	9	16	51	48	+3	43
11	Everton	42	16	10	16	62	68	-6	42
12	Huddersfield Tn	42	14	13	15	63	68	-5	41
13	Sheffield Utd	42	17	7	18	70	86	-16	41
14	Preston NE	42	16	8	18	83	64	+19	40
15	Charlton Ath	42	15	10	17	76	75	+1	40
16	Tottenham H	42	16	8	18	72	73	-1	40
17	West Brom	42	16	8	18	76	96	-20	40
18	Bolton Wdrs	42	13	13	16	62	69	-7	39
19	Blackpool	42	14	10	18	60	64	-4	38
20	Cardiff City	42	13	11	18	62	76	-14	37
21	Leicester City	42	12	11	19	74	86	-12	35
22	Sheffield Wed	42	8	10	24	63	100	-37	26

Note: 2 points for a win

Total league appearances (42 games)
Parsons 42, Saunders 42, Bentley 41, McNichol 40, Armstrong 39, Willemse 36, Harris 31, Stubbs 27, Robertson 26, Blunstone 23, Greenwood 21, P. Sillett 21, Wicks 21, Lewis 17, Thomson 16, O'Connell 10, Smith 4, Brabrook 3, Dicks 1, Edwards 1

Total league goals (81)
Bentley 21, McNichol 14, Parsons 11, O'Connell 7, Lewis 6, P. Sillett 6 (5 pens), Stubbs 5, Blunstone 3, Armstrong 1, Saunders 1, Wicks 1, Willemse 1, own goals 4

League Games Played

Date	Opponents	Venue	Score
21 Aug	Leicester City	A	1-1
23 Aug	Burnley	H	1-0
28 Aug	Bolton Wdrs	H	3-2
31 Aug	Burnley	A	1-1
4 Sep	Cardiff City	H	1-1
6 Sep	Preston NE	H	0-1
11 Sep	Manchester City	A	1-1
15 Sep	Preston NE	A	2-1
18 Sep	Everton	H	0-2
20 Sep	Sheffield Utd	A	2-1
25 Sep	Newcastle Utd	A	3-1
2 Oct	West Brom	H	3-3
9 Oct	Huddersfield Tn	A	0-1
16 Oct	Manchester Utd	H	5-6
23 Oct	Blackpool	A	0-1
30 Oct	Charlton Ath	H	1-2
6 Nov	Sunderland	A	3-3
13 Nov	Tottenham H	H	2-1
20 Nov	Sheffield Wed	A	1-1
27 Nov	Portsmouth	H	4-1
4 Dec	Wolves	A	4-3
11 Dec	Aston Villa	H	4-0
18 Dec	Leicester City	H	3-1
25 Dec	Arsenal	A	0-1
27 Dec	Arsenal	H	1-1
1 Jan	Bolton Wdrs	A	5-2
22 Jan	Manchester City	H	0-2
5 Feb	Everton	A	1-1
12 Feb	Newcastle Utd	H	4-3
26 Feb	Huddersfield Tn	H	4-1
5 Mar	Aston Villa	A	2-3
9 Mar	West Brom	A	4-2
12 Mar	Blackpool	H	0-0
19 Mar	Charlton Ath	A	2-0
23 Mar	Cardiff City	A	1-0
29 Mar	Sunderland	H	2-1
2 Apr	Tottenham H	A	4-2
8 Apr	Sheffield Utd	H	1-1
9 Apr	Wolves	H	1-0
16 Apr	Portsmouth	A	0-0
23 Apr	Sheffield Wed	H	3-0
30 Apr	Manchester Utd	A	1-2

2004–05 FA PREMIER LEAGUE CHAMPIONS

Manager: José Mourinho; Captain: John Terry

League Table

		P	W	D	L	F	A	Gd	Pts
1	Chelsea	38	29	8	1	72	15	+57	95
2	Arsenal	38	25	8	5	87	36	+51	83
3	Man Utd	38	22	11	5	58	26	+32	77
4	Everton	38	18	7	13	45	46	-1	61
5	Liverpool	38	17	7	14	52	41	+11	58
6	Bolton Wdrs	38	16	10	12	49	44	+5	58
7	Middlesbrough	38	14	13	11	53	46	+7	55
8	Man City	38	13	13	12	47	39	+8	52
9	Tottenham H	38	14	10	14	47	41	+6	52
10	Aston Villa	38	12	11	15	45	52	-7	47
11	Charlton Ath	38	12	10	16	42	58	-16	46
12	Birmingham City	38	11	12	15	40	46	-6	45
13	Fulham	38	12	8	18	52	60	-8	44
14	Newcastle Utd	38	10	14	14	47	57	-10	44
15	Blackburn R	38	9	15	14	32	43	-11	42
16	Portsmouth	38	10	9	19	43	59	-16	39
17	West Brom	38	6	16	16	36	61	-25	34
18	Crystal Palace	38	7	12	19	41	62	-21	33
19	Norwich City	38	7	12	19	42	77	-35	33
20	Southampton	38	6	14	18	45	66	-21	32

Note: 3 points for a win

Total league appearances (38 games)

Lampard 38, Makelele 36, Terry 36, Cech 35, Gudjohnsen 30+7, Ferreira 29, Duff 28+2, Gallas 28, Carvalho 22+3, Tiago 21+13, J. Cole 19+9, Drogba 18+8, Robben 14+4, Johnson 13+4, Bridge 12+3, Smertin 11+5, Kežman 6+19, Gérémi 6+7, Huth 6+4, Jarošík 3+11, Babayaro 3+1, Cudicini 3, Parker 1+3, N. Morais 0+2, Mutu 0+2, Forssell 0+1, Grant 0+1, Oliveira 0+1, Pidgeley 0+1, Watt 0+1

Total league goals (72)

Lampard 13 (3 pens), Gudjohnsen 12 (1 pen), Drogba 10, J. Cole 8, Robben 7, Duff 6, Kežman 4 (1 pen), Tiago 4, Terry 3, Gallas 2, Carvalho 1, Makelele 1, own goals 1

League Games Played

Date	Opponents	Venue	Score
15 Aug	Manchester United	H	1-0
21 Aug	Birmingham City	A	1-0
24 Aug	Crystal Palace	A	2-0
28 Aug	Southampton	H	2-1
11 Sep	Aston Villa	A	0-0
19 Sep	Tottenham Hotspur	H	0-0
25 Sep	Middlesbrough	A	1-0
3 Oct	Liverpool	H	1-0
16 Oct	Manchester City	A	0-1
23 Oct	Blackburn Rovers	H	4-0
30 Oct	West Brom	A	4-1
6 Nov	Everton	H	1-0
13 Nov	Fulham	A	4-1
20 Nov	Bolton Wanderers	H	2-2
27 Nov	Charlton Athletic	A	4-0
4 Dec	Newcastle United	H	4-0
12 Dec	Arsenal	A	2-2
18 Dec	Norwich City	H	4-0
26 Dec	Aston Villa	H	1-0
28 Dec	Portsmouth	A	2-0
1 Jan	Liverpool	A	1-0
4 Jan	Middlesbrough	H	2-0
15 Jan	Tottenham Hotspur	A	2-0
22 Jan	Portsmouth	H	3-0
2 Feb	Blackburn Rovers	A	1-0
6 Feb	Manchester City	H	0-0
12 Feb	Everton	A	1-0
5 Mar	Norwich City	A	3-1
15 Mar	West Brom	H	1-0
19 Mar	Crystal Palace	H	4-1
2 Apr	Southampton	A	3-1
9 Apr	Birmingham City	H	1-1
20 Apr	Arsenal	H	0-0
23 Apr	Fulham	H	3-1
30 Apr	Bolton Wanderers	A	2-0
7 May	Charlton Athletic	H	1-0
10 May	Manchester United	A	3-1
15 May	Newcastle United	A	1-1

2005–06 FA PREMIER LEAGUE CHAMPIONS
Manager: José Mourinho; Captain: John Terry

League Table

		P	W	D	L	F	A	Gd	Pts
1	Chelsea	38	29	4	5	72	22	+50	91
2	Man Utd	38	25	8	5	72	34	+38	83
3	Liverpool	38	25	7	6	57	25	+32	82
4	Arsenal	38	20	7	11	68	31	+37	67
5	Tottenham H	38	18	11	9	53	38	+15	65
6	Blackburn R	38	19	6	13	51	42	+9	63
7	Newcastle Utd	38	17	7	14	47	42	+5	58
8	Bolton Wdrs	38	15	11	12	49	41	+8	56
9	West Ham	38	16	7	15	52	55	-3	55
10	Wigan Ath	38	15	6	17	45	52	-7	51
11	Everton	38	14	8	16	34	49	-15	50
12	Fulham	38	14	6	18	48	58	-10	48
13	Charlton Ath	38	13	8	17	41	55	-14	47
14	Middlesbrough	38	12	9	17	48	58	-10	45
15	Man City	38	13	4	21	43	48	-5	43
16	Aston Villa	38	10	12	16	42	55	-13	42
17	Portsmouth	38	10	8	20	37	62	-25	38
18	Birmingham City	38	8	10	20	28	50	-22	34
19	West Brom	38	7	9	22	31	58	-27	30
20	Sunderland	38	3	6	29	26	69	-43	15

Note: 3 points for a win

Total league appearances (38 games)
Terry 36, Lampard 35, Cech 34, Gallas 33+1, Makelele 29+2, Essien 27+4, J Cole 26+8, Del Horno 25, Carvalho 22+2, Robben 21+7, Crespo 20+10, Drogba 20+9, Duff 18+10, Ferreira 18+3, Gudjohnsen 16+10, Wright-Phillips 10+17, Gérémi 8+7, Huth 7+6, Johnson 4, Maniche 3+5, Cudicini 3+1, Diarra 2+1, Pidgeley 1, C Cole 0+9, J Smith 0+1.

Total league goals (72)
Lampard 16 (4 pens), Drogba 12, Crespo 10, J Cole 7, Robben 6, Gallas 5, Terry 4, Duff 3, Gérémi 2, Gudjohnsen 2, Essien 2, Carvalho 1, Del Horno 1, own goal 1

League Games Played

Date	Opponents	Venue	Score
14 Aug	Wigan Athletic	A	1-0
21 Aug	Arsenal	H	1-0
24 Aug	West Brom	H	4-0
27 Aug	Tottenham Hotspur	A	2-0
10 Sep	Sunderland	H	2-0
17 Sep	Charlton Athletic	A	2-0
24 Sep	Aston Villa	H	2-1
2 Oct	Liverpool	A	4-1
15 Oct	Bolton Wanderers	H	5-1
23 Oct	Everton	A	1-1
29 Oct	Blackburn Rovers	H	4-2
6 Nov	Manchester United	A	0-1
19 Nov	Newcastle United	H	3-0
26 Nov	Portsmouth	A	2-0
3 Dec	Middlesbrough	H	1-0
10 Dec	Wigan Athletic	H	1-0
18 Dec	Arsenal	A	2-0
26 Dec	Fulham	H	3-2
28 Dec	Manchester City	A	1-0
31 Dec	Birmingham City	H	2-0
2 Jan	West Ham	A	3-1
15 Jan	Sunderland	A	2-1
22 Jan	Charlton Athletic	H	1-1
1 Feb	Aston Villa	A	1-1
5 Feb	Liverpool	H	2-0
11 Feb	Middlesbrough	A	0-3
25 Feb	Portsmouth	H	2-0
4 Mar	West Brom	A	2-1
11 Mar	Tottenham Hotspur	H	2-1
19 Mar	Fulham	A	0-1
25 Mar	Manchester City	H	2-0
1 Apr	Birmingham City	A	0-0
9 Apr	West Ham	H	4-1
15 Apr	Bolton Wanderers	A	2-0
17 Apr	Everton	H	3-0
29 Apr	Manchester United	H	3-0
2 May	Blackburn Rovers	A	0-1
7 May	Newcastle United	A	0-1

DIVISION TWO CHAMPIONSHIPS

1983–84 FOOTBALL LEAGUE DIVISION TWO CHAMPIONS
Manager: John Neal; Captain: Colin Pates

Chelsea finished with 88 points, ahead of Sheffield Wednesday on goal difference and eight points ahead of third-placed Newcastle United.

Total league appearances (42 games)
Dixon 42, Niedzwiecki 42, Pates 42, McLaughlin 41, Spackman 40, Nevin 38, J. Jones 34, Speedie 32+5, Bumstead 30+1, Hollins 29, C. Lee 25+8, Canoville 17+3, Thomas 17, McAndrew 13, Rhoades-Brown 6, Walker 6, Hutchings 4, Jasper 3, Dublin 1, Johnstone 0+2

Total league goals (90)
Dixon 28 (3 pens), Nevin 14 (1 pen), Speedie 13, Bumstead 7, Canoville 6, McAndrew 4 (2 pens), Thomas 4, C. Lee 3, Spackman 3 (1 pen), Walker 3, Hollins 1, Hutchings 1, J. Jones 1, Rhoades-Brown 1, own goals 1

1988–89 FOOTBALL LEAGUE DIVISION TWO CHAMPIONS
Manager: Bobby Campbell; Captain: Graham Roberts

With a club record 99 points, Chelsea finished 17 points ahead of second-placed Manchester City.

Total league appearances (46 games)
Roberts 46, K. Wilson 43+3, Dorigo 40, Dixon 39, Nicholas 39, Clarke 36, Durie 32, McLaughlin 31, C. Wilson 29+3, McAllister 28+8, Bumstead 27+2, Beasant 22, Wood 21+1, Freestone 21, Hall 17+5, D. Lee 12+8, Pates 10, Mitchell 6, Hazard 4, Hitchcock 3, Dodds 0+2, Monkou 0+2, Le Saux 0+1

Total league goals (96)
Dixon 25, Durie 17, Roberts 15 (12 pens), K. Wilson 13, Dorigo 6, McAllister 6, D. Lee 4, C. Wilson 3, Bumstead 2, Nicholas 1, Pates 1, Wood 1, own goals 2

FA CUP WINS

1969–70 FA CUP WINNERS
Manager: Dave Sexton; Captain: Ron Harris

Results

Date	Opponents (Round)	Venue	Score
3 Jan	Birmingham City (3rd round)	H	3-0
24 Jan	Burnley (4th round)	H	2-2
27 Jan	Burnley (4th round replay)	A	3-1 aet
7 Feb	Crystal Palace (5th round)	A	4-1
21 Feb	QPR (6th round)	A	4-2
14 Mar	Watford (Semi-final)	*	5-1
11 Apr	Leeds United (Final)	**	2-2 aet
29 Apr	Leeds United (Final replay)	†	2-1 aet

* Played at White Hart Lane, ** Played at Wembley,
† Played at Old Trafford

Total FA Cup appearances (8 games)
Bonetti 8, Dempsey 8, Harris 8, Hollins 8, Houseman 8, Hutchinson 8, McCreadie 8, Webb 8, Osgood 7, Cooke 6, Hudson 6, Baldwin 5, Hinton 0+2

Total FA Cup goals (25)
Osgood 8, Houseman 6, Hutchinson 5, Webb 3, Baldwin 1, Dempsey 1, Hollins 1

FA Cup final line-up
Bonetti, Webb, McCreadie, Hollins, Dempsey, Harris (c) (Hinton), Baldwin, Houseman, Osgood, Hutchinson, Cooke. *Scorers*: Houseman, Hutchinson. *Attendance*: 100,000

FA Cup final replay line-up
Bonetti, Harris (c), McCreadie, Hollins, Dempsey, Webb, Baldwin, Cooke, Osgood (Hinton), Hutchinson, Houseman. *Scorers*: Osgood, Webb. *Attendance*: 62,000

1996–97 FA CUP WINNERS

Manager: Ruud Gullit; Captain: Dennis Wise

Results

Date	Opponents (Round)	Venue	Score
4 Jan	West Brom (3rd round)	H	3-0
26 Jan	Liverpool (4th round)	H	4-2
16 Feb	Leicester City (5th round)	A	2-2
26 Feb	Leicester City (5th round replay)	H	1-0 aet
9 Mar	Portsmouth (6th round)	A	4-1
13 Apr	Wimbledon (Semi-final)	*	3-0
17 May	Middlesbrough (Final)	**	2-0

* Played at Highbury ** Played at Wembley

Total FA Cup appearances (7 games)
Clarke 7, Di Matteo 7, Lebœuf 7, Wise 7, Zola 7, M. Hughes 6+1, Minto 6, Newton 6, Petrescu 6, Sinclair 6, Grodås 5, Hitchcock 2, Vialli 1+4, Burley 1+2, Johnsen 1+2, Duberry 1, P. Hughes 1, Gullit 0+1

Total FA Cup goals (19)
M. Hughes 5, Zola 4, Wise 3, Di Matteo 2, Vialli 2, Burley 1, Lebœuf 1 (pen), Newton 1

FA Cup final line-up
Grodås; Sinclair, Lebœuf, Clarke, Minto; Petrescu, Newton, Di Matteo, Wise (c); Zola (Vialli), M. Hughes
Subs not used: Myers, Hitchcock. *Scorers:* Di Matteo, Newton. *Attendance:* 79,160

1999–2000 FA CUP WINNERS

Manager: Gianluca Vialli; Captain: Dennis Wise

Results

Date	Opponents (Round)	Venue	Score
11 Dec	Hull City (3rd round)	A	6-1
19 Jan	Nottingham Forest (4th round)	H	2-0
30 Jan	Leicester City (5th round)	H	2-1
20 Feb	Gillingham (6th round)	H	5-0
9 Apr	Newcastle United (Semi-final)	*	2-1
20 May	Aston Villa (Final)	*	1-0

* Played at Wembley

Total FA Cup appearances (6 games)
De Goey 6, Deschamps 6, Poyet 6, Harley 5, Wise 5, Zola 4+1, Desailly 4, Lebœuf 4, Weah 4, Sutton 3+1, Di Matteo 3, Lambourde 3, Flo 2+4, Terry 2+2, Petrescu 2+1, Ferrer 2, Høgh 2, Morris 1+3, Babayaro 1, Melchiot 1, Ambrosetti 0+1, Clement 0+1, Percassi 0+1

Total FA Cup goals (18)
Poyet 6, Di Matteo 2, Weah 2, Wise 2, Flo 1, Lebœuf 1, Morris 1, Sutton 1, Terry 1, Zola 1 (pen)

FA Cup final line-up
De Goey; Melchiot, Desailly, Lebœuf, Babayaro; Poyet, Wise (c), Deschamps, Di Matteo; Weah (Flo), Zola (Morris)
Subs not used: Terry, Harley, Cudicini. *Scorer:* Di Matteo. *Attendance:* 78,217

LEAGUE CUP WINS

1964–65 LEAGUE CUP WINNERS

Manager: Tommy Docherty; Captain: Terry Venables

Results

Date	Opponents (Round)	Venue	Score
23 Sep	Birmingham City (2nd round)	A	3-0
26 Oct	Notts County (3rd round)	H	4-0
11 Nov	Swansea City (4th round)	H	3-2
26 Nov	Workington (5th round)	A	2-2
16 Dec	Workington (5th round replay)	H	2-0
20 Jan	Aston Villa (Semi-final, 1st leg)	A	3-2
10 Feb	Aston Villa (Semi-final, 2nd leg)	H	1-1
15 Mar	Leicester City (Final, 1st leg)	H	3-2
5 Apr	Leicester City (Final, 2nd leg)	A	0-0

League Cup final, 1st leg line-up
Bonetti, Hinton, R. Harris, Hollins, Young, Boyle, Murray, Graham, McCreadie, Venables (c), Tambling.
Scorers: Tambling, Venables (pen), McCreadie. *Attendance:* 20,690

Total League Cup appearances (9 games)
Bonetti 9, Mortimore 8, Graham 7, Tambling 7, R. Harris 6, Hinton 6, Hollins 6, Murray 6, Bridges 5, McCalliog 5, McCreadie 5, Venables 5, Boyle 4, Upton 4, Fascione 3, Houseman 3, Watson 3, A. Harris 2, Brown 1, Knox 1, Osgood 1, Shellito 1, Young 1

Total League Cup goals (21)
Tambling 6, Graham 4, Bridges 3, Osgood 2, Boyle 1, Brown 1, A. Harris 1, McCalliog 1, McCreadie 1, Venables 1

League Cup final, 2nd leg line-up
Bonetti, Hinton, McCreadie, R. Harris, Mortimore, Upton, Murray, Boyle, Bridges, Venables (c), Tambling.
Attendance: 26,957

1997–98 LEAGUE CUP WINNERS

Managers: Ruud Gullit and Gianluca Vialli; Captain: Dennis Wise

Results

Date	Opponents (Round)	Venue	Score	
15 Oct	Blackburn Rovers (3rd round)	H	1-1	(aet, won 4-1 on penalties)
19 Nov	Southampton (4th round)	H	2-1 aet	
7 Jan	Ipswich Town (5th round)	A	2-2	(aet, won 4-1 on penalties)
28 Jan	Arsenal (Semi-final, 1st leg)	A	1-2	
18 Feb	Arsenal (Semi-final, 2nd leg)	H	3-1	
29 Mar	Middlesbrough (Final)	*	2-0 aet	

* Played at Wembley

League Cup final line-up

De Goey; Sinclair, Duberry, Lebœuf, Le Saux; Petrescu (Clarke), Wise (c), Newton, Di Matteo; M. Hughes (Flo), Zola.
Sub not used: Hitchcock. *Scorers:* Sinclair, Di Matteo. *Attendance:* 77,698

Total League Cup appearances (6 games)

Clarke 4+2, Sinclair 4+1, De Goey 4, Di Matteo 4, Lebœuf 4, Le Saux 4, Wise 4, Zola 4, M. Hughes 3+3, Flo 3+1, Gullit 3+1, Newton 3+1, Duberry 3, Granville 3, Lambourde 3, Petrescu 3, Vialli 2+1, Hitchcock 2, Nicholls 2, Babayaro 1+1, Crittenden 1, Morris 1, Myers 1, Lee 0+2, Charvet 0+1, Hampshire 0+1.

Total League Cup goals (11)

Di Matteo 3, Flo 2, M. Hughes 2, Le Saux 1, Morris 1, Petrescu 1, Sinclair 1
(*Penalty shoot-out scorers:* Lebœuf 2, Clarke 1, Di Matteo 1, M. Hughes 1, Nicholls 1, Sinclair 1, Zola 1)

2004–05 LEAGUE CUP WINNERS

Manager: José Mourinho; Captain: John Terry

Results

Date	Opponents (Round)	Venue	Score
27 Oct	West Ham United (3rd round)	H	1-0
10 Nov	Newcastle United (4th round)	A	2-0 aet
30 Nov	Fulham (5th round)	A	2-1
12 Jan	Man Utd (Semi-final, 1st leg)	H	0-0
26 Jan	Man Utd (Semi-final, 2nd leg)	A	2-1
27 Feb	Liverpool (Final)	*	3-2 aet

* Played at the Millennium Stadium

Total League Cup appearances (6 games)

Duff 5+1, Ferreira 5, Gallas 5, Terry 5, J. Cole 4+2, Bridge 4, Cudicini 4, Makelele 4, Tiago 4, Lampard 3+3, Drogba 3+1, Robben 3+1, Carvalho 3, Parker 3, Kežman 2+2, Johnson 2+1, Cech 2, Gudjohnsen 1+5, Jarošík 1+2, Babayaro 1, Gérémi 1, Smertin 1

Total League Cup goals (10)

Duff 2, Kežman 2, Lampard 2, Drogba 1, Gudjohnsen 1, Robben 1, own goals 1

League Cup final line-up

Cech; Ferreira, Carvalho, Terry (c), Gallas (Kežman); Jarošík (Gudjohnsen), Makelele, Lampard; J. Cole (Johnson), Drogba, Duff.
Subs not used: Tiago, Pidgeley. *Scorers:* Gerrard og, Drogba, Kežman. *Attendance:* 71,622

EUROPEAN SILVERWARE

1970–71 EUROPEAN CUP-WINNERS' CUP WINNERS

Manager: Dave Sexton; Captain: Ron Harris

Results

Date	Opponents (Round)	Venue	Score
16 Sep	Aris Salonika (1st round, 1st leg)	A	1-1
30 Sep	Aris Salonika (1st round, 2nd leg)	H	5-1
21 Oct	CSKA Sofia (2nd round, 1st leg)	A	1-0
4 Nov	CSKA Sofia (2nd round, 2nd leg)	H	1-0
10 Mar	Bruges (Quarter-final, 1st leg)	A	0-2
24 Mar	Bruges (Quarter-final, 2nd leg)	H	4-0 aet
14 Apr	Manchester City (Semi-final, 1st leg)	H	1-0

Total Cup-Winners' Cup appearances (10 games)

Webb 10, Harris 9, Hudson 9, Weller 8+1, Cooke 8, Hollins 8, Houseman 8, Dempsey 7, Osgood 7, Bonetti 6, Boyle 5+2, Mulligan 5+1, Baldwin 4+3, Phillips 4, Smethurst 3+1, Hinton 3, Hutchinson 3, McCreadie 2, Droy 1

Total Cup-Winners' Cup goals (17)

Osgood 4, Hutchinson 3, Hollins 2, Baldwin 2, Dempsey 1, Houseman 1, Hinton 1, Smethurst 1, Webb 1, own goals 1

28 Apr	Manchester City (Semi-final, 2nd leg)	A	1-0
19 May	Real Madrid (Final)	*	1-1 aet
21 May	Real Madrid (Final replay)	*	2-1

* Played at the Karaiskaki Stadium, Piraeus, Greece

European Cup-Winners' Cup final replay line-up
Bonetti, Boyle, Harris (c), Cooke, Dempsey, Webb, Weller, Baldwin, Osgood (Smethurst), Hudson, Houseman
Scorers: Dempsey, Osgood. Attendance: 24,000

European Cup-Winners' Cup final line-up
Bonetti, Boyle, Harris (c), Hollins (Mulligan), Dempsey, Webb, Weller, Hudson, Osgood (Baldwin), Cooke, Houseman
Scorer: Osgood. Attendance: 45,000

1997–98 EUROPEAN CUP-WINNERS' CUP WINNERS
Managers: Ruud Gullit and Gianluca Vialli; Captain: Dennis Wise

Results

Date	Opponents (Round)	Venue	Score
18 Sep	Slovan Bratislava (1st round, 1st leg)	H	2-0
2 Oct	Slovan Bratislava (1st round, 2nd leg)	A	2-0
23 Oct	Tromsø (2nd round, 1st leg)	A	2-3
6 Nov	Tromsø (2nd round, 2nd leg)	H	7-1
5 Mar	Real Betis (Quarter-final, 1st leg)	A	2-1
19 Mar	Real Betis (Quarter-final, 2nd leg)	H	3-1
2 Apr	Vicenza (Semi-final, 1st leg)	A	0-1
16 Apr	Vicenza (Semi-final, 2nd leg)	H	3-1
13 May	Stuttgart (Final)	*	1-0

* Played at the Rasunda Stadium, Stockholm, Sweden

Total European Cup-Winners' Cup appearances (9 games)
De Goey 9, Lebœuf 9, Wise 9, Di Matteo 8, Vialli 8, Zola 7+1, Petrescu 7, Clarke 6+1, Newton 6+1, Duberry 6, Sinclair 5, Poyet 4, Flo 3+2, Granville 3+1, Le Saux 3, Babayaro 2+1, Lambourde 1+2, Myers 1+2, Morris 1+1, P.Hughes 1, M.Hughes 0+3, Nicholls 0+2, Charvet 0+1

Total European Cup-Winners' Cup goals (22)
Vialli 6, Zola 4, Di Matteo 3, Flo 2, Petrescu 2, Granville 1, M.Hughes 1, Lebœuf 1 (pen), Poyet 1, Sinclair 1

European Cup-Winners' Cup final line-up
De Goey; Clarke, Duberry, Lebœuf, Granville; Wise (c); Petrescu, Poyet (Newton); Di Matteo; Vialli, Flo (Zola).
Subs not used: M.Hughes, Myers, Charvet, Morris, Hitchcock. Scorer: Zola. Attendance: 30,216

1998 UEFA SUPER CUP WINNERS
Manager: Gianluca Vialli; Captain: Dennis Wise

Results

Date	Opponents (Round)	Venue	Score
28 Aug	Real Madrid	*	1-0

* Played at the Stade Louis II, Monaco

UEFA Super Cup final line-up
De Goey; Ferrer, Duberry, Lebœuf, Le Saux; Wise (c), Desailly, Di Matteo (Poyet), Babayaro; Zola (Laudrup), Casiraghi (Flo).
Subs not used: Lambourde, Newton, Morris, Hitchcock. Scorer: Poyet. Attendance: 9,762

OTHER CUP FINALS

FA CUP RUNNERS-UP

24 April 1915 – lost 0-3 to Sheffield United at Old Trafford
Molyneux, Bettridge, Harrow (c), Taylor, Logan, Walker, Ford, Halse, Thomson, Croal, McNeil. *Attendance: 49,557*

20 May 1967 – lost 1-2 to Tottenham Hotspur at Wembley Stadium
Bonetti, A.Harris, McCreadie, Hollins, Hinton, R.Harris (c), Cooke, Baldwin, Hateley, Tambling, Boyle
Reserve not used: Kirkup. Scorer: Tambling. Attendance: 100,000

14 May 1994 – lost 0-4 to Manchester United at Wembley Stadium
Kharine; Clarke, Kjeldbjerg, Johnsen, Sinclair; Burley (Hoddle), Newton, Peacock, Wise (c); Stein (Cascarino), Spencer
Sub not used: Hitchcock. Attendance: 79,634

4 May 2002 – lost 0-2 to Arsenal at the Millennium Stadium
Cudicini; Melchiot (Zenden), Gallas, Desailly (c), Babayaro (Terry); Grønkjær, Lampard, Petit, Le Saux; Hasselbaink (Zola), Gudjohnsen
Subs not used: De Goey, Jokanovic. *Attendance:* 73,963

LEAGUE CUP RUNNERS-UP

4 March 1972 – lost 1-2 to Stoke City at Wembley Stadium
Bonetti, Mulligan (Baldwin), Harris (c), Hollins, Dempsey, Webb, Cooke, Garland, Osgood, Hudson, Houseman
Scorer: Osgood. *Attendance:* 100,000

FA CHARITY/COMMUNITY SHIELD

14 September 1955 – beat Newcastle 3-0 at Stamford Bridge
Robertson, P. Sillett, Willemse, Armstrong, Wicks, Saunders, Parsons, Brabrook, Bentley (c), Stubbs, Blunstone
Scorers: Bentley, Blunstone, McMichael og. *Attendance:* 12,802

8 August 1970 – lost 1-2 to Everton at Stamford Bridge
Bonetti, Webb, Harris (c), Hollins, Mulligan, Hinton, Weller, Hudson, Osgood, Hutchinson, Houseman
Sub not used: Smethurst. *Scorer:* Hutchinson. *Attendance* 43,547

3 August 1997 – lost 2-4 on penalties after a 1-1 draw to Manchester United at Wembley Stadium
De Goey; Sinclair, Lebœuf, Clarke, Granville; Wise (c), Morris (Petrescu), Poyet, Di Matteo; M. Hughes (Vialli), Zola
Subs not used: Gullit, P. Hughes, Nicholls, Clement, Hitchcock. *Scorer:* M. Hughes. *Penalty shoot-out scorers:* Zola, Lebœuf. *Attendance:* 73,636

13 August 2000 – beat Manchester United 2-0 at Wembley Stadium
De Goey; Melchiot, Lebœuf, Desailly, Babayaro; Stanic, Wise (c), Di Matteo (Morris), Poyet (Le Saux); Hasselbaink, Zola (Gudjohnsen)
Subs not used: Ambrosetti, Flo, Lambourde, Cudicini. *Scorers:* Hasselbaink, Melchiot. *Attendance:* 65,148

7 August 2005 – beat Arsenal 2-1 at the Millennium Stadium
Cech; Ferreira, Gallas, Terry (c), Del Horno; Gudjohnsen (Tiago), Makelele, Lampard (Geremi); Duff (J. Cole), Drogba (Crespo), Robben (Wright-Phillips)
Subs not used: Cudicini, Carvalho
Scorer: Drogba 2. *Attendance:* 58,014

FULL MEMBERS CUP FINALS

23 March 1986 – beat Manchester City 5-4 at Wembley Stadium
Francis, Wood, Rougvie, Pates (c), McLaughlin, Bumstead, Nevin, Spackman, C. Lee, Speedie, McAllister
Subs not used: Hazard, Dublin. *Scorers:* Speedie 3, Lee 2. *Attendance:* 67,236

25 March 1990 – beat Middlesbrough 1-0 at Wembley Stadium
Beasant, Hall, Dorigo, Bumstead, Johnsen, Monkou, McAllister, Nicholas (c), Dixon, Durie, K. Wilson
Subs not used: D. Lee, C. Wilson. *Scorer:* Dorigo. *Attendance:* 76,369

WAR CUP FINALS

London Victory Challenge Cup final at Highbury
26 April 1919 – Chelsea 3 Fulham 0

Football League South Cup finals at Wembley Stadium
15 April 1944 – Chelsea 1 Charlton Athletic 3
7 April 1945 – Chelsea 2 Millwall 0

COMPLETE LEAGUE AND CUP RECORD

Season	Div	P	W	D	L	F	A	Gd	Pts	Pos	Top League Scorer	FA Cup	LC	Europe	Other
												Round Reached			
1905–06	Two	38	22	9	7	90	37	53	53	3rd	Frank Pearson 18	P Rd 3			
1906–07	Two	38	26	5	7	80	34	46	57	2nd	George Hilsdon 27	Rd 1			
1907–08	One	38	14	8	16	53	62	-9	36	13th	George Hilsdon 24	Rd 2			
1908–09	One	38	14	9	15	56	61	-5	37	11th	George Hilsdon 25	Rd 2			
1909–10	One	38	11	7	20	47	70	-23	29	19th	Jimmy Windridge 6	Rd 2			
1910–11	Two	38	20	9	9	71	35	36	49	3rd	Bob Whittingham 30	SF			
1911–12	Two	38	24	6	8	64	34	30	54	2nd	Bob Whittingham 26	Rd 2			
1912–13	One	38	11	6	21	51	73	-22	28	18th	Vivian Woodward 10	Rd 2			
1913–14	One	38	16	7	15	46	55	-9	39	8th	Harold Halse 10	Rd 1			
1914–15	One	38	8	13	17	51	65	-14	29	19th	Bob Thomson 12	RU			
1919–20	One	42	22	5	15	56	51	5	49	3rd	Jack Cock 21	SF			
1920–21	One	42	13	13	16	48	58	-10	39	18th	Jack Cock 12	QF			
1921–22	One	42	17	12	13	40	43	-3	46	9th	Jack Cock 13	Rd 1			
1922–23	One	42	9	18	15	45	53	-8	36	19th	Harry Ford, Buchanan Sharp 10	Rd 2			
1923–24	One	42	9	14	19	31	53	-22	32	21st	Andy Wilson 5	Rd 1			
1924–25	Two	42	16	15	11	51	37	14	47	5th	William Whitton 16	Rd 1			
1925–26	Two	42	19	14	9	76	49	27	52	3rd	Bob Turnbull 29	Rd 4			
1926–27	Two	42	20	12	10	62	52	10	52	4th	Bob Turnbull 17	QF			
1927–28	Two	42	23	8	11	75	45	30	54	3rd	Jimmy Thompson 25	Rd 3			
1928–29	Two	42	17	10	15	64	65	-1	44	9th	George Biswell, Andy Wilson 9	Rd 5			
1929–30	Two	42	22	11	9	74	46	28	55	2nd	George Mills 14	Rd 3			
1930–31	One	42	15	10	17	64	67	-3	40	12th	Hughie Gallacher 14	QF			
1931–32	One	42	16	8	18	69	73	-4	40	12th	Hughie Gallacher 24	SF			
1932–33	One	42	14	7	21	63	73	-10	35	18th	Hughie Gallacher 19	Rd 3			
1933–34	One	42	14	8	20	67	69	-2	36	19th	George Mills 14	Rd 5			
1934–35	One	42	16	9	17	73	82	-9	41	12th	Dick Spence 19	Rd 3			
1935–36	One	42	15	13	14	65	72	-7	43	8th	Joe Bambrick 15	Rd 5			
1936–37	One	42	14	13	15	52	55	-3	41	13th	George Mills 22	Rd 4			
1937–38	One	42	14	13	15	65	65	0	41	10th	George Mills 13	Rd 3			
1938–39	One	42	12	9	21	64	80	-16	33	20th	Joe Payne 17	QF			
1945–46												Rd 5			
1946–47	One	42	16	7	19	69	84	-15	39	15th	Tommy Lawton 26	Rd 4			
1947–48	One	42	14	9	19	53	71	-18	37	18th	Ken Armstrong, Bobby Campbell 11	Rd 4			
1948–49	One	42	12	14	16	69	68	1	38	13th	Roy Bentley 20	Rd 5			
1949–50	One	42	12	16	14	58	65	-7	40	13th	Roy Bentley, Hugh Billington 17	SF			
1950–51	One	42	12	8	22	53	65	-12	32	20th	Roy Bentley 8	Rd 5			
1951–52	One	42	14	8	20	52	72	-20	36	19th	Roy Bentley, Jimmy D'Arcy 12	SF			
1952–53	One	42	12	11	19	56	66	-10	35	19th	Roy Bentley 12	Rd 5			
1953–54	One	42	16	12	14	74	68	6	44	8th	Roy Bentley 21	Rd 3			
1954–55	One	42	20	12	10	81	57	24	52	1st	Roy Bentley 21	Rd 5			
1955–56	One	42	14	11	17	64	77	-13	39	16th	Roy Bentley 14	Rd 5			CS WIN
1956–57	One	42	13	13	16	73	73	0	39	13th	John McNichol, Ron Tindall 10	Rd 4			
1957–58	One	42	15	12	15	83	79	4	42	11th	Jimmy Greaves 22	Rd 4			
1958–59	One	42	18	4	20	77	98	-21	40	14th	Jimmy Greaves 32	Rd 4		FC Rd 2	
1959–60	One	42	14	9	19	76	91	-15	37	18th	Jimmy Greaves 29	Rd 4			
1960–61	One	42	15	7	20	98	100	-2	37	12th	Jimmy Greaves 41	Rd 3	Rd 4		
1961–62	One	42	9	10	23	63	94	-31	28	22nd	Bobby Tambling 20	Rd 3	N/A		
1962–63	Two	42	24	4	14	81	42	39	52	2nd	Bobby Tambling 35	Rd 5	N/A		
1963–64	One	42	20	10	12	72	56	16	50	5th	Bobby Tambling 17	Rd 4	Rd 2		

Season	Div	P	W	D	L	F	A	Gd	Pts	Pos	Top League scorer	FA Cup	LC	Europe	Other
												Round Reached			
1964–65	One	42	24	8	10	89	54	35	56	3rd	Barry Bridges 20	SF	WIN		
1965–66	One	42	22	7	13	65	53	12	51	5th	George Graham 17	SF	N/A	FC SF	
1966–67	One	42	15	14	13	67	62	5	44	9th	Bobby Tambling 21	RU	Rd 3		
1967–68	One	42	18	12	12	62	68	-6	48	6th	Peter Osgood 16	QF	Rd 2		
1968–69	One	42	20	10	12	73	53	20	50	5th	Bobby Tambling 17	QF	Rd 3	FC Rd 2	
1969–70	One	42	21	13	8	70	50	20	55	3rd	Peter Osgood 23	WIN	Rd 4		
1970–71	One	42	18	15	9	52	42	10	51	6th	Keith Weller 13	Rd 4	Rd 4	ECWCWIN	CS RU
1971–72	One	42	18	12	12	58	49	9	48	7th	Peter Osgood 18	Rd 5	RU	ECWC Rd 2	
1972–73	One	42	13	14	15	49	51	-2	40	12th	Chris Garland, Peter Osgood 11	QF	SF		
1973–74	One	42	12	13	17	56	60	-4	37	17th	Tommy Baldwin 9	Rd 3	Rd 2		
1974–75	One	42	9	15	18	42	72	-30	33	21st	Ian Hutchinson 7	Rd 4	Rd 3		
1975–76	Two	42	12	16	14	53	54	-1	40	11th	Ray Wilkins 11	Rd 5	Rd 2		
1976–77	Two	42	21	13	8	73	53	20	55	2nd	Steve Finnieston 24	Rd 3	Rd 4		
1977–78	One	42	11	14	17	46	69	-23	36	16th	Tommy Langley 11	Rd 5	Rd 2		
1978–79	One	42	5	10	27	44	92	-48	20	22nd	Tommy Langley 15	Rd 3	Rd 2		
1979–80	Two	42	23	7	12	66	52	14	53	4th	Clive Walker 13	Rd 3	Rd 2		
1980–81	Two	42	14	12	16	46	41	5	40	12th	Colin Lee 15	Rd 3	Rd 2		
1981–82	Two	42	15	12	15	60	60	0	57	12th	Clive Walker 16	QF	Rd 3		
1982–83	Two	42	11	14	17	51	61	-10	47	18th	Mike Fillery 9	Rd 4	Rd 3		
1983–84	Two	42	25	13	4	90	40	50	88	1st	Kerry Dixon 28	Rd 3	Rd 3		
1984–85	One	42	18	12	12	63	48	15	66	6th	Kerry Dixon 24	Rd 4	SF		
1985–86	One	42	20	11	11	57	56	1	71	6th	Kerry Dixon, David Speedie 14	Rd 4	QF		FMC WIN
1986–87	One	42	13	13	16	53	64	-11	52	14th	Kerry Dixon 10	Rd 4	Rd 3		FMC Rd 4
1987–88*	One	40	9	15	16	50	68	-18	42	18th	Gordon Durie 12	Rd 4	Rd 2		FMC Rd 3
1988–89	Two	46	29	12	5	96	50	46	99	1st	Kerry Dixon 25	Rd 3	Rd 2		FMC Rd 3
1989–90	One	38	16	12	10	58	50	8	60	5th	Kerry Dixon 20	Rd 4	Rd 3		FMCWIN
1990–91	One	38	13	10	15	58	69	-11	49	11th	Gordon Durie 12	Rd 3	SF		FMC Rd 3
1991–92	One	42	13	14	15	50	60	-10	53	14th	Dennis Wise 10	QF	Rd 2		FMC SF
1992–93	FAPL	42	14	14	14	51	54	-3	56	11th	Mick Harford, Graham Stuart 9	Rd 3	QF		
1993–94	FAPL	42	13	12	17	49	53	-4	51	14th	Mark Stein 13	RU	Rd 3		
1994–95	FAPL	42	13	15	14	50	55	-5	54	11th	John Spencer 11	Rd 4	Rd 3	ECWC SF	
1995–96	FAPL	38	12	14	12	46	44	2	50	11th	John Spencer 13	SF	Rd 2		
1996–97	FAPL	38	16	11	11	58	55	3	59	6th	Gianluca Vialli 9	WIN	Rd 3		
1997–98	FAPL	38	20	3	15	71	43	28	63	4th	Tore André Flo, Gianluca Vialli 11	Rd 3	WIN	ECWC WIN	CS RU
1998–99	FAPL	38	20	15	3	57	30	27	75	3rd	Gianfranco Zola 13	QF	QF	ECWC SF	SC WIN
1999–00	FAPL	38	18	11	9	53	34	19	65	5th	Tore André Flo, Gustavo Poyet 10	WIN	Rd 3	UCL QF	
2000–01	FAPL	38	17	10	11	68	45	23	61	6th	Jimmy Floyd Hasselbaink 23	Rd 5	Rd 3	UC Rd 1	CS WIN
2001–02	FAPL	38	17	13	8	66	38	28	64	6th	Jimmy Floyd Hasselbaink 23	RU	SF	UC Rd 2	
2002–03	FAPL	38	19	10	9	68	38	30	67	4th	Gianfranco Zola 14	QF	QF	UC Rd 1	
2003–04	FAPL	38	24	7	7	67	30	37	79	2nd	Jimmy Floyd Hasselbaink 12	Rd 5	QF	UCL SF	
2004–05	FAPL	38	29	8	1	72	15	57	95	1st	Frank Lampard 13	Rd 5	WIN	UCL SF	
2005–06	FAPL	38	29	4	5	72	22	50	91	1st	Frank Lampard 16	SF	Rd 3	UCL Rd of 16	CS WIN
Total		3690	1472	968	1250	5610	5197	413	4355						
1987–88* PO		4	3	0	1	7	3								

NB: 3 points for a win started in 1981–82

HEAD TO HEAD

Chelsea's complete record in all competitions:
Includes League, Play-offs, FA Cup, League Cup, UEFA Champions League, UEFA Cup, European Cup-Winners' Cup, UEFA Super Cup, Inter-Cities Fairs Cup, FA Charity/Community Shield and Full Members Cup.

Opponents	P	W	D	L	F	A	Opponents	P	W	D	L	F	A
1st Grenadiers	1	1	0	0	6	1	Gillingham	5	5	0	0	17	4
Accrington Stanley	1	1	0	0	7	2	Glossop	8	6	1	1	20	7
Anderlecht (Bel)	2	2	0	0	3	0	Grimsby Town	43	21	8	14	77	49
Aris Salonika (Gr)	2	1	1	0	6	2	Hapoel Tel Aviv (Is)	2	0	1	1	1	3
Arsenal	163	47	49	67	204	240	Hartlepool United	1	1	0	0	1	0
Aston Villa	130	48	29	53	184	198	Helsingborg (Swe)	2	1	1	0	1	0
Atvidaberg (Swe)	2	0	2	0	1	1	Hereford United	2	1	1	0	7	3
Barcelona (Sp)	9	3	1	5	13	20	Hertha Berlin (Ger)	2	1	0	1	3	2
Barnet	2	1	1	0	4	0	Huddersfield Town	63	27	9	27	92	91
Barnsley	32	17	5	10	62	47	Hull City	35	23	8	4	64	23
Barrow	1	1	0	0	5	0	Ipswich Town	43	22	12**	9	78	53
Bayern Munich (Ger)	2	1	0	1	6	5	Jeunesse Hautcharage (Lux)	2	2	0	0	21	0
Besiktas (Tur)	2	1	0	1	2	2	Lazio (It)	4	2	1	1	7	3
Birmingham City	87	39	24	24	142	116	Leeds City	8	5	3	0	18	6
Blackburn Rovers	97	36	26*	35	138	130	Leeds United	101	33	29	39	129	143
Blackpool	81	36	15	30	138	116	Leicester City	100	47	29	24	173	120
Bolton Wanderers	102	40	26	36	165	153	Levski Sofia (Bul)	2	2	0	0	5	0
Bournemouth	5	4	0	1	7	3	Leyton	2	1	1	0	2	0
Bradford City	36	18	8	10	61	54	Leyton Orient	32	16	7	9	51	34
Bradford Park Avenue	16	10	1	5	34	16	Lincoln City	8	5	2	1	24	6
Brentford	11	6	1	4	15	13	Liverpool	142	49	29	64	204	222
Brighton & Hove Albion	8	6	1	1	14	4	Luton Town	43	17	13†	13	68	55
Bristol City	26	8	11	7	36	29	Manchester City	131	53	36	42	183	168
Bristol Rovers	11	6	2	3	13	9	Manchester United	144	39	41*	64	173	238
Bruges (Bel)	4	2	0	2	6	3	Mansfield Town	2	1	1	0	4	2
Burnley	87	30	21	36	115	139	Marseille (Fr)	2	1	0	1	1	1
Burton United	4	3	0	1	9	4	Middlesbrough	107	48	29	30	157	124
Bury	11	5	1	5	21	18	Milan AC (It)	5	1	3	1	5	5
Cambridge United	10	8	1	1	20	4	Millwall	17	5	6†	6	26	21
Cardiff City	40	15	10	15	56	52	Monaco (Fra)	2	0	1	1	3	5
Carlisle United	12	6	2	4	16	12	Morton (Sco)	2	2	0	0	9	3
Charlton Athletic	69	30	17†	22	120	99	MŠK Žilina (Slov)	2	2	0	0	5	0
Chester City	2	1	1	0	5	4	Munich 1860 (W Ger)	2	1	1	0	3	2
Chesterfield	7	4	2	1	17	4	Newcastle United	139	57	35*	47	209	178
Colchester United	1	1	0	0	3	1	Newport County	1	1	0	0	4	2
Coventry City	56	27	14	15	93	71	Northampton Town	3	3	0	0	8	3
Crewe Alexandra	4	1	1	2	4	4	Norwich City	40	14	12	14	51	48
Crystal Palace	42	19	15	8	68	45	Nottingham Forest	90	36	28	26	117	128
CSKA Moscow (Rus)	2	2	0	0	3	0	Notts County	37	15	8	14	60	58
CSKA Sofia (Bul)	2	2	0	0	2	0	Oldham Athletic	49	20	13	16	79	60
Darlington	6	1	4	1	14	14	Oxford United	17	8	5	4	35	27
Derby County	102	35	29	38	144	152	Paris Saint-Germain (Fr)	2	1	1	0	3	0
Doncaster Rovers	2	2	0	0	9	0	Peterborough United	2	2	0	0	10	1
DWS Amsterdam (Hol)	2	0	2	0	0	0	Plymouth Argyle	17	9	6	2	37	18
Everton	148	56	44	48	234	219	Port Vale	14	7	4	3	29	13
Exeter City	2	1	1	0	3	1	Porto (Por)	2	1	0	1	4	3
FC Copenhagen (Den)	2	1	1	0	2	1	Portsmouth	73	29	23	21	128	108
Feyenoord (Hol)	2	2	0	0	6	2	Preston North End	73	30	17	26	108	95
FK Austria (Aus)	2	0	2	0	1	1	Queens Park Rangers	46	16	17	13	59	60
Frem (Den)	2	2	0	0	7	2	Reading	14	6	5	3	20	18
Fulham	63	36	18	9	104	60	Real Betis (Sp)	4	3	0	1	9	3
Gainsborough Trinity	8	5	1	2	15	8	Real Madrid (Sp)	3	2	1	0	4	2
Galatasaray (Tur)	2	2	0	0	6	0	Real Mallorca (Sp)	2	0	1	1	1	2

Opponents	P	W	D	L	F	A
Real Zaragoza (Sp)	2	1	0	1	3	4
Rochdale	1	1	0	0	3	2
Roma (It)	2	1	1	0	4	1
Rotherham United	7	3	1	3	7	12
Scarborough	3	1	1	1	4	4
Scunthorpe United	5	2	1	2	9	10
Sheffield United	78	36	15	27	125	107
Sheffield Wednesday	123	37	45	41	160	184
Shrewsbury Town	15	8	2	5	29	20
Skonto Riga (Lat)	2	1	1	0	3	0
Slovan Bratislava (Slo)	2	2	0	0	4	0
South Shields	8	2	4	2	14	10
Southampton	88	35	25	28	125	117
Southend United	2	2	0	0	6	2
Southern United	1	1	0	0	1	0
Sparta Prague (Cz)	2	1	1	0	1	0
St Gallen (Swi)	2	1	0	1	1	2
Stockport County	12	6	4	2	17	13
Stoke City	78	32	19	27	107	114
Stuttgart (Ger)	3	2	1	0	2	0
Sunderland	104	45	21	38	170	157
Swansea City	19	8	6	5	32	22

Opponents	P	W	D	L	F	A
Swindon Town	13	9	2	2	26	15
Tottenham Hotspur	130	55	30	45	191	190
Tranmere Rovers	9	5	3	1	23	14
Tromsø (Nor)	2	1	0	1	9	4
Vålerenga (Nor)	2	2	0	0	6	2
Vicenza (Sp)	2	1	0	1	3	2
Viking FK (Nor)	2	1	0	1	4	5
Viktoria Zizkov (Cz)	2	1	1	0	4	2
Ville de Belgrade (Yug)	2	1	0	1	2	4
Walsall	11	9	1	1	34	5
Watford	22	9	4	9	38	34
West Bromwich Albion	121	48	33*	40	188	181
West Ham United	87	35	16	36	136	144
Wiener Sport-Club (Aus)	2	1	0	1	2	1
Wigan Athletic	6	3	1	2	11	7
Wimbledon	30	12	11	7	47	39
Wolverhampton Wanderers	97	34	26	37	162	172
Workington Town	3	2	1	0	8	4
Worksop	1	1	0	0	9	1
Wrexham	9	4	3	2	14	8
York City	5	2	2	1	7	3

* 1 drawn cup tie won on pens,† 1 drawn cup tie lost on pens
** 2 drawn cup ties won on pens,• 1 drawn CS match lost on pens

50 MATCHES IN A SEASON

Season	Player	Matches	Season	Player	Matches	Season	Player	Matches
1951–52	Billy Gray	51•		David Webb	52	1991–92	Graeme Le Saux	48+2
	Bill Robertson	50		Keith Weller	47+5	1993–94	Dmitri Kharine	51
1964–65	Peter Bonetti	55	1971–72	John Hollins	58•		Steve Clarke	50
	Ron Harris	53		Ron Harris	57	1994–95	Gavin Peacock	51
	John Hollins	52		David Webb	57	1999–00	Ed de Goey	59
	Barry Bridges	51		Alan Hudson	52		Dennis Wise	48+2
	Marvin Hinton	51		Peter Osgood	52		Gianfranco Zola	44+9
	Bert Murray	51		Charlie Cooke	49+3		Gustavo Poyet	42+11
1965–66	Peter Bonetti	56	1972–73	John Hollins	54•		Tore André Flo	37+20
	John Hollins	56		Ron Harris	52	2001–02	Frank Lampard	49+4
	Marvin Hinton	55		Peter Osgood	50		Mario Melchiot	47+3
	Ron Harris	52	1981–82	Colin Pates	52		Gianfranco Zola	28+22
	George Graham	50	1984–85	Nigel Spackman	55•	2003–04	Frank Lampard	56+2
1966–67	Ron Harris	52•		Kerry Dixon	53		John Terry	51
1968–69	David Webb	54•		Pat Nevin	53		Joe Cole	25+25
	Peter Bonetti	53		Eddie Niedzwiecki	52	2004–05	Frank Lampard	53+5
	Ron Harris	52	1985–86	Pat Nevin	55+1		John Terry	53
	Alan Birchenall	51		Nigel Spackman	52+3		Claude Makelele	50
	Eddie McCreadie	50		Kerry Dixon	51		Eidur Gudjohnsen	42+15
1969–70	John Hollins	54•		Joe McLaughlin	51		Tiago	31+20
	Peter Houseman	54•		Colin Pates	50	2005–06	John Terry	50
1970–71	John Hollins	56	1987–88	Tony Dorigo	50		Frank Lampard	48+2
	Ron Harris	55	1988–89	Graham Roberts	52•			
	Peter Houseman	52+1		Kevin Wilson	48+4			

• Started every first team match

THE 300 APPEARANCES CLUB

	Player	Games	Total	League	PO	FAC	LC	Eur	CS	FMC
1	Ron Harris	795	784+11	646+9		64	46+2	27	1	
2	Peter Bonetti	729	729	600		57	45	26	1	
3	John Hollins	592	592	465		51	48	27	1	
4	Dennis Wise	445	434+11	322+10		38	30	37+1	2	5
5	Steve Clarke	421	407+14	321+9	4	34+2	24+2	11+1	1	12
6	Kerry Dixon	420	413+7	331+4	4	18+2	40+1			20
7	Eddie McCreadie	410	405+5	327+4		41	21+1	16		
8	John Bumstead	409	379+30	314+24	4	20+1	29+5			12
9	Ken Armstrong	402	402	362		39			1	
10	Peter Osgood	380	376+4	286+3		34	30	25+1	1	
11	Charlie Cooke	373	360+13	289+10		32+2	22+1	17		
12	George Smith	370	370	351		19				
13	Bobby Tambling	370	366+4	298+4		36	18	14		
14	Roy Bentley	367	367	324		42			1	
15	John Harris	364	364	326		38				
16	Harold Miller	363	363	337		26				
17	Frank Blunstone	347	347	317		24	3	2	1	
18	Colin Pates	346	345+1	280+1	4	20	32			9
19	Marvin Hinton	344	328+16	257+8		30+3	22+3	18+2	1	
20	Peter Houseman	343	325+18	252+17		25	32+1	15	1	
21	Jack Harrow	333	333	304		29				
22	Tommy Law	319	319	293		26				
23	Gary Locke	317	315+2	270+2		24	21			
24	Micky Droy	313	302+11	263+9		21	17+2	1		
25	Graeme Le Saux	312	280+32	210+20		25+3	17+6	20+1	0+1	8+1
26	Gianfranco Zola	312	260+52	185+44		28+3	10+3	35+2	2	
27	Jackie Crawford	308	308	288		20				
28	Bob McNeil	307	307	279		28				

EVER-PRESENTS

Players that have appeared in every first team game in a season. Players in bold have appeared in every league game, but not every first team game.

1906–07	Tommy Miller
1910–11	**Bob Whittingham**
1921–22	Bob McNeil
1922–23	Tommy Meehan, George Smith
1926–27	Willie Ferguson, George Smith
1932–33	Vic Woodley
1934–35	Allan Craig
1947–48	Ken Armstrong
1951–52	Billy Gray
1954–55	Eric Parsons, Derek Saunders
1955–56	**Stan Wicks**
1957–58	Reg Matthews
1958–59	**Jimmy Greaves**
1962–63	John Mortimore, Terry Venables
1964–65	**Ron Harris**
1966–67	Ron Harris
1967–68	Peter Osgood
1968–69	David Webb
1969–70	John Hollins, Peter Houseman
1971–72	John Hollins
1972–73	**Ron Harris**, John Hollins
1973–74	John Hollins
1974–75	Ron Harris
1975–76	Ray Wilkins
1976–77	Ray Lewington, Gary Locke, Ray Wilkins
1980–81	Petar Borota
1981–82	Colin Pates
1983–84	Kerry Dixon, Eddie Niedzwiecki, Colin Pates
1984–85	Nigel Spackman
1987–88	**Tony Dorigo**
1988–89	Graham Roberts, Kevin Wilson
1989–90	Dave Beasant, Kerry Dixon
2002–03	William Gallas, Frank Lampard, **Gianfranco Zola**
2003–04	**Frank Lampard**
2004–05	**Frank Lampard**

CLEAN SHEETS AND GOALKEEPING RECORDS

	Player (years at club)	C Sheet	Games		Player (years at club)	C Sheet	Games
1	Peter Bonetti (1960–79)	208	729 (29%)	30	John Jackson (1933–42)	5	51
2	Carlo Cudicini (1999–06)	78	178+4 (44%)	31	Neil Sullivan (2003–04)	4	7+1
3	Sam Millington (1926–32)	78	245 (32%)	32	Marco Ambrosio (2003–04)	4	12
4	Jim Molyneux (1910–22)	77	239 (32%)	33	John Dunn (1962–66)	3	16
5	Ed de Goey (1997–03)	72	178+1 (40%)	34	Steve Sherwood (1971–76)	3	17
6	Vic Woodley (1931–45)	60	272 (22%)	35	Ronald Brebner (1906–13)	3	19
7	Eddie Niedzwiecki (1983–88)	55	175 (31%)	36	Mark Bosnich (2001–03)	2	7
8	Dmitri Kharine (1992–99)	51	146 (35%)	37	Wilson Marsh (1921–24)	2	12
9	Petr Cech (2004–06)	50	90 (55%)	38	Bob Mackie (1905–08)	1	1
10	Dave Beasant (1989–93)	41	157 (26%)	39	Alex Stepney (1966)	1	1
11	Jack Whitley (1907–14)	39	138 (28%)	40	David Webb (1968–74)	1	1
12	Bill G Robertson (1946–60)	38	215 (18%)	41	Frank Higgs (1928–30)	1	2
13	Ben Howard-Baker (1921–26)	36	93 (38%)	42	Craig Forrest (1997)	1	2+1
14	Petar Borota (1979–82)	36	114 (32%)	43	Perry Digweed (1988)	1	3
15	Colin Hampton (1914–25)	32	82 (39%)	44	Tommy Hughes (1965–71)	1	11
16	Harry Medhurst (1946–52)	32	157 (20%)	45	Bob Iles (1978–83)	1	14
17	Kevin Hitchcock (1988–01)	30	131+4 (22%)	46	Gerry Peyton (1993)	0	0+1
18	John Phillips (1970–80)	30	149 (20%)	47	Jim Barron (1965–66)	0	1
19	Peter McKenna (1924–31)	25	66 (38%)	48	Nick Colgan (1992–98)	0	1
20	Steve Francis (1981–87)	21	88 (24%)	49	Mike Collins (1951–57)	0	1
21	Reg Matthews (1956–61)	21	148 (14%)	50	Les Fridge (1985–87)	0	1
22	Bob Whiting (1906–08)	18	54 (33%)	51	Stan MacIntosh (1930–36)	0	1
23	Willie Foulke (1905–06)	17	35 (48%)	52	Mike Pinner (1961–62)	0	1
24	Charlie Thomson (1952–57)	16	59	53	Kingsley Whiffen (1966–67)	0	1
25	Tony Godden (1986–87)	12	38	54	Lenny Pidgeley (2003–06)	0	1+1
26	Roger Freestone (1987–91)	10	53	55	James Saunders (1909–10)	0	2
27	Frode Grodås (1996–97)	8	26+1	56	Arthur Robinson (1908–10)	0	3
28	Bill H Robertson (1945–48)	8	43	57	Michael Byrne (1905–06)	0	5
29	Peter Pickering (1948–51)	5	35	58	Errol McNally (1961–63)	0	9

Chelsea have kept 1,238 clean sheets in 4,336 first team games. The list does not include substitute or emergency keepers as the starting keeper is always credited with the clean sheet. Substitute goalkeepers were introduced in 1992 and on seven occasions have shared a clean sheet. They are Carlo Cudicini 3, Kevin Hitchcock 2, Ed de Goey 1 and Lenny Pidgeley 1. Prior to the 1992–93 season outfield players acted as emergency keepers in the event of an injury or dismissal. Here is a selection of those – William Cartwright, Willie Russell, Reg Williams, Ian MacFarlane, Bert Murray, Ron Tindall, David Webb, Bill Garner, Tommy Langley, John Coady, David Speedie, Vinnie Jones and Glen Johnson. Reg Williams and David Webb have shared a clean sheet.

MOST CONSECUTIVE CLEAN SHEETS
7 in 1905–06, 2003–04 and 2005–06 (twice)
Home: 10 in 1926–27 (8) + 1927–28 (2)
Home top-flight: 7 in 1999–00
Away: 5 in 1910–11 and 2004–05

MOST CONSECUTIVE LEAGUE CLEAN SHEETS
10 in 2004–05 (top-flight record). Petr Cech played 1024 minutes without conceding a goal (top-flight record)
Home: 9 in 1926–27 (7) + 1927–28 (2)
Home top-flight: 7 in 2004–05
Away: 5 in 1999–00 and 2004–05

MOST CONSECUTIVE INDIVIDUAL CLEAN SHEETS
9 in 1905–06 (Willie Foulke)
Top-flight: 7 in 2003–04 (Carlo Cudicini) and 2004–05 (Petr Cech)

MOST CONSECUTIVE CLEAN SHEETS AT THE START OF THE SEASON
4 in 1911–12 and 1926–27
Top-flight: 3 in 1996–97 and 2004–05

MOST CONSECUTIVE LEAGUE CLEAN SHEETS AT THE START OF THE SEASON
6 in 2005–06 (top-flight record)

MOST CLEAN SHEETS IN A SEASON
34 in 59 games in 2004–05
Home: 20 in 2004–05
Away: 17 in 2003–04

MOST LEAGUE CLEAN SHEETS IN A SEASON
25 in 38 games in 2004–05 (Premiership record)
Home: 14 in 1910–11 and 2004–05
Away: 11 in 2004–05 (Premiership record)

MOST CLEAN SHEETS IN A SEASON BY AN INDIVIDUAL
28 in 48 games by Petr Cech in 2004–05

FEWEST CLEAN SHEETS IN A SEASON
2 in 47 games in 1960–61

FEWEST LEAGUE CLEAN SHEETS IN A SEASON
1 in 42 games in 1960–61
Home: 0 in 21 games in 1960–61
Away: 0 in 21 games in 1948–49

WORST RUN WITHOUT A CLEAN SHEET
31 games: November 1960 – August 1961
Home: 27 in 1959–60 (3) + 1960–61 (23) + 1961–62 (1)
Away: 20 in 1960–61 (13) + 1961–62 (7)

MOST GOALS CONCEDED IN A MATCH
8 by Bill G. Robertson v Wolves on 26 September 1953

GOALKEEPERS EVER-PRESENT IN A SEASON
Woodley 1932–33 (43 games), Matthews 1957–58 (45),
Borota 1980–81 (45), Niedzwiecki 1983–84 (48),
Beasant 1989–90 (49)

LONGEST UNBROKEN RUN
84 games by Dave Beasant from Jan 1989 to Oct 1990

SCORING GOALKEEPER
Ben Howard-Baker is Chelsea's only goalkeeper to score,
a penalty in November 1921 v Bradford City. Chelsea won 1-0

MOST PENALTY SAVES
Bill G. Robertson: faced 39, saved 7, conceded 30, off-target 2
Peter Bonetti: faced 55, saved 7, conceded 46, off-target 2
Carlo Cudicini: faced 13, saved 6, conceded 7

MOST GOALKEEPERS USED IN A SEASON
5 in 1996–97: Kharine, Hitchcock, Grodås, Colgan and Forrest

FULL INTERNATIONAL GOALKEEPERS
Foulke, Howard-Baker, Woodley, Jackson, Matthews, Bonetti,
Stepney, Roberts (reserve player), Phillips, Borota, Niedzwiecki,
Freestone, Beasant, Kharine, Peyton, Grodås, Forrest, Colgan,
De Goey, Bosnich, Macho (injured during his one year at
Chelsea), Sullivan, Cech

OUTFIELD GOALKEEPERS
Two outfield players have played the whole game in goal.
David Webb was forced to start a game in goal when he played
a full match at home to Ipswich Town on 27 December 1971.
Peter Bonetti and John Phillips were both ruled out through
injury and Steve Sherwood missed his debut by a matter of
minutes because of delays in heavy fog. He had made a
desperate dash by road from Selby, Yorkshire, where he had
gone to spend Christmas at home. Webb kept a clean sheet in
a 2–0 win. Bob Mackie also kept a clean sheet on 28 October
1905. Chelsea beat Southern United 1-0 away in the FA Cup.

THE 50 GOALS CLUB

	Player	Total	League	PO	FAC	LC	Eur	CS	FMC
1	Bobby Tambling	202	164		25	10	3		
2	Kerry Dixon	193	147	1	8	25			12
3	Roy Bentley	150	128		21			1	
4	Peter Osgood	150	105		19	10	16		
5	Jimmy Greaves	132	124		3	2	3		
6	George Mills	123	116		7				
7	George Hilsdon	107	98		9				
8	Barry Bridges	93	80		9	3	1		
9	Tommy Baldwin	92	74		5	6	7		
10	Jimmy Floyd Hasselbaink	87	69		7	7	3	1	
11	Hughie Gallacher	81	72		9				
12	Bob Whittingham	80	71		9				
13	Gianfranco Zola	80	59		11	1	9		
14	Eidur Gudjohnsen	78	54		10	6	8		
15	Dennis Wise	76	53		9	6	6		2
16	Ron Tindall	69	67		2				
17	Frank Lampard	69	50		5	2	12		
18	John McNichol	66	59		7				
19	Dick Spence	65	62		3				
20	Clive Walker	65	60		3	2			
21	John Hollins	64	48		4	7	5		
22	David Speedie	64	47		5	7			5
23	Gordon Durie	63	51	3	1	7			1
24	Andy Wilson	62	59		3				
25	Jimmy Windridge	58	54		4				
26	Bob Turnbull	58	51		7				
27	Ian Hutchinson	58	44		6	4	3	1	
28	Peter Brabrook	57	47		4	4	2		
29	Kevin Wilson	55	42	2	1	4			6
30	Frank Blunstone	54	47		4	2		1	
31	Jack Cock	53	47		6				
32	Albert Thain	50	44		6				
33	Tore André Flo	50	34		1	3	12		

INDIVIDUAL SCORING FEATS

MOST GOALS IN A SEASON
43 Jimmy Greaves in 1960–61

MOST LEAGUE GOALS IN A SEASON
41 Jimmy Greaves in 1960–61

FASTEST RECORDED GOALS
12 seconds Keith Weller v Middlesbrough (h) League Cup, 7 October 1970
Roberto Di Matteo scored the fastest ever FA Cup Final goal at Wembley, 43 seconds v Middlesbrough 17 May 1997

MOST PENALTIES IN A SEASON
13 Graham Roberts in 1988–89

MOST SUCCESSFUL PENALTY TAKERS
Jimmy Floyd Hasselbaink 12 from 12
Terry Venables 10 from 10

FA CUP FACT
Peter Osgood scored in every round of Chelsea's FA Cup success in 1970 – the last time this has been achieved

MOST GOALS IN A MATCH
6 George Hilsdon v Worksop (h) FA Cup, 11 January 1908. Won 9-1
5 George Hilsdon v Glossop (h) Division Two, 1 September 1906. Won 9-2
5 Jimmy Greaves v Wolves (h) Division One, 30 August 1958. Won 6-2
5 Jimmy Greaves v Preston NE (a) Division One, 19 December 1959. Won 5-4
5 Jimmy Greaves v West Brom (h) Division One, 3 December 1960. Won 7-1
5 Bobby Tambling v Aston Villa (a) Division One, 17 September 1966. Won 6-2
5 Peter Osgood v Jeunesse Hautcharage (h) European Cup-Winners' Cup, 29 September 1971. Won 13-0
5 Gordon Durie v Walsall (a) Division Two, 4 February 1989. Won 7-0

BEST GOAL AVERAGE (AMONGST LEADING SCORERS)
Jimmy Greaves 0.78 goals per game

HAT-TRICKS
Chelsea have scored 128 hat-tricks. 104 league, 10 FA Cup, 6 League Cup, 5 Europe and 3 Full Members Cup.
59 players have achieved hat-tricks for the club including a double hat-trick by George Hilsdon in 1908.
They are as follows: Greaves 13, Hilsdon 10, Dixon 8, Tambling 8, Osgood 5, Bambrick 4, Windridge 4, Baldwin 3, Hasselbaink 3,
Mills 3, Spence 3, Thompson 3, B. Turnbull 3, Vialli 3, Whittingham 3, Bentley 2, Bridges 2, Durie 2, Gallacher 2, J. Lewis 2,
James Robertson 2, C. Walker 2, Whitton 2, Argue 1, K. Armstrong 1, Blunstone 1, W. Brown 1, Canoville 1, Cheyne 1,
Cock 1, D'Arcy 1, Davies 1, Dickens 1, Dodd 1, Finnieston 1, Flo 1, Ford 1, Frost 1, Garland 1, Graham 1, Gudjohnsen 1,
M. Hughes 1, Langley 1, Lawton 1, C. Lee 1, McNichol 1, H. Miller 1, O'Connell 1, Payne 1, Peacock 1, Poyet 1, B. Smith 1,
Speedie 1, B. Thomson 1, Tindall 1, Venables 1, Webb 1, Woodward 1, Zola 1

BEST SCORING SEQUENCES
Roy Bentley: 9 in 8 consecutive Division One games, September – October 1952 (7 ones and a two).
Mark Stein: 9 in 7 consecutive Premier League games, December 1993 – February 1994 (5 ones and 2 twos).
George Mills: 8 in 7 consecutive Division One games, April – September 1936 (6 ones and a two).
Bobby Tambling: 12 in 6 consecutive Division Two games, October – November 1962 (2, 3, 1, 2, 2, 2).
Jimmy Thompson: 7 in 6 consecutive Division Two games, October – November 1927 (5 ones and a two).
Bob Whittingham: 6 in 6 consecutive Division Two games, March – April 1911 (6 ones).
Joe Payne: 6 in 6 consecutive Division One games, April – May 1939 (6 ones).
Jimmy Greaves: 6 in 6 consecutive Division One and FA Cup games, January – February 1959 (6 ones).
John Hollins: 6 in 6 consecutive Division One, League Cup and Cup-Winners' Cup games, August – September 1971 (6 ones).

YOUNGEST CENTURY
On completion of his hat-trick at home to Manchester City on 19 November 1960, Jimmy Greaves scored his 100th league
goal for Chelsea, still before the age of 21. The youngest ever player to do so.

TOP SCORER BY SEASON IN ALL COMPETITIONS

Season	Div	Player	Goals	Season	Div	Player	Goals
1905–06	Two	Frank Pearson & Jimmy Windridge	18	1961–62	One	Bobby Tambling	22
1906–07	Two	George Hilsdon	27	1962–63	Two	Bobby Tambling	37
1907–08	One	George Hilsdon	30	1963–64	One	Bobby Tambling	19
1908–09	One	George Hilsdon	27	1964–65	One	Barry Bridges	27
1909–10	One	Jimmy Windridge	6	1965–66	One	George Graham & Bobby Tambling	23
1910–11	Two	Bob Whittingham	34	1966–67	One	Bobby Tambling	28
1911–12	Two	Bob Whittingham	26	1967–68	One	Peter Osgood	17
1912–13	One	Bob Whittingham	12	1968–69	One	Bobby Tambling	19
1913–14	One	Harold Halse	10	1969–70	One	Peter Osgood	31
1914–15	One	Bob Thomson	18	1970–71	One	Keith Weller	14
1919–20	One	Jack Cock	24	1971–72	One	Peter Osgood	31
1920–21	One	Jack Cock	15	1972–73	One	Peter Osgood	17
1921–22	One	Jack Cock	13	1973–74	One	Tommy Baldwin	9
1922–23	One	Harry Ford & Buchanan Sharp	10	1974–75	One	Ian Hutchinson	9
1923–24	One	Andy Wilson	6	1975–76	Two	Ray Wilkins	12
1924–25	Two	William Whitton	16	1976–77	Two	Steve Finnieston	26
1925–26	Two	Bob Turnbull	30	1977–78	One	Tommy Langley	13
1926–27	Two	Bob Turnbull	23	1978–79	One	Tommy Langley	16
1927–28	Two	Jimmy Thompson	25	1979–80	Two	Mike Fillery & Clive Walker	13
1928–29	Two	George Biswell, Andy Wilson & Jimmy Thompson	9	1980–81	Two	Colin Lee	16
1929–30	Two	George Mills	14	1981–82	Two	Clive Walker	17
1930–31	One	Hughie Gallacher	14	1982–83	Two	Mike Fillery	12
1931–32	One	Hughie Gallacher	30	1983–84	Two	Kerry Dixon	34
1932–33	One	Hughie Gallacher	19	1984–85	One	Kerry Dixon	36
1933–34	One	Hughie Gallacher	16	1985–86	One	Kerry Dixon	23
1934–35	One	Dick Spence	19	1986–87	One	Kerry Dixon	12
1935–36	One	Joe Bambrick	19	1987–88	One	Gordon Durie	20
1936–37	One	George Mills	23	1988–89	One	Kerry Dixon	28
1937–38	One	George Mills	13	1989–90	One	Kerry Dixon	25
1938–39	One	Joe Payne	19	1990–91	One	Kerry Dixon & Gordon Durie	15
1946–47	One	Tommy Lawton	30	1991–92	One	Dennis Wise	14
1947–48	One	Ken Armstrong	13	1992–93	FAPL	Mick Harford	11
1948–49	One	Roy Bentley	22	1993–94	FAPL	Gavin Peacock & Mark Stein	14
1949–50	One	Roy Bentley	22	1994–95	FAPL	Paul Furlong & John Spencer	13
1950–51	One	Roy Bentley	11	1995–96	FAPL	John Spencer	14
1951–52	One	Roy Bentley	17	1996–97	FAPL	Mark Hughes	14
1952–53	One	Roy Bentley	17	1997–98	FAPL	Gianluca Vialli	19
1953–54	One	Roy Bentley	21	1998–99	FAPL	Gianfranco Zola	15
1954–55	One	Roy Bentley	21	1999–00	FAPL	Tore André Flo	19
1955–56	One	Roy Bentley	16	2000–01	FAPL	Jimmy Floyd Hasselbaink	26
1956–57	One	John McNichol	11	2001–02	FAPL	Jimmy Floyd Hasselbaink	29
1957–58	One	Jimmy Greaves	22	2002–03	FAPL	Gianfranco Zola	16
1958–59	One	Jimmy Greaves	37	2003–04	FAPL	Jimmy Floyd Hasselbaink	17
1959–60	One	Jimmy Greaves	30	2004–05	FAPL	Frank Lampard	19
1960–61	One	Jimmy Greaves	43	2005–06	FAPL	Frank Lampard	20

CHAIRMEN

Chairmen	Dates in Office
Claude Kirby	1905–35
Charles Pratt Senior	1935–36
Lieutenant-Colonel Charles Doland Crisp	1936–40
Joe Mears	1940–66
Charles Pratt Junior	1966–68
Leslie Withey	1968–69
Brian Mears	1969–81
Viscount Chelsea	1981–82
Ken Bates	1982–2003
Bruce Buck	2003–

MANAGERS

Managers	Achievements
John Tait Robertson 1905–06	
William Lewis 1906–07	Division Two runners-up 1907
David Calderhead 1907–33	FA Cup semi-finalists 1911, 1920, 1932
	Division Two runners-up 1912, 1930
	FA Cup runners-up 1915
	3rd in Division One 1920
	(London Victory Challenge Cup winners 1919 – wartime)
Leslie Knighton 1933–39	FA Cup quarter-finalists 1939
William Birrell 1939–52	FA Cup semi-finalists 1950, 1952
	(Football League South Cup winners 1945, runners-up 1944 – wartime)
Ted Drake 1952–61	League Champions 1955
	Charity Shield winners 1955
Tommy Docherty 1961–67	Division Two runners-up 1963
	League Cup winners 1965
	FA Cup semi-finalists 1965, 1966
	3rd in Division One 1965
	Inter-Cities Fairs Cup semi-finalists 1966
	FA Cup runners-up 1967
Dave Sexton 1967–74	FA Cup winners 1970
	Charity Shield runners-up 1970
	3rd in Division One 1970
	European Cup-Winners' Cup winners 1971
	League Cup runners-up 1972
	League Cup semi-finalists 1973
Ron Suart 1974–75	
Eddie McCreadie 1975–77	Division Two runners-up 1977
Ken Shellito 1977–78	
Danny Blanchflower 1978–79	
Geoff Hurst 1979–81	
John Neal 1981–85	FA Cup quarter-finalists 1982
	Division Two champions 1984
	League Cup semi-finalists 1985
John Hollins 1985–88	Full Members Cup winners 1986
	League Cup quarter-finalists 1986
Bobby Campbell 1988–91	Division Two champions 1989
	Full Members Cup winners 1990
	League Cup semi-finalists 1991
Ian Porterfield 1991–93	FA Cup quarter-finalists 1992
	League Cup quarter-finalists 1993
David Webb 1993 (Feb–May)	
Glenn Hoddle 1993–96	FA Cup runners-up 1994
	European Cup-Winners' Cup semi-finalists 1995
	FA Cup semi-finalists 1996

Managers	Achievements
Ruud Gullit 1996–98	FA Cup winners 1997
	Charity Shield runners-up 1997
Gianluca Vialli 1998–2000	League Cup winners 1998
	European Cup-Winners' Cup winners 1998
	4th in Premier League 1998
	European Super Cup winners 1998
	3rd in Premier League 1999 – qualified for Champions League
	European Cup-Winners' Cup semi-finalists 1999
	FA Cup winners 2000
	Champions League quarter-finalists 2000
	Charity Shield winners 2000
Claudio Ranieri 2000–04	FA Cup runners-up 2002
	League Cup semi-finalists 2002
	4th in Premier League 2003 – qualified for Champions League
	Champions League semi-finalists 2004
	Premier League runners-up 2004 – qualified for Champions League
José Mourinho 2004–	Premier League Champions 2005 and 2006 – qualified for Champions League
	League Cup winners 2005
	Champions League semi- finalists 2005
	Community Shield winners 2005
	FA Cup semi-finalists 2006

ATTENDANCES

STAMFORD BRIDGE CAPACITY 2006
42,360 (West Stand 13,432, East Stand 11,218, Matthew Harding Stand 10,884, Shed End 6,826)

ATTENDANCE RECORDS AT STAMFORD BRIDGE

Highest ever: 82,905 v Arsenal, Division One, 12 October 1935

(In 1945 the Chelsea v Moscow Dynamo friendly had an estimated 100,000 in the ground but because some gates were broken down an exact figure could not be ascertained)

Highest	Attendance, Opponents and Date
Division Two	67,000 v Manchester Utd, 13 April 1906
FA Cup	77,952 v Swindon Town, 4th round, 13 March 1911
League Cup	43,330 v Tottenham, Semi–final, 1st leg, 22 December 1971
Europe	59,541 v AC Milan, Fairs Cup 3rd round, 2nd leg, 16 Feb 1966
All seater	42,328 v Newcastle, Premiership, 4 December 2004
Aggregate	1,014,352 in 1954–55
Lowest	Attendance, Opponents and Date
Top-flight	(pre-war) 6,801 v Liverpool, Division One, 24 December 1938
	(post-war) 7,148 v Southampton, Division One, 12 Feb 1992
Division Two	(pre-war) 3,000 v Lincoln City, 17 February 1906
	(post-war) 6,009 v Orient, 5 May 1982
FA Cup	5,000 v 1st Grenadiers, 1st preliminary round, 7 October 1905
League Cup	5,630 v Workington, 2nd round, 24 October 1960
Europe	13,104 v Frem, Fairs Cup, 1st round, 2nd leg, 4 November 1958
Post war	3,849 v Luton Town, Full Members Cup, 3rd round, 18 Feb 1991

HIGHEST AVERAGE LEAGUE ATTENDANCE AT STAMFORD BRIDGE
1954–55   48,302

HIGHEST AVERAGE LEAGUE ALL-SEATER ATTENDANCE AT STAMFORD BRIDGE
2005–06   41,901

HIGHEST ATTENDANCE FOR ANY CHELSEA MATCH
100,000 at Wembley three times in cup finals. Tottenham Hotspur (FA Cup), 20 May 1967, Leeds United (FA Cup), 11 April 1970 and Stoke City (League Cup), 4 March 1972

HIGHEST AWAY ATTENDANCE
98,436 at the Nou Camp, Barcelona, Champions League, Round of 16, 2nd leg, 7 March 2006

HIGHEST AWAY LEAGUE ATTENDANCE
68,386 at St James' Park, Newcastle, Division One, 3 September 1930 (still Newcastle's record crowd)

101 YEARS OF FIRST TEAM COMPETITIVE GAMES

Competition	P	W	D	L	F	A
Premiership – Old Division One (71 seasons)	2904	1089	766	1049	4287	4310
Old Division Two (19 seasons)	786	383	202	201	1323	887
League Total (90 seasons)	*3690*	*1472*	*968*	*1250*	*5610*	*5197*
League Play-offs	4	3	0	1	7	3
FA Cup	337	164	84	89	578	377
Football League Cup	155	73	36	46	266	194
UEFA Champions League	50	25	13	12	76	41
UEFA Cup	8	4	1	3	11	10
European Cup-Winners' Cup	39	23	10	6	81	28
UEFA Super Cup	1	1	0	0	1	0
Inter-Cities Fairs Cup	20	10	5	5	33	24
FA Charity/Community Shield	5	3	1	1	9	4
Full Members Cup	27	18	3	6	55	41
TOTAL	4336	1796	1121	1419	6727	5919

MATCHES DECIDED BY PENALTY SHOOT-OUT (REGARDED AS DRAWS)

FA Cup	2	1 win (Newcastle Utd 1995–96), 1 defeat (Millwall 1994–95)
LC	3	2 wins (Blackburn Rovers & Ipswich Town 1997–98), 1 defeat (Charlton 2005–06)
CS	1	1 defeat (Man Utd 1997)
FMC	3	2 wins (WBA 1985–86 & Ipswich T 1991–92), 1 defeat (Luton T 1990–91)

WINS, DEFEATS AND SEQUENCES

BIGGEST WINS

Top-flight	7-1	Leeds United (h) 16 March 1935
	7-1	West Brom (h) 3 December 1960
	6-0	Leeds United (h) 8 April 1933
	6-0	Everton (h) 11 September 1948
	6-0	Barnsley (a) 24 August 1997
Old Division Two	9-2	Glossop (h) 1 September 1906
	7-0	Burslem Port Vale (h) 3 March 1906
	7-0	Lincoln City (h) 29 October 1910
	7-0	Portsmouth (h) 21 May 1963
	7-0	Walsall (a) 4 February 1989
FA Cup	9-1	Worksop (h) 1st round, 11 January 1908
Away FA Cup	6-1	Hull City 3rd round, 11 December 1999
	5-0	Wigan 3rd round replay, 26 January 1985
League Cup	7-0	Doncaster Rovers (a) 3rd round, 16 November 1960
Europe	13-0	Jeunesse Hautcharage (Luxembourg) (h) Cup-Winners' Cup 1st round 2nd leg, 29 Sept 1971
		(The biggest win in the Champions League is 5-0 v Galatasaray (a) 1st group stage, 20 Oct 1999)
Away Europe	8-0	Jeunesse Hautcharage Cup-Winners' Cup 1st round 1st leg, 15 September 1971
		(The 21-0 aggregate score was a new record in European football)

LONGEST WINNING SEQUENCE
9 games: 7 August to 28 September 2005
Home: 10 in 1910–11 and 1919–20
Away: 7 in 1988–89
Away top-flight: 6 in 2004–05 (twice) and 2005–06
(Away Europe: 6 in 2003–04 – most away wins in a season in Champions League history)

LONGEST WINNING LEAGUE SEQUENCE
10 games: 19 November 2005 to 22 January 2006 (8 consecutive wins in 2004–05 with a clean sheet equalled the all-time top-flight
European record set by Partizan Belgrade and Skonto Riga)
Home: 13 in 1910–11 and 2004–05 (2) + 2005–06 (11)
Away: 9 in 2004–05 (Premiership record)

BEST START TO A SEASON
9 successive wins in 2005–06
Away: 5 successive wins in 2003–04

BEST START TO A LEAGUE SEASON
9 successive wins in 2005–06
Away: 4 successive wins in 2005–06

LONGEST SEQUENCE WITHOUT A WIN
15 games: 3 February to 21 April 1951
Home: 11 in 1985–86 (6) + 1986–87 (5)
Away: 26 in 1992–93 (14) + 1993–94 (12), a complete calendar year, (1993), without an away win

LONGEST LEAGUE SEQUENCE WITHOUT A WIN
21 games: 3 November 1987 to 9 April 1988
Home: 12 in 1994–95
Away: 22 in 1913–14 (3) + 1914–15 (19), 1951–52 (6) + 1952–53 (16) and 1992–93 (12) + 1993–94 (10)

MOST WINS IN A SEASON
42 in 2004–05
Home: 24 in 2005–06
Away: 20 in 2003–04 and 2004–05

MOST LEAGUE WINS IN A SEASON
29 in 1988–89, 2004–05 and 2005–06 (Premiership record)
Home: 18 in 1906–07 and 2005–06 (Our record in 2005–06 won 18, drawn 1, lost 0 equalled Newcastle's top-flight record in 1906–07 of fewest matches not won when undefeated. In 1891–92 when leagues were smaller Sunderland won all 13 of their home games)
Away: 15 in 2004–05 (Premiership record)

FEWEST LEAGUE WINS IN A SEASON
5 in 1978–79
Home: 3 in 1978–79
Away: 0 in 1914–15

1000TH LEAGUE WIN
Leyton Orient 3 Chelsea 7, 10 November 1979

1000TH TOP-FLIGHT LEAGUE WIN
Chelsea 3 Leeds United 2, 28 January 2003

MOST NUMBER OF POINTS
99 in 1988–89
Top-flight: 95 in 2004–05 (English top-flight record)

FEWEST NUMBER OF POINTS
20 in 1978–79
3 points for a win: 42 in 1987–88

LONGEST UNBEATEN SEQUENCE
19 games: 14 January to 31 August 1984, 22 August to 1 December 1998 and 7 May to 1 November 2005 (the 18th game was a drawn League Cup tie but lost on penalties)
Home: 58 in 2003–04 (9) + 2004–05 (29) + 2005–06 (20)(the 46th game was a drawn League Cup tie but lost on penalties)
Away: 15 in 1985–86

LONGEST UNBEATEN LEAGUE SEQUENCE
40 games: 23 October 2004 to 6 November 2005 (the third longest in English top-flight history behind Arsenal 49 in 2003–04, and Nottingham Forest 42 in 1977–78)
Home: 44 unbroken in 2003–04 (6) + 2004–05 (19) + 2005–06 (19) and will continue into 2006–07
Away: 19 in 2004–05 (14) + 2005–06 (5)

UNBEATEN IN A LEAGUE SEASON
Home: 1910–11 (19), 1976–77 (21), 2004–05 (19), 2005–06 (19)

LONGEST UNBEATEN LEAGUE SEQUENCE AT THE START OF THE SEASON
14 games in 1925–26. Top flight: 11 in 2005–06

SUCCESSIVE DEFEATS
7 games: 1 November to 26 December 1952 and 10 December 1960 to 14 January 1961
Home: 4 in 1978–79
Away: 10 in 1909–10 and 1960–61 (3) + 1961–62 (7)

SUCCESSIVE LEAGUE DEFEATS
7 games: 1 November to 26 December 1952
Home: 4 in 1978–79
Away: 10 in 1909–10 and 1960–61 (3) + 1961–62 (7)

MOST DEFEATS IN A SEASON
29 in 1978–79
Home: 13 in 1978–79
Away: 18 in 1987–88

MOST LEAGUE DEFEATS IN A SEASON
27 in 1978–79
Home: 13 in 1978–79
Away: 16 in 1961–62

FEWEST DEFEATS IN A SEASON
6 in 1998–99 and 2004–05 (all by no more than 1 goal, a club record)
Home: 0 in 1910–11 and 2004–05
Away: 3 in 1983–84
Away top-flight: 4 in 1998–99

FEWEST LEAGUE DEFEATS IN A SEASON
1 in 2004–05
Home: 0 in 1910–11, 1976–77, 2004–05 and 2005–06
Away: 1 in 2004–05
In the history of English League football, Preston NE in 1888–89 (22 games) and Arsenal in 2003–04 (38 games) remained unbeaten throughout the season and Arsenal suffered one defeat in 1990–91 (to Chelsea).

MOST LEAGUE DRAWS IN A SEASON
18 in 1922–23

FEWEST LEAGUE DRAWS IN A SEASON
3 in 1997–98

SUCCESSIVE LEAGUE DRAWS
6 games in 1969–70

BIGGEST LEAGUE GOAL DIFFERENCE
57 in 2004–05 (Premiership record)

WORST LEAGUE GOAL DIFFERENCE
-48 in 1978–79

MOST GOALS IN A SEASON
121 in 56 games in 1964–65 (89 league, 21 LC, 11 FA Cup)
Other seasons with 100 or more – 117 in 1960–61, 109 in 1988–89, 108 in 1997–98, 108 in 2004–05, 105 in 1971–72 and 102 in 2003–04

BIGGEST DEFEATS

Top-flight	1-8	Wolverhampton Wanderers (a) 26 September 1953
	0-7	Leeds United (a) 7 October 1967
	0-7	Nottingham Forest (a) 20 April 1991
Home top-flight	0-6	Notts County, 9 February 1924
Old Division Two	0-6	Rotherham United (a) 31 October 1981
Home Old Division Two	2-5	West Brom, 17 April 1929
	1-4	Rotherham United, 19 March 1982
	0-3	Millwall, 30 March 1929
	0-3	Oldham Athletic, 10 January 1976
	0-3	Barnsley, 26 March 1983
FA Cup	1-7	Crystal Palace (a) 3rd qualifying round, 18 Nov 1905 (this was in effect a reserve side as the first team were playing a league game on the same day)
	0-6	Sheffield Wed (a) 2nd round replay, 5 February 1913
Home FA Cup	0-4	Birmingham City, 5th round, 14 February 1953
League Cup	2-6	Stoke City (a) 3rd round, 2nd replay, 22 October 1974
	1-5	Tottenham Hotspur (a) Semi-final, 2nd leg, 23 January 2002
Home League Cup	1-3	Blackpool, 3rd round replay, 17 October 1966
	1-3	Blackpool, 2nd round, 2nd leg, 25 September 1996
	0-2	Norwich City, Semi-final, 1st leg, 13 December 1972
	0-2	Leicester City, 2nd round, 2nd leg, 25 October 1983
	0-2	QPR, 5th round replay after extra time, 29 January 1986
	0-2	Sheffield Wed, semi-final, 1st leg, 24 February 1991
Europe	0-5	Barcelona (a) Fairs Cup semi-final play-off, 25 May 1966
		The heaviest in the Champions League is 1-5 after extra time v Barcelona (a) quarter-final, 2nd leg, 18 April 2000
Home Europe	0-2	Besiktas, Champions League group stage, 1 October 2003

MOST LEAGUE GOALS IN A SEASON
98 in 1960–61
Home: 61 in 1960–61
Away: 46 in 1988–89
Away top-flight: 41 in 1964–65

MOST GOALS CONCEDED IN A SEASON
107 in 1958–59

MOST LEAGUE GOALS CONCEDED IN A SEASON
100 in 1960–61

FEWEST GOALS SCORED IN A SEASON
32 in 1923–24

FEWEST LEAGUE GOALS SCORED IN A SEASON
31 in 1923–24

FEWEST GOALS CONCEDED IN A SEASON
34 in 2004–05 and 2005–06

FEWEST LEAGUE GOALS CONCEDED IN A SEASON
15 in 2004–05 (English top-flight record. Preston NE also conceded 15 goals in 1888–89 when only 22 matches were played)

CONSECUTIVE GOALSCORING RUNS
27 games from 31 August to 17 December 1985

CONSECUTIVE LEAGUE GOALSCORING RUNS
27 games from 31 August 1985 to 29 March 1986 and 29 October 1988 to 15 April 1989

FAILED TO SCORE IN A SEASON
Best: 4 games in 1959–60
Worst: 23 games in 1923–24

FAILED TO SCORE IN A LEAGUE SEASON
Best: 4 games in 1906–07 and 1959–60
Worst: 22 games in 1923–24

LONGEST TIME WITHOUT SCORING A GOAL
9 games from 14 March 1981 until the end of the season in the old Division Two, a total of 876 minutes. Of the last 22 league games from 6 December Chelsea scored in only three of them.
Home: 4 games from 21 March 1981 to the end of the season
Away: 9 games from 10 January 1981 to the end of the season

LONGEST TIME WITHOUT SCORING A LEAGUE GOAL
9 games from 14 March 1981 until the end of the season in the old Division Two, a total of 876 minutes. Of the last 22 league games from 6 December, Chelsea scored in just three of them.
Home: 4 games from 21 March 1981 to the end of the season
Away: 11 games from 13 December 1980 to the end of the season

LONGEST TIME WITHOUT SCORING A GOAL AT THE START OF THE SEASON
3 games (275 minutes) in 1995–96 (all league)

MISCELLANEOUS FACTS

MOST DEBUTANTS IN A MATCH

11	Stockport (a) 2 September 1905
9	Leicester City (h) 5 January 1946
6	MŠK Žilina (a) 13 August 2003
6	Man Utd (h) 15 August 2004

DEBUT SCORERS

79 players have scored on their debut for the club. The first was James Robertson on 30 September 1905 and the most recent was Adrian Mutu on 23 August 2003. George Hilsdon scored five on his in 1906 and Seamus O'Connell three in 1954.

Nine other players scored two. They are Frank Pearson 1905, Jack Cock 1919, Buchanan Sharp 1920, Sidney Bidewell 1937, Jimmy Bowie and Bobby Campbell 1947, Peter Osgood 1964, David Speedie 1982 and Kerry Dixon 1983.

The highest number of debut scorers in any one season is four in 1991–92.

YOUNGEST PLAYER

Ian Hamilton at 16 years, 138 days made his debut against Tottenham (a) on 18 March 1967. He headed Chelsea's goal in a 1-1 draw. Other 16-year-old debutants:
Kingsley Whiffen 16y, 157 days on 9 May 1967
Tommy Langley 16y, 274 days on 9 November 1974
John Sparrow 16y, 283 days on 13 March 1974
Michael Harrison 16y, 360 days on 13 April 1957

OLDEST PLAYER

Dick Spence at 39 years, 57 days became the oldest player when he made his 246th and final appearance against Bolton (h) on 13 September 1947.

Graham Rix at 36 years, 327 days became the oldest player to make his debut when he appeared as an 89th minute substitute against Viktoria Zizkov (a) on 15 September 1994.

FIRST LEAGUE MATCH

Stockport 1 Chelsea 0, 2 September 1905

FIRST HOME LEAGUE MATCH

Chelsea 5 Hull City 1, 11 September 1905. Chelsea's first ever match at Stamford Bridge was on 4 September 1905 in a friendly against Liverpool. Chelsea won 4-0.

FIRST LEAGUE GOAL

John Tait Robertson, Blackpool 0 Chelsea 1, 9 September 1905

FIRST PENALTY SAVE

Willie Foulke saved the first penalty awarded against Chelsea in the very first match at Stockport in 1905.

FIRST FLOODLIT MATCH

Chelsea 2 Sparta Prague 0, friendly, 19 March 1957

FIRST EUROPEAN MATCH

Frem, Copenhagen 1 Chelsea 3, Fairs Cup, 30 September 1958

FIRST TO FLY

Chelsea were the first club to travel by air to a league game. They flew back from a match at Newcastle on Good Friday 1957 for a game against Everton at Stamford Bridge the following day.

FIRST TO HAVE NUMBERS

Chelsea (and Arsenal) were the first British clubs to wear shirt numbers. The numbers trial was on 25 August 1928 when Chelsea beat Swansea Town 4-0 at Stamford Bridge. Arsenal lost at Hillsborough to Sheffield Wednesday.

FIRST TO HAVE FENCES

Chelsea became the first British club to erect wire fences. In October 1972, 8ft high wire mesh was put up behind each goal to keep supporters off the pitch.

FIRST FOREIGN SELECTION

The first occasion all 11 starting players selected were non-British was away at Southampton on Boxing Day, 1999. Chelsea won 2-1. The line-up was: De Goey (Holland), Ferrer (Spain), Thome (Brazil), Lebœuf (France), Babayaro (Nigeria), Petrescu (Romania), Di Matteo (Italy), Deschamps (France), Ambrosetti (Italy), Poyet (Uruguay), Flo (Norway).

FIRST KIT

Chelsea's original shirts in 1905 were light blue, the racing colours of the then President, the Earl of Cadogan.

In 1990–91 five different shirts were worn: royal blue, red and white diamonds, plain white, jade and red.

TELEVISION COVERAGE

Chelsea were involved in the first European match transmitted live back to England on closed circuit TV. It was the Fairs Cup semi-final play-off away at Barcelona on 25 May 1966. A crowd of 9,008 watched the match at Stamford Bridge relayed on six 30 x 40ft screens.

Chelsea's first game broadcast live on UK TV was away to Manchester City on 4 May 1984.

41 games in 2004–05 were broadcast live on UK TV – a club record.

MOST RED CARDS IN A SEASON

Seven on three occasions: 1991–92: Allen, Boyd, Cundy, Hitchcock, Matthew, Monkou, Townsend.
1998–99: Wise 3, Di Matteo, Lebœuf, Le Saux, Vialli.
1999–00: Lebœuf 2, Wise 2, Babayaro, Desailly, Sutton.

LEADING CAPTAINS

Ron Harris 324 games, Dennis Wise 298 games

MOST CAPTAINS IN A SEASON

Seven players in 1999–2000 started as captain: Frank Lebœuf, Graeme Le Saux, Jody Morris, Gustavo Poyet, Chris Sutton, Dennis Wise and Gianfranco Zola.

RECORD TRANSFERS

Purchase: Andriy Shevchenko from AC Milan in May 2006 for an undisclosed fee.
Sale: £12m Tore André Flo to Rangers in November 2000.

GROUNDS

Since our first fixture at Edgeley Park, Stockport in 1905, Chelsea have played at 163 different venues. The most recent being against Anderlecht in 2005 at the Stade Constant Vanden Stock, Brussels.

PLAYERS USED IN A SEASON IN THE LEAGUE
Fewest: 19 in 1969–70
Most: 34 in 1909–10

MOST CONSECUTIVE APPEARANCES
John Hollins 167 games from 14 August 1971 to 25 September 1974 (135 league, 10 FA Cup, 18 League Cup, 4 European Cup-Winners' Cup)

MOST CONSECUTIVE LEAGUE APPEARANCES
Frank Lampard 164 games from 13 October 2001 to 26 December 2005 (Premiership record).

MOST APPEARANCES IN A SEASON
59 Ed de Goey in 1999–00

MOST INTERNATIONALS IN A CHELSEA TEAM
The first occasion 11 full internationals started a game was away at Coventry on 15 August 1998. Chelsea lost 2-1. De Goey, Ferrer, Desailly, Lebœuf, Le Saux, Poyet, Wise, Di Matteo, Babayaro, Vialli, Casiraghi.

The first time all 14 players involved were full internationals was at FC Copenhagen on 5 November 1998. Chelsea won 1-0. De Goey, Ferrer, Desailly, Leboeuf, Le Saux, Laudrup (Petrescu), Di Matteo, Wise, Babayaro, Zola (Flo), Casiraghi (Poyet).

On 7 August 2005 against Arsenal in the Community Shield, all 16 players involved were full internationals. Chelsea won 2-1. Cech; Ferreira, Gallas, Terry, Del Horno; Gudjohnsen (Tiago), Makelele, Lampard (Gérémi); Duff (J Cole), Drogba (Crespo), Robben (Wright-Phillips)

In 2004–05, every player that appeared in the Premiership up to Chelsea winning the league at Bolton on 30 April 2005 was an international (35 games) – a club record.

MOST GOALSCORERS IN A SEASON
19 in 1996–97, 1999–00 and 2003–04 (including own goals as one entry)

FEWEST GOALSCORERS IN A SEASON
Seven in 1938–39

THE GOAL THAT NEVER WAS
On 26 September 1970 Alan Hudson hit a 20-yard shot that struck the side netting and spun back onto the pitch, as subsequently confirmed on BBC film. Amazingly, the referee awarded a goal that proved to be the winner in the league match at home to Ipswich Town.

SHARED OWN GOAL
Chelsea's second goal in the 3-1 win against Leicester City at Stamford Bridge on 18 December 1954 was officially recorded as a 'Froggatt and Milburn shared own goal' and the only joint own goal in professional English football.

LEAGUE DOUBLES ACHIEVED
Chelsea have achieved 274 doubles. Chelsea have beaten the League Champions elect on two occasions. They are Wolves in 1958–59 and Man Utd in 1993–94. The highest number in a season is 12 in 2004–05. (Premiership record)

MOST DOUBLES
Fulham 10, Tottenham Hotspur 10, Wolves 10, Manchester City 9, Birmingham City 8, Blackpool 8, Derby County 8, Everton 8, Stoke City 8, Sunderland 8, West Brom 8, Arsenal 7, Manchester United 7, Newcastle United 7.

LEAGUE DOUBLES AGAINST
Chelsea have suffered 186 doubles by other clubs.

Five relegated teams have achieved doubles against Chelsea. They are Charlton Ath 1956–57, Leeds Utd 1959–60, Cardiff City 1961–62, Oldham Ath 1993–94 and West Ham 2003–04. The highest number against Chelsea in a season is 7 in 1978–79

MOST AGAINST
Man Utd 13, Arsenal 10, Wolves 9, Leeds Utd 8, Liverpool 8, Sheffield Wed 8, Aston Villa 7, Bolton Wdrs 7, Burnley 7, Tottenham H 7, West Ham 7

MOST GOALS IN A GAME

13 once			
Chelsea	13-0	Jeunesse Hautcharage	29 Sep 1971
11 on five occasions			
Chelsea	9-2	Glossop	1 Sep 1906
Liverpool	7-4	Chelsea	7 Sep 1946
Chelsea	5-6	Man Utd	16 Oct 1954
Chelsea	7-4	Portsmouth	25 Dec 1957
Chelsea	6-5	Newcastle United	10 Sep 1958

FIVE GAMES OR MORE AGAINST THE SAME TEAM IN A SEASON
7 Burnley in 1955–56 (2 league, 5 FA Cup);
6 West Brom in 1952–53 (2 league, 4 FA Cup) and Leeds United in 1969–70 (2 league, 2 FA Cup, 2 League Cup);
5 Arsenal in 1946–47 (2 league, 3 FA Cup), Manchester City in 1970–71 (2 league, 2 European Cup-Winners' Cup, 1 FA Cup), Stoke City in 1974–75 (2 league, 3 League Cup), Wrexham in 1981–82 (2 league, 3 FA Cup), Sheffield Wednesday in 1984–85 (2 league, 3 League Cup), Tottenham Hotspur in 2001–02 (2 league, 2 League Cup, 1 FA Cup), Arsenal in 2003–04 (2 league, 2 UEFA Champions League, 1 FA Cup), Liverpool in 2004–05 (2 league, 2 UEFA Champions League, 1 League Cup), Liverpool in 2005–06 (2 league, 2 UEFA Champions League, 1 FA Cup)

PLAYED IN BOTH FA AND LEAGUE CUPS IN THE SAME SEASON
1969–70 Leeds Utd, 1971–72 Bolton Wdrs, 1977–78 Liverpool, 1984–85 Millwall, 1990–91 Oxford Utd, 2001–02 Tottenham H, 2004–05 Newcastle United

LONGEST CUP TIE
January – February 1956, FA Cup 4th round v Burnley stretched 19 days and 9 hours of play before Chelsea finally beat Burnley 2-0 in the 4th replay.

MOST COMPETITIVE GAMES IN A SEASON
61 in 1999–00 (38 league, 16 UEFA Champions League, 6 FA Cup and 1 League Cup)

TENSE FINISHES TO A SEASON
1914–15: Chelsea finished 19th in Division One and were due to be relegated. They were reprieved when the division was extended to 22 clubs when the league resumed after the First World War in 1919.

1950–51: By beating Bolton 4-0 in the last match Chelsea escaped relegation by 0.044 of a goal.

1962–63: By beating Portsmouth 7-0 in the final game Chelsea achieved promotion to the First Division on goal average by 0.401 of a goal.

INTERNATIONALS

142 players (35 nationalities) have won full international caps while in the service of Chelsea.

The list comprises 40 capped by England, 18 by Scotland, 10 by Northern Ireland and Wales, 7 by the Republic of Ireland, 6 by Denmark, France and Holland, 4 by Portugal, 3 by Norway, 2 by Argentina, Czech Republic, Germany, Italy, Romania, Russia and Spain and 1 by Australia, Cameroon, Canada, Croatia, Finland, Georgia, Ghana, Iceland, Ivory Coast, Jamaica, Liberia, Nigeria, Serbia and Montenegro, South Africa, Switzerland, Ukraine, Uruguay and Yugoslavia.

Caps and goals listed are for internationals played while at Chelsea and not their complete international career.

Pierre Issa and Warren Cummings played for Chelsea reserves and did not make an appearance in the first team.

Player	Country	Caps	Goals		Starts+sub
Aleksidze, Rati	Georgia	10	2	2000–02	3+7
Armstrong, Ken	England	1	0	1955	1
Babayaro, Celestine	Nigeria	21	0	1998–2004	19+2
Baker, Ben-Howard	England	1	0	1925	1
Ballack, Michael	Germany	2	1	2006	2
Bambrick, Joe	Northern Ireland	4	2	1935–38	4
Beasant, Dave	England	2	0	1989	0+2
Bentley, Roy	England	12	9	1949–55	12
Blunstone, Frank	England	5	0	1954–56	5
Bogarde, Winston	Holland	1	0	2000	1
Bonetti, Peter	England	7	0	1966–70	7
Boyd, Tom	Scotland	2	0	1991	2
Brabrook, Peter	England	3	0	1958–60	3
Bridge, Wayne	England	11	1	2003–06	6+5
Bridges, Barry	England	4	1	1965	4
Buchanan, Peter	Scotland	1	1	1937	1
Burley, Craig	Scotland	20	0	1995–97	17+3
Cameron, Jock	Scotland	1	0	1909	1
Campbell, Bobby	Scotland	3	1	1950	3
Carvalho, Ricardo	Portugal	15	1	2004–06	14+1
Cascarino, Tony	Republic of Ireland	15	3	1992–94	6+9
Cech, Petr	Czech Republic	18	0	2004–06	18
Clarke, Steve	Scotland	6	0	1987–94	6
Cock, Jack	England	1	0	1920	1
Cole, Joe	England	22	4	2003–06	12+10
Cooke, Charlie	Scotland	14	0	1966–75	13+1
Crawford, Jackie	England	1	0	1931	1
Crespo, Hernán	Argentina	17	10	2003–06	17
Cummings, Warren	Scotland	1	0	2002	0+1
D'Arcy, Jimmy	Northern Ireland	2	0	1952	2
De Goey, Ed	Holland	2	0	1998	1+1
Del Horno, Asier	Spain	3	0	2005–06	3
Dempsey, John	Republic of Ireland	12	0	1969–72	12
Desailly, Marcel	France	74	1	1998–2004	73+1
Deschamps, Didier	France	16	0	1999–2000	13+3
Di Matteo, Roberto	Italy	19	2	1996–98	18+1
Dickson, Billy	Northern Ireland	9	0	1951–53	9
Dixon, Kerry	England	8	4	1985–86	5+3
Donaghy, Mal	Northern Ireland	15	0	1992–94	15
Dorigo, Tony	England	6	0	1989–91	2+4
Douglas, Angus	Scotland	1	0	1911	1
Drogba, Didier	Ivory Coast	20	14	2004–06	20
Duff, Damien	Republic of Ireland	22	3	2003–06	22
Durie, Gordon	Scotland	12	2	1987–91	8+4
Essien, Michael	Ghana	6	2	2005–06	6
Evans, Bobby	Scotland	3	0	1960	3
Ferreira, Paulo	Portugal	16	0	2004–06	13+3
Ferrer, Albert	Spain	2	0	1998–99	2

Player	Country	Caps	Goals		Starts+sub
Ferris, Jim	Ireland	2	0	1920–21	2
Flo, Tore André	Norway	38	15	1997–2000	34+4
Forrest, Craig	Canada	1	0	1997	1
Forssell, Mikael	Finland	33	12	1999–2005	28+5
Gallacher, Hughie	Scotland	1	0	1934	1
Gallas, William	France	40	1	2002–06	37+3
Gérémi	Cameroon	22	4	2003–06	22
Goldbæk, Bjarne	Denmark	9	0	1999	6+3
Greaves, Jimmy	England	15	16	1959–61	15
Grodås, Frode	Norway	10	0	1996–97	10
Grønkjær, Jesper	Denmark	35	5	2001–04	28+7
Gudjohnsen, Eidur	Iceland	36	15	2000–06	36
Hall, Gareth	Wales	9	0	1988–92	7+2
Harrow, Jack	England	2	0	1922–23	2
Hasselbaink, Jimmy F	Holland	15	7	2000–02	7+8
Hewitt, Tom	Wales	3	0	1913	3
Hilsdon, George	England	8	14	1907–09	8
Høgh, Jes	Denmark	8	0	1999–2000	8
Hollins, John	England	1	0	1967	1
Hughes, Mark	Wales	9	4	1995–97	9
Huth, Robert	Germany	16	2	2004–06	13+3
Irving, Sam	Northern Ireland	2	0	1928–31	2
Issa, Pierre	South Africa	4	0	2001	4
Jackson, Johnny	Scotland	4	0	1934–35	4
Jarošík, Jiří	Czech Republic	3	0	2005	1+2
Johnsen, Erland	Norway	10	1	1990–95	10
Johnson, Glen	England	5	0	2003–05	2+3
Jokanovic, Slavisa	Yugoslavia	8	1	2001–02	8
Jones, Evan	Wales	2	0	1910	2
Jones, Joey	Wales	19	1	1982–85	19
Kežman, Mateja	Serbia & Montenegro	5	1	2004–05	2+3
Kharine, Dmitri	Russia	23	0	1993–98	19+4
Kirwan, Johnny	Ireland	4	0	1906–07	4
Kjeldbjerg, Jakob	Denmark	7	0	1993–94	5+2
Lampard, Frank	England	38	11	2001–06	31+7
Laudrup, Brian	Denmark	5	2	1998	5
Law, Tommy	Scotland	2	0	1928–30	2
Lawton, Tommy	England	11	14	1946–47	11
Le Saux, Graeme	England	16	0	1997–2000	14+2
Lebœuf, Frank	France	32	1	1996–2001	21+11
Makelele, Claude	France	19	0	2003–06	18+1
Maniche	Portugal	1	1	2006	1
McCreadie, Eddie	Scotland	23	0	1965–69	23
Meehan, Tommy	England	1	0	1923	1
Melchiot, Mario	Holland	11	0	2000–04	7+4
Middelboe, Nils	Denmark	3	0	1914–20	3
Mills, George	England	3	3	1937	3
Mitchell, Billy	Northern Ireland	11	0	1933–37	11
Mitchell, Dave	Australia	1	0	1989	1
Moore, Graham	Wales	3	0	1962–63	3
Mulligan, Paddy	Republic of Ireland	11	1	1969–72	11
Mutu, Adrian	Romania	10	9	2003–04	10
Nevin, Pat	Scotland	6	0	1986–87	3+3
Nicholas, Peter	Wales	15	0	1988–91	14+1
Niedzwiecki, Eddie	Wales	2	0	1985–87	1+1
O'Dowd, Peter	England	3	0	1932–33	3
Osgood, Peter	England	4	0	1970–73	2+2
Parker, Scott	England	1	0	2004	0+1

Player	Country	Caps	Goals		Starts+sub
Petit, Emmanuel	France	13	2	2001–03	12+1
Petrescu, Dan	Romania	44	7	1995–2000	44
Phelan, Terry	Republic of Ireland	8	0	1995–96	7+1
Phillips, John	Wales	4	0	1973–77	3+1
Poyet, Gustavo	Uruguay	5	0	1997–2000	4+1
Priestley, Tom	Northern Ireland	1	0	1933	1
Robben, Arjen	Holland	10	4	2004–06	10
Shellito, Ken	England	1	0	1963	1
Shevchenko, Andriy	Ukraine	1	1	2006	0+1
Sillett, Peter	England	3	0	1955	3
Sinclair, Frank	Jamaica	8	0	1998	7+1
Smertin, Alexey	Russia	20	0	2003–06	20
Speedie, David	Scotland	5	0	1985–86	4+1
Spence, Dick	England	2	0	1936	2
Spencer, John	Scotland	13	0	1994–96	7+6
Stanic, Mario	Croatia	14	0	2000–03	7+7
Steffen, Willi	Switzerland	1	0	1947	1
Tambling, Bobby	England	3	1	1962–66	3
Terry, John	England	24	1	2003–06	23+1
Thomas, Mickey	Wales	9	1	1984–85	9
Tiago	Portugal	6	0	2004–05	2+4
Townsend, Andy	Republic of Ireland	22	3	1990–93	22
Venables, Terry	England	2	0	1964	2
Verón, Juan Sebastián	Argentina	4	1	2003	1+3
Warren, Ben	England	9	1	1909–11	9
Weah, George	Liberia	2	0	2000	2
Whittaker, Dick	Republic of Ireland	1	0	1959	1
Wilkins, Ray	England	24	1	1976–79	22+2
Wilson, Kevin	Northern Ireland	22	3	1987–92	17+5
Windridge, Jimmy	England	8	7	1908–09	8
Wise, Dennis	England	21	1	1991–2000	16+5
Woodley, Vic	England	19	0	1937–39	19
Woodward, Vivian	England	2	2	1910–11	2
Wright-Phillips, Shaun	England	4	0	2005–06	3+1
Zenden, Boudewijn	Holland	23	2	2001–04	19+4
Zola, Gianfranco	Italy	9	3	1997	9

Statistics correct up to 8 June 2006. The 2006 World Cup appearances and goals are not included

TOP INTERNATIONAL SCORERS

Player	Goals
Jimmy Greaves	16
Tore André Flo	15
Eidur Gudjohnsen	15
Didier Drogba	14
George Hilsdon	14
Tommy Lawton	14
Mikael Forssell	12
Frank Lampard	11
Hernán Crespo	10
Roy Bentley	9
Adrian Mutu	9

TOP INTERNATIONAL CAPS

Player	Caps
Marcel Desailly	74
Dan Petrescu	44
Tore André Flo	38
William Gallas	37
Eidur Gudjohnsen	36
Frank Lampard	36
Jesper Grønkjær	35
Mikael Forssell	33
Frank Lebœuf	32
Ray Wilkins	24

Most players capped in a season: 26 in 2005–06
Most international appearances in a season: 138 in 2003–04 – record to be broken during 2006 World Cup
Most international goals in a season: 30 in 2004–05 – record to be broken during 2006 World Cup

PLAYERS' INTERNATIONAL HONOURS

Player	Honours
Celestine Babayaro	Olympic Gold medallist 1996
Ronald Brebner	Olympic Gold medallist 1908
Hernán Crespo	Panamerican Gold medallist 1995
Marcel Desailly	World Cup winner 1998 and European Championships winner 2000
Didier Deschamps	World Cup winner 1998 and European Championships winner 2000 both as captain
Albert Ferrer	Olympic Gold medallist 1992
Gérémi	Olympic Gold medallist 2000 and African Cup of Nations winner 2000 and 2002
Ruud Gullit	European Championships winner 1988 as captain and FIFA World Footballer of the Year 1987
Dmitri Kharine	Olympic Gold medallist 1988
Brian Laudrup	European Championships winner 1992
Frank Lebœuf	World Cup winner 1998 and European Championships winner 2000 in squad
Emmanuel Petit	World Cup winner 1998 and European Championships winner 2000
Gustavo Poyet	Copa America winner 1995
George Weah	FIFA World Footballer of the Year 1995
Vivian Woodward	Olympic Gold medallist 1908 and 1912

101 YEARS OF CHELSEA PLAYERS

Chelsea career appearances and goalscorers of all 630 players to represent the Blues from formation in 1905 up to and including season 2005–06. Total includes league, league play-offs, FA Cup, League Cup, UEFA Champions League, UEFA Cup, European Cup-Winners' Cup, UEFA Super Cup, Inter-Cities Fairs Cup, FA Charity/Community Shield and Full Members Cup matches.

Player	Period at club	LEAGUE Apps	Gls	TOTAL Apps	Gls
ABRAMS, Laurence	1914–20	44	7	49	7
ALEKSIDZE, Rati	2000–02	0+2	0	0+3	0
ALEXANDER, David	1939–45	1	0	1	0
ALLEN, Clive	1991–92	15+1	9	22+2	9
ALLEN, Les	1954–59	44	11	49	11
ALLISTER, Jack	1949–52	4	1	4	1
ALLON, Joe	1991–92	3+11	2	4+14	3
ALLUM, Leonard	1932–39	93	2	102	2
AMBROSETTI, Gabriele	1999–2003	9+7	0	11+12	1
AMBROSIO, Marco	2003–04	8	0	12	0
ANDERSON, George	1927–29	9	0	9	0
ANDERTON, Sylvan	1959–62	76	2	82	2
ARGUE, Jimmy	1933–47	118	30	125	35
ARMSTRONG, James	1922–28	29	9	31	10
ARMSTRONG, Ken	1946–57	362	25	402	30
ASHFORD, James	1920–25	8	0	8	0
AYLOTT, Trevor	1975–79	26+3	2	29+3	2
BABAYARO, Celestine	1997–2005	118+14	5	177+20	8
BAIN, Jimmy	1945–47	9	1	14	1
BAKER, Ben-Howard	1921–26	92	1	93	1
BALDWIN, Tommy	1966–74	182+5	74	228+11	92
BAMBRICK, Joe	1934–38	59	33	66	37
BANNON, Eamonn	1979	25	1	27	1
BARBER, George	1930–41	262	0	294	1
BARKAS, Ned	1937–39	27	0	28	0
BARNARD, Darren	1990–95	18+11	2	20+13	2
BARNESS, Anthony	1992–96	12+2	0	16+3	0
BARRACLOUGH, William	1934–37	74	8	81	11
BARRETT, Fred	1920–27	64	6	70	6
BARRON, Jim	1965–66	1	0	1	0
BASON, Brian	1972–77	18+1	1	20+2	1

CHELSEA FC 1905–2006

Player	Period at club	LEAGUE Apps	LEAGUE Gls	TOTAL Apps	TOTAL Gls
BATHGATE, Sid	1946–53	135	0	147	0
BAXTER, Thomas	1919–20	1	0	1	0
BEASANT, Dave	1989–93	133	0	157	0
BELL, Dr John	1920–23	42	9	44	10
BELLETT, Walter	1954–58	35	1	35	1
BENNETT, Walter	1922–24	5	0	5	0
BENTLEY, Roy	1948–56	324	128	367	150
BERRY, Paul	1953–60	3	0	3	0
BETTRIDGE, Walter	1909–22	224	0	255	0
BIDEWELL, Sidney	1937–46	4	2	4	2
BILLINGTON, Hugh	1948–51	82	28	89	32
BIRCHENALL, Alan	1967–70	74+1	20	95+1	28
BIRNIE, Ted	1906–10	101	3	108	3
BISHOP, Sid	1928–33	103	5	109	6
BISWELL, George	1928–29	24	10	25	10
BLOCK, Michael	1957–62	37	6	40	6
BLUNSTONE, Frank	1953–64	317	47	347	54
BODLEY, Mickey	1985–89	6	1	8	1
BOGARDE, Winston	2000–04	2+7	0	4+8	0
BOLLAND, Gordon	1960–62	2	0	2	0
BONETTI, Peter	1959–79	600	0	729	0
BOROTA, Petar	1979–82	107	0	114	0
BOSNICH, Mark	2001–03	5	0	7	0
BOWER, A G 'Baishe'	1923–25	9	0	9	0
BOWIE, Jimmy	1944–51	76	18	84	22
BOWMAN, Andy	1951–55	1	0	1	0
BOYD, Tom	1991–92*	22+1	0	31+1	0
BOYLE, John	1964–73	188+10	10	253+13	12
BRABROOK, Peter	1955–62	251	47	271	57
BRADBURY, Terry	1957–62	29	1	29	1
BRADSHAW, James	1909–10	6	3	6	3
BRAWN, Billy	1907–11	93	10	99	11
BREBNER, Ronald	1906–07; 1912–13	18	0	19	0
BRIDGE, Wayne	2003–06	45+3	1	70+5	3
BRIDGEMAN, Billy	1906–19	147	20	160	22
BRIDGES, Barry	1958–66	174+2	80	203+2	93
BRITTAN, Harold	1913–20	24	7	24	7
BRITTON, Ian	1971–82	253+10	33	279+10	34
BROLLY, Mike	1971–74	7+1	1	8+1	1
BROOKS, Johnny	1959–61	46	6	52	7
BROWN, Dennis	1962–64	10	1	13	2
BROWN, John	1912–15	16	4	16	4
BROWN, William	1924–29	54	20	57	21
BROWN, William Y	1911–13	9	2	10	2
BROWNING, John	1919–20	5	1	6	2
BUCHANAN, Peter	1936–46	39	6	40	6
BUCHANAN, Robert	1911–13	3	0	3	0
BUMSTEAD, John	1976–91	314+24	38	379+30	44
BURGESS, Harry	1935–45	142	33	155	37
BURLEY, Craig	1989–97	85+28	7	105+32	11
BUSH, Robert	1906–07	4	1	4	1
BUTLER, Dennis	1960–63	18	0	18	0
BUTLER, Geoff	1967–68	8+1	0	8+1	0
BYRNE, Michael	1905–06	4	0	5	0
CALDERHEAD, David Jnr	1907–14	34	1	43	1
CAMERON, David	1920–26	73	2	81	2
CAMERON, Jock	1907–13	179	0	194	0

Player	Period at club	LEAGUE Apps	Gls	TOTAL Apps	Gls
CAMPBELL, Bobby	1947–54	188	36	213	40
CANOVILLE, Paul	1981–86	53+26	11	67+36	15
CARR, John	1928–31	1	0	1	0
CARTER, Robert	1929–33	18	1	18	1
CARTWRIGHT, William	1908–13	44	0	46	0
CARVALHO, Ricardo	2004–06	44+5	2	69+5	4
CASCARINO, Tony	1992–94	35+5	8	39+6	8
CASEY, Len	1954–58	34	0	37	0
CASIRAGHI, Pierluigi	1998–2000	10	1	13+2	1
CASTLE, Sidney	1923–26	32	2	32	2
CECH, Petr	2004–06	69	0	90	0
CHARVET, Laurent	1998	7+4	2	7+6	2
CHEYNE, Alec	1930–32; 1934–36	62	12	69	13
CHITTY, Wilf	1931–38	45	16	46	16
CHIVERS, Gary	1978–83	128+5	4	143+5	4
CLARE, Jimmy	1977–81	0+1	0	0+1	0
CLARKE, Steve	1987–98	321+9	7	407+14	10
CLEMENT, Neil	1995–2000	1	0	1+3	0
CLISS, David	1956–62	24	1	24	1
COADY, John	1986–88	9+7	2	10+9	3
COCK, Jack	1919–23	99	47	110	53
COLE, Carlton	2000–06	4+21	4	6+26	8
COLE, Joe	2003–06	63+34	16	93+51	22
COLGAN, Nick	1992–98	1	0	1	0
COLLINS, Michael	1951–57	1	0	1	0
COMPTON, John	1955–60	12	0	12	0
COOKE, Charlie	1966–72; 1974–78	289+10	22	360+13	30
COPELAND, David	1905–07	26	9	26	9
COPELAND, James	1932–37	2	1	2	1
CORTHINE, Peter	1957–60	2	0	2	0
COURT, Colin	1954–59	0	0	1	0
CRAIG, Allan	1933–39	196	0	211	0
CRAIGIE, James	1905–07	0	0	2	0
CRAWFORD, Jackie	1923–34	288	26	308	27
CRESPO, Hernán	2003–06	33+16	20	47+26	25
CRITTENDEN, Nick	1997–2000	0+2	0	1+2	0
CROAL, Jimmy	1914–22	113	22	130	26
CROWTHER, Stan	1958–61	51	0	58	0
CUDICINI, Carlo	1999–2006	119+3	0	178+4	0
CUNDY, Jason	1988–92	40+1	2	56+1	2
DALE, George	1919–22	49	1	52	1
DALLA BONA, Sam	1998–2002	42+13	6	51+22	6
D'ARCY, Jimmy	1951–52	23	12	31	13
DAVIDSON, Alex	1946–48	2	0	2	0
DAVIES, Gordon	1984–85	11+2	6	13+2	6
DE GOEY, Ed	1997–2003	123	0	178+1	0
DE LUCAS, Quique	2002–03	17+8	0	21+10	1
DEL HORNO, Asier	2005–06	25	1	32+2	1
DEMPSEY, John	1969–78	161+4	4	200+7	7
DESAILLY, Marcel	1998–2004	156+2	6	219+3	7
DESCHAMPS, Didier	1999–2000	24+3	0	44+3	1
DI MATTEO, Roberto	1996–2002	108+11	15	155+20	26
DIARRA, Lassana	2005–06	2+1	0	4+3	0
DICKENS, Alan	1989–93	39+9	1	46+9	4
DICKIE, Murdoch	1945–46	1	0	1	0
DICKIE, William	1919–21	35	0	40	0
DICKS, Alan	1951–58	33	1	38	1

CHELSEA FC 1905–2006

Player	Period at club	LEAGUE Apps	Gls	TOTAL Apps	Gls
DICKSON, Bill	1947–53	101	4	119	4
DIGWEED, Perry	1988	3	0	3	0
DIXON, Kerry	1983–92	331+4	147	413+7	193
DOCHERTY, Jim	1979	2+1	0	2+1	0
DOCHERTY, Tommy	1961–62	4	0	4	0
DODD, George	1911–13	29	8	31	9
DODDS, Billy	1986–89	0+3	0	0+5	0
DOLBY, Hugh	1909–12	2	0	2	0
DOLDING, Len	1945–48	26	2	27	2
DONAGHY, Charles	1905–07	2	1	3	1
DONAGHY, Mal	1992–94	63+5	3	72+6	3
DONALD, Alexander	1930–32	24	1	24	1
DORIGO, Tony	1987–91	146	11	180	12
DOUGLAS, Angus	1908–13	96	11	103	11
DOW, Andy	1993–96	14+1	0	17+1	0
DOWNING, Sam	1909–14	134	9	144	10
DRIVER, Phil	1980–83	25+19	4	25+21	4
DROGBA, Didier	2004–06	38+17	22	59+23	32
DROY, Micky	1970–85	263+9	13	302+11	19
DUBERRY, Michael	1993–99	77+9	1	106+9	3
DUBLIN, Keith	1983–87	50+1	0	66+2	0
DUDLEY, Sam	1932–34	1	0	1	0
DUFF, Damien	2003–06	63+18	14	95+30	19
DUFFY, Bernard	1923–27	3	0	3	0
DUNN, John	1962–66	13	0	16	0
DURIE, Gordon	1986–91	115+8	51	145+8	63
DYKE, Charles	1947–51	24	2	25	2
EDWARDS, Robert	1951–55	13	2	13	2
ELLIOT, Sidney	1928–30	30	9	30	9
ELLIOTT, Paul	1991–94	42	3	54	3
ELMES, Timmy	1980–82	2+2	0	2+2	0
ESSIEN, Michael	2005–06	27+4	2	37+5	2
EVANS, Bobby	1960–61	32	0	37	1
FAIRGRAY, Norman	1907–14	79	5	84	5
FALCO, Mark	1982	3	0	3	0
FASCIONE, Joe	1962–69	22+7	1	27+7	1
FEELY, Peter	1970–73	4+1	2	4+1	2
FERGUSON, Chris	1927–30	1	0	1	0
FERGUSON, Edward	1920–23	2	0	2	0
FERGUSON, Willie	1921–33	272	11	294	11
FERREIRA, Paulo	2004–06	47+3	0	68+6	1
FERRER, Albert	1998–2003	71+5	0	105+8	1
FERRIS, James	1920–22	33	8	39	9
FILLERY, Michael	1978–83	156+5	32	176+5	41
FINLAYSON, William	1920–23	5	1	5	1
FINNIESTON, Steve	1971–78	78+2	34	86+4	37
FLECK, Robert	1992–95	35+5	3	43+5	4
FLETCHER, James	1905–06	1	0	1	0
FLO, Tore André	1997–2000	59+53	34	94+69	50
FORD, Harry	1912–24	222	41	248	46
FORREST, Craig	1997	2+1	0	2+1	0
FORSSELL, Mikael	1998–2005	6+27	5	12+41	12
FOSS, Dick	1936–52	41	3	48	3
FOULKE, Willie	1905–06	34	0	35	0
FRANCIS, Steve	1981–87	71	0	88	0
FREEMAN, Charlie	1907–20	95	21	105	22
FREESTONE, Roger	1987–91	42	0	53	0

Player	Period at club	LEAGUE		TOTAL	
		Apps	Gls	Apps	Gls
FREW, James	1922–27	42	0	43	0
FRIDGE, Les	1985–87	1	0	1	0
FROST, James	1906–07	22	4	22	4
FROST, Lee	1976–80	11+3	5	12+3	5
FURLONG, Paul	1994–96	44+20	13	59+26	17
GALLACHER, Hughie	1930–34	132	72	144	81
GALLAS, William	2001–06	147+12	12	213+12	14
GALLON, James	1919–21	2	0	2	0
GALLOWAY, John	1946–49	4	0	4	0
GARLAND, Chris	1971–75	89+3	22	111+3	31
GARNER, Bill	1972–78	94+11	31	105+14	36
GÉRÉMI	2003–06	33+20	3	51+30	3
GIBBS, Derek	1955–60	23	5	25	6
GIBSON, George	1933–39	130	23	142	24
GILKES, Michael	1992	0+1	0	0+2	0
GODDARD, Ray	1946–48	14	1	15	1
GODDEN, Tony	1986–87	34	0	38	0
GOLDBÆK, Bjarne	1998–2000	15+14	5	21+19	5
GOODWIN, Joe	1905–06	0	0	2	0
GOULDEN, Len	1945–50	99	17	111	19
GRAHAM, George	1964–66	72	35	102	46
GRANT, Anthony	2005–06	0+1	0	0+1	0
GRANVILLE, Danny	1997–98	12+6	0	19+7	1
GRAY, Billy	1949–53	146	12	172	15
GREAVES, Jimmy	1957–61	157	124	169	132
GREENWOOD, Ron	1952–55	65	0	66	0
GREGG, Bob	1933–38	48	5	51	6
GRIFFITHS, Robert	1931–41	42	0	45	0
GRODÅS, Frode	1996–98	20+1	0	26+1	0
GRØNKJÆR, Jesper	2000–04	56+32	7	77+42	11
GUDJOHNSEN, Eidur	2000–06	126+60	54	177+86	78
GULLIT, Ruud	1995–98	37+12	4	50+14	7
HALES, Kevin	1979–83	18+2	2	25+2	2
HALL, Gareth	1986–96	120+18	4	148+23	5
HALSE, Harold	1913–21	96	23	111	25
HAMILTON, Ian	1967–68	3+2	2	3+2	2
HAMPSHIRE, Steven	1997–2000	0	0	0+1	0
HAMPTON, Colin	1914–25	79	0	82	0
HANSON, Alf	1938–46	37	8	43	9
HARDING, Augustus	1906–13	4	0	5	0
HARFORD, Mick	1992–93	27+1	9	33+1	11
HARLEY, Jon	1997–2001	22+8	2	30+12	2
HARMER, Tommy	1962–67	8	1	9	1
HARRIS, Allan	1960–64; 1966–67	82+2	0	98+4	1
HARRIS, Charles	1905–09	1	0	2	0
HARRIS, John	1945–56	326	14	364	14
HARRIS, Ron	1961–80	646+9	13	784+11	14
HARRISON, Michael	1957–62	61	8	64	9
HARROW, Jack	1911–26	304	5	333	5
HARWOOD, Jack	1912–13	4	0	4	0
HASSELBAINK, Jimmy Floyd	2000–04	119+17	69	156+21	87
HATELEY, Tony	1966–67	26+1	6	32+1	9
HAY, David	1974–80	107+1	2	118+2	3
HAYWOOD, William	1921–24	23	2	23	2
HAZARD, Micky	1985–90	78+3	9	94+9	12
HENDERSON, George	1905–09	60	1	64	1
HEWITT, Tom	1911–13	8	0	8	0

Player	Period at club	LEAGUE Apps	Gls	TOTAL Apps	Gls
HIGGS, Frank	1928–30	2	0	2	0
HILSDON, George	1906–12	150	98	164	107
HINSHELWOOD, Wally	1951	12	1	14	1
HINTON, Marvin	1963–76	257+8	3	328+16	4
HITCHCOCK, Kevin	1988–2001	92+4	0	131+4	0
HODDINOTT, Frank	1921–23	31	4	32	4
HODDLE, Glenn	1993–95	19+12	1	22+17	1
HØGH, Jes	1999–2001	6+3	0	11+6	0
HOLDEN, Arthur	1908–10	20	1	20	1
HOLLINS, John	1963–75; 1983–84	465	48	592	64
HOLTON, Pat	1959–60	1	0	1	0
HOPE, James	1930–32	1	0	1	0
HOPKIN, David	1992–95	21+19	1	24+22	1
HORN, George	1909–13	2	0	2	0
HORTON, Jack	1933–37	59	15	66	15
HOUSEMAN, Peter	1962–75	252+17	20	325+18	39
HOUSTON, Stewart	1967–72	6+3	0	10+4	0
HOWARD, Terry	1984–87	6	0	6	0
HUDSON, Alan	1968–74; 1983–84	144+1	10	188+1	14
HUGHES, Billy	1948–51	93	0	105	0
HUGHES, Harry	1951–52	1	0	1	0
HUGHES, Mark	1995–98	88+7	25	109+14	39
HUGHES, Paul	1994–2000	13+8	2	15+8	2
HUGHES, Tommy	1965–71	11	0	11	0
HUMPHREYS, Percy	1908–09	45	13	46	13
HUNTER, George	1913–14	30	2	32	2
HUTCHESON, John	1934–37	22	1	22	1
HUTCHINGS, Chris	1980–83	83+4	3	97+4	3
HUTCHINSON, Ian	1968–76	112+7	44	137+7	58
HUTH, Robert	2001–06	23+19	0	32+30	2
HUXFORD, Cliff	1955–59	6	0	7	0
ILES, Bob	1978–83	14	0	14	0
IRVING, Sam	1928–32	89	5	97	5
ISAAC, Robert	1983–87	9	0	13	0
JACKSON, Alex	1930–32	65	25	77	29
JACKSON, John	1933–42	49	0	51	0
JACKSON, William	1928–31	26	6	26	6
JAROŠÍK, Jiri	2005–06	3+11	0	6+14	0
JASPER, Dale	1982–86	10	0	13+2	0
JENKINS, Richard	1924–25	4	0	4	0
JENKINS, Thomas	1949–51	5	0	5	0
JOHNSEN, Erland	1989–97	135+10	1	170+13	1
JOHNSON, Gary	1977–80	16+3	9	18+4	9
JOHNSON, Geoffrey	1911–13	4	0	5	0
JOHNSON, Glen	2003–06	34+6	3	59+10	4
JOHNSTONE, Derek	1983–85	1+3	0	1+3	0
JOKANOVIC, Slavisa	2000–02	19+20	0	28+25	0
JONES, Benny	1947–53	55	11	62	13
JONES, Evan	1909–11	21	4	21	4
JONES, Joey	1982–85	76+2	2	89+2	2
JONES, Keith	1983–87	43+9	7	57+12	10
JONES, Vinnie	1991–92	42	4	52	7
KEENAN, Joe	1999–2006	0+2	0	0+3	0
KELL, Len	1952–54	3	0	3	0
KEMBER, Steve	1971–75	125+5	13	144+6	15
KENNEDY, George	1908–09	10	0	12	0
KEVAN, Derek	1963	7	1	7	1
KEY, George	1905–09	54	2	56	2

Player	Period at club	LEAGUE Apps	Gls	TOTAL Apps	Gls
KEŽMAN, Mateja	2004–05	6+19	4	14+27	7
KHARINE, Dmitri	1992–99	118	0	146	0
KIRKUP, Joe	1966–68	48+5	2	62+7	2
KIRWAN, Jack	1905–08	73	17	76	18
KITAMIRIKE, Joel	2001–04	0	0	1	0
KITCHENER, Ray	1954–56	1	0	1	0
KJELDBJERG, Jakob	1993–96	52	2	65+1	2
KNIGHT, Leon	1999–2003	0	0	0+1	0
KNOX, Tommy	1962–65	20	0	21	0
LAKE, George	1913–18	1	0	1	0
LAMBOURDE, Bernard	1997–2001	29+11	2	43+17	3
LAMPARD, Frank	2001–06	182+4	50	252+15	69
LANGLEY, Tommy	1974–80	129+13	40	139+13	43
LANGTON, Joe	1919–22	3	0	3	0
LAUDRUP, Brian	1998	5+2	0	8+3	1
LAVERICK, Robert	1955–59	7	0	7	0
LAW, Tommy	1925–39	293	15	319	19
LAWTON, Tommy	1945–47	42	30	53	35
LEADBETTER, James	1949–52	3	0	3	0
LEBOEUF, Frank	1996–2001	142+2	17	200+4	24
LEE, Colin	1980–87	167+18	36	200+23	41
LEE David	1988–98	119+32	11	148+46	13
LEE, John	1920–24	7	1	7	1
LE SAUX, Graeme	1987–93; 1997–03	210+20	12	280+32	16
LEWINGTON, Ray	1974–79	80+5	4	87+5	4
LEWIS, Fred	1946–53	23	0	26	0
LEWIS, Jim	1952–58	90	38	95	40
LINFOOT, Fred	1920–24	34	1	41	1
LIVESEY, Charlie	1959–61	39	17	42	18
LIVINGSTONE, Steve	1993–94	0+1	0	0+1	0
LIVINGSTONE, William	1955–59	20	0	22	0
LLOYD, Barry	1966–69	8+2	0	8+2	0
LOCKE, Gary	1972–82	270+2	3	315+2	4
LOGAN, Tommy	1913–20	107	7	117	8
LUKE, George	1967–68	1	0	1	0
LYON, Frank	1907–08	6	0	6	0
MACAULAY, James	1946–51	86	5	94	5
MACAULAY, Bob	1932–36	66	1	74	1
MACFARLANE, Ian	1956–58	40	0	43	0
MACHIN, Alex	1944–48	53	8	61	9
MACINTOSH, Stanley	1930–36	1	0	1	0
MACKIE, Bob	1905–08	44	1	48	1
MAIR, Tommy	1909–10	9	1	9	1
MAKELELE, Claude	2003–06	91+6	1	130+7	1
MALCOLM, Andy	1961–62	27	1	28	1
MANICHE	2006	3+5	0	5+6	0
MARSH, Wilson	1921–24	10	0	12	0
MARSHALL, Owen	1913–20	34	0	36	0
MATTHEW, Damian	1989–94	13+8	0	19+8	0
MATTHEWS, Reg	1956–61	135	0	148	0
MAYBANK, Teddy	1974–76	28	6	32	6
MAYES, Alan	1980–83	61+5	19	71+5	24
MAYES, Arnold	1935–42	12	0	13	0
McALLISTER, Kevin	1985–91	78+28	7	101+39	13
McANDREW, Tony	1982–84	20	4	23	4
McCALLIOG, Jim	1963–65	7	2	12	3
McCARTNEY, David	1906–07	1	0	3	0
McCONNELL, English	1910–11	21	0	21	0

Player	Period at club	LEAGUE Apps	Gls	TOTAL Apps	Gls
McCREADIE, Eddie	1962–74	327+4	4	405+5	5
McDERMOTT, Tom	1905–07	31	10	32	11
McEWAN, Marshall	1909–11	33	3	35	3
McEWAN, Bob	1905–06	19	0	20	0
McFARLANE, Alex	1913–15	4	0	4	0
McINNES, John	1947–51	37	5	37	5
McKENNA, Peter	1924–31	62	0	66	0
McKENZIE, Duncan	1978–79	15	4	16	4
McKENZIE, Ken	1910–11	1	0	1	0
McKENZIE, Ken W	1920–23	21	0	22	0
McKNIGHT, Philip	1947–54	33	1	33	1
McLAUGHLIN, Joe	1983–89	220	5	268	7
McMILLAN, Eric	1958–60	5	0	5	0
McMILLAN, Paul	1967–68	1	0	1	0
McNALLY, Errol	1961–63	9	0	9	0
McNAUGHT, John	1986–87	9+1	2	12+1	2
McNEIL, Bob	1914–27	279	27	307	32
McNICHOL, John	1952–58	181	59	202	66
McROBERTS, Bob	1905–09	104	10	106	10
MEDHURST, Harry	1946–52	143	0	157	0
MEEHAN, Tommy	1920–24	124	4	133	4
MELCHIOT, Mario	1999–2004	117+13	4	149+16	5
MEREDITH, John	1928–30	23	6	23	6
MIDDELBOE, Nils	1913–21	41	0	46	0
MILLAR, John	1984–87	11	0	11	0
MILLER, Harold	1923–39	337	41	363	44
MILLER, Tommy	1905–09	112	0	120	0
MILLINGTON, Sam	1926–32	223	0	245	0
MILLS, George	1929–43	220	116	239	123
MINTO, Scott	1994–97	53+1	4	70+2	5
MITCHELL, David	1988–91	7	0	8	0
MITCHELL, Frank	1949–52	75	1	85	1
MITCHELL, Billy	1933–45	108	2	117	3
MOLYNEUX, Jim	1910–22	210	0	239	0
MONKOU, Ken	1989–92	92+2	2	117+2	2
MOORE, Graham	1961–63	68	13	72	14
MORAIS, Nuno	2004–06	0+2	0	1+3	0
MORAN, Martin	1905–08	63	7	67	8
MORRIS, Jody	1995–2003	82+42	5	113+60	9
MORRISON, William	1924–27	1	0	1	0
MORTIMORE, John	1956–65	249	8	279	10
MULHOLLAND, Jimmy	1962–64	11	2	12	3
MULLIGAN, Paddy	1969–72	55+3	2	74+5	2
MURPHY, Jerry	1985–88	34	3	39	3
MURRAY, Bert	1961–66	156+4	39	179+4	44
MUTU, Adrian	2003–04	21+6	6	30+8	10
MYERS, Andy	1991–99	74+10	2	89+17	2
NEVIN, Pat	1983–88	190+3	36	237+5	45
NEWTON, Eddie	1990–99	139+26	8	181+33	10
NICHOLAS, Tony	1955–60	59	18	63	20
NICHOLAS, Brian	1955–58	26	1	29	1
NICHOLAS, Peter	1988–91	79+1	2	92+1	2
NICHOLLS, Mark	1995–2001	11+25	3	16+36	3
NICOLAS, Alexis	2001–04	1+1	0	2+1	0
NIEDZWIECKI, Eddie	1983–88	136	0	175	0
NUTTON, Michael	1977–83	77+2	0	81+2	0
OAKTON, Eric	1932–37	107	27	112	28
O'CONNELL, Seamus	1954–56	16	11	17	12

Player	Period at club	LEAGUE Apps	LEAGUE Gls	TOTAL Apps	TOTAL Gls
ODELL, Leslie	1924–36	101	7	103	7
O'DOWD, Peter	1931–34	80	0	87	0
OELOFSE, Ralph	1951–53	8	0	8	0
O'HARA, Francis	1905–06	1	0	3	3
O'HARE, John	1932–41	102	0	108	0
OLIVEIRA, Filipe	2001–05	0+5	0	0+8	0
ORD, Tommy	1972–74	3	1	3	1
ORMISTON, Alec	1909–15	95	1	102	1
O'ROURKE, John	1962–63	0	0	1	0
OSGOOD, Peter	1964–74; 1978–79	286+3	105	376+4	150
PANUCCI, Christian	2000–01	7+1	0	9+1	1
PARKER, Paul	1997	1+3	0	1+3	0
PARKER, Scott	2004–05	8+7	1	19+9	1
PARSONS, Eric	1950–56	158	37	177	42
PATES, Colin	1979–88	280+1	10	345+1	10
PATON, John	1946–47	18	3	23	3
PAYNE, Joe	1938–46	36	21	47	23
PEACOCK, Gavin	1993–96	92+11	17	119+15	27
PEARCE, Ian	1991–93	0+4	0	0+5	0
PEARSON, Frank	1905–06	29	18	30	18
PEARSON, George	1926–33	197	33	215	35
PERCASSI, Luca	1998–2000	0	0	0+2	0
PETIT, Emmanuel	2001–04	52+3	2	71+5	3
PETRESCU, Dan	1995–2000	134+16	17	186+22	23
PEYTON, Gerry	1993	0+1	0	0+1	0
PHELAN, Terry	1995–96	13+2	0	21+3	0
PHILLIPS, John	1970–80	125	0	149	0
PICKERING, Peter	1948–51	27	0	35	0
PIDGELEY, Lenny	2003–06	1+1	0	1+1	0
PINNER, Mike	1961–62	1	0	1	0
PLUM, Seth	1924–26	26	1	27	1
PORTER, William	1905–07	2	0	2	0
POTRAC, Tony	1970–73	1	0	1	0
POYET, Gustavo	1997–2001	79+26	36	110+35	49
PRIESTLEY, John	1920–28	191	18	204	19
PRIESTLEY, Tom	1933–34	23	1	27	2
PROUDFOOT, Peter	1906–07	12	0	12	0
PROUT, Stanley	1932–34	16	3	17	3
RANDALL, Ernie	1950–53	3	1	3	1
RANKIN, John	1930–34	62	9	66	9
READ, William	1911–13	3	0	4	0
REID, Ernest	1937–39	1	0	1	0
REILLY, Edward	1908–09	1	0	1	0
RHOADES–BROWN, Peter	1979–84	86+10	4	97+12	5
RICHARDSON, Fred	1946–47	2	0	2	0
RIX, Graham	1994–95	0+1	0	1+3	0
ROBBEN, Arjen	2004–06	35+11	13	50+19	16
ROBERTS, Graham	1988–90	70	18	83	22
ROBERTSON, Bill G	1946–60	199	0	215	0
ROBERTSON, Bill H	1945–48	37	0	43	0
ROBERTSON, James	1905–07	29	21	31	22
ROBERTSON, John Tait	1905–06	36	4	39	4
ROBINSON, Arthur	1908–10	3	0	3	0
ROBSON, Bryan 'Pop'	1982–83	11+4	3	12+5	5
ROBSON, Tom	1965–66	6+1	0	6+1	0
ROCASTLE, David	1994–98	27+2	0	37+3	2
RODGER, George	1924–31	119	2	122	2
ROFE, Dennis	1980–82	58+1	0	61+2	0

Player	Period at club	LEAGUE Apps	Gls	TOTAL Apps	Gls
ROUGVIE, Doug	1984–87	74	3	100	3
ROUSE, Fred	1907–09	38	11	42	11
RUSSELL, Robert	1944–48	2	0	4	0
RUSSELL, Willie	1927–36	150	6	160	6
SALES, Arthur	1924–28	7	0	7	0
SALMOND, Bob	1938–45	24	0	29	0
SAUNDERS, Derek	1953–59	203	9	223	9
SAUNDERS, James	1909–10	2	0	2	0
SAUNDERS, John	1948–54	52	0	60	0
SCOTT, Mel	1956–63	97	0	104	0
SHARP, Buchanan	1919–23	65	20	72	23
SHARP, James	1912–15	61	0	64	0
SHAW, Colin	1961–63	1	0	1	0
SHEARER, Duncan	1983–86	2	1	2	1
SHEERIN, Joe	1997–2000	0+1	0	0+1	0
SHELLITO, Ken	1957–69	114	2	123	2
SHERBORNE, Jack	1936–45	5	0	5	0
SHERWOOD, Steve	1971–76	16	0	17	0
SHIPPERLEY, Neil	1992–95	26+11	7	35+13	9
SILLETT, John	1954–62	93	0	102	1
SILLETT, Peter	1953–62	260	29	288	34
SIMNER, Joe	1947–49	1	0	1	0
SINCLAIR, Billy	1964–66	1	0	1	0
SINCLAIR, Frank	1990–98	163+6	7	211+7	13
SISSONS, John	1974–75	10+1	0	12+1	0
SITTON, John	1977–80	11+2	0	12+2	0
SMALE, Douglas	1937–45	9	0	9	0
SMART, Jim	1965–66	1	0	1	0
SMERTIN, Alexey	2003–06	11+5	0	19+6	1
SMETHURST, Derek	1968–71	14	4	18+1	5
SMITH, Arthur	1938–45	45	0	49	0
SMITH, George	1921–32	351	0	370	0
SMITH, James	1951–55	19	3	23	3
SMITH, Jimmy	2005–06	0+1	0	0+1	0
SMITH, Philip	1910	1	0	1	0
SMITH, Bobby	1950–55	74	23	86	30
SMITH, Stephen	1921–23	22	1	23	1
SORRELL, Dennis	1962–64	3	0	4	1
SPACKMAN, Nigel	1983–87; 1992–96	199+9	12	254+13	14
SPARROW, John	1974–81	63+6	2	68+6	2
SPECTOR, Miles	1952–53	3	0	6	0
SPEEDIE, David	1982–87	155+7	47	197+8	64
SPENCE, Dick	1934–50	221	62	246	65
SPENCER, John	1992–96	75+28	36	100+37	43
SPOTTISWOOD, Joe	1919–20	1	0	1	0
STANIC, Mario	2000–04	39+20	7	54+26	10
STANLEY, Garry	1971–79	105+4	15	115+5	15
STARK, Jimmy	1907–08	30	2	32	2
STEER, William	1912–15	4	1	4	1
STEFFEN, Willi	1946–47	15	0	20	0
STEIN, Mark	1993–98	46+4	21	57+6	25
STEPNEY, Alex	1966	1	0	1	0
STONE, George	1924–28	25	2	25	2
STRIDE, David	1976–79	35	0	37	0
STUART, Graham	1989–93	70+17	14	89+21	18
STUBBS, Les	1952–58	112	34	123	35
SULLIVAN, Neil	2003–04	4	0	7+1	0
SUTTON, Chris	1999–2000	21+7	1	27+12	3

Player	Period at club	LEAGUE Apps	LEAGUE Gls	TOTAL Apps	TOTAL Gls
SWAIN, Kenny	1973–78	114+5	26	127+5	29
TAMBLING, Bobby	1958–70	298+4	164	366+4	202
TAYLOR, Fred	1909–19	155	4	171	4
TENNANT, Albert	1934–53	2	0	8	0
TERRY, John	1998–2006	174+12	14	254+18	30
THAIN, Albert	1922–31	144	44	153	50
THOMAS, Mickey	1984–85	43+1	9	53+1	11
THOME, Emerson	1999–2000	19+2	0	20+2	0
THOMPSON, Jimmy	1927–29	37	33	42	34
THOMSON, Charlie	1952–57	46	0	59	0
THOMSON, Jim	1965–68	33+6	1	40+7	1
THOMSON, Bob	1911–22	83	23	95	29
TIAGO	2004–05	21+13	4	31+21	4
TICKRIDGE, Sid	1951–55	61	0	73	0
TINDALL, Ron	1953–61	160	67	174	69
TOOMER, James	1905–06	0	0	1	0
TOWNROW, Jack	1927–32	130	3	140	3
TOWNSEND, Andy	1990–93	110	12	138	19
TUCK, Peter	1951–54	3	1	3	1
TURNBULL, Bob	1925–28	80	51	87	58
TURNBULL, James	1912–13	20	8	22	8
TYE, Edward	1914–15	1	0	1	0
UPTON, Frank	1961–65	74	3	86	3
VENABLES, Terry	1960–66	202	26	237	31
VERÓN, Juan Sebastián	2003–06	5+2	1	11+3	1
VIALLI, Gianluca	1996–2000	46+12	21	69+19	40
VILJOEN, Colin	1980–82	19+1	0	22+1	0
WALDRON, Colin	1967	9	0	10	0
WALKER, Andy	1913–20	18	2	23	2
WALKER, Clive	1975–84	168+30	60	191+33	65
WALKER, Tommy	1946–48	98	23	105	24
WALTON, Joe	1906–11	53	0	53	0
WARD, Joe	1920–22	14	0	16	0
WARREN, Ben	1908–14	92	4	101	5
WARREN, Robert	1948–51	1	0	1	0
WATSON, Ian	1962–65	5	1	9	1
WATSON, James	1905–06	13	0	14	0
WATT, Steven	2002–06	0+1	0	1+1	0
WEAH, George	2000	9+2	3	13+2	5
WEAVER, Reg	1929–32	20	8	20	8
WEAVER, Sam	1936–45	116	4	125	4
WEBB, David	1968–74	230	21	299	33
WEGERLE, Roy	1986–88	15+8	3	18+10	4
WELLER, Keith	1970–71	34+4	14	49+5	15
WEST, Colin	1985–90	8+8	4	8+8	4
WHIFFEN, Kingsley	1966–67	1	0	1	0
WHITE, Alex	1937–48	17	0	18	0
WHITEHOUSE, Ben	1906–08	10	1	13	2
WHITING, Bob	1906–08	52	0	54	0
WHITLEY, Jack	1907–14	127	0	138	0
WHITTAKER, Dick	1952–60	48	0	51	0
WHITTINGHAM, Bob	1909–19	119	71	129	80
WHITTON, William	1923–26	38	19	39	19
WICKS, Stan	1954–56	71	1	81	1
WICKS, Steve	1974–79; 1986–88	149+1	6	163+1	8
WILDING, Harry	1914–28	241	22	265	25
WILEMAN, Arthur	1909–11	14	5	14	5
WILKINS, Graham	1972–82	136+1	1	148+1	1

Player	Period at club	LEAGUE		TOTAL	
		Apps	Gls	Apps	Gls
WILKINS, Ray	1973–79	176+3	30	193+5	34
WILLEMSE, Stan	1949–56	198	2	221	2
WILLIAMS, Bill	1927–28	2	0	2	0
WILLIAMS, Ernest	1909–10	6	0	8	1
WILLIAMS, Paul	1980–83	1	0	1	0
WILLIAMS, Reg	1945–51	58	13	74	17
WILSON, Andy	1923–31	238	59	253	62
WILSON, Clive	1987–90	68+13	5	85+18	5
WILSON, Kevin	1987–92	124+28	42	155+36	55
WINDRIDGE, Jimmy	1905–11	143	54	152	58
WINTER, Danny	1945–51	131	0	155	0
WISE, Dennis	1990–2001	322+10	53	434+11	76
WOLFF, Frank	1905–06	0	0	1	0
WOLLEASTON, Robert	1998–2003	0+1	0	0+2	0
WOOD, Darren	1984–89	134+10	3	167+11	4
WOODLEY, Vic	1931–45	252	0	272	0
WOODWARD, Vivian	1909–15	106	30	116	34
WOOSNAM, Max	1914	3	0	3	0
WOSAHLO, Roger	1964–67	0+1	0	0+1	0
WRIGHT-PHILLIPS, Shaun	2005–06	10+17	0	15+24	0
YOUNG, Allan	1961–69	20	0	26	1
ZENDEN, Boudewijn	2001–04	24+19	4	30+29	4
ZOLA, Gianfranco	1996–2003	185+44	59	260+52	80

SUBSTITUTES

Substitutes were introduced to English football in 1965. Chelsea's first used substitute was John Boyle who replaced George Graham at Fulham on 28 August 1965. Chelsea won 3-0.

Top substitute appearances	
Eidur Gudjohnsen	86
Tore André Flo	69
Jody Morris	60
Gianfranco Zola	52
Joe Cole	51

Scoring substitutes

64 players have scored after coming on as a substitute. Jimmy Floyd Hasselbaink is the only one to score a hat-trick v Wolves (h) in March 2004.

Top scoring substitutes	
Tore André Flo	12
Eidur Gudjohnsen	11
Mikael Forssell	9
Joe Cole	8
Hernán Crespo	7
Jimmy Floyd Hasselbaink	6
Didier Drogba	5
Mateja Kežman	5
Gianfranco Zola	5

Seven players – Chris Hutchings, David Lee, Joe Allon, Eddie Newton, Paul Hughes, Tore André Flo and George Weah – scored on their debuts after coming on as sub.

Mikael Forssell scored a goal in four successive substitute appearances in January 2002 – a club record.

Kevin Hitchcock holds the record for the number of selections as a substitute with a total of 244 times, including four as a playing substitute.

INDEX

RESOURCES AND PICTURE CREDITS

Among many others, I would like to draw attention to the following resources, which contributed immensely to my new understanding of Chelsea's first 100 years:

Archives:
1837online.com, Access to Archives, Archivo General de la Nación, Argentina, British Library, British Library Newspapers, British Pathé, *Buenos Aires Herald*, Derbyshire Records Office, *El Dia* (Uruguay), The Football League, the *Guardian*, Guildhall Library, Greater Manchester Records Office, Hammersmith and Fulham Archives and Family History Centre, Historical Directories, University of Leicester, the *Independent*, London Metropolitan Archives, National Archives, National Football Museum, Preston, Oswald Stoll Foundation, Soccerbase.com, *The Times*, Westminster Libraries

Books:
A History Of Chelsea F.C., Finn, Ralph L, Pelham, 1969
Chelsea, Groves, Reg, Famous Football Clubs, 1947
Chelsea – A Complete Record 1905-1991, Cheshire, Scott, Breedon Books, 1991
Chelsea – An Illustrated History, Cheshire, Scott, Breedon Books, 1994
Chelsea, Champions!, Sewell, Albert, Phoenix Sports Books, 1955
Chelsea FC Players Who's Who with 1989 Supplement, Cheshire, Scott, 1989
Chelsea Football Club – the Full Statistical Story 1905-1986, Cheshire, Scott and Ron Hockings, 1986
Colossus – the True Story of William Foulke, Phythian, Graham, Tempus, 2005
England, Their England, Harris, Nick, Pitch Publishing, 2003
Football in London, Prole, David, Robert Hale, 1964
Football is my Business, Lawton, Tommy, Sporting Handbooks Ltd, 1948
Going for Goal, Bentley, Roy, Museum Press, 1955
The Hughie Gallacher Story, Joannou, Paul, Breedon Books, 1989
José Mourinho – Made in Portugal, Lourenço, Luis, Dewi Lewis Media, 2004
Ninety Years of the Blues, Hockings, Ron, 1995
Ossie the Wizard, Osgood, Peter., Stanley Paul, 1969
Rhapsody in Blue – the Chelsea Dream Team, Glanvill, Rick, Mainstream, 1996
The Bridge – the History of Stamford Bridge, Benson, Colin, Chelsea, 1987
The Chelsea Football Book Nos 1-5, Ed. by Albert Sewell, Stanley Paul, 1970-4
Upfront with Chelsea, Westcott, Chris, Mainstream Publishing, 2001

Other publications:
Chelsea Chronicles and matchday programmes 1905-2005
Chelsea F.C. handbooks and yearbooks 1905-2004
F.A. Book for Boys
Match, Shoot!, Topical Times annuals

Picture credits:
Pages 6, 11, 167, 279, 309, 337, 355 Empics; page 113 Getty Images, page 221 Alan Tomkins, Picture sections – Section One: page 1 (top) Colorsport, (bottom) Empics, pages 2 (bottom) and 3 (top) courtesy Albert Sewell, page 3 (bottom) Getty Images, page 4 (top) both Empics, page 5 (top) Getty Images, (bottom) Colorsport, pages 6 and 7 Empics (all), page 8 (top) Colorsport, (bottom) Getty Images. Section Two: Page 1 (top right) British Library, (bottom) Getty Images, page 2 (top left) Getty Images, (top right) London Metropolitan Archive, (below) Getty Images (both), page 3 (top) Empics, page 4 (top) British Film Institute, page 5 (top) Empics, (bottom left) Empics, (bottom right) Getty Images, page 6 (bottom left) Empics, (bottom right) Getty Images, page 7 (top) Colorsport, (below) Empics (both), page 8 (top left) Getty Images, (top right) Empics, (bottom left) Getty Images, (bottom right) Empics. Section Three: page 1 (bottom left) courtesy Richard Coburn, (bottom right) Reuters, page 2 (top left) Getty Images, (top right) Empics, page 3 (top) Colorsport, (bottom) Empics, pages 4 and 5 Empics (all), pages 6 and 7 Empics (all) except page 7 (top right) Colorsport, page 8 (top left and bottom) City of Westminster Archives, (top right) Empics